TRADE LIBERALISATION

Impact on Growth and Trade in Developing Countries

Ashok Parikh
University of East Anglia, UK

TRADE LIBERALISATION

Impact on Growth and Trade in Developing Countries

World Scientific

NEW JERSEY • LONDON • SINGAPORE • BEIJING • SHANGHAI • HONG KONG • TAIPEI • CHENNAI

Published by

World Scientific Publishing Co. Pte. Ltd.
5 Toh Tuck Link, Singapore 596224
USA office: 27 Warren Street, Suite 401-402, Hackensack, NJ 07601
UK office: 57 Shelton Street, Covent Garden, London WC2H 9HE

Library of Congress Cataloging-in-Publication Data
Parikh, Ashok K.
Trade liberalisation : impact on growth and trade in developing countries / Ashok Parikh.
p. cm.
Includes bibliographical references.
ISBN-13 978-981-270-502-0 -- ISBN-10 981-270-502-3
1. Free trade. 2. Developing countries--Commerce. 3. Developing countries--Economic conditions. I. Title.

HF1713.P387 2007
382'.3091724--dc22

2006052292

British Library Cataloguing-in-Publication Data
A catalogue record for this book is available from the British Library.

Typeset by Stallion Press
Email: enquiries@stallionpress.com

Printed in Singapore.

Acknowledgements

While proposing and writing the collection of essays, most of them previously published in journals, I have benefited from various co-authors. I would like to express my gratitude to all my co-authors: Dr. Uma Kambhampati, Reading University, Reading, Berkshire, UK; Dr. Rajesh Mehta, Research and Information Systems, New Delhi, India; Dr. Haishun Sun, Government of Australia, Canberra, Australia; Dr. Miyuki Shibata, University of East Anglia, Norwich, UK; Mr. Corneliu Stirbu, Hamburg Institute of International Economics, Hamburg, Germany; Professor Korkut Boratov, Ankara University, Ankara, Turkey and Dr. Alberto Gabriele, UNCTAD, Geneva, Switzerland. The Leverhulme Trust kindly financed the Emeritus Fellowship during the 2002–2004 period, which facilitated the preparation and publication of papers in journals. Professors Manoranjan Dutta of Rutgers Univrsity, New Jersey, USA and T.R. Gourvish of the London School of Economics, London, UK kindly gave comments on the first chapter of the book and improved both the content and the presentation.

The author is very grateful to Ms. Sandhya of World Scientific Publishing for excellent and painstaking editing on the entire book.

I thank the publishers who granted reprint permissions for the following chapters:

Chapter 2: Disciplining Firms: The Impact of Trade Reforms on Profit Margins in Indian Industry. *Applied Economics*, 35(4), 2003, pp. 461–470, Reprinted by permission of Taylor & Francis Ltd.

Chapter 3: Has Liberalisation Affected Profit Margins in the Indian Industry? *Bulletin of Economic Research*, 57(3), July 2005, pp. 273–304, Reprinted by permission of Blackwell Publishing Ltd.

Chapter 5: Impact of Trade Liberalisation on Import Demands in India: A Panel Data Analysis for Commodity Groups. *Applied Economics*, 37(16), 2005, pp. 1851–1863, Reprinted by permission of Taylor & Francis Group.

Chapter 6: Does Trade Liberalisation Accelerate Convergence in Per Capita Incomes in Developing Countries? *Journal of Asian Economics*, 15(1), 2004, pp. 33–48, Reprinted by permission of Elsevier Science Direct, 2003.

Chapter 7: Dynamics of the Relationship between the Terms of Trade and the Trade Balance in Developing Countries of Asia, Africa and Latin America. *Journal of Quantitative Economics*, New series Vol. 2, No. 2, July 2004, pp. 104–121, Reprinted by permission of Editor, *Journal of Quantitative Economics*.

Chapter 9: Relationship between Trade Liberalisation, Growth and Balance of Payments in Developing Countries: An Econometric Study. *International Trade Journal*, Vol. 20, No. 4, Winter 2006, pp. 429–467, Reprinted by permission of Taylor & Francis Group.

Chapter 10: Instability and Volatility of Capital Flows to Developing Countries (co-authored with A. Gabriele and K. Boratov). *World Economy*, 23(8), August 2000, pp. 1031–1056, Reprinted by permission of Blackwell Publishing Ltd.

For my grand-daughters Maya and Ella

Contents

Chapter 1
Introduction

The aim of this book is to bring together key papers on the impact of liberalisation on the economies of both developed and developing countries. Many have appeared in journals and other collections, but by grouping the essays together important insights emerge that are not evident in each of the individual contributions. In the various studies we examine the impact of liberalisation on the structure of both the micro- and the macroeconomy. Liberalisation may impact on research and development at a firm level; it may increase the profitability of enterprises; it may lead to an increase in exports in the long run and it may increase foreign direct and indirect investment and impact on economic growth. Some of these impacts may or may not be realised at a country level and hence a study at the country, region and world level becomes imperative. Theoretically, there are differing opinions on the effects of liberalisation. Some economists strongly believe that free trade promotes economic growth, while others hold that free trade may be harmful to economic growth as increased imports could destroy domestic industries. The use of the terms liberalisation and globalisation is very common in the literature and also in day-to-day conversations. It is important therefore to distinguish between liberalisation and globalisation.

Globalisation and Liberalisation

Globalisation is not just a single phenomenon. It encompasses a range of trends and forces leading to openness, integration and the interdependence of economies. The integration of economies on a worldwide basis considers the world as a single market, and production area is simply a subset of regional economies rather than national economies linked by trade and investment flows. Global resources may be used optimally, including the competitive sourcing of inputs to achieve cost competitiveness in production, economies of scale and efficient technology utilisation. Globalisation will lead to easy movement of product and factor flows across borders where trade, services, investment, financial capital, technology and labour freely move. At a firm level, globalisation can lead to a process where firms coordinate their activities across national boundaries with a view to maximising profits and remaining competitive.

Globalisation has both positive and negative aspects. On the positive side, globalisation can provide operational economies of scale, technological and productivity improvements through cross-border specialisation and the utilisation of global factors of production and technology. It may also provide the productive application of capital worldwide, maximising rates of return on savings and investment where national opportunities are limited. On the negative side, there may be a loss of employment where labour intensive production in low-income countries is prevalent. National policies are sacrificed in favour of globalisation, and multilateral global rules might result in a loss of sovereignty.

Trade liberalisation embraces all the elements in the opening of markets and can have one or several of these ingredients. There may be a reduction in tariffs and non-tariff barriers, a relaxation of investment and capital flows between countries and an enhanced transparency of trade policies and trade facilitation measures. Trade liberalisation in a broad sense argues for measures that facilitate an increase in trade and does not necessarily imply free movement of factors of production such as labour and capital. Trade liberalisation means reducing the limits on trade that countries around the world have erected over a number of years. Protectionism aims to ensure that domestic industries are protected from competition from foreign producers and can be implemented through tariffs, quotas and other non-tariff barriers such as regulations and legislation that make hard for foreign competitors to sell goods into another country.

Financial liberalisation refers to market opening measures that can deal with the free movement of financial capital from one country to another. Some deregulatory measures combined with investment opportunities to foreign firms and tax relief to flow of financial capital from foreigners to domestic economy would lead to a liberalisation of finance. In the extreme situation where all controls are removed on foreign private investment, capital will move freely across national borders.

Pro-Liberalisation and Its Opponents

The pro-liberalisation lobby has two strong proponents (Bhagwati, 2004; Wolf, 2004; Bhagwati and Kreuger, 1974) who strongly argue that globalisation and outward-oriented policies contribute to sustained economic growth. Panagariya (2004) has found that the growth miracle countries that grew at a rate of 3 percent per capita or more on a sustained basis between 1961 and 1999 almost always experienced a rapid growth in trade. Moreover, there are few examples of highly-protected countries that managed to grow rapidly on a sustained basis without lowering their level of protection. Countries that have failed to grow had a dismal trade performance. Some serious advocates of free trade argue that openness is by itself sufficient for growth. They are aware that macroeconomic stability, the enforcement of contracts and policy credibility are necessary to register significantly higher economic growth. However, such policies yield better prospects for growth under an open trading environment. Openness serves as a direct stimulus to growth. Even if we ignore the initial stimulus to economic growth, it can be stated that increased growth often leads to increased trade liberalisation and vice versa.

Among the free trade sceptics, Rodriguez and Rodrik (1999) provide a critique of the link between growth and openness. Cross-country regression studies provide weak evidence on the relationship between openness and growth. The South Centre of the United Nations raises severe doubts about the benefits of liberalisation and globalisation and remains critical of the World Bank studies, which according to the Centre are based on a misinterpretation of the facts. Liberalisation and globalisation have progressed at a slower pace in developing countries as compared with advanced countries. However, the pace of liberalisation quickened in the 1980s in many developing countries under the structural adjustment programme of multilateral financial institutions. Liberalisation of capital flows in developing countries has proceeded further than trade policy reform largely to attract foreign direct investment and non-debt-creating equity flows.

Wacziarg and Welch (2003) have constructed a panel data set on income growth and liberalisation, which allowed them to identify both within country and between country variations. They find that, on average, a country grows at a set 1.5 percent per annum higher rate in the liberalised phase than in the protected phase, controlling for country and year effects on the panel data. While assessing the impact of openness on growth, real exchange rate policy is very important. If the real exchange rate is left overvalued when countries liberalize, it maintains the discrimination against traded goods. This would obviously reduce the impact of openness on growth. Stiglitz (2002) raises issues about the speed of liberalisation. His argument rests on two main considerations, namely, that trade liberalisation must be gradual and developed countries need to do their part by removing trade barriers on products of interest to developing countries, especially agriculture, where domestic and export subsidies further harm the interests of developing countries.

Some of the sceptics of free trade do not recommend protectionism, and it seems that on the whole they are not against free trade and liberalisation. The financial crises in Latin American economies and East Asian economies gave perhaps a bad name to trade liberalisation. The collapse of growth in Latin American economies in the 1980s might not be entirely due to financial problems. International financial institutions such as the World Bank and orthodox economists attribute this failure to the insufficient integration of Latin American countries with the international economies and the relatively larger role of the state in these economies. Others argue that Latin America's poor performance is perhaps due to its debt crisis, and this could be also due to changes in the world economy and to external forces over which Latin American economies have no control (United Nations, 2003).

The South Centre and UNCTAD conclude that for developing countries, the first best policy with respect to liberalisation and globalisation is not to seek rapid and close integration but rather to define careful policies of selective integration, which is called strategic integration. If the first best policies are not feasible, then UNCTAD would need to spell out other alternatives for developing countries. During the 1980s and 1990s, many developing countries went for far-reaching market-oriented reforms with the expectation that improved factor allocation would turn out to be an important ingredient in their integration in a globalising economy. However, the reforms were met with low rates of investment and deindustrialisation. The fast pace of trade liberalisation created trade deficits, which added to payment difficulties and increased dependence on capital flows. Capital inflows involved raising interest rates, which hindered domestic investment and slowed growth and currency appreciation, which reduced the international competitiveness of domestic producers and adversely affected trade performance (UNCTAD, 2006).

Chile opened up its economy to trade by reducing tariffs and undertook reforms such as privatisation. Macroeconomic affairs were well managed, and unlike other Latin American economies, macroeconomic stability was maintained. Chile is the only major economy that has maintained a sustained rapid growth in Latin America. In 1981–1991 and 1991–2001, its GDP grew at an annual rate of 5.3 and 5.9 percent, respectively. The experience of China and India during the 1980s and 1990s suggests that outward oriented policies are necessary to achieve higher growth performance. Starting from the 1970s, China began to open its economy to both trade and foreign investment side by side with other policy measures. China's GDP grew at near double-digit rates during both the 1980s and the 1990s with per capita incomes quadrupling over the two decades. Both exports and imports grew at phenomenal rates, and this implies that trade was the engine of economic growth in China.

The economic transitions of Russia and East Germany in Europe, Botswana and Mauritius in Africa and Chile in Latin America strongly suggest that globalisation is a two-edged sword. If a country maintains economic policies that are complementary to the prevailing conditions of the global economy, it is likely to benefit in terms of economic growth. To some extent, the tendency to cast blame on globalisation for domestic economic failures is misplaced. For the longer term, the analysis points to the conclusion that every country must globalize its economy in order to attain high and sustained GDP growth rates (Letiche, 2006). However, the analysis and experience also indicates the need for a greater stabilization of the global economy, and this can be facilitated not only by fundamental reforms of existing international economic institutions, but also by reductions in the developed world of agricultural subsidies and tariffs on imports from the developing nations. The *New Growth Centres* to which Klein (2004) refers to are Russia, India and China, for which he predicts sustainable growth rates. China has grown at a rate of seven to 10 percent annually from 1978 except for the short period 1989–1990. The Indian economy strives to achieve seven percent and hopes to be able to maintain such a rate of growth, while the Russian growth rate will not be as high as that of India and China but will be encouraged by the demonstration effect.

Gains from Trade[a]

Thirlwall (2000) raises doubts about the gains from trade being equitably distributed. Trade is an important engine of economic growth, and there could be both static and dynamic gains from it. In his view, most developing countries are constrained in their growth performance by a shortage of foreign exchange and could grow faster with more exports. Dynamic gains from trade are due to shifts in the production possibility frontier as trade is related to more investment, faster productivity growth with scale economies, learning by doing and the acquisition of new technologies from abroad, especially through foreign direct investment. The modern trade theory (Helpman and Krugman, 1985) and the new growth theory (Grossman and Helpman, 1991) focus on the above-mentioned dynamic gains from trade and provide a causal chain between exports and economic growth. In the new growth theory, all forms of externalities keep the marginal product of capital from falling, and trade improves long-run growth performance. For a small country, with no trade, there is very little scope for large scale investment in advanced capital equipment, and specialisation is limited by the extent of the market. However, if a poor, small country can trade, there is some prospect of industrialisation and of dispensing with traditional methods of production.

[a] The static neoclassical trade theory based on the Ricardian comparative advantage framework assumed perfect competition. In a two-country model, the theory suggested that Portugal should specialise in production of wine while the United Kingdom in textiles in a bilateral trade model. This theory has now lost its relevance as the European Union and common trading blocks have emerged in international trade. Defining each member country of the United Nations by shares of the world output and trade, 175 of 292 member countries are marginal. Prior to the formation of 25 member countries' European Union, USA had dominant shares in the world market (Dutta, 2006). In 2004, (UNCTAD, Handbook of Statistics, 2004) the shares of US exports and imports were 9.12 and 16.50 percent while that of the EU was 40.37 and 38.75 percent, respectively.

Measurement of Liberalisation

Sachs and Warner (1995) constructed a dummy variable for openness based on five individual dummies for specific trade policies. A country was classified as closed if it displayed at least one of the following characteristics: (a) average tariff rates of 40 percent or more (TAR); (b) non-tariff barriers covering 40 percent or more of trade (NTB) (c) a black market exchange rate depreciated by 20 percent or more relative to the official exchange rate on average during the 1970s or the 1980s (BMP); (d) a state monopoly of major exports (XMB) and (e) a socialist economic system (SOC). Table 1 reports data on trade policy for period 1990–1999 and openness is defined as 1, while the state of being not open is given a zero value. Sachs–Warner used this for the decades 1970s and 1980s, and Wacziarg employed the same methodology with some modifications for the classification of open versus closed economies in period 1990–1999. This is presented in Table 1.

There are several possible measures of trade liberalisation or outward orientation, and many investigators (e.g., Leamer, 1988) and organisations (World Bank, 1987) have devised their own measures. Some of the most common are the average import tariff; the average index of non-tariff barriers; an index of the effective rate of protection; an index of relative price distortions or exchange rate misalignment and the average black market exchange rate premium. Most of the African countries are in the moderately and strongly inward oriented categories. When a whole group of countries is relatively inward oriented, it may not be easy to obtain any relationship between the degree of orientation and growth.[b]

Brahmbhatt and Dadush (1996) at the IMF have developed an index of openness with four indicators: (a) the ratio of exports and imports to GDP; (b) the ratio of foreign direct investment to GDP; (c) the share of manufactures in total exports and (d) a country's credit rating. A sample of 93 countries is then divided into four groups — fast, moderate, weak and slow integrators. They find that the fast integrators include most of the rapidly growing East Asian exporting economies, while the weakly

---

[b] The World Bank study inappropriately suggested that the economic performance of the outward oriented economies has been broadly superior to that of inward oriented economies in all respects.

Table 1. Data on trade policy.

Country	OPEN90–99[1]	OPEN90–99 adjusted[2]	Avg. tariff (%)[3]	Core non-tariff barriers (%)[4]	Core non-tariff barriers (%)[4]	All non-tariff barriers (%)[5]	Black market premium (%)[6]	Export marketing board[7]	Socialist[7]
	1 = open; 0 = closed	1 = open; 0 = closed	1990–1999 (average)	1989–1994 (average)	1995–1998 (average)	1999	1990–1999 (average)		
Albania	1	1	15.9				7.53	0	0
Algeria	0	0	23.97			15.8	177.91	0	0
Angola	0	0					23.62	0	0
Argentina	1	1	12.54	3.1	2.10	67.2	9.30	0	0
Armenia	1	1					0.00	0	0
Australia	1	1	7.91			22.2	0.00	0	0
Austria	1	1	6.91			23.4	0.00	0	0
Azerbaijan	1	1					0.00	0	0
Bangladesh	0	0	43.70	54.2		9.8	83.27	0	0
Barbados	1	1	15.58				2.31	0	0
Belarus	0	0	12.63				n/a	1	0
Belgium	1	1	6.91			23.4	0.00	0	0
Benin	1	0	28.61		1.00		1.93	0	0
Bolivia	1	1	10.34	0.0		16.4	1.49	0	0
Botswana	1	0	20.55				7.82	0	0
Brazil	1	0	17.32	16.5	21.60	44	13.76	0	0
Bulgaria	1	1	17.37				7.44	0	0
Burkina Faso	1	0	29.13				1.98	0	0
Burundi	0	0	7.40				29.55	0	0
Cameroon	1	1	18.43	8.2			1.98	0	0

(Continued)

Table 1. (*Continued*).

Country	OPEN90–99[1]	OPEN90–99 adjusted[2]	Avg. tariff (%)[3]	Core non-tariff barriers (%)[4]	Core non-tariff barriers (%)[4]	All non-tariff barriers (%)[5]	Black market	Export marketing board[7]	Socialist[7]
	1 = open; 0 = closed	1 = open; 0 = closed	1990–1999 (average)	1989–1994 (average)	1995–1998 (average)	1999	1990–1999 (average)		
Canada	1	1	6.81			25	0.00	0	0
Cape Verde	1	0	22.05				0.00	0	0
Central African Republic	0	0	12.80				1.55	1	0
Chad	0	0	15.80				1.98	1	0
Chile	1	1	11.33	5.2	5.20	31.4	9.84	0	0
China	0	0	31.06				35.89	0	1
Colombia	1	1	14.30	55.2	10.30	53.4	8.87	0	0
Congo, Dem. Rep.	0	0	25.47				34.67	1	0
Congo, Rep.	0	0	17.97				1.98	1	0
Costa Rica	1	1	10.60		6.20		5.37	0	0
Cote d'Ivoire	1	0	22.00		30.90		1.98	0	0
Croatia	0	0					37.76	0	0
Cyprus	1	0	10.64		21.60		2.16	0	0
Czech Republic	1	1	6.08				0.22	0	0
Denmark	1	1	6.91			23.4	0.00	0	0
Dominican Republic	1	0	16.70		6.20		16.31	0	0
Ecuador	1	1	11.29			25.8	9.34	0	0

(*Continued*)

Table 1. (*Continued*).

Country	OPEN90–99[1]	OPEN90–99 adjusted[2]	Avg. tariff (%)[3]	Core non-tariff barriers (%)[4]	Core non-tariff barriers (%)[4]	All non-tariff barriers (%)[5]	Black market	Export marketing board[7]	Socialist[7]
	1 = open; 0 = closed	1 = open; 0 = closed	1990–1999 (average)	1989–1994 (average)	1995–1998 (average)	1999	1990–1999 (average)		
Egypt, Arab Rep.	1	0	30.23	57.3			12.45	0	0
El Salvador	1	0	9.38		5.20		13.59	0	0
Estonia	0	0	1.12				25.09	0	0
Ethiopia	0	0	22.55				111.43	0	0
Finland	1	1	6.91			23.4	0.00	0	0
France	1	1	6.91			23.4	0.00	0	0
Gabon	0	0	19.87				1.98	1	0
Gambia, The	1	1	13.55				4.69	0	0
Georgia	1	1					0.00	0	0
Germany	1	1	6.91			23.4	0.00	0	0
Ghana	1	1	14.93	3.1			2.96	0	0
Greece	1	1	6.91			23.4	1.24	0	0
Guatemala	1	1	10.27				6.03	0	0
Guinea	1	1					3.99	0	0
Guinea-Bissau	1	1					0.00	0	0
Guyana	0	0	13.70				28.23	0	0
Haiti	0	0	10.00				81.12	0	0
Honduras	1	1	8.90				9.21	0	0
Hong Kong, China	1	1		2.1	2.10	0	−0.02	0	0
Hungary	1	1	12.11			21.2	5.40	0	0

(*Continued*)

Table 1. (*Continued*).

Country	OPEN90–99[1]	OPEN90–99 adjusted[2]	Avg. tariff (%)[3]	Core non-tariff barriers (%)[4]	Core non-tariff barriers (%)[4]	All non-tariff barriers (%)[5]	Black market	Export marketing board[7]	Socialist[7]
	1 = open; 0 = closed	1 = open; 0 = closed	1990–1999 (average)	1989–1994 (average)	1995–1998 (average)	1999	1990–1999 (average)		
Iceland	1	1	3.98			0	1.24	0	0
India	0	0	48.65	99.0	93.80		7.45	0	0
Indonesia	1	0	16.27	53.6	31.30	14	7.10	0	0
Iran, Islamic Rep.	0	0					1199.31	0	0
Iraq	0	0					138,935.90	0	0
Ireland	1	1	3.98			23.4	2.50	0	0
Israel	1	1	7.80				2.09	0	0
Italy	1	1	6.91			23.4	0.00	0	0
Jamaica	1	0	14.68				15.46	0	0
Japan	1	1	5.98			5.7	−0.35	0	0
Jordan	1	1	15.83				3.37	0	0
Kazakhstan	0	0					55.34	0	0
Kenya	1	0	27.47	86.6			15.94	0	0
Korea, Rep.	1	0	11.28	50.0	25.00		0.03	0	0
Kyrgyz Republic	1	1					n/a	0	0
Latvia	1	1	5.73				7.29	0	0
Lesotho	1	1	17.40				3.49	0	0
Liberia	0	0					2306.86	0	0
Lituania	1	1	4.33				7.45	0	0
Luxembourg	1	1	6.91			23.4	0.38	0	0

(*Continued*)

Table 1. (*Continued*).

Country	OPEN90–99[1]	OPEN90–99 adjusted[2]	Avg. tariff (%)[3]	Core non-tariff barriers (%)[4]	Core non-tariff barriers (%)[4]	All non-tariff barriers (%)[5]	Black market	Export marketing board[7]	Socialist[7]
	1 = open; 0 = closed	1 = open; 0 = closed	1990–1999 (average)	1989–1994 (average)	1995–1998 (average)	1999	1990–1999 (average)		
Macedonia, FYR	1	0					18.45	0	0
Madagascar	1	1	7.13				5.93	0	0
Malawi	0	0	19.80				28.83	0	0
Malaysia	1	1	11.70	56.3	19.60		1.35	0	0
Mali	1	1	15.66				1.98	0	0
Malta	1	1	7.23				1.20	0	0
Mauritania	1	0	28.23				1.55	0	0
Mauritius	1	0	27.00		16.70		5.25	0	0
Mexico	1	1	12.53	27.8	13.40	50.9	2.24	0	0
Moldova	1	1					0.00	0	0
Morocco	1	0	23.75	58.3	13.40	5.5	3.54	0	0
Mozambique	1	1	16.25				6.87	0	0
Myanmar	0	0	5.70				2280.77	0	0
Nepal	0	0	15.28				24.23	0	0
Netherlands	1	1	6.91			23.4	0.00	0	0
New Zealand	1	1	6.35			34.8	2.50	0	0
Nicaragua	1	1	9.90			5.6	9.98	0	0
Niger	1	1	18.30				1.87	0	0
Nigeria	0	0	29.74	14.4	11.50		151.32	0	0
Norway	1	1	4.87				0.00	0	0

(*Continued*)

Table 1. (*Continued*).

Country	OPEN90–99[1]	OPEN90–99 adjusted[2]	Avg. tariff (%)[3]	Core non-tariff barriers (%)[4]	Core non-tariff barriers (%)[4]	All non-tariff barriers (%)[5]	Black market	Export marketing board[7]	Socialist[7]
	1 = open; 0 = closed	1 = open; 0 = closed	1990–1999 (average)	1989–1994 (average)	1995–1998 (average)	1999	1990–1999 (average)		
Pakistan	0	0	54.73	17.7			9.74	0	0
Panama	1	1	10.67				0.00	0	0
Papua New Guinea	0	0	16.67				16.57	1	0
Paraguay	1	0	10.91		0.00	22.4	11.83	0	0
Peru	1	1	16.80	6.3		36.8	8.75	0	0
Philippines	1	1	19.09	11.5		14.2	4.36	0	0
Poland	1	1	12.46				2.42	0	0
Portugal	1	1	6.91			23.4	2.04	0	0
Romania	0	0	13.50				104.30	0	0
Russian Ferderation	0	0	11.24				50979.69	1	0
Rwanda	0	0	38.40				50.78	0	0
Senegal	0	0	13.05	10.3			1.98	1	0
Sierra Leone	0	0	30.25				61.47	0	0
Singapore	1	1	0.32	1.0	2.10	0	0.80	0	0
Slovak Republic	1	1	7.35				5.34	0	0
Slovenia	1	0	10.60				10.06	0	0
Somalia	0	0					246.55	0	0
South Africa	1	1	9.05	36.5	8.30	11.1	3.46	0	0
Spain	1	1	6.91			23.4	1.71	0	0
Sri Lanka	1	0	24.34		22.70		7.84	0	0

(*Continued*)

Table 1. (*Continued*).

Country	OPEN90–99[1]	OPEN90–99 adjusted[2]	Avg. tariff (%)[3]	Core non-tariff barriers (%)[4]	Core non-tariff barriers (%)[4]	All non-tariff barriers (%)[5]	Black market	Export marketing board[7]	Socialist[7]
	1 = open; 0 = closed	1 = open; 0 = closed	1990–1999 (average)	1989–1994 (average)	1995–1998 (average)	1999	1990–1999 (average)		
Swaziland	1	1	15.10			12.1	7.62	0	0
Sweden	1	1	6.91			23.4	0.00	0	0
Switzerland	1	1	1.38				0.00	0	0
Syrian Arab Republic	0	0	16.00				279.97	0	0
Taiwan, China	1	1	9.85			11.7	0.95	0	0
Tajikistan	1	1					n/a	0	0
Tanzania	0	0	25.12				22.17	0	0
Thailand	1	0	29.54	36.5	17.50		1.80	0	0
Togo	0	0	15.25				1.98	1	0
Trinidad and Tobago	1	0	14.86			0.92	13.22	0	0
Tunisia	1	0	28.25	54.2			3.67	0	0
Turkey	1	1	15.28	5.2	19.80		1.15	0	0
Turkmenistan	0	0					42.86	1	0
Uganda	1	0	14.37		3.10		19.33	0	0
Ukraine	0	0	9.73				9.02	1	0
United Kingdom	1	1	6.91			23.4	0.00	0	0

(*Continued*)

Table 1. (*Continued*).

Country	OPEN90–99[1]	OPEN90–99 adjusted[2]	Avg. tariff (%)[3]	Core non-tariff barriers (%)[4]	Core non-tariff barriers (%)[4]	All non-tariff barriers (%)[5]	Black market	Export marketing board[7]	Socialist[7]
	1 = open; 0 = closed	1 = open; 0 = closed	1990–1999 (average)	1989–1994 (average)	1995–1998 (average)	1999	1990–1999 (average)		
United States	1	1	5.96			29.6	0.00	0	0
Uruguay	1	1	14.00	32.3	0.00	29.3	9.88	0	0
Uzbekistan	0	0					Dual x rt.	0	0
Venezuela	1	1	14.31		17.70	37.3	4.13	0	0
Yemen, Rep.	1	1	20.00				8.34	0	0
Yugoslavia, FR (Serbia/ Montenegro)	0	0					106.44	0	0
Zambia	0	0	18.43		1.00		62.55	0	0
Zimbabwe	0	0	20.43	22.7			132.81	0	0

[1]Based on application of Sachs Warner criteria.
[2]Adjusted dummy based on adjusted criteria: TAR, NTB>20%, BMP>10%. XMB and SOC criteria unchanged.
[3]Unweighted average tariff, 1990–1999. *Sources*: UNCTAD (2001), World Bank (2000) and WTO (various trade policy reviews).
[4]Core non-tariff barrier frequency on capital good and intermediates includes quotas, licensing, prohibitions and administered pricing. *Source*: Michaelopoulos (1999) and Wacziarg and Welch (2003).
[5]All NTB frequency. All NTBs include core NTBs plus technical measures and automatic licensing. *Source*: UNCTAD (2001).
[6][[(parallel Xrate/official Xrate) – 1]*100]. *Source*: Easterly and Sewadeh (2000).
[7]Based on literature reviews.

and slowly integrating group include most of the low-income countries of sub-Saharan Africa and some of the middle-income countries of Latin America. The high performance of Asian countries is the most spectacular economic success linked to exports despite the crisis in East Asia. The economies of Japan, Korea, Taiwan, Singapore, Hong Kong, Malaysia, Indonesia and Thailand have recorded some of the highest GDP growth rates in the world, averaging approximately six percent since 1965 and some of the highest rates of export growth averaging more than 10 percent per annum. Success was not always based on free trade as Japan and Korea followed both export promotion and import substitution at the same time and Government policy remained interventionist. The World Bank study (1993) of the East Asian Miracle highlighted that there is no single East Asian Model and what is important for economic growth is not whether the free market or government intervention rules but is rather a question of getting the economic fundamentals (a high level of physical and human capital) for growth right. Three policies are identified as contributing to the success of the "tiger" economies, namely industrial policies to promote particular sectors of the economy; government control of financial markets to reduce the cost of capital and to direct credit to strategic sectors of the economy and finally policies to promote exports and protect domestic industry. It is indeed necessary that good governance is applied to all the three policies. Trade as such provides externalities and foreign exchange to keep the process of economic growth going.

Winters (2004) concludes that openness to trade boosts economic growth rates in developing countries but not for ever. He claims that when a country opens up by reducing tariffs and removing other barriers, economic growth increases for a period while incomes climb to their new higher level but then settle back to the underlying rate. Open economies seem to have less corruption and lower inflation, and these factors, along with opportunities to sell goods abroad, help growth by stimulating investment. Since openness promotes investment, it is clearly the engine of economic growth. Trade liberalisation and sound finances obviously go together. Dollar and Kraay (2004) have examined the impact of openness which they called "globalisation" and examined its impact on economic growth, poverty and inequality in a large number of developing countries. The first group of globalisers is based on the top one-third of these developing countries in terms of their growth in trade as a share of GDP at constant prices between 1975–1979 and 1995–1997. These countries are shown in Table 2 and include some well-known economic reformers, namely Malaysia and Thailand in East Asia; China, which has been liberalising trade throughout this period; Bangladesh and India in South Asia with reforms more in the 1990s and several Latin American economies, namely Argentina, Brazil and Mexico. The second group of globalisers is based on absolute declines in average tariff rates. Tariff data are scarce before 1985, and consequently, the reduction in average tariff between the 1985–1989 period and the 1995–1997 period is used, the top one-third of tariff cutters being shown in Table 3. Both Kenya and Pakistan appear here, but neither has shown any upsurge in trade. Six large countries, China, India, Brazil, Thailand, Argentina and Bangladesh, are in both groups. The top one-third of 73 countries in the sample had their share of trade to GDP rise from 16 to 33 percent while tariffs were reduced from 57 to 35 percent (Table 2). Growth in the globalising countries rose from 2.9 percent per annum in the 1970s to 3.1 percent in the 1980s and 5.0 percent in the 1990s. In the non-globalising countries, growth fell from 3.3 percent per annum in the 1970s to 0.8 percent per annum in the 1980s and 1.4 percent in the 1990s.

The Impact of Liberalisation on the Profitability of Enterprises

In Chapters 2 and 3 we analyse the effects of increased trade exposure on the profitability of firms in the Indian industry. While trade reforms are often expected to decrease profit margins as firms struggle to compete in international markets, there is the possibility that increased competition may improve firm efficiency and provide a positive impetus to firm profitability. In this area, this study is different from many others in that it considers both these possibilities. An efficiency index is constructed to directly analyse the impact of changing efficiency levels on firm profit margins. The results of the study indicate that liberalisation has significantly influenced profit margins. However, its main effect is through the impact that it has had on other firm variables — market shares, advertising, research and development and exports, all of which changed after 1991. This implies that the structure of the firm within an industry changes with the trade and other liberalisation measures.

Table 2. Post-1980 globalisers (based on increases in trade volumes).

	Average annual per capita GDP growth (%)						Average trade/GDP (%)						Weighted average tariff rate		
	1970s	1975s	1980s	1985s	1990s	1995s	1970s	1975s	1980s	1985s	1990s	1995s	1985s	1990s	1995s
Argentina	2.3	1.0	−3.2	−2.0	6.8	5.2	11.3	13.2	16.4	15.5	23.7	32.9	27.5	13.9	11.0
Bangladesh	−7.0	3.2	1.2	3.1	3.4	3.7	10.3	11.8	13.8	14.0	18.6	26.7	92.7	54.3	26.0
Brazil	8.8	3.8	−2.9	1.5	0.9	1.6	11.1	10.7	10.3	10.5	13.5	17.9	45.8	21.0	11.5
China	1.4	3.4	3.9	1.7	8.6	7.8	12.5	14.1	26.7	28.5	30.1	34.2	38.8	39.9	20.9
Colombia	4.0	3.5	0.0	2.5	2.4	0.6	33.8	30.9	33.4	33.1	45.0	58.9	29.4	16.6	12.2
Costa rica	3.4	3.6	−3.6	2.0	2.0	−0.1	74.5	77.1	71.3	82.0	108.3	128.1	19.5	12.6	11.2
Dominican Rep.	7.6	1.7	−2.1	3.5	1.8	5.6	38.7	31.5	41.3	40.3	56.3	92.3	—	17.8	16.2
Haiti	1.4	3.4	−3.4	−2.2	−7.3	−0.3	32.2	43.0	47.7	50.8	67.0	98.9	11.6	—	10.0
Hungary	5.9	2.8	1.2	1.4	−2.8	3.3	40.9	47.1	48.4	52.7	57.6	74.0	18.0	9.9	14.8
India	−1.2	0.7	3.3	4.1	2.6	4.4	12.7	13.7	15.9	16.3	17.0	22.1	99.4	61.9	38.3
Ivory coast	1.6	5.1	−3.8	−3.6	−3.4	3.3	54.4	52.7	70.4	67.5	68.0	76.4	26.3	23.8	20.7
Jamaica	2.5	−3.8	−0.1	3.4	−0.8	−2.7	80.0	75.9	76.5	106.6	109.2	125.9	18.4	19.6	10.9
Jordan	8.2	10.8	1.1	−4.3	1.4	−1.6	—	94.2	118.2	104.0	162.2	166.2	16.3	15.8	16.0
Malaysia	6.5	6.6	3.8	3.0	5.8	5.4	89.3	91.7	106.8	120.8	173.9	219.8	14.9	14.3	8.9
Mali	0.8	4.5	−1.3	1.1	−1.8	2.3	28.6	29.9	42.8	51.3	51.6	51.3	—	—	18.8
Mexico	4.5	3.3	−2.3	−0.2	2.4	4.2	17.0	17.7	21.2	23.2	33.5	49.9	16.7	12.8	12.8
Nepal	0.7	11.0	1.0	2.0	3.0	2.2	16.5	25.4	31.0	32.2	42.0	60.3	21.8	16.1	11.0
Nicaragua	2.7	−9.8	0.5	−7.5	−2.2	—	49.1	52.9	65.6	51.0	68.5	85.1	22.1	12.7	10.7
Paraguay	3.7	5.2	−4.2	−0.7	1.0	−0.2	28.2	32.1	32.0	37.8	77.3	99.4	10.9	13.1	9.3
Philippines	3.1	3.3	−3.1	2.9	−0.6	3.1	40.5	41.6	52.2	56.2	75.5	106.1	27.8	24.5	17.2
Rwanda	−0.9	2.8	0.4	−1.5	−14.9	0.3	19.1	22.9	26.4	29.5	46.5	37.4	33.0	38.4	—
Thailand	1.8	6.2	3.0	6.9	6.0	1.5	47.4	47.1	49.8	59.1	84.6	94.6	41.0	36.6	23.1
Uruguay	0.1	2.8	−6.3	4.1	4.9	4.3	35.5	42.6	47.3	50.0	66.4	84.3	33.7	18.9	9.6
Zimbabwe	5.8	−3.1	0.0	−0.9	0.4	3.1	—	43.8	44.2	44.8	59.4	77.1	9.2	17.2	21.5

Source: Dollar and Kraay (2004).

Table 3. Post-1980 globalisers (based on reductions in tariffs).

Country	Average annual per capita GDP growth (%)						Average trade/GDP (%)						Weighted average tariff rate		
	1970s	1975s	1980s	1985s	1990s	1995s	1970s	1975s	1980s	1985s	1990s	1995s	1985s	1990s	1995s
Argentina	2.3	1.0	−3.2	−2.0	6.8	5.2	11.3	13.2	16.4	15.5	23.7	32.9	27.5	13.9	11.0
Bangladesh	−7.0	3.2	1.2	3.1	3.4	3.7	10.3	11.8	13.8	14.0	18.6	26.7	92.7	54.3	26.0
Benin	−0.2	0.1	−1.9	−4.6	1.4	2.6	78.7	87.2	88.7	63.9	51.8	45.8	42.8	41.0	12.7
Brazil	8.8	3.8	−2.9	1.5	0.9	1.6	11.1	10.7	10.3	10.5	13.5	17.9	45.8	21.0	11.5
Burkina Faso	1.2	2.6	0.9	1.2	−0.9	3.2	42.4	48.1	48.5	46.1	43.1	37.9	60.8	—	28.5
Cameroon	2.9	5.5	4.0	−2.2	−7.2	2.1	53.6	46.7	59.3	61.3	68.5	65.0	32.0	18.6	18.1
Central Afr. R	−0.9	0.9	−3.2	−1.9	−2.8	−0.2	40.7	43.1	48.1	44.3	46.9	42.1	32.0	—	18.6
China	1.4	3.4	3.9	1.7	8.6	7.8	12.5	14.1	26.7	28.5	30.1	34.2	38.8	39.9	20.9
Colombia	4.0	−3.5	0.0	2.5	2.4	0.6	33.8	30.9	33.4	33.1	45.0	58.9	29.4	16.6	12.2
Dominica	—	—	5.7	5.9	1.4	1.8	—	109.6	108.9	114.5	118.5	112.3	31.9	28.0	15.0
Ecuador	8.3	4.0	−2.8	−1.1	1.1	0.6	49.8	54.9	46.9	47.0	52.5	57.5	34.3	10.6	11.7
Egypt	0.3	4.1	3.7	−0.6	0.1	3.3	84.0	98.7	83.6	64.6	61.6	59.7	39.7	35.3	28.1
Ethiopia	0.3	0.8	−0.3	1.9	−1.2	5.0	—	—	27.7	28.6	22.9	25.4	29.6	28.8	16.3
India	−1.2	0.7	3.3	4.1	2.6	4.4	12.7	13.7	15.9	16.3	17.0	22.1	99.4	61.9	38.3
Indonesia	5.5	5.6	5.7	2.5	4.3	4.5	58.0	69.4	60.1	48.6	50.2	57.0	27.9	20.1	13.2
Kenya	9.2	2.7	−2.2	3.5	−0.6	0.6	109.5	79.9	56.6	51.4	60.7	78.2	39.4	33.3	13.5
Nicaragua	2.7	−9.8	0.5	−7.5	−2.2	—	49.1	52.9	65.6	51.0	68.5	85.1	22.1	12.7	10.7
Pakistan	−2.4	3.3	2.1	2.5	0.8	−0.3	47.6	37.1	35.7	33.4	34.9	34.5	69.2	59.8	41.7
Peru	3.4	−3.1	−2.8	−3.3	2.7	3.0	47.0	43.7	45.3	37.8	44.3	52.7	45.0	19.0	13.3
Thailand	1.8	6.2	3.0	6.9	6.0	1.5	47.4	47.1	49.8	59.1	84.6	94.6	41.0	36.6	23.1
Uganda	−0.8	−1.9	1.9	0.4	1.6	4.2	—	—	35.3	37.8	31.4	43.1	25.0	17.1	13.0
Uruguay	0.1	2.8	−6.3	4.1	4.9	4.3	35.5	42.6	47.3	50.0	66.4	84.3	33.7	18.9	9.6
Venezuela	−1.1	2.2	−3.7	−1.3	2.3	0.2	61.4	51.5	42.6	42.8	47.2	54.7	31.1	15.8	12.7
Zambia	2.0	−6.9	−4.0	−1.7	−1.4	2.4	194.2	145.8	98.3	87.6	78.9	78.3	29.9	26.4	17.0

Source: Dollar and Kraay (2004).

As mentioned in the previous paragraph, the determinants of firm-level profit margins are analysed in the Indian manufacturing sector in this chapter. The model we estimate is rich in its dynamic characterisation allowing as it does for lagged terms, trend movements, business cycle effects and a structural break in 1991. We hypothesise that the reforms undertaken by the government in 1991 constitute a structural break that influences a firm's independence to react to other firms as well the extent of competition faced by these firms. Inserting this into the standard industrial organisation model of profits, a dynamic market model is obtained. Estimating this model for the 1980–1998 period, it was found that the 1991 reforms did have a significant impact on profit margins in the Indian industry. The reforms have worked through their impact on firms' behavioural variables — advertising, research and development, capital-output ratios and managerial remuneration — though the precise variables that were significant varied from sector to sector. We find that relatively inefficient firms make significantly lower profits than others both before and after the liberalisation, as one would expect.

The Impact of Liberalisation on Exports and Imports in China and India

In Chapter 4, we turn our attention to exports at a country level for the Chinese economy. Trade liberalisation may indeed play a direct role in encouraging export growth, and in China, performance was closely associated with trade promotions, and liberalisation schemes, both regional and national. The relationship between exports and economic growth is strong in developing economies. Both the externality effects of exports on the non-exports sector and the higher marginal productivity of the exports sector relative to the non-exports sector play an important role in promoting exports and the GDP growth. The underlying theoretical model of Feder (1982) is used with the data of the Chinese provinces, and it is shown that the economic structure, degree of openness and policy environment have a significant role in the relationship between exports, and economic growth. Coastal regions in China have shown a tremendous improvement in exports, and export processing zones have led to both the growth in exports and the growth in domestic output at an unprecedented rate in these regions of China.

As exports are stimulated with export promotion policy and liberalisation, the removal and relaxation of tariff and non-tariff barriers can improve the performance of imports and import price elasticities. In Chapter 5, we examine the impact of liberalisation on the price elasticities of imports at a commodity level for broad commodity groups and at an aggregate level for the Indian economy over period 1993–1997. Liberalisation is implemented by reducing tariff and non-tariff barriers and relaxing exchange controls. The impact of tariffs and a market-based exchange rate is introduced in the import price of the commodity. Relative price (import/domestic) elasticities for each commodity group are estimated using panel data for six countries over five years. For the Indian economy, relative price elasticities for each of the years at an aggregate level are obtained using data for 20 commodity groups as observations, and these show that the price elasticity tends to rise with the increase in liberalisation when tariff rates are reduced.

Liberalisation, Growth Rates and Terms of Trade

Chapter 6 examines whether trade and/or financial liberalisation results in the acceleration or deceleration of convergence of per capita real incomes in Africa, Asia and Latin America. Do countries that have low per capita income experience higher economic growth after liberalisation as compared with pre-liberalisation? Data for 14 Asian countries, 30 African countries and 20 Latin American countries are available, some of which did not liberalise during period 1970–1999. The panel data methodology and the concepts of beta-convergence and sigma convergence are used for each of the regions. The study concludes that liberalisation has accelerated convergence in real per capita incomes to their regional income levels for Asian and Latin American economies, while for African countries, liberalisation seems to have produced a divergence of real per capita incomes from their mean level. This suggests that in Africa conditions are probably not right for achieving higher economic growth despite some liberalisation attempts.

Terms of trade play a very important role in enhancing trade. Primary producing countries have faced unfavourable terms of trade for a long period of time. In Chapter 7, we, therefore, examine the relationship between the terms of trade and trade balance to GDP ratios for a large number of developing economies using data on the barter terms of trade, real exchange rate and trade balances. The literature on the subject postulates a J-curve or S-curve[c] between the terms of trade and trade balance, and we examine whether there is any evidence of a J-curve or S-curve relationship in time series data over period 1970–1999. We find that for a few economies in Asia, Africa and Latin America, the existence of an S-curve is supported. However, for a large number of countries, neither a strict J-curve nor an S-curve relationship holds.

Liberalisation, Growth and Trade Balance

In Chapter 8, we study the relationship between liberalisation and economic growth for as many developing countries as possible over three decades. This is a study of 42 developing countries of Asia, Africa and Latin America in which we first examine the impact of trade liberalisation on economic growth, the investment share of GDP, openness, the trade balance and current account (as a percentage of GDP). Both panel data and country-by-country data are used to measure the impact of liberalisation on domestic economic growth measured in PPP terms from the data available in the Summers *et al.* (2001) study. Domestic economic growth is often positively related to liberalisation for many countries in our sample. Next we analyse the impact of growth on the trade balance and current account to examine whether higher economic growth due to liberalisation leads to an adverse effect on the balance of trade. Trade balance is normalised by GDP to take into account different country sizes. We also allow control variables in both sets of regressions such as the terms of trade, advanced countries' growth rates, liberalisation and debt related variables. This is studied rigorously in the next chapter.

The balance of payments constrained growth model uses a foreign exchange constraint that limits growth, and using the Harrod multiplier, Thirlwall and Hussain (1982) derived a growth equation, which is

---

[c] Depreciation of exchange rate causes the trade deficit to widen initially and then to narrow after some delay. This is known as the J-curve effect since a graph of trade surplus will resemble a J if this happens. An S-curve is a slight extension of the J-curve in the sense that the impact of exchange rate depreciation wears out after a while and there is no further improvement when all impacts are realized. Hence, at the top of the curve, the slope is zero or negative.

apparently constrained by the balance of payments. We use this model in the first part as a behavioural equation and establish that liberalisation promotes growth, with output growth in the pre-liberalisation period lower than that in the post-liberalisation period. With panel data for 42 countries, an analysis is conducted on the relationship between growth and liberalisation using regional panels for three regions (fixed effect and random effect models) and country-by-country (OLS regression) data. These relationships suggest that liberalisation promotes growth but growth itself may have negative effect on the trade balance for a large majority of countries.

Liberalisation can affect trade balance adversely in the short run as some evidence shows from the previous chapter. Hence, we study the impact of liberalisation on growth and trade deficits and current accounts of developing countries in Chapter 9. It is expected that trade liberalisation would promote economic growth from the supply side by leading to a more efficient use of resources, by encouraging competition and by increasing the flow of ideas and knowledge across national boundaries. Trade liberalisation could lead to faster import growth than export growth, and hence the supply side benefits may be offset by the unsustainable balance of the payment position. This study uses panel data for 42 countries (both time-series and cross-section dimension) to estimate the effect of trade liberalisation on growth and growth on trade balance while controlling for other factors such as income terms of trade. The major finding of the study is that trade liberalisation promotes growth in most countries, but the growth itself has a negative impact on the trade balance. Countries following trade liberalisation could have high real exchange rates, a worsening savings-investment balance and consequently a worsening current account and trade balance. This chapter uses the dynamic stochastic model of current account in which the principle of consumption smoothing is applied to rational forward-looking agents acting under inter-temporal budget constraints.

One of the models in a cross-section regression study makes use of political and security variables and concludes that the convergence or "catching-up" hypothesis is supported and extreme political repression tends to constrain growth. One unit change in the liberalisation index leads, on average, to a 1.62 percentage point change in growth rates, *ceteris paribus*.

Financial Instability and Volatility

So far, we have looked at the impact of trade liberalisation. In the last chapter (Chapter 10), financial liberalisation and its instability are examined. The study aims to examine the instability and volatility of various components of capital inflows/outflows to developing economies. It is indeed the case that both instability and volatility in these areas have increased during period 1990–1998 in relation to previous decades. Contagion and herd behaviours among private investors have contributed to financial instability and crises. International coordination of official financial and development assistance among donor countries and multilateral agencies may help to decrease the probability of future financial crises.

References

Bhagwati, J and A Kreuger (eds.) (1974). *Foreign Trade Regimes and Economic Development: A Special Conference Series on Foreign Trade Regimes and Economic Development*. New York: Cambridge University Press.

Bhagwati, J (2004). *In Defence of Globalisation*. Oxford: Oxford University Press.

Brahmbhatt, M and U Dadush (1996). Disparities in global integration. *Finance and Development*, 33(3), 1–4.

Dollar, D and A Kraay (2004). Trade, growth and poverty. *Economic Journal*, 114(493), F22–F49.

Dutta, M (2006). *China's Industrial Revolution and Economic Presence*. Singapore: World Scientific Publishers.

Feder, G (1982). On exports and economic growth. *Journal of Development Economics*, 12, 59–73.

Grossman, G and E Helpman (1991). *Innovation and Growth in the Global Economy*. Cambridge, MA: MIT Press.

Helpman, E and P Krugman (1989). *Trade Policy and Market Structure*. Cambridge, MA: MIT Press.

Klein, LR (2004). New growth centres in this globalized economy. *Journal of Policy Modelling*, 26(4), 499–505.

Leamer, E (1988). Measures of openness. In *Trade Policy and Empirical Analysis*, R Baldwin (Ed.), Chicago: Chicago University Press.

Letiche, JM (2006). Positive economic incentives, new behavioural economics and successful economic transition. *Journal of Asian Economics*, 17(5), 775–796.

Michaelopoulos, C (1999). Trade Policy and Market Access Issues for Developing Countries. World Bank PRWP No. 2214.

Panagariya, A (2004). Miracles and debacles: in defence of trade openness. *The World Economy*, 27(8), 1149–1171.

Rodriguez, F and D Rodrik (1999). Trade policy and economic growth: A skeptic's guide to cross-national evidence. NBER Working Paper No. W7081.

Sachs, J and A Warner (1995). Economic reform and the process of global integration. *Brookings Papers on Economic Activity*, 1, 1–118.

Stiglitz, J (2002). *Globalization and Its Discontents*. W.W. Norton & Company.

Summers, R, A Heston and B Aten (2001). *Penn World Table Version 6.0*. Center for International Comparisons at the University of Pennsylvania (CICUP).

Thirlwall, AP (2000). Trade, trade liberalisation and economic growth: Theory and evidence, pp. 1–27 Economic Research Paper No. 63, African Development Bank.

Thirlwall, AP and Hussain, NM (1982). The balance of payments constraint, capital flows and economic growth rate differences between developing countries. *Oxford Economic Papers*, 34(3), 498–509.

United Nations (2003). *Liberalisation and Globalisation: The Issues at Stake for the South and for UNCTAD*, pp. 1–60, Geneva, Switzerland; South Centre, United Nations.

UNCTAD (2001). *Trade Analysis and Information System*, CD ROM, Version 8.0. Geneva, Switzerland: United Nations.

UNCTAD (2004). *Handbook of Statistics*. Geneva, Switzerland: United Nations.

UNCTAD (2006). *Trade and Development Report, 2006*. Geneva, Switzerland: United Nations.

Wacziarg, R and KH Welch (2003). *Trade Liberalisation and Growth: New Evidence*. pp. 1–75, Working Paper No. 10152, National Bureau of Economic Research, Cambridge, MA.

Winters, LA (2004). Trade liberalisation and economic performance: An overview. *Economic Journal*, 114(493), F4–F21.

Wolf, M (2004). *Why Globalisation Works*. Connecticut, USA: Yale University Press.

World Bank (1987). *World Bank Development Report 1987*. Washington, DC.

World Bank (1993). *The East Asian Miracle: Economic Growth and Public Policy*. Washington, DC: World Bank Policy Research Report.

World Bank (2000). *International Trade and Development: Data on Import Tariff and NTBs*. Washington, DC.

Chapter 2

Disciplining Firms: The Impact of Trade Reforms on Profit Margins in Indian Industry*

Uma S. Kambhampati

Department of Economics, University of Reading, UK
les98usk@reading.ac.uk

Ashok Parikh

Department of Economics, University of East Anglia, UK
A.Parikh@uea.ac.uk

Introduction

In this paper, we analyse the effects of increased trade exposure on the profitability of firms in the Indian industry. The 1991 liberalisation in India sought to deregulate industries and expose firms to international competition. It represented both a challenge and an opportunity to the hitherto protected manufacturing sector in India. Such reforms are often expected to decrease profit margins as firms struggle to compete in international markets. There is, however, the possibility that increased competition may improve firm efficiency and provide a positive impetus to firm profitability (Singh *et al.*, 1999). The net effect would then be uncertain. In this area,

* We would like to thank the Reserve Bank of India for the data that has made this study possible. We are also grateful to Prof. Steve Davies and an anonymous referee for their comments on the previous version of this chapter.

this paper is different from many others in that it considers both these possibilities. An efficiency index, albeit a limited one, is created directly to analyse the impact of changing efficiency levels on firm profit margins.

Many studies of trade policy have found that increased exposure to international competition results in a dampening effect on profit margins in imperfectly competitive industries. Most of these studies have considered the pro-competitive effects of imports. Devarajan and Rodrik (1989) find that "liberalisation has an output-expanding, pro-competitive effect in key manufacturing industries" in Cameroon. An increase in import competition erodes the market power of domestic firms, leading them to increase output, i.e., the marginal revenue curve faced by domestic firms becomes flatter. Though the demand curve also shifts inwards (because the market share of imports has increased), the former decreases the incentive of domestic firms to withhold sales and increase prices. Levinsohn (1993) also confirms that imports provide market discipline in Turkey. Krishna and Mitra (1998) found that in the case of India, mark-ups not only decreased in the post-reform period in three (out of four) industries but also decreased to a level that leaves firms making losses. They rationalise this on the grounds that, "in the presence of adjustment and sunk costs, a firm may lose money while it adapts to a new trading environment". Since the study was able to access only two years of data after the reforms, it was unable to consider what might happen after firms had adapted to these conditions. Chand and Sen (1999) studying the case of India in an earlier period (1973–1988) also find that increased exposure to trade had a pro-competitive effect on domestic pricing.

In addition to squeezing profit margins in this way, trade reforms may increase efficiency and enable firms to maintain profit margins even while decreasing prices. This is particularly important because increased openness to trade enables domestic firms to import new technology and therefore improve the quality and efficiency both of products and of processes. Improvements in efficiency are also likely to occur, because increased competition decreases levels of X-inefficiency and slack amongst firms. Thus, although firms of quite different efficiency levels can survive simultaneously in a protected environment, such efficiency dispersion is likely to decrease once an economy is exposed to international competition

(Tybout, 1998). Nickell (1996) maintains that while the theoretical reasons for believing that increased competition would improve firm performance are not overwhelming, there is considerable empirical support for this view. Analysing efficiency in Indian manufacturing firms, Driffield and Kambhampati (forthcoming) find that efficiency has increased in five out of the six sectors that they studied since the reforms in 1991. Balakrishnan *et al.* (2000), however, in their study of total factor productivity growth in 2300 firms between 1988–1989 and 1997–1998 conclude that there was no evidence of any acceleration in productivity growth after liberalisation. Thus, there is, as yet, no consensus regarding the impact of reforms on the efficiency or the performance of firms.

Hypotheses and Data

In this paper we are interested in three main hypotheses:

- Has liberalisation influenced the profitability of firms in the Indian industry? More specifically, has increased international competition squeezed profit margins in India?
- To what extent has the effect of the reforms manifested itself through changes in a firm's behaviour, i.e., through its advertising expenditure, R&D, export and import ratios? Does liberalisation have a direct effect on profit margins or does it affect profit margins because it influences these behavioural variables?
- Do more efficient firms have larger profit margins than less efficient firms? Again, has the impact of such inefficiency changed since 1991?

To answer these questions, panel data on large and medium firms in the Indian manufacturing over a 19-year period (1980–1998) is used. The dataset is obtained from the Reserve Bank of India on tape and provides accounting information on these firms. It is a unique dataset providing information on a very large sample and across a long time period. The data covers firms across a number of industries in India. However, the panel is not balanced because some firms exit while others do not submit their returns on time. While we have been able to use the entire dataset for the analysis in Tables 1 and 2, we have created a much smaller *balanced* panel of firms that appear in every year for the econometric analysis in Table 3.

Table 1. Trend changes in sales and exports in indian industries.

	Log(sales) $= \alpha + \beta$ trend + γ dummy + δ trend*dummy		Log(exports) $= \alpha_x + \beta_x$ trend + γ_x dummy + δ_x trend*dummy	
	γ	δ	γ_x	δ_x
Insignificant	34	28	26	26
Above 0	17	25	15	26
Below 0	34	23	25	14
Total	85	76	66	66

Note: The dummy variable was included in all the industry sales equations, but the trend*dummy term was only included in 76 industries, because in the other nine industries, including it reduced the significance of all the other variables.

Table 2. Changes in exports, imports and profits.

	1980–1990, exports/sales		1992–1998, exports/sales	
	> 0.045	< 0.045	> 0.045	< 0.045
Exports/sales	0.1408	0.006	0.1624	0.008
Imports/sales	0.0817	0.051	0.098	0.048
Profit1	0.2025	0.2006	0.2292	0.09
Profit2	0.2427	0.2473	0.2720	0.1432

Note: Profit1 = sales – (raw materials + stores + fuel + salaries + repairs + rent + other manufacturing expenses); Profit2 = sales – (raw materials + stores + fuel + salaries), where export/sales = 0.045 is the sample average.

The period covered in the dataset includes 1991, which was a period of policy reforms in India. It is also the focus of our study. However, this structural change, together with the small, longitudinal size of the sample, has meant that we have had to assume that the series is stationary without conducting unit root tests. Before we go any further, however, it is worth considering the nature of the reforms and their effect on firms' activities.

Reforms and Their Effect in India

In 1991, the Indian government's structural adjustment programme encompassed the first sustained attempts to increase the autonomy of the private sector. The programme attempted to deregulate foreign trade and the labour market. The reforms have been extensively discussed, and further details can be obtained from Ahluwalia *et al.* (1996), Bhaduri and Nayyar (1996) and Joshi and Little (1996). While exit continues to be difficult,[a] the government has begun to decrease its support of inefficient firms and has accepted, de facto, the need for redundancies.

Given the decreasing levels of protection of domestic firms as well as increased freedom for firms to import, expand and lay off labour, one might expect levels of economic activity to have changed considerably since the reforms. To capture the pattern of these changes, we estimate simple trend equations for each of the industries in our sample for the sales and export variables. The equations were of the following generic specification:

$$\text{Log(sales)} = \alpha + \beta \text{ trend } + \gamma \text{ dummy } + \delta \text{ trend}^{*}\text{dummy},$$
$$\text{Log(exports)} = \alpha_x + \beta_x \text{ trend } + \gamma_x \text{ dummy } + \delta_x \text{ trend}^{*}\text{dummy},$$

where trend is the simple time trend over the 19 years, dummy $= 1$ for year > 1991; else $= 0$. The interactive term is included to pick up the post-1991 change in trend.

Initial estimations revealed that in some industries, the trend*dummy term was insignificant and including it reduced the significance of both the β and γ coefficients. Therefore, two separate specifications, one with this interaction term and one without, were tested, and the one that was most significant was chosen. Table 1 presents the results only for those industries where at least one term in the equation was significant.[b] Column 2 in the table indicates the number of industries in which the γ coefficient (the coefficient of the 1991 dummy) is insignificant, above 0 and below 0 for the sales variable. Column 3, on the other hand, summarises the results for the δ coefficient (the coefficient of the post-1991 trend). Columns 4 and 5 repeat this for the exports variable.

Table 1 indicates that sales decreased in 1991 in 34 industries (γ coefficient is negative) and increased in only 17 industries. The exports equation, on the other hand, indicates that while a few industries saw a one-off increase

---

[a] A firm that wishes to exit has to be "declared" bankrupt by the Board for Industrial and Financial Restructuring. The process can take up to two to three years and sometimes as long as 10 years (Ahluwalia *et al.*, 1996).

[b] While at least one term was significant in 85 industries for the sales equations, this was true in only 66 industries for the exports equations.

in exports (15/66) in 1991, more (26/66) experienced an increasing trend after 1991.

Table 2 summarises the export and import sales ratios as well as profit margin figures over this period. The table is divided into the pre-and post-1991 period and on the basis of the average export sales ratio in our sample (Expsal = 0.045). It shows that both exports and imports as a proportion of sales are generally higher in the post-1991 period.

Table 2 generally reflects the poor export performance of most Indian firms (Lall, 1999), with even the firms that have above-average exporting figures showing an export sales ratio of only 0.14 (1980–1990). Although export to sales ratios do not change significantly after the reforms, the profit margins of firms that export less than the average decrease in the post-1991 period. Thus, the difference between the profit margins of the above- and below-average exporters increased significantly after the reforms.

The table therefore seems to indicate that the profit performance of below-average exporters was worse than that of the above-average exporters. What is not clear from this table, however, is whether exports increase profit margins or whether there is some self-selection in that the more profitable firms enter the export market. In fact, the differential profit margin incorporates three effects — the effect of the reforms on profit margins generally, the effect of these reforms on export levels and the effect of the increases in exports on profit margins. These effects cannot be separated in the table. This requires a more detailed analysis of the effect of exports on profit margins, which we undertake in the following section when we estimate our regression model. It is found there that, once the effect of all other variables is taken into account, contrary to the results given in Table 2, exports actually have a depressing impact on profit margins as many early studies have found. Thus, the association highlighted in Table 2 is not confirmed by our multivariate analysis in the next section.

Empirical Estimation

As already indicated, we have three hypotheses of interest in this paper. An attempt was made to test these hypotheses using a balanced panel of 281 firms across 19 years. Since both cross-sectional variation and inter-temporal variation can provide useful information in such estimation, variables are classified into one of three types: firm time-invariant, time firm-invariant and firm-time varying variables. The firm-time invariant variables are constant over time but specific for the cross-sectional units: a textile firm compared to a steel firm has very specific characteristics that are reflected in firm specific constants. The time firm-invariant variable is the same for cross-sectional units at a given point of time, but they vary through time. One example of this would be neutral technological change considered by year effects. In this study, the 1991 liberalisation could have caused changes in the firm's behaviour, which may be captured by time-effect-dummies since 1991. The firm-time varying variables are the ones that vary across cross-sectional units at a point in time and exhibit variations through time. Most of the variables are time varying in this study.

In order to test our hypotheses using this data, we estimated the following basic equation:

$$\begin{aligned}\text{Profit margin} = {} & f(\text{MS, KO, ADS, RDS, MANREMS, EXPS, IMPS,}\\ & \text{Dum, Trend, DEVAC, DEVAC*Dum}),\end{aligned}$$

where profit margin = Profit1 or Profit2,

$$\begin{aligned}
\text{Profit1} &= (\text{sales} - (\text{raw materials} + \text{fuel} + \text{salaries} + \text{repairs} + \text{rent}\\
&\quad + \text{other manufacturing expenses}))/\text{sales and}\\
\text{Profit2} &= (\text{sales} - (\text{raw materials} + \text{fuel} + \text{salaries}))/\text{sales}\\
\text{MS} &= \text{share of the firm's sales in a given industry}\\
\text{KO} &= \text{gross fixed assets/sales of the firm}\\
\text{ADS} &= \text{advertising/sales ratio}\\
\text{RDS} &= \text{R\&D/sales ratio}\\
\text{MANREMS} &= \text{managerial remuneration/sales}\\
\text{EXPS} &= \text{exports/sales ratio}\\
\text{IMPS} &= \text{imports/sales ratio}\\
\text{Dum} &= \text{dummy which is 1 for year} > 1991 \text{ and}\\
&= 0 \text{ for all other years}\\
\text{Trend} &= \text{time trend}\\
\text{DEVAC} &= \text{average cost of the firm} - \text{minimum average}\\
&\quad\ \text{cost in the sample}\\
\text{DEVACD} &= \text{DEVAC*Dum}
\end{aligned}$$

Most of these variables have the standard interpretations. Thus, market share (MS) could lead to higher profit margins, because it enables firms to take advantage of economies of scale and reduce costs. It also helps increase a firm's market power. The capital–output (KO) ratio normalises for the capital intensity of production of a firm. Advertising (ADS) and R&D (RDS) intensity denote the ability of a firm to differentiate its output. They can be seen (as in traditional industrial organisation theories) as barriers to entry, which enable incumbents to earn supernormal profits. Alternatively, they can be seen as endogenous sunk costs (Sutton, 1991, 1998), which reflect a consumer's willingness to pay. Within the latter framework, AD would not necessarily always be profitable. Within the latter framework, AD is most likely to increase profits in high concentration industries and when the increase in advertising expenditure is not a "local deviation" but a "discrete jump" to some high level (Sutton, 1991). Managerial remuneration is often expected to increase profit margins because it is seen as a proxy for good management. There is considerable literature (Nickell, 1996) that indicates that an increase in competition of the kind that would arise with liberalisation increases managerial effort and improves firms' performance.

Before we go any further, it is worth considering the possible endogeneity of some of these independent variables. The potential dual causality between the dependent and independent variables in any analysis of profit margins has long been recognised. Thus, while AD may affect profit margins, the level of profitability will also determine the AD expenditure. Similarly, while exports may influence profit margins, it is equally possible that only profitable firms enter export markets. This is true for a number of variables in models of profitability, including managerial remuneration. Thus, while managerial remuneration may increase managers' efficiency and therefore profit margins, it is equally possible that firms with higher profit margins pay managers higher salaries. One way to get round this problem is to distinguish the timing of the effect. Thus, while the effect of AD on profit margins is contemporaneous, profitability in its turn is only likely to influence the *future* AD expenditure. Similarly, while the impact of profitability on exports is lagged, the impact of exports on profitability is contemporaneous. Finally, while the effect of MANREM on profit margins is current, current profits are only likely to influence managerial remuneration in the future. The use of panel data helps us to separate out some of these effects.

In addition to these industrial structure and conduct variables, we also have a number of liberalisation-related variables. Exports (EXPS) are included, because a number of studies have shown that the competition unleashed by liberalisation squeezes profit margins. Additionally, exports themselves are expected to have increased after 1991 for some firms. On the other hand, however, Table 2 seems to reject this hypothesis, because it indicates that the profit margins of exporting firms in India are larger, and increasing, relative to those of non-exporting firms. Returning to the discussion of causality amongst variables, it is sometimes argued that profits influence exports, rather than the other way round. Thus, firms that are more profitable enter export markets. This might be because they are better able to undertake the investment and marketing costs required for entry into the international market. Also, they may simply have deeper pockets and so can sustain losses, if necessary. As noted earlier, however, while the impact of exports on profits is contemporaneous, the reverse impact of profits on exports is likely to be lagged.[c]

One of the advantages of liberalisation has been cited as the ability to import up-to-date technology (Howell and Kambhampati, 1998, 1999). Such technology could be expected to increase the product quality and the efficiency of the firm production. Imports (IMPS) are therefore included in the model, and a positive relationship is hypothesised between this variable and the profit margin. A dummy variable for the post-1991 years (Dum) is also included to capture all other changes that occurred in 1991.

A second hypothesis stated that profit margins might vary not only because market shares, advertising expenditures or R&D expenditures vary across firms but also because these variables may, in their turn, be systematically affected by the reforms. More specifically, it is possible that AD expenditures may have increased after the reforms and that, though, profit margins may otherwise have been unaffected; this "discrete" change in the AD expenditure (Sutton, 1991) may have pushed margins upwards. A similar argument could be made for market shares, capital–output ratios, RDS or managerial remuneration. In the case of exports too, it is possible that

[c] In the latter case, it is the past profitability of the firm that will influence current exports.

some firms may have managed to increase their export volumes, while others lag behind. The effect of liberalisation on the former would be larger than on the latter (which remain more domestic-market oriented). To allow for such effects, Eqs. (2) and (4) were estimated, where interaction terms between our post-1991 dummy and each of these variables were included.

To consider the third hypothesis — the impact of *relative efficiency* on profit margins — we created a relative efficiency index. The efficiency index is based on the observed minimum cost per unit value of output for each year. The distance from this observed minimum cost per unit value of output is regarded as the inefficiency of that firm from the most efficient manufacturing firm for that year.[d] This can be seen as a deterministic measure of inefficiency.[e] The hypothesis was that firms that are furthest from the most efficient firm would have lower profit margins than those closer to the most efficient firm. If this is not the case, then it implies that these firms have significant market power that enables them to maintain high margins even when they are inefficient. To test this hypothesis, we included three separate efficiency[f] terms. The first, DEVAC, is the distance of each firm from the most efficient in the sample. The larger the deviation from the minimum cost per unit of value added, the smaller one would expect the profitability to be. In addition, DEVAC*Dum and DEVAC*exports were included to consider whether the effect of efficiency changed after 1991

[d] As we consider the unit value of output rather than the physical volume of output, the measure can be used for the entire manufacturing sector. The cost *per unit value* of output must be similar in all industries and high value goods in general have high costs (though this may be affected by profit margins varying across industries). This is especially significant because the firms do not remain in the same industry classification over the entire period of 19 years.

[e] Farrell's (1957) measure of efficiency is defined as the minimum cost per unit of physical output for homogenous goods. We have the whole manufacturing sector, where there is heterogeneity, and hence we chose the minimum cost per unit value of output in each period for the entire manufacturing sector.

[f] Initially, we attempted to compile inefficiency as the deviation of average cost of a firm from the minimum of average cost *within an industry*. This, however, posed two problems: (a) the firms within an industry do not remain in the same industry classification throughout the period, and (b) when the industry measure of inefficiency is computed, sometimes there were only two or three firms in a given industry in some years. We therefore decided to conduct a separate industry-level analysis of industry 451. This industry (Machinery) is chosen because it is one of the few in our balanced panel sample with a sufficiently large sample size.

or amongst the export-oriented firms. DEVAC*exports was found to be insignificant in most estimations, and therefore it was excluded from the results presented in Table 3.

Results

The use of panel data dictates that the model is estimated using both random and fixed effects estimation methods. Within the latter is included both the "within-effects" and the "between-effects" estimation. While the within-effects estimation takes firm-specific fixed effects, where the focus is on the time-series dimension in the data, into account, the "between-effects" model explores the cross-sectional dimension by using only the firm means over time. The two specifications were tested to see which fits better using an F-test, and it was found that in most cases, the within estimation (fixed effects) dominates over the between-effects model. In all cases, the estimated slope coefficients were restricted to be identical across firms.[g] Finally, the random effect estimator was estimated, which in general is specified as follows:

$$y_{it} = X_{it}\beta + \varepsilon_{it}, \quad \text{where } \varepsilon_{it} = \alpha_i + \eta_{it}.$$

The error term consists of firm specific effects and a combined firm and time varying error. The random effect estimator is preferred over the within (or fixed effect) estimation if the time-invariant firm specific dummy variables α_i are uncorrelated with X_{it}. When the true model is the random effect model, OLS will yield consistent estimates of β, but the standard errors will be underestimated. Hence, a Generalised Least Squares procedure is used.[h]

[g] The panel data has a number of advantages: (a) it increases the number of observations; (b) it adds more variability and more information; (c) it permits the data to be treated in two dimensions separately, provided there are enough time periods for which data are available and (d) it makes econometric specification rich so that we can use a fixed effect and a random effect model.

[h] When there is no uncorrelated firm-specific component of variance, the random effect estimator reduces to a pooled estimator. The pooled estimator weighs all observations equally. The OLS estimator on the pooled data does not use the information about heteroscedasticity that can result from repeated observations. The random effect estimator is a combination of the between and within estimator with GLS weights. The random effect model assumes that the explanatory variables are independently distributed of both the error term and the firm effect, where the latter is randomly distributed with a common mean and

Table 3. Regression results for the four models.

Variable	Profit1				Profit2			
	Equation (1)		Equation (2)		Equation (3)		Equation (4)	
	Coeff.	t	Coeff.	t	Coeff.	t	Coeff.	t
Market share	−0.009	−0.45	0.01	0.61	−0.02	−1.18	−0.002	−0.08
Dum	0.016	1.60	−0.22	−8.91	0.017	1.72	−0.24	−9.36**
Trend	0.0011	1.25	−0.003	−2.68**	0.0007	0.78	−0.003	−3.42**
Trend*Dum			0.02	11.5**			0.02	11.98**
Dum*market share			−0.03	−1.73			−0.03	−1.82
ADS	1.85	6.74**	2.12	6.52**	1.94	7.05**	2.18	6.65**
Dum*ADS			−0.46	−1.62			−0.45	−1.57
MANREMS	−59.25	−399.6**	−24.5	−17.8**	−58.05	−389.9**	−23.77	−17.22**
Dum*MANREMS			−35.0	−25.4**			−34.53	−25.0**
RDS	7.42	12.06**	2.15	2.02*	8.54	13.82**	2.24	2.1*
Dum*RDS			7.01	5.92**			8.36	7.03**
Exports	−0.13	−3.32**	−0.12	−2.25*	−0.11	−2.60**	−0.09	−1.78
Imports	0.21	5.08**	−0.009	−0.18	0.20	4.69**	−0.08	−1.51
Dum*imports			0.13	2.50**			−0.03	−0.62
Dum*exports			−0.09	−1.55			0.14	2.68**
KO	−0.03	−377.6**	−0.06	−9.43**	−0.03	−373.6**	−0.05	−9.11**
Dum*KO			0.02	3.57**			0.20	3.31**
DEVAC[1]	−0.001	−1.84*	−0.0004	−0.78	−0.001	−2.07*	−0.001	−0.99
DEVAC*Dum	0.003	1.29	0.0008	0.41	0.0035	1.55	0.001	0.63
Adj-$R2$	0.9855		0.9876		0.9851		0.9873	
S.E. of regression	0.1759		0.1625		0.1766		0.1631	
Hausman Chi-square[2]	85.63	0.000*	220.65	0.000*	84.29	0.000*	195.49	0.000*
F-test	26.8	0.000*	17.58	0.000*	31.63	0.000*	22.52	0.000*

* Implies significance at the 10 percent level and ** at the 5 percent level.
[1] For DEVAC and DEVAC*Dum, we use slightly different definitions in the Profit1 and Profit2 equations.
[2] In the Hausman test, the null hypothesis is the random effect model, and this is rejected by the presented test statistic in the table.

The fixed effect model was tested against the random effect model using the Hausman test, and it was found that in the entire sample, the fixed effect model dominates. However, in our single industry (451) sample, the random effect specification dominates, perhaps not surprisingly, because firms are likely to be more homogeneous in a well-defined industry group and individual firm effects will not be correlated with the explanatory variables. This suggests that, provided sufficient observations are available to create a balanced panel (as was possible in the case of industry 451), a disaggregate industry-level analysis may remove heterogeneity and provide better results.

Four different model specifications were estimated. The basic model includes a single post-1991 dummy and trend term (Eqs. (1) and (3) in Table 3 below). It is estimated using Profit1 and Profit2 as our dependent variables, respectively. While the Profit1 variable is the profit margin after all costs have been excluded, the Profit2 variable measures the profit margin after raw materials, fuel and wage costs have been excluded. Results are presented using both variables because there is considerable controversy, especially in the case of India, over the way in which interest, rent and other manufacturing costs are presented in balance sheets. It is found, however, that results do not vary significantly or systematically between two measures of profitability. Equations (2) and (4) include dummy *interaction* terms between each variable and the 1991 dummy to see if the variable behaved differently after 1991 (see hypothesis 2).

As already indicated, an F-test indicates that the within-effects estimation was preferred to the "between-effects" one. In addition, the Hausman test indicates that the fixed effect model was better than the random effect specification in the overall sample. We therefore present these results in Table 3.

The results of Table 3 indicate that the post-1991 dummy is positive but only marginally significant in Eqs. (1) and (3), implying that though profit margins may have increased after the reforms, this effect was neither large nor systematic across firms in the sample. In fact, when the effect of

---

variance. This specification implies a homoscedastic variance for all i and t. However, the specification allows serial correlation over time only between the disturbances of the same firm, and this is identical for all firms.

the reforms is allowed to be divided into the effects caused by changes in each of the other variables after the reforms, it is found that the residual effect of the liberalisation on profit margins becomes negative and highly significant. Thus, the coefficient of Dum (in Eqs. (2) and (4) in the table) becomes negative once the dummy interaction terms are included. The post-liberalisation trend (Trend*Dum) is positive and significant in the case of both Profit1 and Profit2, implying that profit margins have generally shown an increasing trend in the post-1991 period. For the most general model related to Profit1 in Table 3, (column 4) the Generalised Method of Moments (GMM) estimation using one and two period lags in a dynamic panel set-up (Arellano and Bond, 1991) was also used. The results obtained were qualitatively (signs of the regression coefficients) similar to the results presented in Table 3.

Results indicate that the market share variable was not significant in any of these specifications (though it becomes significant in the intra-industry equation estimated for industry 451). The firm profitability across the sample therefore seems to have been driven by factors unrelated to market share or structure power. Both advertising (ADS) and R&D (RDS) have a consistently positive and significant effect on profitability. This is not surprising, and it reflects the increasing importance of these variables in the firm's arsenal of competitive instruments since the reforms (see Ghoshal *et al.*, 2001, for case study based confirmation of this intuition). Firms have begun to use these variables not only to increase consumers' willingness to pay (Sutton, 1991)[i] but also as competitive instruments against other firms, creating market niches and differentiating their products. The effect of R&D expenditure increases even further in the post-1991 period while that of AD shows no significant trend.

The table also indicates that firms with the higher capital intensity of production (KO) and higher managerial salary bill related to sales (MANREM) tend to make smaller profits. This seems to imply that neither capital nor managers are being as productively employed as they could be. Note, however, that the two variables react very differently after the reforms. Thus,

---

[i] The cases of Bajaj Auto Ltd. and of Hindustan Lever Ltd. and Nirma Detergents (Ghoshal *et al.*, 2001) reflect this trend.

while capital utilisation has improved since the reforms, managerial remuneration continues to have a negative impact on profit margins. This is not surprising, because although cases of firms offering profit-related bonuses and employee-stock option schemes are increasing in India, they are still few and far between. Therefore, managerial salaries and profits are not as closely related in India as they have become in China, where profit-related bonuses are an increasingly large proportion of the salary (Minami and Hondai, 1995). In India, therefore, higher managerial remuneration seems to impose a cost on the firm without providing a commensurate return.

Turning to the trade-related variables, it is found that exports lead to lower profit margins in all four equations. This seems to confirm the "trade as market discipline" hypothesis of many earlier studies (Krishna and Mitra, 1998; Levinsohn, 1993). In the post-1991 period, however, there are some signs, though not conclusive, that exports may be increasing profit margins (see Eq. (4) coefficient on Dum*exports). The effect of imports on profit margins, on the other hand, seems to be less clear. While imports, over the entire sample period, seem to have a positive impact on profitability (Eqs. (1) and (2)), this effect disappears once the effect of the reforms (Eqs. (2) and (4)) is allowed for. This result is confirmed by Driffield and Kambhampati (2003) who find that imports have not significantly increased efficiency in a range of broad industrial sectors in India between 1988 and 1994.[j] Patibandla (1998, p. 421) relates this to the fact that large firms in India do not feel the need to undertake systematic re-organisational efforts in adapting imported technologies to local conditions most efficiently. The residual effect of the reforms on profit margins (after each of the above trade-related effects is taken into account) is negative (coefficient of Dum in Eqs. (2) and (4)) indicating that, in general, the reforms have been pro-competitive.

Finally, our efficiency variable DEVAC has a negative effect on profit margins, indicating that the further away the firm is from the most efficient one in the sample, the smaller is its profit margin. This is as expected.

[j] While it is possible that the causality is reversed, i.e., that more profitable firms are more likely to import up-to-date capital equipment, this relationship is likely to be lagged rather than be contemporaneous as in the current specification. Thus, the last year's profits relationship will influence this year's imports. Therefore, there is no real simultaneity bias in these estimates.

As indicated earlier, this effect is much more significant in the "between" estimation than in the "within" model, implying that inter-firm variations in efficiency are more important than variations across time. Thus, efficiency seems to be a firm time-invariant variable which gives better results in the between-effects specification. It is also found that the coefficients on both the efficiency variables (DEVAC and DEVAC*Dum) are larger and more significant in the "between" estimates.

Thus, there is evidence that liberalisation has had a significant impact on profit margins in our overall sample. To see whether these results are robust within a single industry, the model for industry 451 is estimated, which is one of the few within our sample to have a sufficiently large balanced panel.

Industry 451: machinery manufacturing

Industry 451, the machinery manufacturing industry in India, is one of the few industries for which a sufficiently large sample (26 firms over 19 years) is available (Table 4). The only difference in our model for this industry relative to the models in Table 3 relates to the efficiency term, which is constructed here on the basis of the distance from the most efficient firm *within* this industry and not on the basis of the most efficient within the entire sample[k] (as in the case of Table 3).

It is found that market shares have a positive effect on profit margins in this industry (Eq. (2)), unlike in the overall sample. This is not surprising since the variable is likely to be more comparable across firms within an industry. This effect decreases after 1991. Contrary to the results in Table 3, R&D initially has a negative effect on profit margins, though after 1991, there is a positive trend. Similarly, imports also have a negative effect on profit margins, confirming the results for the larger sample (Table 3).[l] Given that the example is the machinery industry, it is not surprising that advertising expenditure was not a significant determinant of profit margins. As expected, at this intra-industry level, the efficiency term becomes extremely

[k] The measure of inefficiency is at an industry level. It is the deviation of the actual average cost of a firm from the minimum cost at an industry level.

[l] In their analysis of the determinants of industrial efficiency, Driffield and Kambhampati (2003) also find that imports decrease efficiency in the wider Machine and Machine Tools sector.

Table 4. Results for industry 451.

Variable	Profit1				Profit2			
	Equation (1)		Equation (2)		Equation (3)		Equation (4)	
	Coeff.	*t*	Coeff.	*t*	Coeff.	*t*	Coeff.	*t*
Market share	0.16	0.38	1.53	2.7**	−0.10	−0.25	0.8	1.46
Dum	−0.001	−0.06	−0.02	−0.88	0.0008	0.08	−0.02	−1.04
Trend	0.002	2.30*	0.001	0.73	0.0018	2.58**	0.001	1.04
Trend*Dum			0.002	1.21			0.002	0.98
Dum*market share			−1.45	−3.6**			−1.04	−2.67**
ADS	0.83	1.03	0.93	1.10	0.58	0.75	0.65	0.79
Dum*ADS			−0.21	−0.18			−0.12	−0.11
MANREMS	−0.36	−0.38	−0.89	−0.60	−0.20	−0.22	−0.74	−0.49
Dum*MANREMS			0.43	0.29			0.53	0.37
RDS	0.42	0.72	−1.41	−1.9*	−0.03	−0.05	−1.21	−1.72*
Dum*RDS			3.92	3.6**			2.74	2.62**
Exports	−0.07	−1.22	−0.15	−1.53	0.01	0.20	−0.03	−0.31
Imports	−0.16	−4.10**	−0.22	−4.43**	−0.15	−3.98**	0.07	0.77
Dum*imports			0.10	1.66			−0.23	−4.79**
Dum*exports			0.12	1.20			0.15	2.49*
KO	−0.01	−1.45	−0.001	−0.12	−0.0061	−0.83	0.0008	0.1
Dum*KO			−0.01	−0.85			0.0003	0.02
DEVAC[1]	−0.81	−18.3**	−0.79	−18.3**	−0.85	−22.1**	−0.83	−21.53**
DEVAC*Dum	0.04	0.79	0.03	0.71	0.04	0.96	0.04	0.88
Constant			0.29	19.0**			0.34	23.49
Adj-$R2$	0.8093		0.4880		0.8427		0.5892	
S.E. of regression	0.0457		0.0751		0.0433		0.0701	
Hausman Chi-square[2]	18.43	0.0305	23.34	0.1387	15.37	0.0814	21.18	0.1715
F-test	27.04	**		**	26.24	**		

* implies significance at the 10 percent level and ** at the 5 percent level.
[1] For DEVAC and DEVAC*Dum, we use slightly different definitions in the Profit1 and Profit2 equations.
[2] In the Hausman test, the null hypothesis is the random effect model, and this is rejected by the presented test statistic in the table.

significant and negative (DEVAC), indicating that the firms furthest from the most efficient firm have the lowest profit margins.

Conclusion

These results indicate that liberalisation had a significant impact on firm profit margins. However, its main effect was through other firm variables — market shares, advertising, R&D and exports — all of which changed after 1991. While exports have had a pro-competitive effect on profit margins in the sample, AD and R&D both cause an increase in profit margins. It was also found that neither capital nor managerial capabilities (as proxied by remuneration) are particularly effective in increasing profit margins.

While the efficiency terms had the expected negative effect in the original equation, this effect becomes insignificant once interaction between the dummy and other variables (Eqs. (2) and (3)) are allowed for. However, it is found that in the "between-effects" estimation, where the cross-sectional variation between firms is emphasised, the efficiency terms are more significant. Thus, the difference in efficiency across firms is more significant in influencing profit margins than the variation of this efficiency across time. The efficiency term also becomes very significant in our intra-industry regression (industry 451), indicating once again that it is the "within" industry variation that is most significant.

References

Ahluwalia, IJ, R Mohan and O Goswami (1996). *Policy Reform in India*. New Delhi: Oxford and IBH Publishing Co. Pvt. Ltd.

Arellano, M and S Bond (1991). Some tests of specification for panel data: Monte carlo evidence and an application to employment equations. *Review of Economic Studies*, 58, 277–297.

Balakrishnan, P, K Pushpangadan and M Suresh Babu (2000). Trade liberalisation and productivity growth in manufacturing. *Economic and Political Weekly*, 7 October, 3678–3682.

Bhaduri, A and D Nayyar (1996). *The Intelligent Person's Guide to Liberalisation*. India: Penguin.

Chand, S and K Sen (1999). Competitive pressures from trade exposure: Evidence from Indian manufacturing. *Indian Economic Review*, 34(2), 113–126.

Devarajan, S and D Rodrik (1989). Trade liberalization in developing countries: Do imperfect competition and scale economies matter? *AEA Papers and Proceedings*, 79(2), 283–287.

Driffield, N and US Kambhampati (forthcoming). Trade liberalisation and the efficiency of firms in Indian manufacturing. *Review of Development Economics*, 7, 419–430.

Farrell, M (1957). The measurement of productive efficiency. *Journal of the Royal Statistical Society, Series A, General*, 120(part 3), 253–281.

Ghoshal, S, G Piramal and S Buddhiraja (2001). *World Class in India*. New Delhi: Penguin.

Howell, J and US Kambhampati (1998). Liberalisation and labour: The effect on formal sector workers. *Journal of International Development*, 10(4), 439–452.

Howell, J and US Kambhampati (1999). The challenge of economic reforms: The response of India's firms, presented at the *ASSA Meetings in New York*, January 1999.

Joshi, V and IMD Little (1996). *India's Economic Reforms: 1991–2001*. Delhi: OUP.

Krishna, P and D Mitra (1998). Trade liberalisation, market discipline and productivity growth: New evidence from India. *Journal of Development Economics*, 56, 447–462.

Lall, S (1999). India's manufactured exports: Comparative structure and prospects. *World Development*, 27(10), 1769–1786.

Levinsohn, J (1993). Testing The imports-as-market-discipline hypothesis. *Journal of International Economics*, 35, 1–22.

Minami, R and S Hondai (1995). An evaluation of the enterprise reform in China: Income share of labor and profitability in the machine industry. *Hitotsubashi Journal of Economics*, 36(2), 125–143.

Nickell, SJ (1996). Competition and corporate performance. *Journal of Political Economy*, 104(4), 724–746.

Patibandla, M (1998). Structure, organizational behaviour, and technical efficiency: The case of an Indian industry. *Journal of Economic Behaviour and Organization*, 34, 419–434.

Reserve Bank of India, Data provided on tape for 1700 firms (1980–1998).

Singh, A, J Glen and R Matthias (1999). How intensive is competition in the emerging markets? An analysis of corporate rates of return from nine emerging markets. IMF Working Paper No. WP/99/32.

Sutton, J (1998). *Technology and Market Structure: Theory and History*. Cambridge, MA: MIT Press.

Sutton, J (1991). *Sunk Costs and Market Structure: Price Competition, Advertising and the Evolution of Concentration*. Cambridge, MA: MIT Press.

Tybout, J (1998). Manufacturing firms in developing countries: How well do they do and why? *Mimeo*.

Chapter 3
Has Liberalisation Affected Profit Margins in the Indian Industry?*

Uma S. Kambhampati

Department of Economics, University of Reading, UK
les98usk@reading.ac.uk

Ashok Parikh

Department of Economics, University of East Anglia, UK
A.Parikh@uea.ac.uk

Introduction

Traditionally, profit studies have been nested within a static structure–conduct performance framework, which assumes that the industry is in equilibrium. This has been criticised on the grounds that the data used to estimate these models are not generated from equilibrium positions and may be generated during random or temporary departures from equilibrium (Geroski, 1990, p. 17). Thus, while a policy to control profits in a highly concentrated industry may seem reasonable, it may only reinforce an already existing error-correction mechanism, which functions to bid excess profits

* We are grateful to Mike Utton, Steve Davies and Nigel Driffield for their comments on this chapter. We would also like to thank two anonymous referees for some extremely useful suggestions on this chapter. The second author is grateful to Leverhulme Trust for the award of Emeritus Fellowship which facilitated the completion of this study. We would like to thank the Reserve Bank of India for making the data available to us.

away through increased entry. Schmalensee (1989, p. 356) therefore suggested that "there is a clear need for theoretical work on dynamic market models that can capture both inter-industry and intra-industry differences, particularly in response to cyclical demand shifts". Since then attempts have been made (Conyon and Machin, 1991a; Machin and van Reenen, 1993; Geroski, 1990; Geroski and Jacquemin, 1988) to model profit margins within a dynamic setting.

In this chapter, we make use of firm-level panel data to analyse profit margins in the Indian industry. The chapter makes a number of contributions to the existing literature. First, it uses panel data over an 18-year period to estimate a dynamic market model for profit margins in the Indian manufacturing. The length of the time period of our sample implies that we can consider both the cyclical behaviour of profits and other dynamic patterns (captured by the lag terms, trend and dummies for the 1991 structural break). Second, the chapter explicitly considers whether a structural break (in terms of policy as well as increased competitiveness such as the one that occurred in India in 1991) is likely to change the impact that a firm's behaviour (advertising, research and development expenditure, efficiency, utilisation of managerial staff and capital) has on its profit margins. To do this, we model the conjectural variations of firms as being determined by relative market shares (Clarke and Davies, 1982) as well as by the reforms in 1991 (see section "Data"). Third, we analyse firm-level profit margins, while taking account of industry-level differences. To do this, we estimate our models across firms but also divide our sample into nine broad industrial sectors. Fourth, the methodology we employ (Arellano and Bond, 1991) to estimate our dynamic model across panel data allows us to take into account a long-standing criticism of cross-sectional profit margin studies that market structure (and conduct) variables like market share, advertising and product differentiation may not be exogenous. Fifth, this methodology (Arellano and Bond, 1991) also helps us to overcome problems of autocorrelation and lags in economic behaviour that are inherent in most profit studies. We can therefore be more confident that our estimates are consistent and are asymptotically efficient. Sixth, we explicitly include relative efficiency (or distance from the most efficient firm in the sector). This enables us to consider the extent of managerial slack in the firm and, with the inclusion of the post-1991 dummy, helps us to test whether such slack is reduced in the face of increased competition. Finally, to our knowledge, a comprehensive analysis of profit margins has not been done at the firm level for India, certainly not since the reforms in 1991.

In the second section, we provide a brief literature review. In the third section, we discuss the dynamic context of this study. The fourth section puts forward the modelling structure while the fifth section provides a summary of the available data. In the sixth section, the dynamic panel model and estimation procedures are explained, while in the seventh section, the results are discussed. In the last section, summary and conclusions both at a sectoral (industry) level and manufacturing sector are drawn.

Literature

Much empirical work on profit margins is founded on the Cowling and Waterson (1976) model that shows profit margins to be a function of market shares, a conjectural variation term and the industry price elasticity of demand. As the conjectural variation is unobservable, it has been modelled as a function of the firm's market share on the grounds that a firm's response will depend upon the ratio of its market share relative to that of other firms. In essence, the conjectural variation term was seen as a function of the extent of market power in an industry. In addition, by assuming that the price elasticity of demand is constant, a positive relationship between the market share (or industry concentration) and profit margins is hypothesised. Testing this relationship formed the mainstay of profit studies for a long time. Recent studies, however, have found that the hypothesised relationship does not always materialise (Conyon and Machin, 1991b). The relationship seems to depend upon the definition of profit margins chosen, industry characteristics and upon business cycle conditions.

More comprehensive models of profit margins attempt to allow for variations in industry characteristics by including a number of other structural and conduct variables (including economies of scale, advertising, product differentiation, labour market variables and trade variables). These models are eclectic and include a combination of variables that influence both prices and costs.

In cross-sectional analyses, the potential endogeneity of concentration (and even advertising) was taken into account by estimating a system of equations (Geroski, 1982). With the increasing availability of panel data, however, the endogeneity is being corrected using an instrumental variable methodology wherein lagged values of variables can be used to instrument for the endogenous variables. Such data also facilitate the estimation of dynamic market models of profitability. Many of these models (Geroski, 1990; Geroski and Jacquemein, 1988) consider whether market concentration (power) allows firms to earn supernormal profits over long periods of time. They therefore included a lagged dependent variable to allow for partial adjustment to shocks in the persistence of profits. Within such models, the entry decisions of firms are explicitly modelled as a function of excess profits (the difference between long-run and actual profitability) in the industry (Geroski, 1990). Other dynamic analyses consider the influence of business cycles on profit margins (Machin and van Reenen, 1993; Haskel and Martin, 1992; Schmalensee, 1989). These studies have found that profit margins are sensitive to business cycles, and the magnitude and direction of the effect depends upon industry concentration.

In this chapter, we are concerned with analysing the determinants of profit margins in the Indian industry. Unlike earlier studies, however, we are also concerned with the behaviour of profit margins in the context of quite significant competitive shocks that struck the Indian industry in the 1990s. Our analysis of this structural break is aided by the availability of firm-level panel data over the 1980–1998 period. The model we estimate is rich in its dynamic characterisation, taking into account the long-run trend, two period lagged adjustments as well as dummies for the structural break in 1991 and dummies for every year to capture business cycle effects. In addition, the model is also comprehensive in including a number of standard industrial organisation variables (like market share, advertising, R&D) as well as less standard managerial and trade-related variables. It also distinguishes between the pre- and post-1991 determinants of profit margins within our sample.

The Dynamic Context of the Study

Till the mid-1980s India followed a strategy of planned economic development based on import substitution. The 1951 Industrial Development Regulation Act (on which much of the Indian industrial policy is based) dictated the direction and the volume of investment through the licensing of private industrial investment, a large public sector and foreign exchange controls. Planned import substitution tilted investment flows initially towards heavy and capital goods industries and later towards chemicals, petroleum and durable consumer goods.

The 1991 reforms attempted to change this system. They were characterised by *external* liberalisation, and provided some firms with the opportunity of entering global markets through technical modernisation (Bhaduri and Nayyar, 1996; Joshi and Little, 1996). As part of this programme of reforms, the government undertook extensive industrial reforms simplifying its licensing regime and relaxing anti-trust rules so that large firms no longer required licenses for expansion and diversification. The reforms eased the entry and expansion of incumbent firms by de-licensing capacity expansion for firms with assets below a moderate threshold; firms located in "backward" areas, firms in scale critical industries and firms that were "modernising". Modernisation through the import of capital equipment and technical know-how was encouraged. Licenses were "broadbanded" so that enterprises could adjust their product mixes more easily to changing market conditions. Restrictions on "monopoly houses", especially those in "priority industries", were relaxed (Ahluwalia *et al.*, 1996; Srivastava, 1996; Economic Survey, 1985–1986). These initiatives generally increased the freedom of incumbent firms to expand. Encouragement of *de novo* entry was less effective. Finally, sectors reserved for the public sector were thrown open to the private sector entry and competition.[a]

This was also the first sustained attempt at trade liberalisation in India following the balance of the payments crisis of 1989. The trade reforms were recommended by the Tax Reforms Committee (1991), and led to a reduction in the general level of tariffs, a reduction of the spread of dispersion of tariff rates, the abolition of numerous exemptions and concessions and the abolition of making changes through notifications. When the tariff rates for 1987–1988 are compared with those in the 1992–1997 period (Nouroz, 2001) we find significant changes. In 1992–1993, the first year

[a] However, reservations for small-scale industry continued. While the government also accepted the need for redundancies, and began a process of withdrawal from involvement in employer–employee negotiations, few significant steps have been taken towards the removing of exit barriers.

when the reforms were introduced, the peak tariff rates were brought down to 110 percent, and in 1994–1995 they were further reduced to 65 percent. In 1997–1998, the peak tariff rate was further reduced to 40 percent, but a special additional duty of 2 percent was charged. In addition to these reductions, there was also an overall change in the structure of tariffs. In 1992–1993, the import weighted tariff rates for capital goods, intermediate goods and consumer goods were 66, 69 and 75 percent, respectively. In 1994–1995, these rates declined to 41 percent for capital goods, 42 percent for intermediate goods and to 46 percent for consumer goods, and they were further reduced to 32 percent for consumer and intermediate goods and to 25 percent for capital goods in 1997–1998 (Mehta, 2003).

Another aspect of the trade policy reform was the reduction in quantitative restrictions. Since 1991, the Indian government has decreased the number of items for which import licences are required and has eliminated quantitative restrictions for capital and intermediate goods. Exports have been encouraged through the devaluation of the Rupee and through concessions that have been offered to 100 percent export-oriented units. The government has also broadened and simplified export incentives and has removed many export restrictions. Procedures for foreign direct investment were simplified and trade tariffs were reduced.[b]

The reforms in the early 1990s also deregulated the financial sector. In 1992, interest rates were decontrolled, reserve and liquidity requirements were cut and priority-sector lending was overhauled. In addition, better capitalised and more technologically advanced private and foreign banks were allowed to enter, and the existing nationalised banks were also slowly being privatised. The stock market was deregulated in the early 1990s and is now regulated by the Securities and Exchange Board of India (SEBI). The financial sector reforms made it easier for foreign financial institutions

[b] In 1987–1988, 39 percent of items were on a restricted list, whereas in 1992–1993 only 21 percent of imports were in this category. Under the open general licence category, there was a sharp general increase in the items covered in this category in 1997–1998 (Nouroz, 2001, p. 48). Nouroz calculated effective rates of protection for several industries in India and compared them to other Asian countries. She found that despite considerable reforms there were negative rates of protection in some industries. The estimates of effective rates of protection also showed considerable bias against exports.

(FFIs) to enter the country and eased rules regarding the ownership of firms. While the earlier FERA regulations only allowed 49 percent foreign ownership (and this also only in limited sectors), the new regulations allowed 51 percent foreign ownership and even completely foreign owned firms.

Many other reforms have been suggested and discussed, but little headway has been made in implementing them. Thus, while the government has accepted the need for redundancies, it still maintains a pro-labour rhetoric. At a practical level, however, it is increasingly permissive of firms making people redundant and is explicitly withdrawing from involvement in employer–employee negotiations (Howell and Kambhampati, 1998). While this ambiguity creates its own problems, it has certainly provided firms with the opportunity to restructure, should they wish to do so. These changes might be expected to increase efficiency in the industry, both by driving out marginal firms and by forcing firms to restructure and increase efficiency to survive.

Trade liberalisation and firm performance

At an empirical level, many studies of trade policy have found that increased exposure to international competition results in a reduction in profit margins in imperfectly competitive industries. Devarajan and Rodrik (1989) find that "liberalisation has an output-expanding, pro-competitive effect in key manufacturing industries" in Cameroon. An increase in import competition erodes the market power of domestic firms, leading them to increase output, i.e., the marginal revenue curve faced by domestic firms becomes flatter. Although the demand curve also shifts inwards (because the market share of imports has increased), the former decreases the incentive of domestic firms to withhold sales and increase prices. Levinsohn (1993) confirms that imports provide market discipline in Turkey. Krishna and Mitra (1998) find that in the case of India, mark-ups not only decrease in the post-reform period in three (out of four) industries, but also decrease to a level that leaves firms making losses. They rationalise this on the grounds that, "in the presence of adjustment and sunk costs, a firm may lose money while it adapts to a new trading environment", (p. 454). Since the study was able to access only two years of data after the reforms, it was unable to consider what might happen after firms had adapted to these conditions. Chand and Sen (1999) studying the case of India in an earlier period (1973–1988) also found that increased exposure to trade had a pro-competitive effect on domestic pricing.

Before we consider the factors determining these margins, we will look at the data and empirical methodology in the next two sections.

Data

In this study, we use panel data on large and medium firms in the Indian manufacturing over a 19-year period (1980–1998). The dataset is obtained from the Reserve Bank of India and provides accounting information on these firms. It is a unique dataset providing information on a very large sample and across a long time period. The data covers firms across a number of industries in India. However, the panel is not balanced, because some firms exit while others do not submit their returns on time. We create a balanced panel of firms that exist in every year from 1980 to 1998 for our analysis of the entire manufacturing sector.[c] However, we also then divide our sample into nine broad industrial sectors, for which we estimate separate regressions. In these sectors, we work with unbalanced panels.

The period covered in the dataset includes 1991, which was a period of policy reforms in India. It is also the focus of our study. However, this structural change, together with the small, longitudinal size of the sample, has meant that we have had to assume that the series is stationary without conducting unit root tests.[d] The availability of panel data is also helpful because it allows us to control for time-invariant unobservables via firm-specific fixed effects. To some extent, therefore, it enables us to overcome the omitted variable bias that often affects studies of this kind (Machin and van Reenen, 1993).

---

[c] Balance sheet data do not have price information, and we too do not have information on prices of products produced by firms in various years. Data on input prices such as wage rates, raw-material prices, etc. are not available at a firm level.

[d] Our econometric estimation uses first differenced models, and hence the unit root problem in case it existed is taken into account as first differences will be stationary in case the original profit to sales ratio and other normalised variables are unit root non-stationary.

A very preliminary consideration of summary statistics indicates that profit margins in the Indian industry increased from 0.24 in 1980–1990 to 0.27 in 1991–1998 for the relatively export-intensive firms, while they decreased from 0.25 to 0.14 for the firms that did not export very much (Kambhampati and Parikh, 2003).

Mean profit margins for the entire manufacturing sector were 0.18 when all costs were excluded (Profit1) and were 0.23 when only labour, raw material and fuel costs were excluded (Profit2). By both measures, sector 1 (Plantations) showed the highest profit margins (greater than 30 percent by the Profit 1 measure), while sector 4 (textiles) showed the lowest margins (less than 3 percent by the Profit1 measure) (Tables 1 and 2).

In the next section, we will consider the modelling structure that we employ before discussing the empirical methodology in the sixth section.

Table 1. Summary statistics for profit margins.

Sector/no. of firms	Sector description	Number of observations	Profit1		Profit2	
			Mean	SD	Mean	SD
1 23/24	Plantations	454	0.350	0.180	0.420	0.179
3 17/18	food, alcohol, Tobacco	317	0.198	0.150	0.226	0.153
4 30/35	Textiles	630	0.027	2.771	0.057	2.754
5 23/24	Metal products	454	0.170	0.109	0.216	0.112
7 50/54	Machine tools	975	0.204	0.101	0.240	0.107
8 42/45	Chemicals and pharmaceuticals	832	0.203	0.139	0.233	0.127
10 13/14	Cement	257	0.240	0.166	0.285	0.159
11 12/13	Paper and printing	235	0.191	0.110	0.226	0.128
13 8/13	Trading	188	0.131	0.194	0.148	0.197
All manufacturing		5339	0.181	1.461	0.227	1.445

Notes:
Profit1 = (sales – (raw materials + fuel + salaries + repairs + rent + other manufacturing expenses))/sales.
Profit2 = (sales – (raw materials + fuel + salaries))/sales.
Sectors, which have less than seven firms are not considered although they are included in "all manufacturing".
The number of firms varies from year to year within a sector, and the minimum and maximum number of firms are shown in column 2 of the table.

Table 2. Summary statistics for all variables: all manufacturing.

Variable names	Mean 1980–1998	Mean 1980–1990	Mean 1991–1998	Standard deviation 1980–1998	Standard deviation 1980–1990	Standard deviation 1991–1998
Sales	9,220,817	4,074,531	1.73e+07	2.94e+07	8974276	4.53e+07
DEVAC1	1.7481	2.5566	0.6429	4.95875	6.2183	1.8826
MKTSHARE	0.2349	0.2308	0.2403	0.2944	0.2903	0.3004
Profit1	0.1810	0.2047	0.1359	1.4615	0.1363	2.4010
Profit2	0.2274	0.2499	0.1873	1.4447	0.1602	2.3708
XS	0.0440	0.0331	0.0609	0.0918	0.0777	0.1087
MS	0.0601	0.0573	0.6527	0.09099	0.0861	0.1000
ADS	0.0058	0.0048	0.0074	0.0168	0.0143	0.0201
RDS	0.0015	0.0007	0.0026	0.0048	0.0031	0.0064
MANREMS	0.0021	0.0016	0.0029	0.0171	0.0029	0.0280
DumMAN	0.0117	0	0.0029	0.0171	0	0.0280
DumADS	0.00305	0	0.0074	0.01329	0	0.0201
DumRDS	0.0011	0	0.0026	0.0042	0	0.0064
DumXS	0.0248	0	0.0061	0.0750	0	0.1088
KO	1.1193	0.7054	1.8372	27.039	0.6626	44.5370
DumKO	0.7109	0	1.8372	27.0428	0	44.5370
MktDum	0.1012	0	0.2403	0.2279	0	0.3005
DumMS	0.0269	0	0.0653	0.0705	0	0.1000
DumDEV1	0.2678	0	0.6429	1.1854	0	1.8826

Notes: MKTSHARE, market share; XS, exports/sales ratio; MS, imports/sales ratio; ADS, advertising–sales ratio; RDS, R&D/sales ratio; MANREMS, managerial remuneration/sales ratio; KO, capital–output ratio.

Modelling Structure

Following Cowling and Waterson (1976), the profit margin for a profit maximising[e] firm can be written as

$$\left(\frac{II}{S}\right)_i = \frac{\text{MKT}_i(1+\lambda_i)}{\varepsilon}, \tag{1}$$

where MKT_i = market share, λ_i is the conjectural variation term (i.e., the output changes that firm i would expect from its rivals when it changes output itself) and ε is the industry price elasticity of demand.

[e] Under the assumption of constant returns, price-cost margins are equivalent to $\frac{II}{S}$ in the long run.

Clarke and Davies (1982) model λ_i as a function of the market share of all firms excluding firm i relative to its market share

$$\lambda_i = \frac{\alpha_i(1 - \mathrm{MKT}_i)}{\mathrm{MKT}_i}. \tag{2}$$

Substituting (2) in (1), we get

$$\left(\frac{II}{S}\right)_i = \left[\frac{(1 - \mathrm{MKT}_i)\alpha_i + \mathrm{MKT}_i}{\varepsilon}\right]. \tag{3}$$

As is well known, the two extreme values of α_i in this formulation give us the total collusion ($\alpha_i = 1$) and the Cournot behaviour ($\alpha_i = 0$). α_i, in its turn, has been variously modelled as a linear function of the industry concentration (Kwoka and Ravenscraft, 1986) and as a function of more general industry variables (concentration, import intensity and union power) (Machin and van Reenen, 1993).

In this chapter, however, we suggest that α_i is likely to be influenced by increased competitiveness in the Indian industry following the reforms in 1991. These reforms increased a firm's independence to respond to other firms (by removing constraints on their actions). They also increased entry into, and competition within, an industry. Both these factors are likely to influence the way in which firms react to the actions of other firms and therefore their conjectural variations. We, therefore, hypothesise that α_i is a function of liberalisation in India.[f] If this is the case, we can write

$$\alpha_{it} = \theta_1 \mathrm{LIBDUM}_t. \tag{4}$$

Inserting (4) in (3), we get

$$\left(\frac{II}{S}\right)_{it} = \left[\frac{(1 - \mathrm{MKT}_{it})(\theta_1 \mathrm{LIBDUM})_t + \mathrm{MKT}_{it}}{\varepsilon}\right], \tag{5a}$$

which can be rewritten as

$$\begin{aligned}\left[\frac{II}{S}\right]_{it} &= \beta_1 \mathrm{LIBDUM}_{it} + \beta_2(\mathrm{MKT} * \mathrm{LIBDUM})_{it} \\ &\quad + \beta_3 \mathrm{MKT}_{it} + \mu_{it} + \nu_t + \zeta_{it}.\end{aligned} \tag{5b}$$

---

[f] The liberalisation variable takes the value of 1 after 1991 and 0 before 1991. This variable is firm invariant.

μ_{it} consists of two sets of effects, namely firm-specific effects constant over time and firm-specific time varying effects. ν_t is the business cycle effects, which are not firm specific but varying over time.

We then specify panel firm-specific time varying effects in this model in two parts. The first is with respect to all explanatory variables as well as with interaction to liberalisation. The second are the constant firm-specific fixed effects, which do not vary over time. Thus, in (5b), we have,

$$\mu_{it} = \Phi_i + f(\text{KO, ADS, RDS, MANREMS, XS, MS, Trend, DEVAC and interactions with liberalisation}), \tag{6}$$

where KO is gross fixed assets/sales of the firm, ADS is the advertising–sales ratio, RDS is the R&D/sales ratio, MANREMS is the managerial remuneration/sales ratio, XS is the exports/sales ratio, MS is the imports/sales ratio, Trend is time trend and DEVAC is (average cost of the firm — minimum average cost in the sample).

Given the lags in economic behaviour of agents, we introduce two period lags of the dependent variable, namely profit–sales ratios as additional variables, which makes the model dynamic in nature. We then obtain the following estimable equation:

$$\begin{aligned}\left[\frac{II}{S}\right]_{it} &= \phi_i + \nu_t + \beta_1\text{LIBDUM}_t \\ &\quad + \beta_2(\text{MKTSHARE} * \text{LIBDUM})_{it} + \beta_3\text{MKTSHARE}_{it} \\ &\quad + \beta_4\left[\frac{II}{S}\right]_{it-1} + \beta_5\left[\frac{II}{S}\right]_{it-2} + \beta_6\text{KO}_{it} + \beta_7\text{ADS}_{it} \\ &\quad + \beta_8\text{RDS}_{it} + \beta_9\text{MANREMS}_{it} + \beta_{10}\text{XS}_{it} + \beta_{11}\text{MS}_{it} \\ &\quad + \beta_{12}\text{TREND} + \beta_{13}\text{DEVAC}_{it} \\ &\quad + \text{Coeffs} * \text{ Interactions with Liberalisation}).\end{aligned} \tag{7}$$

Our profit measure here is a proxy for the price-cost margin that is the theoretically appropriate variable to use in this context. The controversy surrounding accounting rates of return is well known in the literature and relates to a number of issues. First, the way in which assets are valued especially in the context of inflation can lead to considerable bias in accounting measures of profits. Second, there is disagreement over whether advertising and R&D are investment costs yielding returns over a long period or are current costs. In developing countries, there is also considerable variation in the costs that are actually included in the advertising and R&D categories. Third, firms follow different conventions with respect to depreciation, with some firms pursuing a policy of accelerated depreciation. To take these problems into account, we have used a very limited measure of profits [sales revenue – (salaries + raw material costs + fuel costs)]. This variable does not exclude controversial and hard-to-measure costs like advertising, R&D or depreciation, making it easier to compare profits across firms.

Empirical Estimation

The above model (7) with the profit/sales ratio as the dependent variable can then be written in matrix-vector notation as follows:

$$Y_{it} = \alpha_1 Y_{it-1} + \alpha_2 Y_{it-2} + \mathbf{x_{it}b} + \nu_t + \phi_i + \xi_{it}, \quad i = 1, 2, \ldots, N, \quad t = 1, 2, \ldots, T, \tag{8}$$

where α_1 and α_2 are parameters with respect to lagged (profit/sales) variables. Y_{it} is profit to sales ratio for firm i in year t. $\mathbf{x_{it}}$ is a $1 \times k$ vector of exogenous variables and their interactions with liberalisation variable and

$$\mathbf{x_{it}} = \begin{bmatrix} \mathbf{x}'_{i1} \\ \mathbf{x}'_{i2} \\ \vdots \\ \mathbf{x}'_{iT} \end{bmatrix}.$$

$\mathbf{b}$ is a $1 \times k$ vector of parameters to be estimated.

ϕ_i are the random effects that are independent and identically distributed over the firms with variance σ_ϕ^2. ν_t are the time effects or the intercept for each year due to business cycle effects on profits. ξ_{it} are independently identically distributed over the whole sample with variance σ_ξ^2.

It is assumed that ϕ_i and ξ_{it} are independent for each i over all t. First differencing the equation removes ϕ_i and produces an equation that is estimable by instrumental variables. Ordinary Least Squares (OLS) estimates in the dynamic model are biased and inconsistent. Arellano and Bond (1991) derive a Generalized Method of Moments Estimator (GMM) for α_1

and α_2 and **b** using the lagged levels of the first differenced profit variable and the differences of strictly exogenous variables **x**. The null hypothesis of no first-order autocorrelation in the differenced residuals will be normally rejected if the original errors are by assumption serially uncorrelated. This means that the presence of first-order autocorrelation in the differenced residuals does not imply that the estimates are inconsistent. However, the presence of second-order autocorrelation would imply that the estimates are inconsistent. Arellano and Bond developed the tests for first- and second-order autocorrelation and the application of the Sargan test to test whether overidentifying restrictions are valid.

When the assumption of strict exogeneity of the right-hand side variables does not hold, we use the lagged values of these variables as instruments and one-step, robust and two-step estimates are obtained.[g] In this study, we estimate both the one-step and two-step (instrumental variables) results and choose the former as they satisfy the Arellano–Bond second-order autocorrelation test and the Sargan test of overidentifying restrictions for most of the nine sectors.

In the first differenced version, firm effects will cancel out, and a constant term will be the time trend coefficient. The model with a constant term and time dummies will be as follows:

$$\begin{aligned}\Delta Y_{it} &= \text{Constant} + \text{Year Dummies } + \alpha_1 \Delta Y_{it-1} + \alpha_2 \Delta Y_{it-2} \\ &\quad + \Delta \mathbf{x_{it}} \mathbf{b} + \Delta \varepsilon_{it}. \end{aligned} \tag{9}$$

When we take first differences, three observations are lost due to lags and differencing. $\Delta \mathbf{x}_{it}$ will serve as its own instrument in estimating the first difference equation. Assuming that ε_{it} are not autocorrelated for each i at time $t = 4$, Y_{i1} and Y_{i2} are valid instruments for lagged variables. We also estimated the first differenced model without lags using Instrumental Variables (IV) procedure, and the model equation (1) in *static* form (without lagged dependent variables) as fixed effect and random effect models using

---

[g] Both one-step and two-step estimation with lagged values of exogenous variables as instruments were tried, but the results in most cases were similar. One of the limitations of this is the increase in the instrument matrix size and the GMM estimators with too many over identifying restrictions perform poorly. Inference on coefficients is based on single step estimation.

instruments (Table 3). For the All Manufacturing sample, therefore, we present the one-step dynamic estimation results as well as the random and fixed effect static estimation results for comparison purposes (Table 3). We find that they are very similar. For our other subsamples, however, we only present the one-step results as they pass all the relevant diagnostic tests. The one-step estimation procedure treats all Δx_{it} variables as endogenous and used lagged values as instruments.

We test for second-order autocorrelation in the first differenced model[h] as the first-order serial correlation is due to first differences when original errors are serially uncorrelated. The presence of first-order autocorrelation in the differenced residuals does not imply that the estimators are inconsistent.

The standard model (market share, KO, ADS, RD, MANREM)

Most of these variables have the standard interpretations. Thus, market share (MKTSHARE) could lead to higher profit margins because it enables firms to take advantage of economies of scale and to reduce costs. It also helps increase a firm's market power. The capital–output (KO) ratio normalises for the capital intensity of production of the firm. The Advertising (ADS) and the R&D (RDS) intensity denote the ability of a firm to differentiate its output. They can be seen (as in traditional industrial organisation theories) as barriers to entry, which enable incumbents to earn supernormal profits. Alternatively, they can be seen as endogenous sunk costs (Sutton, 1991), which reflect a consumer's willingness to pay. Within the latter framework, AD would not necessarily always be profitable. In fact, within this framework, AD is most likely to increase profits in high concentration industries and when the increase in advertising expenditure is not a "local deviation" but a "discrete jump" to some high level (Sutton, 1991, p. 63). Managerial remuneration (MANREM) is expected to increase profit margins because it is seen as a proxy for good management.

[h] In the first differenced model when original errors are not autocorrelated, the reduced form errors will be serially correlated. $E(\varepsilon_{it} - \varepsilon_{it-1}, \varepsilon_{it-1} - \varepsilon_{it-2}) = E((-\varepsilon_{it-1})^2) = E(-\varepsilon_{it}^2) \neq 0$.

Dynamic variables

As indicated earlier, our model is rich in its dynamic characterisation. We include two lagged dependent variables (ProfitLD and ProfitL2D), which help account for any partial adjustment in changes in profit margins over time, as well as correct for any autocorrelation that may exist in the estimation. In addition, we include a trend term (Trend), which will capture trend increases or decreases in profit margins. Finally, we include annual dummies for the years 1985–1998 (years 5–19). These dummies are expected to capture firm-invariant fixed effects like business cycles that affect all firms in the industry similarly.

Trade-related variables

In addition to the above variables, we also include a number of liberalisation-related variables. Exports (XS) are included, because a number of studies have shown that the competition in export markets is likely to squeeze profit margins. It is, however, equally possible that exports may actually increase a firm's experience and allow it to learn faster. If this were the case, exports may increase profit margins in the medium term. We also include imports (MS) in our model because one of the advantages of liberalisation has been cited as the ability of the firms to import up-to-date technology (Howell and Kambhampati, 1999). Such technology could be expected to increase the product quality and the efficiency of the firm production. We therefore hypothesise a positive relationship between this variable and the profit margin.

In addition to the above variables, we include interaction terms between a dummy variable for the post-1991 years (Dum = 1) and all the other variables, to capture the impact of the reforms after 1991. Thus, we have MKTDum, DumADS, DumRDS and so on, which will capture changes in the impact that market share, advertising and R&D have on profit margins in the post-1991 period. More specifically, it is possible that AD expenditures may have increased after the reforms and that, though, profit margins may otherwise have been unaffected, this discrete change in the AD expenditure may have pushed margins upwards. It is equally possible that while advertising expenditures have remained unchanged, the *impact* that these expenditures have had has changed considerably. A similar argument could be made for market shares, KO, RDS or MANREM.

Relative efficiency variables

The efficiency index is based on the observed minimum cost per unit value of output for each year. The distance from this observed minimum cost per unit value of output is regarded as the inefficiency of that firm from the most efficient firm in that sector for that year. This can be seen as a deterministic measure of inefficiency.[i] Our hypothesis was that firms that are furthest from the most efficient firm would have lower profit margins than those closer to the most efficient firm. If this is not the case, then it implies that these firms have significant market power that enables them to maintain high margins even when they are inefficient. To test this hypothesis, we include DEVAC, the distance of each firm from the most efficient in the sample. The larger the deviation from the minimum cost per unit of value added, the smaller we would expect the profit margins to be. In addition, we also included DEVAC*Dum (DumDEV1) to consider whether the effect of efficiency changed after 1991.

Results

All manufacturing

The estimation for all manufacturing is based on a balanced panel of 282 firms over the entire time period. We estimate the model over this sample using the one-step dynamic panel methodology as well as the fixed and random effects static methodology. The results are presented in Table 3. We note that they are very similar to each other. However, the dynamic models are chosen in preference to the static models because they help to capture any inertia in the firm's behaviour and performance.[j] In what follows, we will discuss the results of the one-step estimation.

Our results indicate that MANREMS had a negative impact on profit margins both before and after the reforms. As we will see later, this may

---

[i] Farrell's (1957) measure of efficiency is defined as the minimum cost per unit of physical output for homogenous goods. We have the whole manufacturing sector, where there is heterogeneity, and hence we chose the minimum cost per unit value of output in each period for the entire manufacturing sector and for the sectoral level analysis, the distance of the average cost from the minimum in that sector.

[j] While the two-step results seem to provide better Z-scores, the one-step estimation is preferred because it satisfies the Arellano–Bond second-order autocorrelation test and the Sargan test of overidentifying restrictions in more sectors than the two-step estimation does.

Table 3. Results for the all manufacturing sample.

	One-step		Fixed effects		Random effects	
	Coeff	Z	Coeff	Z	Coeff	Z
ProfitLD	−0.004	−0.450				
ProfitL2D	−0.004	−0.870				
Dum			0.168	7.290**	0.181	7.610**
Trend	0.008	2.670**	−0.003	−1.870*	−0.002	−1.540
MKTSHARE	−0.145	−1.480	0.012	0.600	0.009	0.510
DummKT	−0.049	−1.390	−0.028	−1.710*	−0.030	−1.800*
ADS	1.381	1.520	2.111	6.470**	1.770	5.790**
DumADS	−0.245	−0.390	−0.473	−1.650*	−0.397	−1.350
MANREMS	−18.141	−3.470**	−24.614	−17.880**	−19.496	−14.180**
DumMAN	−39.020	−7.830**	−34.878	−25.330**	−39.853	−28.960**
RDS	5.908	2.130**	2.144	2.020**	1.903	1.750*
DumRDS	9.613	2.990**	7.068	5.960**	7.022	5.780**
XS	−0.036	−0.220	−0.118	−2.290**	−0.083	−1.630
DumXS	0.004	0.020	−0.083	−1.510	−0.094	−1.670*
MS	0.011	0.080	−0.009	−0.180	−0.051	−1.070
DumMS	−0.029	−0.230	0.130	2.450**	0.136	2.490**
KO	−0.051	−3.570**	−0.056	−9.340**	−0.042	−7.060**
DumKO	0.016	1.140	0.021	3.490**	0.007	1.210
DEVAC1	0.035	0.830	0.006	0.890	0.005	0.640
DumDEV1	0.006	0.100	−0.006	−0.810	−0.004	−0.590
Year 1	−0.009	−0.800				
Year 2	−0.008	−0.700	−0.010	−0.760	−0.010	−0.710
Year 3	−0.780	−0.860	−0.024	−1.910*	−0.022	−1.700
Year 4	−0.037	−2.350**	−0.014	−1.120	−0.014	−1.100
Year 5	−0.048	−2.610**	−0.008	−0.640	−0.008	−0.640
Year 6	−0.058	−2.810**	−0.003	−0.270	−0.003	−0.270
Year 7	−0.055	−2.450**	−0.157	−1.010	−0.120	−0.750
Year 8	−0.037	−1.710*	−0.013	−1.070	−0.013	−1.030
Year 9	−0.053	−2.810**	−0.015	−1.170	−0.015	−1.140
Year 10	−0.062	−3.230**	−0.014	−1.110	−0.014	−1.040
Year 11	−0.025	−1.370	(Dropped)		(Dropped)	
Year 12	−0.004	−0.230	−0.137	−8.130**	−0.134	−7.720**
Year 13	0.005	0.300	−0.137	−8.530**	−0.135	−8.130**
Year 14	−0.026	−1.300	−0.137	−8.890**	−0.135	−8.500**
Year 15	(Dropped)		−0.087	−5.850**	−0.086	−5.580**
Year 16	0.008	2.670**	−0.054	−3.770**	−0.053	−3.550**
Year 17	−0.145	−1.480	−0.041	−2.890**	−0.039	−2.700**
Year 18	−0.049	−1.390	−0.047	−3.400**	−0.047	−3.280**
Year 19	1.381	1.520	(Dropped)		(Dropped)	

(*Continued*)

Table 3. (*Continued*).

	One-step		Fixed effects		Random effects	
	Coeff	Z	Coeff	Z	Coeff	Z
Constant	−0.245	−0.390	0.297	22.100	0.281	18.540
Sargan test[1] $\chi^2(646)$	919.89	(0.00)	$R^2 = 0.9877$			
A–B serial correlation[2]	−0.34	(0.7363)				
Wald test(1): χ^2	123,579.48	(0.00)			377,498.66	Df: 34
Wald test(2): χ^2	94871.73	(0.00)				

Notes:
MKTSHARE, market share; XS, exports/sales ratio; MS, imports/sales ratio; ADS, advertising–sales ratio; RDS, R&D/sales ratio; MANREMS, managerial remuneration/sales ratio; KO, capital–output ratio.
Wald test(1) is the joint tests of significance of all parameters.
Wald test(2) is the test of the null hypothesis that all coefficients excepting the constant and time dummies are zero. ( ) refers to probability level in the Z column.
[1] The Sargan test of overidentifying restrictions is from the two-step estimation.
[2] Refers to the null of the second-order serial correlation.
Z-statistic follows a normal distribution, and 5 percent critical value is –1.96 or + 1.96.
In the fixed effect model, the fixed effects are correlated with the error term, while in the random effects, they are assumed to be uncorrelated. The assumption of zero correlation is rejected by the F-test ($F(34, 5024) = 11, 831.90$). We reject the random effect model.
All the right-hand side variables excepting trend are used as endogenous variables, and two period lags of each of these right-hand side variables are used as instruments. This includes the interactions of liberalisation with the right-hand side variables.
*Significant at 10 percent level; **significant at 5 percent level; ***significant at 1 percent level.

be explained by the fact that the best paid managers might well be targeting growth, given the lifting of restrictions on the firm's growth. R&D increases profit margins both before and after the reforms, while capital intensity decreases margins. At the all-manufacturing level, we find that profit margins were decreasing year on year before the liberalisation, but after the reforms, profit margins stabilised. The results, however, vary from sector to sector. We will therefore not discuss these results in any detail. Instead, we will concentrate on the sectoral results in what follows.

Sectoral results

As indicated earlier, we estimated each of the above models for nine broad sectors — plantations, food processing, textiles, paper, metal products, machine tools, chemicals, cement and trading. The sectoral classification is provided in Appendix A. We choose the one-step results because they satisfied the diagnostic tests in most sectors, while the two-step estimations did not (Tables 4–6).

The trend (Trend) in profit margins in most of our sectors is generally positive. There are only two sectors (out of nine) in which the trend is negative (textiles and trading). Considering the annual time dummies (years 5–19), we find the patterns more varied. These time dummies correct for time-varying fixed effects like business cycle effects. We find that there are positive fixed effects of time, that is, profit margins increase in the years after liberalisation in paper, food, chemicals, cement and plantations. The results for a majority of our industries, therefore, seem to negate the general intuition that profit margins will be squeezed by the increase in competition generated by such reforms (Krishna and Mitra, 1998). In the Indian case, we find a year-on-year increase in profit margins even after the liberalisation in four out of nine industries and an improvement over the pre-liberalisation situation in two further industries. There is a worsening in profit margins only in textiles and trading. The worsening in textiles is not surprising as this is a sector in which the efficiency effects of reforms showed up in the mid-1980s when much of the industry was reformed but the effect of trade liberalisation in the 1990s was to increase competition and therefore squeeze profit margins considerably (Howell and Kambhampati, 1999).

Our results also indicate that the impact of market shares on profit margins is insignificant across all sectors. Market shares in such studies proxy both for market power (large firms have greater market power) and for market efficiency (larger firms are more efficient). In this chapter, we have extracted the market efficiency effect into the DEVAC terms, and, therefore, the market share variable simply is a market power term. The insignificance of this variable might arise from the fact that powerful firms are prioritising growth (i.e., an increase in their size) over profit margins, and, therefore, larger firms are not using their market power to increase profit margins. This

Table 4. Consumer good industries.[k]

	Food		Textiles		Paper	
	Coeff.	*Z*	Coeff.	*Z*	Coeff.	*Z*
ProfitLD	−0.116	−2.580 ∗ ∗	0.001	1.000	−0.017	−0.350
ProfitL2D	−0.1563	−3.03	0.000	−0.470	0.101	1.800∗
Trend	0.000	0.110	−0.007	−3.390∗∗	0.006	2.450∗∗
MKTSHARE	0.030	0.430	0.063	1.430	−0.022	−1.240
DumMKT	−0.055	−1.290	−0.013	−0.270	0.015	0.920
ADS	−0.160	−0.560	−1.639	−1.640∗	−2.988	−3.730∗∗
DumADS	−0.057	−0.200	3.192	3.010∗∗	2.930	3.290∗∗
MANREMS	2.517	0.400	−8.022	−1.310	7.264	2.040∗∗
DumMAN	−14.523	−0.990	7.279	0.900	−8.552	−2.190∗∗
RDS	−12.079	−1.690∗	−10.714	−1.400	13.360	4.490∗∗
DumRDS	10.828	1.260	17.379	2.250∗∗	−15.854	−5.660∗∗
XS	−0.055	−0.970	0.010	0.140	0.016	0.120
DumXS	0.071	1.030	0.093	1.580	−0.046	−0.310
MS	−0.073	−0.310	−0.193	−1.490	−0.055	−1.410
DumMS	1.156	1.510	0.248	1.450	0.071	1.710∗
KO	0.032	2.680 ∗ ∗	−0.027	−0.790	−0.011	−1.140
DumKO	−0.068	−3.600∗∗∗	−0.008	−0.250	0.026	0.850
DEVAC1	−1.076	−15.210∗∗∗	−0.337	−2.140∗∗	−0.989	−30.970∗∗
DumDEV1	−0.197	−3.610∗∗∗	0.305	1.930∗	0.058	3.020∗∗
Year 5	0.022	1.360	0.027	1.000	−0.027	−1.990∗∗
Year 6	0.146	8.430∗∗∗	0.035	1.300	−0.053	−5.020∗∗
Year 7	−0.159	−6.800∗∗∗	0.094	2.970∗∗	−0.085	−8.770∗∗
Year 8	−0.180	−6.350∗∗∗	0.093	2.950∗∗	−0.086	−5.330∗∗
Year 9	−0.123	−6.020∗∗∗	0.104	3.510∗∗	−0.069	−4.770∗∗
Year 10	0.175	5.880∗∗∗	0.086	2.970∗∗	−0.059	−4.280∗∗
Year 11	0.198	5.750∗∗∗	0.115	5.350∗∗	−0.104	−6.560∗∗
Year 12	0.260	7.870∗∗∗	0.016	0.820	−0.106	−11.690∗∗
Year 13	0.212	8.100∗∗∗	−0.012	−0.910	−0.004	−0.540
Year 14	0.204	9.020∗∗∗	0.005	0.300	−0.071	−6.900∗∗
Year 15	0.258	8.510∗∗∗	0.022	1.310	−0.009	−0.630
Year 16	0.155	5.460∗∗∗	−0.024	−1.680∗	−0.064	−5.100∗∗
Year 17	0.212	9.890∗∗∗	−0.026	−1.810∗	0.028	3.160∗∗
Year 18	0.018	0.690	0.011	0.750	−0.002	−0.420

(*Continued*)

[k] This classification into consumer and capital goods industries is not dependent upon input–output analyses of any kind. It is only done to make the presentation and analysis of the results easier.

Table 4. (*Continued*).

	Food		Textiles		Paper	
	Coeff.	Z	Coeff.	Z	Coeff.	Z
Constant	(Dropped)		(Dropped)		(Dropped)	
Sargan test[1] $\chi^2(646)$	0.00	(1.00)	437.27	(1.00)	0.00	(1.00)
A–B serial correlation[2]	0.98	(0.3258)	0.20	(0.8392)	−0.71	(0.4750)
Wald test(1): $\chi^2 df = 33$	4.59e+9	(0.00)	1.27e+6	(0.00)	578.22	(0.00)
Wald test(2) : $\chi^2 df = 15$	233.48	(0.00)	2.3e+7	(0.00)	2233.73[3]	(0.00)

Notes:
MKTSHARE, market share; XS, exports/sales ratio; MS, imports/sales ratio; ADS, advertising–sales ratio; RDS, R&D/sales ratio; MANREMS, managerial remuneration/sales ratio; KO, capital–output ratio.
Wald test(1) is the joint tests of significance of all parameters.
Wald test(2) is the test of the null hypothesis that all coefficients
excepting the constant and time dummies are zero. ( ) refers to probability level in the Z column.
[1] The Sargan test of overidentifying restrictions is from the two-step estimation.
[2] Refers to the null of the second-order serial correlation.
[3] 12 degrees of freedom
Z-statistic follows a normal distribution, and 5 percent critical value is –1.96 or +1.96.
In the fixed effect model, the fixed effects are correlated with the error term, while in the random effects, they are assumed to be uncorrelated. The assumption of zero correlation is rejected by the F-test ($F(34, 5024) = 11,831.90$). We reject the random effect model.
All the right-hand side variables excepting trend are used as endogenous variables, and two period lags of each of these right-hand side variables are used as instruments. This includes the interactions of liberalisation with the right-hand side variables.
* Significant at 10 percent level, **significant at 5 percent level, ***significant at 1 percent level.

would, of course, make the market share endogenous, and the endogeneity of this variable is taken into account in the methodology we use.

Our results also indicate that an increase in advertising (ADS) decreased profit margins in three sectors (textiles, paper and chemicals) and was insignificant in determining profit margins in all others. This might reflect the fact that advertising in India before 1991 was often undertaken with a view providing information about the product rather than as a competitive strategy amongst firms. Thus, advertising was a cost without a

Table 5. Capital and intermediate goods industries.

	Metals		Mach. tools		Chemicals		Cement	
	Coeff.	*Z*	Coeff.	*Z*	Coeff.	*Z*	Coeff.	*Z*
ProfitLD	0.021	0.55	−0.043	−1.73*	−0.003	−0.12	−0.029	−0.90
Profit2LD	0.059	1.61	0.004	0.20	−0.032	−5.22**	−0.028	−1.22
Trend	0.006	1.92*	0.008	6.26**	0.010	11.84**	0.010	7.74**
MKTSHARE	−0.010	−0.26	0.032	0.82	−0.016	−0.68	0.012	0.61
DumMKT	0.005	0.42	0.001	0.14	−0.006	−0.42	−0.010	−0.29
ADS	−1.323	−0.68	−0.920	−0.93	−0.212	−1.95*	−0.924	−0.86
DumADS	−4.095	−2.88**	1.449	1.54	−0.062	−0.74	0.899	0.70
MANREMS	3.606	1.60	0.763	0.59	0.139	0.05	−3.294	−0.74
DumMAN	−4.815	−1.80*	−2.672	−2.17**	−4.317	−1.49	0.324	0.06
RDS	−1.105	−1.20	−1.298	−2.03**	−0.499	−0.85	1.298	1.45
DumRDS	−0.784	−0.44	0.455	0.49	−0.507	−0.50	−0.346	−0.17
XS	−0.172	−2.68**	−0.119	−2.64**	0.052	1.05	−0.113	−1.22
DumXS	0.087	1.26	0.050	1.58	−0.001	−0.03	−0.003	−0.03
MS	−0.007	−0.19	−0.102	−2.53**	−0.155	−3.75**	−0.069	−1.11
DumMS	0.025	0.60	−0.003	−0.07	0.034	0.86	−0.104	−1.10
KO	−0.008	−0.71	−0.014	−1.56	−0.001	−0.10	−0.003	−0.69
DumKO	0.008	0.67	−0.003	−0.27	−0.010	−1.29	−0.011	−1.33
Dum DEVAC1	−0.625	−5.12**	−0.713	−7.14**	−0.986	−22.5**	−1.103	−40.3**
DumDEV1	−0.144	−1.03	−0.115	−1.22	−0.057	−1.45	0.048	0.93
Year 5	−0.003	−0.45	−0.023	−3.66**	0.030	4.46**	−0.049	−3.67**
Year 6	−0.017	−1.78*	−0.026	−4.01**	0.014	2.33**	−0.063	−6.94**

(Continued)

Table 5. (*Continued*).

	Metals		Mach. tools		Chemicals		Cement	
	Coeff.	*Z*	Coeff.	*Z*	Coeff.	*Z*	Coeff.	*Z*
Year 7	−0.050	−5.64**	−0.019	−1.81*	0.013	1.68*	0.022	2.73**
year 8	−0.052	−3.39**	0.030	1.95*	0.006	1.08	−0.046	−4.31**
Year 9	−0.004	−0.32	0.072	3.16**	0.055	6.01**	−0.159	−6.28**
Year 10	−0.032	−1.39	0.064	3.37**	−0.006	−0.89	−0.037	−2.39**
Year 11	−0.035	−1.49	0.021	0.90	−0.054	−5.81**	0.024	1.37
Year 12	0.018	0.93	0.068	5.60**	−0.044	−9.16**	0.066	6.45**
Year 13	−0.002	−0.15	0.052	4.49**	−0.025	−4.90**	0.065	3.34**
Year 14	−0.014	−1.35	0.075	6.51**	−0.032	−4.55**	−0.009	−0.78
Year 15	0.027	1.20	0.062	7.81**	0.028	4.52**	−0.006	−0.71
Year 16	−0.005	−0.26	0.017	2.27**	0.029	5.45**	0.027	2.19**
Year 17	0.040	4.66**	0.022	3.10**	0.106	15.66**	0.035	4.02**
Year 18	−0.029	−2.15**	0.015	1.68*	0.014	1.60	0.005	0.31
Year 19								
Constant	(Drop)		(Drop)		(Drop)		(Drop)	
Sargan test[1] $\chi^2(646)$	0.00	(1.00)	22.37	(1.00)	13.38	(1.00)	0.00	(1.00)
A–B serial correlation[2]	−0.38	(0.704)	1.62	(0.105)	1.13	(0.258)	1.88	(0.059)

(*Continued*)

Table 5. (*Continued*).

	Metals		Mach. tools		Chemicals		Cement	
	Coeff.	Z	Coeff.	Z	Coeff.	Z	Coeff.	Z
Wald test(1): χ^2	2.93e+09	(0.0)	3349.20	(0.00)	894,482	(0.00)	911.31	(0.00)
Wald test(2): χ^2	434.30	(0.00)	223.85	(0.00)	807.79	(0.00)	253.47	(0.00)

Notes:
MKTSHARE, market share; XS, exports/sales ratio; MS, imports/sales ratio; ADS, advertising–sales ratio; RDS, R&D/sales ratio; MANREMS, managerial remuneration/sales ratio; KO, capital–output ratio.
Wald test(1) is the joint tests of significance of all parameters.
Wald test(2) is the test of the null hypothesis that all coefficients excepting the constant and time dummies are zero.
( ) refers to probability level in the Z column.
[1] The Sargan test of overidentifying restrictions is from the two-step estimation.
[2] Refers to the null of the second-order serial correlation.
Z-statistic follows a normal distribution and 5 percent critical value is –1.96 or +1.96.
In the fixed effect model, the fixed effects are correlated with the error term, while in the random effects, they are assumed to be uncorrelated. The assumption of zero correlation is rejected by the F-test ($F(34{,}5024) = 11{,}831.90$). We reject the random effect model.
All the right-hand side variables excepting trend are used as endogenous variables, and two period lags of each of these right-hand side variables are used as instruments. This includes the interactions of liberalisation with the right-hand side variables
*Significant at 10 percent level; **significant at 5 percent level; ***significant at 1 percent level.

Table 6. Service sectors.

	Plantations		Trading	
	Coeff.	*Z*	Coeff.	*Z*
ProfitLD	0.033	1.60	−0.025	−0.67
Profit2LD	−0.021	−0.69	0.033	1.07
Trend	−0.004	−1.61	−0.001	−0.43
MKTSHARE	0.104	1.84*	−0.348	−2.09 **
DumMKT	−0.016	−0.83	0.151	0.71
ADS	−0.424	−0.36	−0.862	−1.20
DumADS	1.119	0.97	−0.848	−0.94
MANREMS	−1.259	−0.62	8.193	0.91
DumMAN	−2.440	−1.02	−0.675	−0.06
RDS	12.453	2.52 **	57.226	3.54 **
DumRDS	−12.224	−2.08 **	−50.968	−1.84*
XS	−0.092	−1.63	−0.079	−0.71
DumXS	−0.016	−0.23	−0.023	−0.14
MS	0.772	1.17	0.935	1.23
DumMS	−1.083	−1.39	−0.658	−0.81
KO	−0.017	−1.82*	−0.608	−12.55 **
DumKO	0.025	1.41	0.557	9.37 **
DEVAC1	−0.966	−20.10 **	−1.046	−16.69 **
DumDEV1	0.034	0.77	−0.069	−1.15
Year 5	0.131	9.06 **	0.104	9.35 **
Year 6	−0.003	−0.23	0.177	8.24 **
Year 7	−0.003	−0.21	0.132	7.69 **
Year 8	−0.015	−1.12	0.146	6.40 **
Year 9	−0.055	−3.23 **	−0.078	−4.78 **
Year 10	−0.006	−0.40	0.080	3.82 **
Year 11	0.011	0.64	0.111	4.61 **
Year 12	−0.048	−3.08 **	0.027	1.34
Year 13	0.019	1.17	−0.057	−3.51 **
Year 14	−0.026	−1.80*	0.101	4.05 **
Year 15	0.001	0.09	−0.009	−0.58
Year 16	0.005	0.22	−0.153	−8.18 **
Year 17	0.036	3.36 **	−0.065	−3.98 **
Year 18	0.018	1.63	−0.064	−3.80 **
Constant	(Drop)		(Drop)	
Sargan test[1] χ^2 (150)	0.00	(1.00)	0.00	(1.00)
A–B serial correlation[2]	−1.84	(0.0662)	−0.62	(0.5384)

(*Continued*)

Table 6. (*Continued*).

	Plantations		Trading	
	Coeff.	Z	Coeff.	Z
Wald test(1): χ^2	1.02e+11	(0.00)	154,257	(0.00)
Wald test(2): χ^2	175.39	(0.00)	2.9e+5	(0.00)

Notes:
MKTSHARE, market share; XS, exports/sales ratio; MS, imports/sales ratio; ADS, advertising–sales ratio; RDS, R&D/sales ratio; MANREMS, managerial remuneration/sales ratio; KO, capital–output ratio.
Wald test(1) is the joint tests of significance of all parameters.
Wald test(2) is the test of the null hypothesis that all coefficients excepting the constant and time dummies are zero.
( ) refers to probability level in the Z column.
[1] The Sargan test of overidentifying restrictions is from the two-step estimation.
[2] Refers to the null of the second-order serial correlation.
Z-statistic follows a normal distribution and 5 percent critical value is –1.96 or +1.96.
In the fixed effect model, the fixed effects are correlated with the error term, while in the random effects, they are assumed to be uncorrelated. The assumption of zero correlation is rejected by the F-test ($F(34, 5024) = 11,831.90$). We reject the random effect model.
All right-hand side variables excepting trend are used as endogenous variables, and two period lags of each of these right-hand side variables are used as instruments. This includes the interactions of liberalisation with the right-hand side variables.
*Significant at 10 percent level; **significant at 5 percent level; ***significant at 1 percent level.

commensurate return (Kambhampati, 1996). After the liberalisation, there is some evidence of the increasing use of advertising as a competitive strategy amongst large firms. This is revealed in three industries — textiles, machine tools and paper — in our sample.

As indicated earlier, we included MANREM as a proxy for the quality of managers. Our implicit hypothesis then was that well-paid managers are likely to work harder and have a more positive impact on the firm performance than do poorly paid managers, an efficiency wage type effect. Our results indicate that this was only true in the paper sector before liberalisation. In all other sectors, this variable was insignificant. After the liberalisation, firms that increased their managers' salaries in the paper, machine tools and metals sectors actually saw a decrease in profit margins. We conjecture that this might arise from the fact that in the post-liberalisation scenario, controls on the firm growth were loosened (both in terms of broadbanding sectors across which firms could grow and in terms of allowing larger shares for firms before they were considered monopolistic). This might have increased the motivation of firms for growth rather than profits, leading them to reward managers better for growth than for profits. Anecdotal evidence in India (as the case of Reliance Industries; Ghoshal *et al.*, 2000)) suggests that this may well be the case. In this situation, highly paid managers may actually aim for higher growth than for profits. In most other industries, however, this effect was not very significant.

Like advertising, the R&D expenditure is used as a competitive instrument by firms in many Western economies, and firms that spend more on R&D may be expected to increase profits as R&D proves to be a barrier to entry and enables them to diversify products. In fact, Sutton (2001) argues that the main impact of trade liberalisation is from two basic mechanisms — an intensification of price competition and a consequent narrowing of the "capability" window in which firms operate, as the minimum level consistent with viability increases. A firm's optimal response to these pressures, according to Sutton (2001), will involve injecting resources to increase capabilities, for instance, through R&D expenditures. Hence, the importance of R&D may be expected to increase post-liberalisation. In the context of developing countries, however, the R&D expenditure is much smaller and less likely to operate in this manner. Our results indicate that firms that increased spending on R&D saw an increase in profit margins in three sectors — paper, plantations and trading — before liberalisation. After liberalisation, however, this pattern reversed, and firms that spent more on R&D actually had lower profit margins. Since neither plantations nor trading is an R&D intensive industry, this result might arise from the fact that firms often include miscellaneous expenditure on IT services and product improvements into their R&D variable. The reversal in the pattern, post-liberalisation, may therefore arise from the fact that firms scrap and scale down their R&D (product-development) programmes in the face of such deregulation and focus on increasing the efficiency through investment in modern (imported) equipment (which is reflected in MS, i.e., imports) and the adoption of organisation practices. In the machine tools sector, too, an increase in R&D led to a decrease in profit margins. This is surprising, given that the machine tools sector is likely to be a research-intensive industry.

Our results indicate that neither of our trade-related variables (exports or imports) has a significant effect on profit margins in most industries. Thus, the increase in imports largely as capital and intermediate inputs into firms, for instance, did not seem to improve profit margins as expected. In one sector, machine tools, it actually led to a decrease in profit margins. The increase in competition caused by the entry into export markets squeezed profit margins significantly in three sectors — metals, machine tools and plantations. However, this effect does not change after the liberalisation. In fact, there is no significant post-liberalisation effect of either variable in *any* of our nine industries.

Capacity utilisation had an insignificant impact on profit margins in a majority of industries. There were only two sectors — plantations and trading — in which it had a negative effect on profits. Since these are service type sectors, it is not surprising that firms with higher capital–output ratios had lower profit margins. Post-liberalisation, however, this trend reversed, implying that there was an improvement in capacity utilisation. Only in the food industry is the trend different.

Finally, we included the efficiency of the firm relative to others in the industry (DEVAC). The more inefficient the firm relative to others in the industry is, the lower would we expect its profit margin to be. Our results confirm this quite comprehensively (the variable is significantly negative in all nine sectors), indicating that few firms have sufficient market power to offset the impact of inefficiency on profit margins. Post-liberalisation, we find that this effect is reversed, though in all industries the magnitude of the post-liberalisation effect is much smaller than that for the entire period so that the net effect in the post-liberalisation period is small. This implies that while inefficient firms were able to improve their profit positions in the post-liberalisation period, they were unable to significantly offset the effect of their inefficiency on profit margins.

Significance of the behavioural variables in determining profit margins

As indicated earlier, we conducted Wald tests to consider the impact of each individual explanatory variable on profit margins after the liberalisation. To do this, the slope coefficients of a variable before and after liberalisation (for example, the coefficient of ADS and the coefficient of DumADS) are summed before a Wald test of the joint significance of these coefficients is carried out. The results are presented in Table 7.

Table 7. Joint tests.

	All-India		Sector 1		Sector 3		Sector 4		Sector 5		Sector 7		Sector 8		Sector 10		Sector 11		Sector 13	
	χ^2	P	χ^2	P	χ^2	P	χ^2	P	χ^2	P	χ^2	P	χ^2	P	χ^2	P	χ^2	P	χ^2	P
MKTSHARE	2.79	0.095	2.48	0.1156	0.10	0.75	0.53	0.47	0.02	0.89	0.66	0.41	1.00	0.32	0.00	0.95	0.14	0.71	2.70	0.10
ADS	1.02	0.313	3.54	0.059	0.78	0.38	10.34	0.001	11.49	0.00	0.63	0.43	3.66	0.06	0.00	0.97	0.06	0.81	3.17	0.07
MANREM	239.42	0.00	26.17	0.00	0.43	0.51	0.05	0.82	1.16	0.28	3.38	0.06	6.94	0.01	2.01	0.16	0.34	0.56	2.40	0.12
RDS	32.69	0.00	0.02	0.87	0.15	0.70	4.46	0.04	1.34	0.25	1.52	0.22	2.02	0.15	0.43	0.51	11.97	0.00	0.06	0.81
XS	0.03	0.87	3.23	0.07	0.17	0.68	4.92	0.02	4.46	0.035	1.66	0.20	0.99	0.32	3.44	0.06	0.07	0.79	1.84	0.17
MS	0.01	0.92	0.59	0.44	2.20	0.13	0.29	0.59	0.28	0.58	11.92	0.00	6.74	0.01	2.20	0.14	0.36	0.55	1.56	0.20
KO	17, 221.8	0.00	0.27	0.60	2.91	0.08	[1]	0.00	0.00	0.95	1.65	0.20	3.01	0.08	4.32	0.04	14.16	0.00	1.61	0.20
DEVAC	0.63	0.43	387.70	0.00	227.07	0.00	129.87	0.00	85.52	0.00	196.31	0.00	472.48	0.00	1343.26	0.00	222.29	0.00	467.80	0.00

[1] 9.3×10^5

The table indicates that the significance of the behavioural variables varies from sector to sector. However, we can see from the table that in plantations, textiles and chemicals, a number of the behavioural variables are significant, while in metals, machine tools, cement, paper and trading, only a small number of these variables are significant.

The variable that is universally significant (in all nine sectors) is DEVAC, implying that inefficient firms are never highly profitable. Our results, therefore, indicate that the most efficient firm is also likely to be the most profitable, indicating that market power is not so significant in any industry that it enables a firm to override the impact of efficiency. This is further reinforced by the insignificance of the market share as a determinant of profit margins in our estimates.

The next most significant variables are AD and KO, both of which are significant in five industries. In these industries, therefore, it is clear that the overall impact of this variable (pre- and post-liberalisation) is important. Other significant variables are MANREMS and RD.

Post-liberalisation determinants of profit margins

Turning now to analyse whether liberalisation has had a significant impact on profit margins or not, we consider the test of the joint significance of all the dummy variable terms. Our results indicate that these tests are significant in all sectors. Thus, liberalisation seems to have had a significant effect on profit margins in every sector. The conduit through which this effect is operationalised varies, however, as we have seen in our results. In some sectors, it is through the impact of advertising expenditures after the reforms (dumads), in others through RD (dumrds), MANREM (dumman) and so on (Table 8).

Our time dummies too reflect this pattern. We find a year-on-year increase in profit margins after the liberalisation in three out of nine industries (food, chemicals and machine tools). In all three sectors, the year 12–19 dummies are significant and positive. In addition, in three industries (paper, metals and cement), there was an improvement over the pre-liberalisation situation, though this did not imply increases in profit margins. Instead, it reversed the earlier declines and resulted in insignificant changes. Thus, our results for a majority of our industries (six of 10) seem to negate the

Table 8. Joint tests of all dummies.

Sector	All India	
	χ^2	P
	12.39	0.0885
Plantations	74.05	0.00
Food	41.64	0.00
Textiles	84.61	0.00
Metals	25.22	0.00
Machine tools	6.48	0.00
Chemicals	8.52	0.00
Cement	29.52	0.00
Paper	73.43	0.00
Trading	708.82	0.00

Notes: MKTSHARE, market share; XS, exports/sales ratio; MS, imports/sales ratio; ADS, advertising–sales ratio; RDS, R&D/sales ratio; MANREMS, managerial remuneration/sales ratio; KO, capital–output ratio.

general intuition that profit margins will be squeezed by the increase in competition generated by such reforms (Krishna and Mitra, 1998).

Conclusion

In this study, we analyse the determinants of firm-level profit margins in the Indian manufacturing. We hypothesise that the reforms undertaken by the government in 1991 have influenced the behaviour of Indian firms and therefore their reaction to each other. Inserting this into the standard industrial organisation model of profits, we obtain a model that is rich in its dynamics and allows us to consider changes in the determinants over time as well as in the face of significant structural breaks. Estimating this model for the 1980–1998 period, we find that the 1991 reforms did have a significant impact on profit margins in the Indian industry. This is not surprising, given that these reforms increased a firm's independence to react to other firms, as well as increased the extent of competition faced by these firms. The impact of the reforms therefore has worked through its impact on firms' behavioural variables — advertising, R&D, KO, MANREM and so on. We find that relatively inefficient firms make significantly lower profits than others both before and after the liberalisation as expected.

Appendix A

Sector	Industries[1]	Name
1	110–190	Plantations
3	31–342	Food, alcohol, tobacco
4	351–359	textiles
5	410–430, 451–457	Metal products
7	445–451	Machine tools
8	461–470	Chemicals and pharmaceuticals
10	521–532	Cement
11	551–573	Paper and printing
13	640	Trading

Note: [1]This column provides the RBI classification of industries.

References

Ahluwalia, IJ, R Mohan and O Goswami (1996). *Policy Reform in India*. New Delhi: Oxford and IBH Publishing Co. Pvt. Ltd.

Arellano, M and S Bond (1991). Some tests of specification for panel data: Monte Carlo evidence and an application to employment equations. *Review of Economic Studies*, 58, 277–298.

Bhaduri, A and D Nayyar (1996). *The Intelligent Person's Guide to Liberalisation*. India: Penguin.

Chand, S and K Sen (1999). Competitive pressures from trade exposure: Evidence from Indian manufacturing. *Indian Economic Review*, 34(2), 113–126.

Clarke, R and S Davies (1982). Market structure and price-cost margins. *Economica*, 49, 227–287.

Conyon, M and S Machin (1991a). The Determination of profit margins in UK manufacturing. *Journal of Industrial Economics*, 39, 369–382.

Conyon, M and S Machin (1991b) Market structure and the empcrical specification of profit margins. *Economics Letters*, 35, 227–231.

Cowling, K and M Waterson (1976). Price-cost margins and market structure. *Economica*, 43, 267–274.

Devarajan, S and D Rodrik (1989). Trade liberalization in developing countries: Do imperfect competition and scale economies matter? *AEA Papers and Proceedings*, 79(2), 283–287.

Farrell, M (1957). The measurement of productive efficiency. *Journal of the Royal Statistical Society, Series A, General*, 120(3), 253–281.

Geroski, P (1982). Simultaneous equations models of the structure-performance paradigm. *European Economic Review*, 19, 145–158.

Geroski, P (1990). Modelling persistent profitability. In *The Dynamics of Company Profits*, DC Mueller (ed.). Cambridge: Cambridge University Press.

Geroski, P and A Jacquemin (1988). The persistence of profits: An international comparison. *Economic Journal*, 98, 375–379.

Ghoshal, S, G Piramal and CA Bartlett (2000). *Managing Radical Change*. New Delhi: Penguin.

Government of India (1986). *Economic Survey, 1985–86*. New Delhi: Ministry of Finance.

Haskel, J and S Martin (1992). Margins, concentration, unions and the business: Theory and evidence for Britain. *International Journal of Industrial Organisation*, 10(4) 611–632.

Howell, J and US Kambhampati (1998). Liberalisation and labour: The effect on formal sector workers. *Journal of International Development*, 10(4), 439–452.

Howell, J and US Kambhampati (1999). The challenge of economic reforms: The response of India's firms, presented at the *ASSA Meetings in New York*, January 1999.

Joshi, V and IMD Little (1996). *India's Economic Reforms: 1991–2001*. Delhi: Oxford University Press.

Kambhampati, US (1996). *Industrial Structure and Performance: A Study of the Structure, Conduct and Performance of Indian Industry (1970-85)*. Delhi: Oxford University Press.

Kambhampati, US and A Parikh (2003). Disciplining firms?: The impact of trade reforms on profit margins in indian industry. *Applied Economics*, 35(4), 461–470.

Kambhampati, US, P Krishna and D Mitra (1997). The impact of trade policy reforms on labour markets: Evidence from India. *Journal of International Trade and Economic Development*, 6(2), 287–297.

Krishna, P and D Mitra (1998) Trade liberalisation, market discipline and productivity growth: New evidence from India. *Journal of Development Economics*, 56, 447–462.

Kwoka, JE and DJ Ravenscraft (1986). Co-operation v. rivalry: Price-cost margins by line-of-business. *Economica*, 53, 351–363.

Levinsohn, J (1993). Testing the imports-as-market-discipline hypothesis. *Journal of International Economics*, 35, 15–22.

Machin, S and J van Reenen (1993). Profit margins and the business Cycle: Evidence from UK manufacturing firms. *Journal of Industrial Economics*, 41(1) 29–50.

Mehta, R (2003). Indian Industrial tariffs, towards WTO development round negotiations. *Research and Information System for the Non-Aligned and Other Developing Countries*, New Delhi.

Nouroz, H (2001). *Protection in Indian Manufacturing: An Empirical Study*. New Delhi Macmillan India Press Limited.

Reserve Bank of India (1980–1998). Data provided on tape for 1700 firms.

Schmalensee, R (1989). Intra–industry profitability differences in US manufacturing 1953–1983. *Journal of Industrial Economics*, 37(4) 337–357.

Srivastava, V (1996). *Liberalization, Productivity and Competition*. Delhi: Oxford University Press.

Sutton, J (1991). *Sunk Costs and Market Structure: Price Competition, Advertising and the Evolution of Market Concentration*. Cambridge, MA: MIT Press.

Sutton, J (2001). Rich trades, scarce capabiliites: Industrial development revisited. *Economic and Social Review*, 33(1), 1–22.

Chapter 4

Exports, Inward Foreign Direct Investment and Regional Economic Growth in China*

Haishun Sun

Deakin University, Melbourne, Australia

Ashok Parikh

University of East Anglia, Norwich, UK

Introduction

The relationship between exports, economic growth and development has long been a subject of much interest in development literature. Theoretical consensus on export-led growth emerged among neoclassical economists in the 1970s and 1980s after the successful story of newly industrialised countries (NICs). The export-led growth hypothesis has not only been widely accepted among academic scholars (see, for example, Chenery, 1980; Feder, 1982; Krueger, 1985, 1990) and evolved into a "new conventional wisdom" (Tyler, 1981), but also shaped the development policies of a number of countries and the World Bank (see World Bank Development Report, 1987, 1992). However, empirical investigations to date have presented mixed or even contradictory results. Asian Newly Industrialised Countries (NICs) such as Taiwan, Hong Kong, South Korea and Singapore are broadly cited

* The authors would like to thank two anonymous referees for helpful comments on the previous version of this chapter.

as successful examples of the export-led growth model of development (see, for example, Chen and Tang, 1990; Dutt and Ghosh, 1996). There is less consensus on the impact of export expansion on economic growth for other countries, particularly if they are larger and undergoing transition from a centrally planned system to a market economy like China.

The reasons for these different observations have been discussed in some recent studies (e.g., Kohli and Singh, 1989; Moschos, 1989; Boulding, 1992; Greenaway and Sapsford, 1994; Poon, 1995; Yaghmaian, 1994; Yaghmaian and Ghorashi, 1995). They argue that the relationship between exports and economic growth depends on the level of development and economic structure. At a very low level of development, export expansion may not be able to affect economic growth effectively. On the other hand, when economic development reaches a high level, the contribution of exports to economic growth will be less significant compared to middle-income countries. For exports to effectively affect economic growth, a country should attain a minimum level of development, with an outward-oriented development policy. This is the so-called minimum development level hypothesis. Furthermore, some authors (e.g., Yaghmaian and Ghorashi 1995; McNab and Moore, 1998) maintain that both exports and economic growth are preceded by a long and complex process of structural change and economic development. These indicate that the differential impact of exports on economic growth across different countries and regions depends on the level of development and economic structure and is subject to a dynamic interactive process of economic development and structural change.

China, the largest developing country in the world, is undergoing economic transition from a centrally planned system to a market economy. Its economy is characterised by a regional dualistic development pattern and structural divergence. These conditions are likely to influence the relationship between exports and economic growth, and shape a development pattern that is distinguishable from both mature market economies and small, open and newly industrialised countries. To date, several empirical studies have been undertaken to investigate the relationship between exports and economic growth in the case of China by several authors; they are, among others, Li and Leung (1994), Lardy (1995), Xue (1995), Demurger (1996) and Liu *et al.* (1997). They find that export expansion and open policies generally have had a positive impact on Chinese economic growth in the past two decades.

However, these studies implicitly assume a constant relationship between export expansion and economic growth across different regions and sectors, without distinguishing the differential impacts of exports on economic growth in different regions where economic structure and degree of openness and policy environment are different. As a result, they failed to assess the impacts of exports on economic growth within different development contexts and therefore are unable to account for the differential impact of exports in different regions and the externalities from the export sector to the non-export sector.

The objectives of this study are to examine whether the economic growth in different regions of China is export led and, if this is the case, whether (i) the marginal productivities in the export and non-export sectors are different and (ii) there exists a strong externality effect of high growth in the export sector on the non-export sector. *A priori*, marginal factor productivities are likely to be lower in the non-export sector. The model used in this study is the Feder (1982) model, which can isolate externality and differential marginal productivity effects. The chapter is organised as follows. The next section presents an analytical framework for the impact of export expansion on economic growth, and discusses the model and data used in the analysis of the effects of exports and foreign investment on economic growth across the different regions of China. The third section presents the results of an empirical investigation and interprets policy implications. Finally, conclusions will be drawn.

Framework of Analysis

There is a large body of literature on the role of exports in economic growth in less developed countries. The underlying hypothesis on the contribution of export expansion to overall economic growth is that export expansion positively influences economic growth because it will increase the resource allocation efficiency, increase capacity utilisation, allow a country to take advantage of scale economies and promote technical change and overall productivity (Balassa, 1985, 1988; Tyler, 1981). In recent years, Edwards (1992, 1993) has considered this last effect, implying that trade will positively affect growth because it exposes the developing country to new ideas and techniques that can be used to improve new production methods and productivity.

In the modern endogenous growth theory (Jones, 1998) spillover effects of knowledge from the export sector to the non-export sector can be regarded as externalities. Goods that are excludable allow their producers to capture the benefits they produce; goods that are not excludable involve substantial beneficial spillovers that are not captured by the producers. Such spillovers are called externalities. In developing economies, the export sector is one of the most advanced sectors with new technologies. The non-export sector gains the spillover effects of new technologies, and these are generally regarded as positive externalities in the traditional literature. The export sector is unable to capture all the benefits it produces to the non-export sector. In the modern growth theory, the productivity of research increases with the stock of ideas. The distortion that markets produce is called a knowledge spillover because some of the knowledge created spills over to other researchers. On the other hand, the market system misses the benefits of new inventions that contribute to the productivity of future research since the market values research according to the stream of profits that are earned from the new design of machines or products.

The most common approach taken in empirical investigations of the export–growth relationship is based on the neoclassical aggregate production function. Assuming Hicks-neutral technological change, the aggregate growth can be written as the sum of the weighted growth rates of factor inputs and the total factor productivity (TFP). In the light of growth theory, export expansion plays a key role in promoting productivity growth in a less developed country (Sharma and Dhakal, 1994). This is because exports not only increase the efficiency of the export sector, but also improve productivity in non-export sectors through positive externalities. Feder (1982) captured the positive externality on the non-export sector and the productivity differential in favour of the export sector in a simple neoclassical model, which generalised Balassa's original model.

The model used in this study is based on Feder's (1982) model, with some modifications. The economy is assumed to consist of two sectors: export and non-export. The overall output is composed of products and services produced by the two sectors. The production functions in the two sectors are

$$N = F(K_n, L_n, X), \tag{1}$$

$$X = G(K_x, L_x), \tag{2}$$

where K_i and L_i $(i = n, x)$ are capital and labour in the non-export and export sectors of the economy. The assumption of a productivity differential is introduced as

$$\left(\frac{G_K}{F_K}\right) = \left(\frac{G_L}{F_L}\right) = 1 + \delta, \tag{3}$$

where G_L, F_L are the marginal productivities of labour in the export and non-export sectors, respectively, and G_K, F_K are the respective marginal productivities of capital. δ measures the difference in productivity in favour of exports. If $\delta = 0$, marginal productivities are equalised across the two sectors. The production function for the non-export sector is augmented by the inclusion of X, the export sector output. If the marginal contribution of the export sector (F_x) is zero, then the externality is not present. The aggregate GDP is the sum of N and X:

$$Y = N + X. \tag{4}$$

Using the results that marginal productivity of labour in the non-export sector is $F_L = \beta(Y/L)$ and marginal productivity of capital is $F_K = \alpha$, the following equation can be derived for the rate of growth of GDP:

$$\frac{\hat{Y}}{Y} = \alpha\left(\frac{I}{Y}\right) + \beta\left(\frac{\hat{L}}{L}\right) + \left[F_x + \frac{\delta}{1+\delta}\right]\left[\frac{\hat{X}}{X} \cdot \frac{X}{Y}\right]. \tag{5}$$

Further, Feder specifies the externality effect to decompose the factor productivity differential by adopting an explicit specification for the term F_x. Assuming that exports affect the production of the non-export sector with constant elasticity, the production function for the sector will be

$$N = F(K_n, L_n, X) = X^{\theta} \cdot F(K_n, L_n), \tag{6}$$

where θ is a parameter. From the above

$$\frac{\partial N}{\partial X} = F_x = \theta\left(\frac{N}{X}\right) \tag{7}$$

and Eq. (5) can be written as

$$\frac{\hat{Y}}{Y} = \alpha\left(\frac{I}{Y}\right) + \beta\left(\frac{\hat{L}}{L}\right) + \left[\frac{\delta}{1+\delta} + \theta\frac{N}{X}\right]\frac{\hat{X}}{X}\cdot\frac{X}{Y}. \tag{8}$$

As $N/Y = 1 - (X/Y)$, we can write

$$\theta\left(\frac{N}{X}\right) = \theta\left(\frac{N/Y}{X/Y}\right) = \frac{\theta}{(X/Y)} - \theta. \tag{9}$$

We obtain after substitution

$$\frac{\hat{Y}}{Y} = \alpha\left(\frac{I}{Y}\right) + \beta\left(\frac{\hat{L}}{L}\right) + \left[\frac{\delta}{1+\delta} - \theta\right]\frac{\hat{X}}{X}\cdot\frac{X}{Y} + \theta\cdot\frac{\hat{X}}{X}. \tag{10}$$

If it is assumed that $\delta/(1+\delta) = \theta$, then the model is

$$\frac{\hat{Y}}{Y} = \alpha\left(\frac{I}{Y}\right) + \beta\left(\frac{\hat{L}}{L}\right) + \theta\left(\frac{\hat{X}}{X}\right). \tag{11}$$

If Eq. (10) is rewritten with separate δs and θ, we can obtain

$$\frac{\hat{Y}}{Y} = \alpha\left(\frac{I}{Y}\right) + \beta\left(\frac{\hat{L}}{L}\right) + \frac{\delta}{1+\delta}\cdot\left[\frac{\hat{X}}{X}\cdot\frac{X}{Y}\right] + \theta\left[\frac{\hat{X}}{X} - \frac{\hat{X}}{X}\cdot\frac{X}{Y}\right]. \tag{12}$$

If $\theta = 0$, Eq. (10) reduces to

$$\frac{\hat{Y}}{Y} = \alpha\left(\frac{I}{Y}\right) + \beta\left(\frac{\hat{L}}{L}\right) + \frac{\delta}{1+\delta}\cdot\left[\frac{\hat{X}}{X}\cdot\frac{X}{Y}\right]. \tag{13}$$

In our study, the investment–output ratio is decomposed into two components, domestic and foreign investment, and hence, the general model on the lines of Eqs. (10) and (12) would be

$$\frac{\hat{Y}}{Y} = \alpha_1\left(\frac{I}{Y}\right) + \alpha_2\left(\frac{\text{FDI}}{Y}\right) + \beta\left(\frac{\hat{L}}{L}\right) + \frac{\delta}{1+\delta} \cdot\left[\frac{\hat{X}}{X}\cdot\frac{X}{Y}\right] + \theta\left[\frac{\hat{X}}{X} - \frac{\hat{X}}{X}\cdot\frac{X}{Y}\right]. \tag{14}$$

In the econometric estimation in the present study, we have estimated Eqs. (10)–(13), augmented by the direct foreign investment to GDP ratio. The earlier regression based analyses (Balassa, 1985; Ram, 1985, 1987) established that the coefficient on the exports growth variable in Eq. (11) was higher in the post-oil shock period. This type of result led Balassa to conclude that there are advantages of following an outward-oriented approach. Later Ram (1987) found that although the relationship between export growth and output growth was positive, the coefficient of export growth was smaller for the post-oil shock period as compared to the pre-oil shock period. It was largely the favourable demand conditions that were responsible for faster economic growth, and both outward orientation and favourable demand conditions can go together. It seems that the work in this area has not provided conclusive evidence that world demand conditions affect the growth between export growth and aggregate growth in GDP. However, world business cycles play some role in the way the export sector interacts with the aggregate GDP.

The other line of inquiry concerns the issue of endogeneity of export growth or the $(\hat{X}/Y)$ variable. This is because the lack of suitable explanatory variables did not permit investigators to estimate another equation in a simultaneous equation model. McNab and Moore (1998) explained export expansion by using trade policy variables, i.e., moderately inward, moderately outward and strongly outward policy variables introduced in the form of dummy variables.

Econometric Estimation of GDP Growth

Empirical results of the basic model

We estimated Eqs. (10)–(13) as alternative models. Equations (10) and (12) are identical algebraic models, and we demonstrated that both yielded identical parameter values. Among the three models (10) or (12), (11) and (13), (12) turned out to be the best estimated growth equation. The data used in this study are panel data, including 29 provinces across three regions of China for a period of 11 years from 1985 to 1995.[a] The principal data

---

[a] Tibet is excluded from the present study because there is no FDI.

sources are statistical yearbooks of each province from 1986 to 1996, where all the data are in the 1984 constant prices.

In general, cross-section and time-series data on their own yield very different estimates of a model. If pooled cross-section and time-series data are available, we have more information, and this in turn avoids a number of problems encountered with either cross-section or time-series alone. In our region-level panel data analysis both cross-sectional and inter-temporal effects can be examined. In the present case, it may be useful to think of three types of effects due to these three types of variables; region time-invariant effects, period region-invariant effects, and region time-varying effects. Our analysis uses the province-level data and then classifies the provinces into main regions. The advantage of panel data comes in a variety of ways: (a) it increases the number of observations; (b) it adds more variability and more information; (c) it permits the data to be treated in two dimensions separately (cross-section and time-series), provided there are enough time periods for which data are available and (d) it makes econometric specification rich such as the fixed effect and random effect model in addition to some exploration on endogeneity issues and restricted estimation.

Equations were estimated with growth in labour force, but it was always insignificant. In Table 1, if we look at the results of Eq. (12), we find that the marginal productivity of domestic capital in the non-export sector is not significantly different from zero, while all other coefficients are positive and statistically significant. The marginal productivity of foreign investment in the non-export sector is 0.74. The differential marginal productivity parameter δ is 0.2395 ($\delta/(1+\delta) = 0.1932$, the coefficient of WEX in Eq. (12), Table 1), while the parameter θ representing the externality effect of the export sector on the non-export sector is 0.0470 (coefficient of ZEX in Eq. (12) of Table 1). Both these effects are small, and the differential marginal productivity parameter is not statistically different from zero at 5 percent level. The externality effect (θ) is positive and significant, and this means that the export sector contributes to the growth of the non-export sector. The study uses panel data, so both the random effect and fixed effect models are estimated. The Hausman test yields the value of $\chi^2(4) = 11.481$, resulting in a clear rejection of the null hypothesis of the random effect against the fixed effect model.

Table 1. Regression results using panel data (29 provinces, 11 years), dependent variable: GRRGDP.

	Constant	GLAB	GEXP	INVGDP	FDIGDP	ZEX	WEX	R^2/F	SEE
With ZEX and GEXP	0.0719	—	0.0470	0.0362	0.7412	0.1462		0.1717	0.0469
Feder: separate effects	(6.4759)		(2.5747)	(0.9025)	(4.8465)	(0.9168)		(2.3821)	
Eq. (10) with GLAB	0.0695	0.10028	0.0560	0.0348	0.8179			0.1714	0.0469
(Balassa) Eq. (11)	(6.1509)	(0.8374)	(4.0217)	(0.8659)	(6.2216)			(2.0827)	
Without GLAB	0.0713		0.05805	0.0358	0.8131			0.1695	0.0469
(Balassa) Eq. (11)	(6.434)		(4.2363)	(0.8934)	(6.1938)			(1.7207)	
With ZEX and WEX	0.0719	—		0.0362	0.7412	0.1932	0.0470	0.1717	0.0469
Modified Feder Eq. (12)	(6.4759)	—		(0.9025)	(4.8465)	(1.3051)	(2.5747)	(2.3831)	
With ZEX	0.0749	—		0.0428	0.6210	0.4173		0.1543	0.0473
Feder Eq. (13)	(6.7268)	—		(1.0612)	(3.4548)	(3.4547)		(1.9648)	

Notes: GRRGDP = growth rate of real GDP; GEXP = growth rate of exports; GLAB = growth rate of labour; INVGDP = domestic fixed capital investment/GDP; FDIGDP = (FDI)/GDP; and ZEX = $[\frac{\hat{X}}{X}\frac{X}{Y}]$, WEX = $[\frac{\hat{X}}{X} - \frac{\hat{X}}{X}\frac{X}{Y}]$.

Table 2. The between and within estimates of the fixed effect model of Eq. (12): Dependent variable GRRGDP.

	Coefficient	t-statistics
Between (OLS on means) estimates		
Constant	−0.1097	6.2928
INVGDP	−0.0743	−1.4329
FDIGDP	0.3578	1.0716
ZEX	0.7064	1.9785
WEX	−0.0262	−0.3874
R^2	0.5336	
SEE	0.0141	
Within estimates (implying that province effects are eliminated)		
INVGDP	0.1981	3.1129
FDIGDP	0.7102	3.8228
ZEX	0.1059	0.6356
WEX	0.0471	2.4396
R^2	0.2688	
SEE	0.0462	

Note: The random effect model is rejected in favour of the fixed effect model by the Hausman test; $\chi^2(4) = 11.481$.

In Table 2, we present the results for GDP growth from the between and within estimates. Since such pooled regression estimates are a weighted average of the between and within estimates, most of the parameters yield t-ratios in excess of 1 but rarely reaching significance at the 5 percent probability level for the between estimates. On the other hand, the marginal productivities of domestic and foreign capital in the non-export sector (when province effects are subtracted out) are 0.198 and 0.710. Both are significant. The externality effect of exports on the non-export sector (θ) is positive and strong, while $\delta/(1+\delta)$ is not significant.

Results of simultaneous equations

The above analysis suggests that provincial GDP growth is largely due to domestic and foreign investment and export expansion and its effects on the non-export sector at the provincial level. For 29 provinces, the effect of externality is strong and cannot be ignored. Indeed, the above results could suffer from a simultaneous equation bias; so we decided to re-specify it as a simultaneous equation model.

$$GRRGDP = a_0 + a_1 INVGDP + a_2 FDIGDP + a_3 \cdot \left(\frac{\hat{X}}{X} \cdot \frac{X}{Y}\right)$$

$$ZEX = \frac{\hat{X}}{X} \cdot \frac{X}{Y} = b_0 + b_1 \cdot GRRGDP + b_2 \cdot REGION1 + b_3 \cdot REGION2.$$

The first equation of the above simultaneous equation model is Feder's Eq. (5), where we estimate externality and differential marginal productivity in favour of the export sector together. We tried with Eq. (12), but a number of parameters were not significant. REGION1 and REGION2 are dummies used for the coastal and non-coastal provinces, respectively. In the above model, INVGDP and FDIGDP are insignificant, as were the region dummies. The model remained underidentified in the estimated form. We then decided to re-specify the above model and instead of the ZEX variable, we used the Balassa Eq. (11) as the first equation of a simultaneous equation model.

The model was estimated by the three stage least squares with panel data of 319 observations. Thus,

$$\underset{}{\mathrm{GRRGDP}} = \underset{(2.9256)}{0.1069} - \underset{(0.7548)}{0.3157}\ \mathrm{GEXP} + \underset{(0.7970)}{0.0852}\ \mathrm{INVGDP} + \underset{(3.1398)}{1.0458}\ \mathrm{FDIGDP},$$

$$\mathrm{SEE} = 0.0855,$$

$$\mathrm{GEXP} = \underset{(0.6454)}{0.0406} + \underset{(1.8513)}{1.3183}\ \mathrm{GRRGDP} - \underset{(1.7511)}{0.0548}\ \mathrm{REGION1} - \underset{(1.2423)}{0.0279}\ \mathrm{REGION2},$$

$$\mathrm{SEE} = 0.1866.$$

The coefficient of the GEXP variable in the first equation is negative but not significantly different from zero. On the other hand, marginal productivity of foreign capital in the non-export sector is positive and significant. There is a significant relationship between GDP growth and export growth, and export growth is largely explained by GDP growth. Regions that have promoted higher exports did not seem to maintain the growth, but, on the other hand, their growth in exports tended to be lower. This is mainly due to the larger exports in the base year providing lower prospects of export growth. Overall, the relationship between exports and GDP growth does not seem to be that strong.

Empirical results across different regions

There are three macro-regions in China, and each consists of a number of provinces and cities. These three regions are the eastern region (the coastal region), the central region and the western region. The three regions are distinguishable from each other in many respects, not only in their distance from the coast, but also in economic structure and the degree of economic openness and policy orientation. The eastern (coastal) region is relatively advanced, and the economic growth center, principal exports provider and foreign investment destination in China, with a higher degree of trade openness. Its economy is dominated by manufacturing and services. In contrast, the economy of the two inland regions is backward, and largely domestic market-oriented, with a lower degree of openness. In the past two decades, the economic growth in the eastern region has outperformed the two inland regions. Export expansion and foreign investment inflows are important determinants of rapid economic growth in the eastern region.

To measure the differential effects of export expansion on economic growth across the three macro-regions in China, we performed regressions for each of these regions, using Feder's model and the data for each region. The regression results are presented in Table 3. It is clear that export expansion played a differing role in regional economic growth. In the eastern (coastal) region, the effect of export growth on GDP growth is positive and significant, while its impact on GDP growth is marginally significant in the central region and insignificant in the western region. It is interesting to note that change in exports as a share of GDP (the ZEX variable) has a positive and significant effect on economic growth in the central region. This indicates that as the degree of trade openness increases (as measured by ZEX), the impact of export expansion on GDP growth becomes increasingly important.

From Table 3, we also find that the growth in labour has almost no impact on GDP growth in two of the three regions, indicating that labour surplus is a basic feature of the Chinese economy and that in many cases labour is overused in the production process. On the other hand, capital

Table 3. Regression results by regions: Fixed effect and random components model.

Variables	Within (fixed effects), estimates		Variance components, (random effects) estimates		Total estimates	
	Coefficient	*t*-statistics	Coefficient	*t*-statistics	Coefficient	*t*-statistics
The eastern region: 132 observations, (12 regions), $\chi^2(5) = 8.1298$*, accept random effects model*						
GLAB	0.0778	0.3629	0.2240	1.12	0.3036	1.5319
INVGDP	0.3200	3.3321	0.2164	2.5469	0.1614	1.9815
FDIGDP	0.5426	2.7291	0.5356	2.9516	0.5158	2.9062
GEXP	0.0471	1.7003	0.0480	1.7886	0.0495	1.5319
ZEX	−0.0289	0.1424	0.0090	0.0475	0.0256	0.1356
Constant			0.0285	1.2132	0.0418	1.8551
R^2	0.3418		0.2015		0.2059	
The central region: 99 observations, (nine regions), $\chi^2(5) = 8.2772$*, accept random effect model*						
GLAB	0.8672	2.8103	0.7598	2.6306	0.6944	2.4105
INVGDP	0.1359	1.0680	0.0713	0.7325	0.0447	0.5008
FDIGDP	6.6418	5.2183	6.2920	5.0238	6.0817	4.7408
GEXP	−0.2002	2.6742	−0.1292	1.8379	−0.0908	1.2986
ZEX	6.2564	1.4295	4.8838	3.6448	4.1380	3.1100
Constant			0.0271	1.0534	0.0347	1.4347
R^2	0.4803		0.3923		0.3939	
The western region: 88 observations: (eight regions), $\chi^2(5) = 7.5584$*, accept random effect model*						
GLAB	−0.1622	1.1774	−0.1732	1.3197	−0.1773	1.3485
INVGDP	0.1992	2.2054	0.1062	1.9857	0.0819	1.7843
FDIGDP	2.4092	1.5498	2.5313	1.9219	2.3730	1.9126
GEXP	0.0705	1.3078	0.0748	1.6391	0.0602	1.3348
ZEX	−1.5597	0.9539	−1.4430	0.9844	−0.9432	0.6473
Constant			0.0476	2.7841	0.0553	3.6742
R^2	0.2430		0.1019		0.1038	

input is a major determinant of economic growth in the Chinese economy. The coefficients of domestic investment as a share of GDP (represented by INVGDP) are positive and significant in the eastern and western regions. FDI plays an important role in Chinese economic growth for the period under study. As shown in Table 3, FDI has a positive impact on GDP growth in each of the three regions. In the central region, export growth has a negative and significant impact on GDP growth, and this can be due to lack of available infrastructure not promoting economic growth but on the contrary taking resources away from the non-export sector. The net effect of the differential marginal productivity and externality impact of the export sector on the non-export sector seems to be negative for the western region.

These findings are virtually consistent with the theoretical hypothesis presented in the first section of the chapter that the impact of export expansion (and foreign investment) on economic growth varies according to regional economic characteristics, including the level of development, economic structure and policy orientations. To a large extent, the differential impacts of exports and foreign investment account for divergent growth performance across different regions. On the other hand, the level of development and structural characteristics and policy orientation shaped the direction and extent of the impact of export expansion and foreign investment. Therefore, it can be maintained that export expansion and economic growth are two interactive processes of economic development.

Sources of growth

Using the results of Table 3 and the mean values of sample variables from the appendix table for various regions, the average rate of growth in the 1985–1995 period can be decomposed so as to identify the contributions of domestic investment, foreign investment, labour force growth and resource shifts in exports. This is presented in Table 4 for all three regions.

The results indicate that the gain in productivity in the coastal region due to allocation associated with the export expansion contributed 0.63 percent to the growth, while domestic and foreign investment contributed more than 7 percent growth. The contribution of exports can be decomposed into two components: (i) the gain due to externalities affecting the non-export sector, $\theta(1-x)\hat{X}/X$, is 0.60 of one percentage point and (ii) the gain due to other elements underlying the higher factor productivity in the export sector, $(\delta/1+\delta)\cdot$ZEX, is 0.1139 of 1 percent. For the central region, we have negative externality effects, while the gain due to higher productivity in the export sector is 1.134. For the western region, the coefficient of ZEX is negative and insignificant, and hence externality and differential marginal

Table 4. Decompositions of sources of growth by regions.

Region	Source	Regression coefficient	Mean growth (1985–1995)	Contribution to growth (%)
Eastern	Constant	0.0285	—	2.850
	GLAB	0.2240	0.0213	0.478
	INVGDP	0.2164	0.2759	5.971
	FDIGDP	0.5356	0.0210	1.126
	GEXP	0.0480	0.1317	0.632
	ZEX	0.0090	0.0187	0.017
Overall				11.074
Central	Constant	0.0271	—	2.710
	GLAB	0.7598	0.0245	1.870
	INVGDP	0.0713	0.2437	1.740
	FDIGDP	6.2920	0.0029	1.846
	GEXP	−0.1292	0.1314	−1.698
	ZEX	4.8838	0.0051	2.507
Overall				8.969
Western	Constant	0.0476	—	4.760
	GLAB	−0.1732	0.0235	−0.406
	INVGDP	0.1062	0.2962	3.145
	FDIGDP	2.5313	0.0022	0.569
	GEXP	0.0748	0.1534	1.148
	ZEX	−1.4430	0.0044	−0.636
Overall				9.392

productivity effects together are insignificant. It is also possible to work out the social marginal productivity of domestic and foreign investment in exports using the share of exports in GDP. The formula for this is

$$\mathrm{SMP}_{x\mathrm{DI}} = F_{x\mathrm{DI}}\left[1 + \frac{\theta(1-x)}{x}\right](1+\delta), \tag{15}$$

$$\mathrm{SMP}_{x\mathrm{FI}} = F_{x\mathrm{FI}}\left[1 + \frac{\theta(1-x)}{x}\right](1+\delta). \tag{16}$$

In Eqs. (15) and (16), $F_{x\mathrm{DI}}$ and $F_{x\mathrm{FI}}$ are the marginal productivity of domestic investment and foreign direct investment in exports while x is the share of exports in the regional GDP. The social marginal productivity of domestic and foreign investment is 0.444 and 1.10, respectively, in the eastern region, which is the most prosperous of all.

Conclusions

This chapter has presented an empirical study into the impact of exports on economic growth in the context of China. Using the modified Feder model, this study investigated the effects of export growth, change in exports as a share of GDP, and domestic investment and foreign investment as a share of GDP on GDP growth rates. It found that export expansion generally has a positive and significant impact on Chinese economic growth. It also established that there is a strong positive externality from the export to the non-export sector and the contribution of export growth to overall economic growth is important.

In addition, this study investigated the regional differential effects of export expansion and foreign investment on GDP growth across the three macro-regions in China within different development contexts. It has been shown that export growth positively affects GDP growth in two of the regions. However, the strength of the positive impact of export on GDP growth varies significantly across the regions. In the eastern (coastal) region, export growth significantly contributed to economic growth, while its impact is negative and marginally significant in the central region and is insignificant in the western region. This finding is consistent with the findings by Fan (1992). Similar results have also been found for FDI.

These results clearly imply that the relationship between exports (and FDI) and economic growth depends on the regional economic and social settings, including the level of development, industrial structure, policy orientation and degree of openness. Without attaining a certain level of development, an outward-looking policy and an established comparative advantage, exports would be unlikely to affect economic growth effectively and would, therefore, not play the role of an engine. The Chinese experience, especially the divergent growth performance and differential impacts of exports and foreign investment, confirms that export expansion and inflows of foreign investment can play an important role in accelerating economic growth within an open policy environment and development context.

References

Balassa, B (1985). Exports, policy choices, and economic growth in developing countries after the 1973 oil shocks. *Journal of Development Economics*, 18, 23–35.

Balassa, B (1988). The lessons of the Asian development: An overview. *Economic Development and Cultural Change*, 36 (supplement 3).

Boulding, KE (1992). Appropriate methodologies for the study of the economy. In *Praxiologies and the Philosophy of Economics: The International Annual of Practical Philosophy and Methodology*, JL Auspitz *et al.* (eds.), Vol. I. News Brunswick, New Jersey: Transaction Publishers.

Chen, T-J and D-P Tang (1990). Export performance and productivity growth: The case of Taiwan. *Economic Development and Cultural Change*, 38(3), 577–585.

Chenery, HB (1980). Interactions between industrialization and exports. *American Economic Review*, 70, 281–287.

Demurger, S (1996). Openness and industrial-growth in Chinese cities. *Revue Economique*, 47(3), 841–850.

Dutt, SD and D Ghosh (1996). The export growth-economic growth nexus: A causality analysis. *The Journal of Developing Areas*, 30(1) 167–182.

Edwards, S (1992). Trade orientation, distortions and growth in developing countries. *Journal of Development Economics*, 39, 31–57.

Edwards, S (1993). Openness, trade liberalization, and growth in developing countries. *Journal of Economic Literature*, 31, 1358–1393.

Feder, G (1982). On export and economic growth. *Journal of Development Economics*, 12, 59–73.

Fan, CC (1992). Regional impact of foreign trade in China, 1984–1989. *Growth and Change*, 23(2), 129–159.

Greenaway, D and D Sapsford (1994). What does liberalization do for exports and growth. *Weltwirtschaftliches Archiv*, 130, 152–174.

Jones, CI (1998). *Introduction to Economic Growth*. New York, London: W.W. Norton.

Kohli, I and N Singh (1989). Exports, growth and causality in developing countries. *Journal of Development Economics*, 26, 55–63.

Krueger, AO (1985). The experiences and lessons of Asia's super-exports. In *Export-Oriented Development Strategies, The Success of Five Newly Industrializing Countries*, V Corbo, AO Krueger and F Ossa (eds.), Boulder: Westview Press.

Krueger, AO (1990). *Perspectives on Trade and Development*. Chicago: University of Chicago Press.

Lardy, NR (1995). The role of foreign trade and investment in China's economic transformation. *The China Quarterly*, December, 1065–1082.

Li, KW and WSC Leung (1994). Causal relationships among economic aggregates in China. *Applied Economics*, 26, 1189–1196.

Liu, X, H Song and P Romilly (1997). An empirical investigation of the causal relationship between openness and economic growth in China. *Applied Economics*, 29(12), 1679–1687.

McNab, RM and RE Moore (1998). Trade policy, export expansion, human capital and growth. *The Journal of International Trade and Economic Development*, 7(2), 237–256.

Moschos, D (1989). Export expansion, growth and level of economic development. *Journal of Development Economics*, 30, 93–102.

Poon, JP (1995). Export expansion, economic growth and economic development revisited. *Journal of Economic Development*, 20(1), 75–90.

Ram, R (1985). Exports and economic growth: Some additional evidence. *Economic Development and Cultural Change*, 33(2), 415–425.

Ram, R (1987). Exports and economic growth in developing countries: Evidence from time series and cross section data. *Economic Development and Cultural Change*, 36(4), 51–72.

Sharma, SC and D Dhakal (1994). Causal analyses between exports and economic growth in developing countries. *Applied Economics*, 26(12), 1145–1158.

Tyler, WG (1981). Growth and export expansion in developing countries, some empirical evidence. *Journal of Development Economics*, 9, 121–130.

World Bank (1987). *World Development Report 1987*. New York: Oxford University Press.

World Bank (1992). *World Development Report 1992*. New York: Oxford University Press.

Xue, J (1995). The export-led growth model and its application in China. *Hitotsubashi Journal of Economics*, 36, 189–206.

Yaghmaian, B (1994). An empirical investigation of exports, development and growth in developing countries: Challenging the neo-classical theory of export-led growth. *World Development*, 22, 1977–1995.

Yaghmaian, B and R Ghorashi (1995). Export performance and economic development: An empirical analysis. *American Economist*, 39(2), 37–46.

Appendix Table. Means, standard deviations and other statistics of eight variables (by regions of China).

Name	Mean	Std. dev.	Skewness	Kurtosis	Variable: Description
China: all regions; number of observations: 319					
GRRGDP	0.09734	0.05122	0.71308	4.2642	Growth in GDP
GLAB	0.02292	0.02235	−1.7024	19.998	Growth in labour
GLEXP	0.13764	0.19292	−0.0668	5.4252	Growth in exports
INVGDP	0.27153	0.06664	1.17722	2.1307	Investment–GDP ratio
EXGDP	0.06661	0.06064	2.59763	9.8755	Exports/GDP ratio
DFIGDP	0.01023	0.02031	3.68109	15.610	Foreign inv–GDP ratio
NEXPGDP	0.97137	0.02606	−2.5976	9.8755	Non-exports/GDP ratio
ZEX	0.01056	0.02455	6.16052	65.419	Change in exports/GDP
Eastern region; number of observations: 132					
GRRGDP	0.11077	0.05446	0.63679	1.37425	Growth in GDP
GLAB	0.02134	0.02196	1.13947	10.5388	Growth in labour
GLEXP	0.13174	0.23010	−0.0581	5.84544	Growth in exports
INVGDP	0.27593	0.05583	1.14941	4.35325	Investement–GDP ratio
EXGDP	0.11339	0.07054	1.91945	6.16522	Exports/GDP ratio
DFIGDP	0.02103	0.02800	2.25426	5.25670	Foreign inv–GDP ratio
NEXPGDP	0.95127	0.03032	−1.9195	6.16522	Non-export/GDP ratio
ZEX	0.01874	0.03579	4.17533	30.4290	Change in exports/GDP
Central region; number of observations: 99					
GRRGDP	0.08968	0.05553	0.68795	7.66680	Growth in GDP
GLAB	0.02456	0.01675	0.89900	1.83275	Growth in labour
GLEXP	0.13146	0.15372	−0.0668	2.41645	Growth in exports
INVGDP	0.24376	0.05382	1.06647	1.45707	Investement–GDP ratio
EXGDP	0.03761	0.01130	1.69695	4.39334	Exports–GDP ratio
DFIGDP	0.00293	0.00391	1.38428	0.58169	Foreign inv–GDP ratio
NEXPGDP	0.98384	0.00486	−1.6967	4.39334	Non-exports–GDP ratio
ZEX	0.00513	0.00802	2.09686	15.3309'	Change in exports/GDP
Western region; number of observations: 88					
GRRGDP	0.08583	0.03432	0.11996	0.32407	Growth in GDP
GLAB	0.02345	0.02786	−4.3004	25.1588	Growth in labour
GLEXP	0.15344	0.17133	0.01720	0.24258	Growth in exports
INVGDP	0.29620	0.08219	0.93051	0.29486	Investement–GDP ratio
EXGDP	0.02908	0.01005	0.10653	−0.8262	Exports/GDP ratio
DFIGDP	0.00225	0.00300	2.05796	3.88481	Foreign inv–GDP ratio
NEXPGDP	0.98750	0.00432	−0.1065	−0.8262	Non-exports/GDP ratio
ZEX	0.00441	0.00536	0.52259	1.88067	Change in export/GDP

Notes to the appendix table:

1. China has three macro-regions, namely the eastern (coastal) region, the central region and the western region. The eastern region consists of 12 provinces and province-level cities. They are Guangdong, Fujian, Jiangsu, Zhejiang, Shanghai, Shandong, Hebei, Beijing, Tianjin, Liaoning, Guangxi and Hainan. The central region includes nine provinces and autonomous regions: Shanxi, Inner Mongolia, Jilin, Heilongjiang, Anhui, Jiangxi, Henan, Hubei and Hunan. The western region consists of nine provinces and autonomous regions. They are Shaanxi, Shichuan, Qinghai, Yunnan, Guizhou, Gansu, Ningxia, Xingjiang and Tibet (Tibet is excluded from this study).
2. The data sources: the primary data sources for this study including the appendix table are statistical yearbooks of all the provinces for the period from 1985 to 1996. The national statistical yearbooks are also used where the provincial data is incomplete.
3. As shown in the appendix table, the export–GDP ratio and foreign investment–GDP ratio are much higher in the coastal region than that in the two inland regions (the central and western regions). These indicate that the impact of export expansion and foreign investment is expected to have different impacts on economic growth across different regions. In other words, the different degrees of economic openness and trade orientation contributed to the different growth performance in different regions of China.
4. Domestic investment is defined as fixed capital investment financed by domestic savings that are separate from the part of fixed capital investment financed by foreign investment. In our computation, domestically financed investment is the total domestic investment less the portion of investment financed by foreign capital.
5. FDI and domestic investment do not overlap with each other. In Chinese official statistics, FDI refers to foreign direct investment that is directly used for establishing and operating enterprises in China. FDI is separate in statistics from other forms of foreign capital inflows such as foreign loans, foreign aid, foreign investment in financial markets (stock and bond markets) and trade compensation. There are two categories of FDI statistics in China: contract (pledged) FDI values and actually arrived

(or used) FDI values. In this study, actually arrived FDI values for the period from 1984 to 1995 are used.

6. All variables are measured at the constant 1984 prices.

Appendix on notations used

^ denotes change in variable

FDI	=	foreign direct investment
FDIGDP	=	foreign direct investment to output ratio
F_x	=	marginal contribution of the export sector
F_L	=	marginal product of labour in the non-export sector
F_K	=	marginal product of capital in the non-export sector
G_L	=	marginal product of labour in the export sector
G_K	=	marginal product of capital in the export sector
GEXP	=	growth in exports
GLAB	=	growth in labour
GRGDP	=	growth rate in gross domestic product
I/Y	=	investment–output ratio
INVGDP	=	investment–output ratio
L	=	labour
K	=	capital
N	=	non-export sector
X	=	export sector
WEX	=	growth in exports times share of non-exports
Y	=	gross domestic product
$\hat{Y}/Y$	=	growth in gross domestic product
ZEX	=	growth in exports times export share
x	=	share of exports in regional GDP

Parameters

δ	=	differential marginal productivity parameter between export and non-export
θ	=	externality effect of export sector on non-exports
α_1	=	marginal productivity of domestic investment
α_2	=	marginal productivity of FDI
β	=	elasticity of output with respect to labour

Chapter 5

Impact of Trade Liberalisation on Import Demands in India: A Panel Data Analysis for Commodity Groups*

Rajesh Mehta

Research and Information Systems for the Non-Aligned and Other Developing Countries, New Delhi, India

Ashok Parikh

University of East Anglia, Norwich, UK

Introduction

The objectives of this study are to assess the impact of trade liberalisation on import demands for a sample of countries during the 1993–1997 period. Our sample consists of both developing and developed countries, namely Brazil, Chile, Japan, India, The European Union and USA. The selected period is 1993–1997 on account of the availability of data and of information on changes that have occurred in tariff and non-tariff barriers. A decline in tariff rates and hence import prices will lead to an increase in import demand.

* We are grateful to Mr. David Bailey, Dr. Kunal Sen and Professor Mark Taylor for their helpful comments. The second author wishes to thank the Leverhulme Trust for the award of an Emeritus Fellowship which facilitated the completion of the above study.

The extent of the increase in import demand owing to a unit change in import prices (on account of a unit change in tariff rates) varies from commodity to commodity. It is expected that liberalisation leading to a decline in import prices could have an impact on price elasticity as the lower expected import prices and greater flexibility in the import structure could induce greater elasticity in demand for imports. Disaggregated estimates of trade elasticities are important to quantify the influence of various determinants of demand and to provide a scientific basis for policy decisions, particularly for those related to demand restraint, devaluation, tariffs, etc. In this chapter, an attempt is made to estimate import demand functions for 20 broad commodity groups at an aggregate level using a panel dataset of countries and commodities over the 1993–1997 period. In the field of international trade, not much work has been done to estimate disaggregated elasticities at a commodity level using panel data for both developing and developed countries. Erkel-Rourse and Mirza (2002) provided a comprehensive survey and found that import price elasticities from gravity type models were around unity. They obtained relatively high trade elasticities for homogeneous goods. Our study attempts to consider the impact that tariff reductions for each commodity have had and, in particular, their impact on import price elasticities. At an aggregate level for India, we use data for 20 commodities in a panel form (over the 1993–1997 period) and estimate year-by-year price elasticities.

This study is organised in six sections. In the second section, we provide the underlying framework to estimate commodity level import demand relationships. In the third section, we discuss the available data and any adjustment and derivation of variables made from the original data. The fourth section discusses the results of the various models, both static and dynamic, on panel data of 20 commodities for five years for the Indian economy, each commodity using data from six countries. In the first model, we are interested in the country-level price elasticity for each commodity. In the fifth section, we look at the price elasticities for the Indian economy over time and examine whether any changes have taken place with liberalisation. We also discuss the results based on a dynamic panel model and estimate the average price elasticity for the Indian economy without considering each commodity group separately. A comparison of estimated elasticities for the Indian economy is made with those of Japan.[a] We summarise and draw conclusions in the final section.

Specification and Functional Form of Demand Functions

India had followed a policy of import substitution in the early days of development, and this strategy of development had resulted in an inefficient production of importables, resulting in a high cost economy. Major reforms in trade policy were implemented in the 1990s following the balance of payments crisis of 1989. The trade reforms were recommended by the Tax Reforms Committee (Government of India, 1991), and led to a reduction in the general level of tariffs, a reduction of the spread of dispersion of tariff rates, the abolition of numerous exemptions and concessions, and the abolition of making changes through notifications. When the tariff rates for 1987–1988 are compared with those in the 1992–1997 period (Nouroz, 2001), we find significant changes. Sharma and Mehta (1997) provide the data for the nominal rate of protection for the 1989–1990 period by input–output sectors. In 1992–1993, the first year when the reforms were introduced, the peak tariff rates were brought down to 110 percent, and in 1994–1995, they were further reduced to 65 percent. In 1997–1998, the peak tariff rate was further reduced to 40 percent, but a special additional duty of 2 percent was charged. In addition to the above reductions in peak rate tariffs, there was an overall change in the structure of tariffs. In 1992–1993 the import weighted tariff rate for capital goods was 66 percent; for intermediate goods, it was 69 percent while for consumer goods it was 75 percent. In 1994–1995, these rates declined for capital goods to 41 percent, for intermediate goods to 42 percent and for consumer goods to 46 percent, and they were further reduced to 32 percent for consumer and intermediate goods and to 25 percent for capital goods in 1997–1998. Another aspect of the trade policy reform was the reduction in quantitative restrictions. In 1987–1988, 39 percent of items were on a restricted list, whereas in 1992–1993 only 21 percent of imports were in this category. Under the

[a] We chose Japan as we have no gaps in observations and Japan's data are more reliable than the European Union (EU), because exchange rate fluctuations are not the same for all the EU countries and the extent of non-tariff barriers vary from country to country in the EU.

open general licence category, there was a sharp general increase in the items covered in this category in 1997–1998 (Nouroz, 2001, p. 48). Nouroz calculated effective rates of protection for several industries in India and compared them to other Asian countries. She found that despite considerable reforms there were negative rates of protection in some industries. The estimates of effective rates of protection also showed considerable bias against exports.

In another study, Das and Pant (1997) attempted to estimate equilibrium real exchange rates for the Indian economy for the period 1960–1993 and estimated import demand and export supply functions. They estimated a linear import demand equation with real GDP and relative import to domestic price and obtained negative and significant results with income and relative prices. They do not provide nor discuss the estimates of price and income elasticities.

In the empirical economic literature, the standard import demand equation is specified by relating the quantity of imports to the relative price of imports to domestic prices and income. For developing countries, however, the specification of the import demand equation has to take account of factors such as restrictions on imports and availability of foreign exchange.

$$M^d = f(\text{Import price/Domestic price, Income and other factors}). \quad (1)$$

As we are dealing at the commodity level, we propose to use a two-level budgeting approach to specify import demand functions at an individual commodity level. These are broad groups of imports for which import demand functions are specified and estimated. At the first stage, the choice of total imports and domestic output for consumption purposes is made. In the second stage, the allocation of total imports to various commodities is made by the consumers.

Under the assumption of strong separability,[b] the direct utility function is made of subutility functions for each group, and they are combined additively (Deaton and Muellbauer, 1980). Assume that we want to maximize

---

[b] In the case of strong separability, the utility functions are additive for each group, and preferences are strongly or additively separable. If any subset of commodities appears only in a separable utility function, then quantities purchased within the group can always be obtained as a function of group expenditure and prices within the group alone.

utility assuming weak separability, namely

$$U = f(v_1(\text{domestic}), v_2(\text{imports})) \tag{2}$$

subject to the constraint $P_d D + P_m M = E$. v_1 and v_2 are subutility functions of domestic and imported goods, respectively. P_d is the price of domestic goods, while P_m is the price of imported goods. D and M refer to the quantity of domestic consumption and imports, respectively. E is the total expenditure.

This will yield

$$D = d(P_d, P_m, E) \quad \text{and} \quad M = m(P_d, P_m, E) \tag{3}$$

In this utility function, it is the preferences that are strongly or additively separable and not the utility function. The consumer can allocate the total expenditure in two stages: at the first or higher stage, the expenditure is allocated to domestically produced goods and imported goods, while at the lower level, group expenditures are allocated to individual commodities.

In the second stage, expenditures on imports are allocated to disaggregated commodity groups.

We assume that imports of broad commodity groups are strongly separable and the prices of other imported goods do not have any effect on the imports of the broad commodity group under consideration. We maximize a subutility function

$$V(M_1 \ldots M_{20}) \quad \text{subject to } P_{m1}M_1 + P_{m2}M_2 + \cdots + P_{m20}M_{20} = P_m M, \tag{4}$$

in which $M_1, M_2, \ldots, M_{20}$ are the quantity of imports while P_{m1}, $P_{m2}, \ldots, P_{m20}$ are corresponding prices of the imports and $P_m M$ is the total value of imports. This yields under the strong separability assumption import demand functions at commodity levels in the following form:

$$\begin{aligned} M_1 &= f(M, P_{m1}, \text{NTM}_1, P_m, \text{ Other variables including} \\ &\quad \text{domestic prices}), \\ M_2 &= f(M, P_{m2}, \text{NTM}_2, P_m, \text{ Other variables including} \\ &\quad \text{domestic prices}), \\ &\ \vdots \\ M_{20} &= f(M, P_{m20}, \text{NTM}_{20}, P_m, \text{ Other variables including} \\ &\quad \text{domestic prices}). \end{aligned} \tag{5}$$

Diagrammatically, we have the total consumer expenditure at the top of the tree.

Total Consumption Expenditure

↓ ↓

Expenditure on Domestically Produced Goods | Expenditure on Imported Goods

↓ ↓ ↓

Imports1 Imports2 Imports20

Data and Empirical Specification of Import Demand Functions

Annual data for the 1993–1997 period for six countries[c] are used in this study for each of the 20 commodity groups. For Brazil, the observation for year 1994 is missing, while for Chile, the observations for years 1993 and 1996 are missing. For USA, the observation for 1994 is not available. We thus have 26 observations for each of the 20 commodities when missing observations are taken into account. If we consider a single country like India, we have 100 observations over 20 commodities with five annual observations.

We have data on imports in current value terms by commodities, the unit value of commodity, the total value of imports, the unit value of total imports, tariff rates, domestic wholesale prices for broad commodity groups and information on non-tariff barriers at a commodity level. The real value of imports in any year will be the total value of imports at a commodity level deflated by the unit value of commodity prices. The relative price variable in year t, P_{jt}, is the ratio of the import price index of commodity j in year t to the wholesale price index of good j in the same year, adjusted for the level of tariff on the commodity. We use subscript c and t to denote country and year. We specify the import demand function for each commodity as a double logarithmic relationship as many studies

[c] There are several advantages in the estimation of price elasticities of import using cross-country data: (a) it will take into consideration lower level of tariffs in our sample periods adopted by countries other than India; (b) it will enable us to capture characteristics of recent vintage that is post-Uruguay round of trade negotiations and (c) it will provide a reasonable number of observations for the estimation procedure.

have used such a functional form (Stone, 1954; Parikh, 1986; Sarmad, 1989).

$$\log M_{jct} = \alpha_j + \upsilon_j \log \mathrm{MT}_{ct} + \gamma_j \log P_{jct} + \delta_j \mathrm{NTM}_{jct} + \varepsilon_{jct} \quad (6)$$

and

$$\varepsilon_{jct} = \mu_{jc} + e_{jct}, \quad (7)$$

where $j = 1, 2, \ldots, 20$; $t = 1, 2, \ldots, 5$ and $c = 1, 2, \ldots, 6$; $M_{jct} =$ import quantity of a commodity group i, of country c in year t, $MT_{ct} =$ total import quantity of a country c in year t, $P_{jct} =$ relative prices (foreign vis-à-vis domestic) of commodity group i of country c in year t, $\mathrm{NTM}_{jct} =$ index of non-tariff barrier for commodity group i for country c in year t, $\mu_{jc} =$ country and commodity specific effects and $e_{jct} =$ error term for commodity i for country c in year t.

In the above equation, the explanatory variable P_{jct} is defined as follows:

$$P_{jct} = \frac{[\mathrm{FP}_{jct} * \mathrm{EXRT}_{ct} * (1 + \mathrm{TR}_{jct})]}{\mathrm{DP}_{jct}} \quad (8)$$

where $\mathrm{FP}_{jct} =$ import unit value index of commodity group j for country c in year t; $\mathrm{EXRT}_{ct} =$ exchange rate of country c in year t (currency of country c/US dollar), units of local currency per unit of dollar; $\mathrm{TR}_{jct} =$ tariff rate of a commodity group j for country c in year t: and $\mathrm{DP}_{jct} =$ domestic price index of a commodity group j for country c in year t.

For NTM we have used some judgement on the basis of qualitative information. There are many types of NTMs, hard core, medium effect and soft core. We only consider hard core non-tariff barriers, which have a significant impact on imports in different countries. Since these hard core NTMs are different in different countries, we opted for a dummy variable instead of an index number form. We have also tried using the coverage ratio defined as the ratio of the number of lines subject to different types of non-tariff barriers in a commodity group j for country c in year t divided by the total number of lines in commodity group j for country c in year t. These proportions did not consider the qualitative categorisation of non-tariff barriers at a commodity level.

The above regression equation is estimated separately for 20 commodity groups ($j = 1, 2, \ldots, 20$) defined by different sections of the Harmonized

System (HS)[d] classification (Mehta, 2003). The estimation of different equations for each commodity group is carried out using two-dimensional panel data, where c = Brazil, Chile, the European Union, India, Japan and the USA and t = 1993, 1994, 1995, 1996 and 1997.

We also considered 20 commodity groups for India and we estimated a similar equation using panel of commodities over time period 1993–1997 with 100 observations. The two dimensions were year and commodity in this model, while in the first model, the two dimensions were time periods and countries for each commodity.

Estimation and Results

The approach to estimation is the use of panel methodology.

$$y_{it} = \log M_{it} = \alpha + \mathbf{X}_{kit}\boldsymbol{\beta}_k + \mu_i + \lambda_t + \eta_{it},$$
$$i = 1, 2, \ldots, 6 \quad \text{and} \quad t = 1, \ldots, 5, \tag{9}$$

where M_{it} is the imports of the ith country at time period t, $\mathbf{X}_{kit}$ is the set of k time-varying variables, namely relative prices, total imports and non-tariff barriers, μ_i is the set of fixed country effects, λ_t are the time effects introduced by time dummies and η_{it} is a time-varying idiosyncratic random error term that is assumed to be independent and identically distributed across individual countries and time with mean zero and variance σ^2. Our interest lies in the estimation of the parameter vector $\boldsymbol{\beta}_k$. We assume that all the variables are independent of the error term η_{it}.

If we treat the unobserved country effects, μ_i, as N fixed unknown parameters, Eq. (9) is a fixed effect model. A common way of estimating this model is to specify the effects as $N-1$ dummy variables. In the context of this analysis, these would represent fixed country effects. Alternatively, if we consider μ_i as drawn from a distribution with mean and variance σ^2, then the model is a random effect model. In the fixed effect specification, the error distribution consists solely of the idiosyncratic error term η_{it}, whereas in the random effect specification, the error disturbance consists of both the

[d] The HS system was developed from Customs Cooperation Council Nomenclature, also known as the Brussels Trade Nomenclature system. The HS was implemented in 1986 for customs tariff and in 1987 for imports.

unobserved country effects μ_i, and the idiosyncratic error term η_{it}. μ_i and η_{it} are assumed to be uncorrelated.

There are advantages and disadvantages of both specifications of the model. The fixed effect model may be unattractive as it includes many more parameters to estimate and is inefficient as it removes one element of variability (that across the countries). It also has the disadvantage of rendering the parameters of the time-invariant regressors unestimable as they are perfectly collinear with the set of $N-1$ dummy variables specified for the fixed effects. There is a simple test to choose between the fixed and random effect specification of the model (Hausman, 1978), and it is based on the null hypothesis that the random effect specification is true.

Both the random effect and fixed effect specifications assume that the presence of μ_i captures all the correlation between the unobservables in different time periods (i.e., that η_{it} is uncorrelated over countries and time) and also the characteristics of different countries. Provided that $\mathbf{X}_{kit}$ can be assumed to be exogenous, the presence of autocorrelation in η_{it} does not result in inconsistency of the estimators. However, it may invalidate the standard errors and resulting tests.

An alternative to imposing the random effect structure of the error term (which correspondingly imposes a structure on the estimated covariance matrix) is to relax this structure and to estimate a covariance matrix that is robust to general forms of heteroscedasticity and autocorrelation. The Generalised Method of Moments estimator resolves this problem.[e]

In Table 1, we provide the results based on the fixed effect model for most commodities using log P as an explanatory variable in the model. The equation also uses a dummy for non-tariff barriers and the log of total imports in the model. Both year and country effects are used in the model. We assume that the slope coefficient for P_{jct} is identical across countries. For each commodity group, price elasticities are negative and significant. For the first two groups, namely live animals and vegetable products, the price elasticity is small. In the panel data models, between countries, within countries and random effect estimators are provided. The between effect regression is to be estimated on country averages, but as there are only

[e] It is possible to use the Flexible Generalised Least Squares provided the estimated covariance matrix is consistent.

Table 1. Fixed effect and random effect models for 20 commodity groups using country-level price variables.

Name of commodity	Model	Constant	NTM	Log P	Log MT	R^2/Obs	σ_u/σ_e	ρ
1. Live animals	Fixed effects	−5.44 (−0.51)	−0.29 (−1.46)	−0.49* (−6.11)	1.064 (1.86)	0.88 (26)	1.986 (0.2438)	0.9851
2. Vegetable products	Fixed effects	−2.24 (−0.07)	−0.19 (−0.31)	−0.65* (−5.99)	0.97 (0.53)	0.81 (26)	2.20 (0.79)	0.8861
3. Animals or vegetable fats and oils	Fixed effects	−19.75 (−0.71)	−0.17 (−0.34)	−0.95* (−8.76)	1.79 (1.22)	0.90 (26)	4.84 (0.64)	0.9832
4. Prepared foodstuffs	Fixed effects	9.697 (0.32)	0.1677 (0.30)	−0.8497* (−7.92)	0.2976 (0.18)	0.86 (26)	2.12 (0.70)	0.9017
5. Mineral products	Fixed effects	16.579* (2.11)	0.1600 (1.12)	−1.023* (−27.31)	−0.0163 (−0.04)	0.9898 (26)	2.847 (0.170)	0.9964
6. Products of chemical or allied industries	Fixed effects	−12.338 (−0.38)	0.1339 (0.23)	−0.8772* (−4.19)	1.5070 (0.87)	0.6529 (26)	3.762 (0.742)	0.9625
7. Plastics and articles thereof	Fixed effects	4.834 (0.18)	−0.7746 (−1.68)	−0.4368* (−1.98)	0.5341 (0.38)	0.4610 (26)	0.9778 (0.5878)	0.7345
8. Raw hides, skins leather and articles thereof	Fixed effects	−16.17 (−0.95)	−0.055 (−0.19)	−0.5882* (−3.73)	1.6008 (1.78)	0.9115 (26)	2.4230 (0.3787)	0.9761

(Continued)

Table 1. *(Continued)*

Name of commodity	Model	Constant	NTM	Log P	Log MT	R^2/Obs	σ_u/σ_e	ρ
9. Wood and articles of wood	Fixed effects	−16.885 (−0.93)	0.0264 (0.08)	−0.7891* (−5.45)	1.6633 (1.73)	0.8343 (26)	3.2038 (0.4123)	0.9837
10. Pulp of wood	Fixed effects	18.916 (0.80)	0.0219 (0.05)	−0.8515* (−9.36)	−0.204 (−0.16)	0.9148 (26)	1.5719 (0.5378)	0.8952
11. Textiles and textile articles	Fixed effects	−8.2978* (−2.15)	−0.0176 (−0.25)	−0.2776* (−4.04)	1.2976 (6.28)	0.9137 (26)	1.067 (0.0885)	0.9932
12. Footwear, headgear, umbrellas, etc.	Fixed effects	3.0890 (0.45)	0.0756 (0.63)	−0.9098* (−20.49)	0.6106 (1.67)	0.9780 (26)	2.2572 (0.1569)	0.9952
13. Articles of stone, plaster, cement, asbestos, etc.	Fixed effects	−1.4508 (−0.19)	0.1432 (1.05)	−0.8493* (−16.47)	0.8321* (1.99)	0.9768 (26)	2.3945 (0.1801)	0.9943
14. Natural or cultured pearls, precious stones, etc.	Fixed effects	−5.9122 (−0.53)	0.1384 (0.74)	−0.9252* (−33.48)	1.0996 (1.83)	0.9951 (26)	3.3276 (0.2460)	0.9946
15. Base metals and articles thereof	Fixed effects	2.1893 (0.23)	0.0393 (0.24)	−0.9274* (−23.45)	0.7455 (1.48)	0.9809 (26)	2.7094 (0.2165)	0.9937

(Continued)

Table 1. (*Continued*)

Name of commodity	Model	Constant	NTM	Log P	Log MT	R^2/Obs	σ_u/σ_e	ρ
16. Machinery and mechanical appliance	Fixed effects	11.2057 (0.34)	0.5788 (0.96)	−0.7650* (−5.05)	0.3282 (0.18)	0.7578 (26)	1.4935 (0.7450)	0.8008
17. Vehicles, aircraft, vessels	Fixed effects	15.0785 (1.09)	0.3915 (1.81)	−0.9538* (−26.71)	0.0663 (0.09)	0.9889 (26)	1.5500 (0.2857)	0.9671
18. Optical, photographic, etc.	Fixed effects	7.7354 (0.55)	0.3009 (1.20)	−0.9811* (−23.81)	0.4093 (0.55)	0.9824 (26)	1.9364 (0.3225)	0.9730
19. Arms and ammunition	Fixed effects	−3.3612 (−0.15)	−0.1786 (−0.47)	−0.9896* (−15.09)	0.7509 (0.64)	0.9620 (26)	2.8733 (0.5003)	0.9706
20. Miscellaneous manufactures	Fixed effects	−5.8267 (−1.07)	0.0048 (0.05)	−0.9474* (−36.95)	1.1022* (3.75)	0.9935 (26)	2.6430 (0.1266)	0.9977

Notes: Year effects and country dummies both are used in these regressions. σ_u is the standard error of the estimated fixed effects or random effects, σ_e is the standard error of the estimated residuals and ρ is the fraction of variance attributed to the variation of fixed effects. If t- or z-value is greater than 1.96 or less than −1.96, it is significant at 5 percent level.
*Significant at 5 percent level.

six countries, we have six observations. This equation is not estimated as the number of parameters with year effects will exceed the number of observations. The fixed effect (or within effects) model uses the country dummies, 26 observations (allowing for missing observations) and nine parameters with five year dummies and a constant term. In the fixed effect model, country effects are fixed. σ_u is the standard deviation of estimated fixed or random country effects μ_i in the model, and σ_e is the estimated standard error of the distribution of η_{it} in Eq. (9). The Hausman test for each commodity favours the fixed effect specification, and hence we do not provide the results for random effect model in this table.

In the subsequent log-log model, we modify Eq. (9) and allow the price elasticities to vary country by country. Our model equation is

$$y_{it} = \log M_{it} = \alpha + \mathbf{X}_{kit}\boldsymbol{\beta}_k + \mu_i + \lambda_t + \eta_{it}, \quad i = 1, 2, \ldots, 6 \text{ and } t = 1, \ldots, 5. \quad (10)$$

In Eq. (10), $\mathbf{X}_{kit}$ consists of interactions between country dummies and the log price variable (CP1 $= \log P_{jct} *$ country1, CP2 $= \log P_{jct} *$ country2 and so on), and this permits the country price elasticities to vary. We have six price variables, one for each country, and we obtain price elasticities by countries in this model whether we use the fixed effect or random effect estimation. For the country of our interest, if we examined price elasticities when they are adjusted for tariff changes, we find that the coefficient of CP4 is significant for almost all commodities. In this equation, X_k is a set of (NTM, CP1, CP2, CP3, CP4, CP5, CP6 and log MT) variables, and country dummies and year dummies are used in the fixed effect model. In the random effect model, country effects are random. We thus have 13 variables in the model, namely log MT, NTM, six price variables, and four year dummies in the random effect model. In the last column of Table 2, we provide the test based on the Hausman test, and the rejection of the null of the random effect model leads us to provide results based on the fixed effect model. In the random effect model, as before, the country effects are random. In order to save space, estimated parameters with respect to year variables are not presented. Our price elasticites for Mineral Products, Plastics, Machinery and Mechanical Appliance, Vehicles, Aircraft, Vessels and Optical Photographic equipments are

Table 2. Fixed effects and random effects models for 20 commodity groups using country-level price variables.

Name of commodity sector no (number of observations)	Model	Constant	NTM	CP1: Brazil	CP2: Chile	CP3: the EU	CP4: India	CP5: Japan	CP6: USA	Log MT	R^2 or Wald χ^2	$\sigma_u/\sigma_e/\rho$	Hausman
1. Live animals (26)	Random effects	−7.68 (−0.85)	−0.08 (−0.37)	−0.98* (−4.22)	0.23 (1.58)	−0.45 (−0.78)	−0.64* (−6.0)	0.95* (2.52)	−0.30 (−0.59)	1.12* (2.16)	1305(W)	0.00 0.31 0.00	13.12
2. Vegetable products (26)	Fixed effects	3.29 (0.19)	0.025 (0.080)	−0.30 (−0.89)	−0.11 (−0.03)	−0.01 (0.00)	−0.86 (−12.52)	−0.21* (−2.28)	−0.63 (−0.49)	0.66 (0.77)	0.9399	1.45 0.46 0.91	NA
3. Animals or vegetable fats and oils (26)	Fixed effects	−27.21 (−1.29)	−0.61 (−1.47)	0.22 (0.36)	2.03 (0.64)	−0.65 (−0.45)	−0.98* (−10.9)	1.68 (0.41)	−0.14 (−0.06)	2.09 (1.94)	0.9233	4.5536 0.5851 0.9837	34.13
4. Prepared foodstuffs (26)	Fixed effects	11.655 (0.39)	0.11 (0.21)	−0.84 (−1.27)	−4.76 (−0.66)	−7.69 (−1.17)	−0.89* (−7.94)	0.45 (0.05)	−0.75* (−2.98)	0.12 (0.09)	0.8747	9.47 0.69 0.99	17.26
5. Mineral products (26)	Fixed effects	9.036 (1.42)	0.007 (0.07)	−0.98* (−5.28)	−1.02* (−32.14)	−0.29 (−0.14)	−0.22 (−1.02)	−1.059* (−10.86)	−1.00* (−8.82)	0.395 (1.15)	0.9939	2.495 0.137 0.997	594.28
6. Products of chemical or allied industries (26)	Random effects	26.00 (4.54)	0.275 (0.66)	0.995* (2.34)	−0.767* (−3.26)	−0.888* (−3.44)	−0.64* (−2.65)	0.66* (2.05)	−0.82 (−2.43)	−0.54 (−1.79)	70.1(W)	0.00 0.72 0.00	10.51
7. Plastics and articles thereof (26)	Random effects	13.24 (1.31)	0.199 (0.63)	−0.62 (−1.53)	−0.054 (−0.34)	−1.089 (−1.51)	−0.30 (−1.64)	0.80 (1.13)	−1.04 (−1.72)	0.032 (0.584)	168.13(W)	0.00 0.71 0.00	1.19
8. Raw hides, skins leather and articles thereof (26)	Fixed effects	4.17 (0.64)	0.096 (0.80)	−0.14 (−1.15)	−0.40 (−1.77)	−0.17 (−0.22)	−0.95* (−9.63)	0.15 (1.06)	−0.96* (−8.27)	0.50 (1.40)	0.9494	1.42 0.16 0.99	−67.28
9. Wood and articles of wood (26)	Fixed effects	8.37 (1.25)	−0.11 (−1.22)	−0.54* (−5.93)	−9.74* (−5.18)	0.64* (2.14)	−0.25* (−3.18)	−1.05* (−12.36)	−0.99* (−18.4)	0.58 (1.78)	0.9851	15.99 0.13 0.99	−119.97

(*Continued*)

Table 2. *(Continued)*

Name of commodity sector no (number of observations)	Model	Constant	NTM	CP1: Brazil	CP2: Chile	CP3: the EU	CP4: India	CP5: Japan	CP6: USA	Log MT	R^2 or Wald χ^2	$\sigma_u/\sigma_e/\rho$	Hausman
10. Pulp of wood (26)	Fixed effects	16.58 (0.66)	0.253 (0.67)	−0.88 (−1.41)	−3.67 (−0.57)	−0.55 (−0.25)	−0.87* (−9.75)	−0.71 (−0.28)	−0.89 (−1.89)	−0.025 (−0.02)	0.9065	4.89 0.59 0.98	20.03
11. Textiles and textile articles (26)	Fixed effects	−3.71 (−1.01)	−0.035 (−0.58)	−0.16 (−1.90)	−1.13 (−1.28)	−0.96 (−1.20)	−0.39* (−3.82)	−0.34 (−0.94)	0.96 (0.46)	1.08* (5.49)	0.9181	2.35 0.09 0.99	19.46
12. Footwear, headgear, umbrellas, etc. (26)	Fixed effects	0.74 (0.19)	−0.013 (−0.21)	−0.96* (−12.43)	−0.90* (−18.2)	−0.72 (−1.73)	−0.42* (−3.89)	−0.57* (−2.73)	−0.95* (−27.4)	0.71* (3.50)	0.9930	2.14 0.092 0.998	141.63
13. Articles of stone, plaster, cement, asbestos, etc. (26)	Fixed effects	2.36 (0.60)	0.079 (1.04)	−0.52* (−5.73)	−0.51 (−0.91)	−0.16 (−0.46)	−0.88* (−29.2)	−3.66* (−3.16)	−0.93* (−13.66)	0.68* (3.21)	0.9914	2.53 0.11 0.99	−11.86
14. Natural or cultured pearls, precious stones, etc. (26)	Fixed effects	5.17 (0.37)	0.02 (0.11)	−0.93* (−28.3)	−1.03* (−9.22)	−0.95* (−18.1)	−0.82* (−5.69)	−0.93* (−3.77)	−0.88* (−4.00)	0.51 (0.69)	0.9929	2.89 0.31 0.99	−31.75
15. Base metals and articles thereof (26)	Fixed effects	12.84 (1.88)	0.20 (0.53)	−0.53* (−3.22)	−0.83* (−7.32)	0.34 (0.59)	−0.96* (−29.1)	−0.27 (−0.21)	−0.97* (−2.22)	0.20 (0.53)	0.9883	1.81 0.18 0.99	−41.36
16. Machinery and mechanical appliance (26)	Fixed effects	−2.13 (−0.09)	−0.13 (−0.30)	−0.43 (−1.00)	−1.01* (−6.33)	0.02 (0.06)	−1.85 (−1.40)	−0.57 (−0.48)	−0.76* (−2.89)	1.11 (0.86)	0.8495	3.47 0.61 0.97	39.66
17. Vehicles, aircraft, vessels (26)	Fixed effects	14.08 (1.34)	0.13 (0.81)	−0.59* (−2.99)	−0.97* (−28.5)	0.18 (0.16)	−0.30 (−1.04)	−0.96 (−1.83)	−1.01* (−14.5)	0.13 (0.22)	0.9918	1.58 0.25 0.97	−21.52
18. Optical, photographic, etc. (26)	Fixed effects	−0.31 (−0.03)	0.03 (0.22)	−0.46* (−3.61)	−1.02* (−15.95)	−0.46 (−1.32)	−0.17 (−0.68)	−1.79* (−2.10)	−0.98* (−34.2)	0.84 (1.71)	0.9938	2.07 0.20 0.99	−6.21

(Continued)

Table 2. *(Continued)*

Name of commodity sector no (number of observations)	Model	Constant	NTM	CP1: Brazil	CP2: Chile	CP3: the EU	CP4: India	CP5: Japan	CP6: USA	Log MT	R^2 or Wald χ^2	$\sigma_u/\sigma_e/\rho$	Hausman
19. Arms and ammunition (26)	Fixed effects	3.85 (0.20)	0.02 (0.06)	−0.38 (−0.99)	−1.17 (−1.16)	−0.70 (−1.22)	−1.28* (−10.1)	−0.80 (−0.54)	−0.94* (−18.1)	0.38 (0.36)	0.9819	2.48 0.36 0.98	740.8
20. Miscellaneous manufactures (26)	Fixed effects	−3.96 (−1.31)	−0.064 (−1.09)	−0.86* (−17.00)	−0.975* (−22.84)	−0.454* (−2.15)	−0.944* (−27.84)	3.85* (2.76)	−0.96* (−43.63)	0.93* (5.73)	0.9973	3.39 0.085 0.99	26.21

Notes: Year dummies were used in the fixed effect model. σ_u is the standard error of the estimated fixed effects or random effects, σ_e is the standard error of the estimated residuals and ρ is the fraction of variance attributed to the variation of fixed effects. *Significant at 5 percent or lower level.
If t- or z-value is greater than 1.96 or less than −1.96, it is significant at 5 percent level. NA = not applicable, W is the value of the Wald test.

not significantly different from zero for the Indian economy. The coefficient of log MT (log of total imports) is significant for a few commodities. For Vegetable Products, a percentage increase in total imports is associated with a 0.86 percent increase in vegetable imports. As we have only 26 observations, we decided not to consider differences in the impacts of total imports by countries. It is expected that with a small number of observations and diversity in countries, all elasticities may not be negative and some heterogeneous products like Miscellaneous Manufactures, Products of Chemical or Allied Industries for Japan turn out to have positive price elasticities. Similarly for Brazil, a couple of elasticities do not turn up with negative signs. For the Indian economy, most elasticities are of reasonable magnitudes.

Price Elasticities for the Indian Economy by Years

In this section, the data for 20 commodities are treated as a panel. We carry out continuous cross-section analysis using data for the Indian economy with 20 observations for 1993, 1994, 1995, 1996 and 1997.

We first did cross-section regressions for each of the above five years and discovered that the tariff variable on its own was never significant once the impact of it was introduced in the log P variable. For each year, total imports against each commodity were identical, and hence it was constant. Our regression contained only one variable, namely log P, and for each of the years the regression coefficient was highly significant and it also showed an increase in the negative price elasticity from year to year. We present the results for the latest year 1997 for the Indian economy, and the price elasticity is about −0.82. The next stage was to conduct a panel with two years and the estimated price elasticity was −0.67 for the two years (1993 and 1994 combined period), while for the latter period, the estimated price elasticity was −0.93. The purpose of this is to demonstrate that as liberalisation through reduction in tariff barriers progresses import demands tend to become more price elastic. These results are presented in the first three rows of Table 3. For Japan, the elasticity was −0.36 whether we use the fixed effect or random effect model. However, when we analysed year-by-year elasticity for Japan, we found that for the latter period the price elasticity in absolute terms shows an increase to −0.57. This is the impact of liberalisation in Japan.

Table 3. All India import demands of 20 commodities 1993–1997 (regression coefficients, t-statistic and/or z-statistic).

Years (no. of observations) country	Model	Constant	Log MT	Log M(−1)	Log M(−2)	YP1=1993 price or Log p	YP2=1994 price	YP3=1995 price	YP4=1996 price	YP5=1997 price	NTM	R^2/Wald χ^2	σ_u, σ_e	ρ	Hausman
1997 (20) India	Cross-section	15.577* (28.29)	—			−0.8282* (−4.02)						0.4729			
1993–1994 (40) India	Random effects	14.7790* (14.72)				−0.6649* (−2.76)						0.3006	2.4537 0.6338	0.9374	0.55, RE accepted
1995–1997 (60) India	Fixed effects	15.5937* (188.77)				−0.9288* (−29.30)						0.9565	2.3443 0.4449	0.9652	Not applicable
100, 20 commodities India	Fixed effects without log tq	15.6362* (141.61)	—			−0.8752* (−19.97)	−0.9483* (−18.82)	−0.8747* (−16.31)	−1.0505* (−17.51)	−0.9403* (−18.35)		0.9178	2.3948 0.5452	0.9507	−36.60, not applicable
100, 20 commodities, Japan	Fixed effects without log tq	16.4835* (152.92)				−0.4239* (−6.61)	−0.2829* (−5.77)	−0.5641* (−9.15)	−0.2835* (−4.48)	−0.5728* (−9.04)	0.6025* (5.76)	0.6495	1.3560 0.2649	0.9632 0.9632	Not applicable
100, 20 commodities India	Fixed effects	−14.8070 (−0.35)	1.7567 (0.73)			−0.7019* (−2.91)	−0.8635* (−6.82)	−0.8770* (−16.27)	−1.0252* (−14.45)	−0.9424* (−18.30)		0.9184	2.38 0.5469	0.9520	−36.29, not applicable
100, 20 commodities, Japan	Fixed effects	−8.3185 (−0.99)	1.277* (2.63)			−0.3084* (−4.07)	−0.2761* (−5.85)	−0.6105* (−9.87)	−0.3608* (−5.33)	−0.5335* (−8.50)	0.4659* (4.11)	0.6799	1.3538 0.2549	0.9657	−4.06, not applicable
60, 20 commodities India	First differences with lags	0.2052 (0.99)	−0.3058* (−3.79)			—	−0.8239* (−4.88)	−0.7828* (−6.61)	−0.9566* (−12.52)	−0.9430* (−16.56)			2.911 0.67	0.9412	
60, 20 commodities, Japan	First differences with lags	0.2931 (4.05)	−0.1922 (−1.85)			—	−0.2655* (−5.49)	−0.4336* (−7.89)	−0.4912* (−7.42)	−0.6924* (−9.20)	0.1180 (1.26)	135.20(W)	1.6732 0.29	0.9704	

(*Continued*)

Table 3. *(Continued)*.

Years (no. of observations) country	Model	Constant	Log MT	Log M(−1)	Log M(−2)	YP1=1993 price or Log p	YP2=1994 price	YP3=1995 price	YP4=1996 price	YP5=1997 price	NTM	R^2/Wald χ^2	σ_u, σ_e	ρ	Hausman
40, 20 commodities India	Dynamic with two lags, first differences	−0.1553 (−1.20)	−1.441 (−1.28)	−0.492* (−2.29)	0.0342 (0.38)	dlogprice −0.9524* (−24.19)	dlogprice(−1) −0.5484* (−2.22)					800.77(W)	−0.414[1] (0.73)[2]		
40, 20 Commodities, Japan	Dynamic with two lags, first differences	−0.0691 (−1.54)	0.3577 (1.81)	0.1296 (1.37)		dlogprice −0.8836* (−5.56)	dlogprice(−1) 0.0986 (1.45)					83.29(W)	0.000* (0.99)		

Commodity dummies for 20 commodities were used in the fixed effect model. Figures in parentheses are t-statistic or z-statistic.

[1] Autocorrelation of order 1.

[2] Probability level in parentheses.

YP1–YP5 are interactions between year and logprice.

With the dynamic model, only one price variable is used. The dynamic model is estimated using the Arellano–Bond (1991) panel data estimator.

σ_u is the standard error of the estimated fixed effects or random effects, σ_e is the standard error of the estimated residuals and ρ is the fraction of variance attributed to the variation of fixed effects. If t- or z-value is greater than 1.96 or less than −1.96, it is significant at 5 percent level.

*Significant at 5 percent level. W is the value of the Wald test.

Alternatively, we can combine the observations for all the five years and conduct a regression model with 100 observations, where commodities and years are the panel of observations. Variable NTM does not vary from commodity to commodity or year by year. Non-tariff barriers were not completely removed for a large number of commodities until 2001, and hence NTM values need not be zero.[f] Interactions between *year* and log P were used for the Indian economy. These are labelled YP1 to YP5.

$$y_{jt} = \log M_{jt} = \alpha + \mathbf{X}_{kjt}\beta_k + \mu_j + \lambda_t + \eta_{jt}, \quad j = 1, \ldots, 20 \text{ and } t = 1, 2, 3, 4, 5. \quad (11)$$

The X_{kjt} matrix of variables consists of log MT and YP1–YP5. The commodity effects are the fixed effects in this model. The fixed effect model dominates over the random effect model. The Hausman test values are not positive, and the present version of the Hausman test is not strictly applicable in this case. Our main results based on the first two equations indicate that the price elasticities for each year for the Indian economy are highly significant, and as tariff reductions take place, the price elasticities tend to increase. This fixed effect regression used the year dummies, but they were not significant; so, in the presented results, only commodity effects and YP1–YP5 are used. In the second model, we used log MT (log of total imports), but as this was not significant, we prefer the results of the first model. The price elasticity for year 1996 is around unity, and this means that liberalisation has tended to increase the price elasticity. It is, however, the case that the relative import price contains the impact of exchange rate, domestic price and tariff changes, so it is not easy to attribute the change or increase in the price elasticity entirely to liberalisation. We used the tariff variable separately in the model Eq. (11), but this was not significant. For Japan, after 1994, we find a pattern of absolute price elasticity showing an

[f] Data on NTMS were collected from India's import policy (Government of India, 1992–1998) while for other countries they came from UNCTAD. The UNCTAD definition was restricted to hard core non-tariff barriers only while India's definition included all types of NTMS that are soft, medium and hard core. As the above data series use the UNCTAD definition and UNCTAD source for India, NTMS are zero for all commodities until 1996. No statistics was available for 1997. Given this limitation of data, we cannot estimate the impact of removal or relaxation of non-tariff barriers with the available information.

increase over time from −0.27 to −0.69 (Table 3, 60 observations, 20 commodities). There was a sharp decline in the price elasticity from −0.42 in 1993 to −0.28 in 1994 (Table 3, 100 observations, 20 commodities).

In the next equation, we decided to use the first difference model in case the commodity imports themselves are unit root non-stationary. It will not be possible to conduct any test given the limited number of observations over time. In this model, we used all variables in the first differenced form and again found that all price elasticities were negative and highly significant. Again, for year 1996, the price elasticity in absolute terms was very high. Similarly, for Japan, the same direction of the price elasticity was found.

The last model which we estimated is the dynamic model on panel data. This indeed results in a loss of observations. We estimate the model in first differences with two lags. Furthermore, instrumental variables are used for lagged dependent variables in the model. As we have a limited number of observations, we are unable to use instruments for price variables.

$$\begin{aligned}\Delta M_{jt} &= \alpha_1 \Delta M_{jt-1} + \alpha_2 \Delta M_{jt-2} + \beta_1 \Delta \log P_{jct-1} \\ &\quad + \beta_2 \Delta \log P_{jct-2} + \gamma \Delta \log \mathrm{MT}_{jt} + \Delta \varepsilon_{jt}, \\ &\qquad j = 1, 2, \ldots, 20 \quad \text{and} \quad t = 1, 2 \ldots, 5. \qquad (12)\end{aligned}$$

First differencing Eq. (9) has removed the fixed effects and produces an equation that is estimable by instrumental variables. Arellano and Bond (1991) have derived a Generalised Method of Moments Estimator for α_1 and α_2, β_1 and β_2 and γ using lagged levels of the dependent variable and the predetermined variables and differences of strictly exogenous variables. The methodology assumes that there is no second-order serial correlation in the first differenced error term. We lose 60 observations, given the first differences and two lags. We find that the coefficient of lagged differences of the price variables are −0.95 and −0.55, and they both are significant and negative. We might state that the lagged effects of price changes are also significant in addition to current effects of price changes. Liberalisation leads to reduction in tariff barriers, and consequently, reduction in import prices leads to an increase in imports in short run, and this impact is present even after a one year lag. For Japan, the lagged effect of the price change was not significant.

Summary and Conclusions

In this study, the impact of liberalisation through relaxation of tariffs and non-tariff barriers on imports is examined. Our main focus is on the measurement of the import price elasticity at an aggregate level and for each broad commodity group. Data for six countries over the 1993–1997 period were obtained for 20 broad commodity groups, and these were used in a panel form to measure the impact of tariff reductions on import prices first and then using the ratio of import prices to domestic prices in a regression model with panel data. The estimated regression equation was derived on the basis of two-level budgeting approach and the assumption of weak or strong separability. Data of other countries included both developing and developed countries, and this increased the range of variation in both tariff and non-tariff barriers and relative prices. The use of non-tariff barriers in the cross-country panel framework permitted the consideration of the additional impact of non-tariff barriers on the quantity of imports. Our approach for the measurement of price elasticity used each commodity group and the assumption of identical price elasticity over countries in the first instance. We conducted a year-by-year cross-section study for the Indian economy and found that the price elasticity shows an increase from the earlier to the later period. The panel study was extended for each broad commodity group, and under the assumption of the differential slope coefficient for each country, we estimated the price elasticity for each broad commodity group for each country. For textiles, the price elasticity was negative but not significant for most countries,[g] while for natural or cultured pearls, the price elasticity was negative and statistically significant for all the six countries. As we are interested in the price elasticity for the Indian economy, we also examined elasticity by years ignoring the commodity differences and found that there seems to be an increase in the absolute value of the price elasticity from earlier to later years as tariff reductions progressed. Most of the obtained price elasticities are less than one. This is small, but they are

[g] This is expected given that a large amount of imports by developed countries is subject to multi-fibre arrangement quotas. Panagariya *et al.* (2001) estimated the import demand elasticity for textiles and apparel and found that the import demand elasticity facing Bangladesh was about 26, which was considerably higher than that obtained in many studies. They used disaggregate data and also the fact that exports under the multi-fibre agreement are subject to binding quotas.

obtained under import controls with partial liberalisation. The price elasticity for textile products is −0.28 for the Indian economy, while for highly differentiated products such as machinery and vehicles they are around −0.76 and −0.95, respectively. This can be explained through large tariff and non-tariff barriers implemented in India before liberalisation. We do not find any consistent pattern on estimated import elasticities for highly differentiated products versus homogenous products, because tariff and non-tariff restrictions remained high even after the commencement of liberalisation. A dynamic panel model was also used to capture the impact of lags while removing the fixed commodity effects in an econometric framework. The lagged price elasticity and current price elasticity were both negative and significant, indicating that the impacts of relative price reductions continue for a longer period than a year on annual data. The price elasticity for the Indian economy was compared with that of Japan, and although such elasticity was lower for Japan, the pattern of increase in the absolute value of the price elasticity with liberalisation efforts continued from 1994–1997. Our study uses unit values rather than prices, and although our dynamic panel estimation with instruments obtains higher estimates of import price elasticities, we do not have sufficient observations to conduct detailed investigation.

References

Arellano, M and S Bond (1991). Some tests of specification for panel data: Monte Carlo evidence and an application to employment equations. *Review of Economic Studies*, 58, 277–298.

Das, SK and M Pant (1997). India's rupee devaluation, trade balance and unemployment: A producer theory approach. *Journal of Asian Economics*, 8, 51–66.

Deaton, A and J Muellbauer (1980). *Economics and Consumer Behaviour.* Cambridge: Cambridge University Press.

Erkel-Rousse, H and D Mirza (2002). Import price elasticities: Reconsidering the evidence. *Canadian Journal of Economics*, 35, 282–306.

Government of India. *Import and Export Policy*, Vol. 1. Ministry of Commerce, Various annual issues from 1992–1998.

Government of India (1991). *Tax Reform Committee*. Interim Report, Ministry of Finance, Chairman: Raja J. Chelliah.

Hausman, JA (1978). Specification tests in econometrics. *Econometrica*, 46, 1251–1271.

Mehta, R (2003). Indian industrial tariffs, towards WTO development round negotiations. *Research and Information System for the Non-Aligned and Other Developing Countries*, New Delhi.

Nouroz, H (2001). *Protection in Indian Manufacturing: An Empirical Study*. New Delhi: Macmillan India Press Limited.

Panagariya, A, S Shah and D Mishra (2001). Demand elasticties in international trade: Are they really low? *Journal of Development Economics*, 64, 313–342.

Parikh, A (1986). *The Estimation and Forecasting of Trade Shares*. Economic and Social Commission for Asia and the Pacific, United Nations, Bangkok.

Sarmad, K (1989). The determinants of import demand in Pakistan. *World Development*, 17, 1619–1625.

Sharma, P and R Mehta (1997). Trade reforms and changes in effective protection on Indian industries. Paper presented in *Int. Conf. on Indian Economic Reforms: Structural Adjustment and Policy Requirement for Long Term Economic Growth*, New Delhi.

Stone, JRN (1954). *The Measurement of Consumers' Expenditure and Behaviour in the United Kingdom, 1920–1938*, Vol. 1. Cambridge: Cambridge University Press.

Appendix A

Name of commodity	Imports in value at constant prices (log MT)		Adjusted price in index (log P)	
	Mean	SD	Mean	SD
1. Live animals	14.31	2.64	0.3152	2.8922
2. Vegetable products	15.56	1.98	0.2504	3.2380
3. Animals or vegetable fats and oils in their cleavage products	13.3794	1.7502	0.2866	2.9126
4. Prepared foodstuffs	14.8389	1.9094	0.8263	2.6348
5. Mineral products	16.7357	2.4035	−0.4241	3.8361
6. Products of the chemical or allied industries	15.8953	1.5217	0.4618	2.6262
7. Plastics and articles thereof	15.1178	1.7188	0.4329	3.0182
8. Raw hides and skins, leather, furskins and articles thereof	13.9945	2.1207	−0.4801	3.1487
9. Wood and articles of wood	14.3957	2.7896	−0.1877	3.2318

(*Continued*)

(Continued)

Name of commodity	Imports in value at constant prices (log MT)		Adjusted price in index (log P)	
	Mean	SD	Mean	SD
10. Pulp of wood or of other fibrous celluslosic material	15.1422	1.7562	−0.1888	2.9071
11. Textiles and textile articles	15.7431	1.8445	0.8304	2.5908
12. Footwear, headgear umbrellas, walking sticks, seat-sticks, whips, riding-crops and parts thereof	14.1023	2.6594	0.4661	2.8788
13. Articles of stone, plaster, cement, asbestos, mica or similar materials	14.2783	1.7536	−0.1352	2.7676
14. Natural or cultured pearls, precious or semi-precious stones, precious metals clad with precious metal and articles thereof	16.4935	3.3135	−1.9605	4.4209
15. Base metals and articles of base metal	15.8797	1.9332	0.2738	3.0889
16. Machinery and mechanical appliances	17.5383	2.1623	−0.2855	3.1841
17. Vehicles, aircraft, vessels and associated transport equipment	16.8435	2.9360	−0.5892	3.3329
18. Optical, photographic, cinematographic measuring, checking, precision, medical or surgical instruments and apparatus	16.0339	3.0845	−0.6778	3.8310
19. Arms and ammunition	11.2356	3.5783	−0.4779	3.7035
20. Miscellaneous manufactured articles	14.7114	3.0730	0.0805	3.5388

Chapter 6

Does Trade Liberalisation Accelerate Convergence in Per Capita Incomes in Developing Countries?*

Ashok Parikh and Miyuki Shibata

University of East Anglia, Norwich, UK

Introduction

The objectives of this chapter are to study the impact of liberalisation on convergence in per capita incomes of less developed economies of Asia, Africa and Latin America. This study is confined to 64 developing countries for which information on the onset of liberalisation is available. Liberalisation in trade promotes exports and imports, and this, in turn, could have an impact in increasing real per capita incomes. However, the convergence of real income cannot be assured through trade liberalisation as some theories argue in favour of divergence of per capita incomes while others suggest that convergence of per capita incomes will result from liberalisation.

In this chapter, we consider two measures of sigma-convergence and one measure of beta-convergence to measure the impact of trade liberalisation on real per capita incomes. The first one is the standard deviations of real per capita incomes before and after liberalisation and the deviations of real income from its regional mean income with and without liberalisation. Both

* The authors wish to thank two anonymous referees for their very helpful comments; Professor Shaun Hargreaves-Heap for editing the chapter; the Editor of the journal "*Journal of Asian Economics*" for reading and commenting on the chapter, and the Leverhulme Trust for the award of Emeritus Fellowship which facilitated this study.

these measures are based on the concept of sigma-convergence proposed by Barro and Sala-i-Martin (1992, 1995). We also use two methodologies namely single difference and difference-in-differences on the sigma-convergence measure. In the difference-in-differences approach, we need to have a control group of countries and, as it is not easy to determine the control group of countries, we have used various permutations and combinations of the control group of countries. The difference-in-differences approach was used by Meyer (1994). Slaughter (2001) obtained results, which sometimes contradicted those of the single-difference approach. Slaughter finds no strong link between trade liberalisation and income convergence. On the other hand, studies based on the single-difference methodology supports the convergence hypothesis.

The chapter uses the "difference-in-differences" methodology, which basically compares the convergence pattern among the liberalising countries before and after liberalisation with the convergence pattern among control countries before and after liberalisation.[a] Our main empirical result is ambiguous, because the methodology based on the difference-in-differences approach needs to use control group, which is similar to the treatment group. This was not possible given that three regions of the world, Asia, Africa and Latin America, are hardly similar to each other. Asian, African and Latin American economies are very different in structure, and hence the comparison of Asian countries with the control group as Latin America might not show any convergence. We have, therefore, more inclination towards accepting the results based on the single-difference methodology.

The chapter has four additional sections. In Section 2, we give a brief review of the literature on the theory of trade convergence in per capita incomes across countries and regions. Section 3 provides a brief description of the data and studies the relationship between per capita incomes' convergence on account of liberalisation region by region. Section 4 uses

[a] There is no obvious way to select control countries, and hence we try various alternative control groups. Some empirical studies focussing on the trade and income convergence attempt to identify trade's effect mainly through a single comparison of two groups of countries. Single comparisons often support the hypothesis that trade converges incomes. The difference-in-differences approach is designed to overcome the ambiguities of the single-difference studies.

both the approaches namely single-difference and difference-in-differences on sigma-convergence measures. Section 5 summarizes the results and indicates brief conclusions.

Brief Review

Various studies have been conducted on the relationship between trade and income convergence. Trade liberalisation can influence each of three ingredients of the national income: factor prices, factor quantities and production technology. The factor price equalization theorem may claim that liberalisation tends to bring factor prices closer. Samuelson (1971) shows that in the standard specific-factor framework, free trade very likely generates convergence.[b] Stiglitz (1970) finds the opposite, because when two countries have different rates of time preferences, free trade tends to make factor prices diverge. Deardorff (1986) provides a two-country-two-factor and four good Heckscher–Ohlin type model in which free trade tends to converge producer prices but diverge factor prices. A number of papers on convergence cannot consider the role of international trade because they assume the Solow[c] world in which countries producing a single aggregate good exist independent of one another (Barro and Sala-i-Martin, 1992). Barro and Sala-i-Martin provide two concepts of convergence namely beta convergence and sigma convergence. Our study uses both of these concepts. With the sigma convergence, the standard deviation of per capita real incomes should become smaller after liberalisation.

Baldwin (1992) formalises how liberalisation can generate dynamic gains from trade for a country well endowed in capital by raising its rate of return and encouraging further investment. For a country relatively poorly endowed with capital, dynamic losses from trade may result as liberalisation lowers the rate of return and thus slows investment. The cross-country implication of these dynamic adjustments is divergence of relative endowments as capital rich countries invest more while capital poor countries invest less.

---

[b] Factor price equalisation is neither necessary nor sufficient for equating per capita incomes across trading countries (Rassekh and Thompson, 1998).

[c] Tsangarides (2002) employed a panel data and finds support for the conditional convergence hypothesis with rates of convergence of 4–5 percent for African economies and 9–13 percent for OECD economies.

Free trade can lead to divergence in cross-country endowments by inhibiting the diminishing marginal returns to investment. Investment could change the output mix, and as a consequence, the rate of return does not decline. Richer countries do not lose their desire to invest under free trade, and this also suggests that endowments do not converge.

The above did not consider the implications of changes in technology. Trade liberalisation can boost technology flows and can facilitate the transfer of technology from one country to another. If technology flows from advanced countries to less advanced countries, the convergence in real incomes is more likely.

However, this may not happen, and Matsuyama (1996) provides a model in which free trade leads poor countries to specialise in products that use low technology. Richer countries can grow richer as they concentrate more on high technology products.

There are a number of studies examining empirically whether free trade results in convergence of real per capita incomes among developed countries. Bernard and Jones (1996) provide some evidence that incomes diverge with freer trade. They suggested that international trade could lead to comparative advantage leading to specialisation, and as countries produce different goods, the production technologies could remain different among countries. Ben David (1993, 1996) and Sachs and Warner (1995) show that international trade causes convergence. The latter study included both developing and developed economies, although the definition of openness was subject to some limitations. Sachs and Warner and Ben David were the first to test the effect of freer trade on convergence of income. These studies identify the effects of trade mainly through a single comparison of two groups of countries.

Data and Methodology

In this section, a brief description of data and the concept of beta convergence are used on two cross-section data sets for the liberalised and pre-liberalised periods.

Data on *real* per capita incomes in the dollar currency is collected from the World Development Indicators of the World Bank for 64 developing countries. The period of liberalisation when it started was obtained from

Sachs and Warner (1995). Sachs and Warner[d] (1995) classify a country as either closed or open using five different criteria: nontariff barrier coverage; tariff rates; black market premia on exchange rates; overall economic system — socialist or capitalist, and the extent of government intervention in the export sector. A country is classified as closed if it fails any one of these five criteria. We found that in our sample of 64 countries, nine Asian countries, 15 African and 16 Latin American countries liberalised during the 1970–1999 period. The other 24 countries did not liberalise at all during this period, and they are excluded from the estimation of the beta-convergence measure.

The degree of liberalisation could be very different from country to country, but this could not be taken account of in the study. The time period when openness or liberalisation took place was also different from country to country. For each country, means and standard deviations for the non-liberalised and liberalised periods are given in Table 1. We use the data on real per capita incomes in the dollar currency at 1995 prices. In almost all cases, the liberalisation period is after a first few years of the non-liberalised period, and hence the liberalisation regime will indeed have a higher real per capita mean income than the previous period. Three African countries, namely Burundi, Gambia and Ghana, do not have a higher mean income in periods after liberalisation as compared to pre-liberalisation. As growth in real per capita income proceeds, the latter period could have both autonomous and liberalisation effects on an increase in real per capita incomes.

Beta convergence

We use the concept of unconditional beta convergence[e] next. This concept means that if a poor economy tends to grow faster than a rich one, the poor country tends to catch up with the rich one in terms of the level of per

---

[d] A country has a closed policy if it has one of the following characteristics: (a) nontariff barriers covering 40 percent or more of trade; (b) average tariff rates of 40 percent or more; (c) a black market exchange rate that is depreciated by 20 percent or more; (d) a socialist economic system and (e) a state monopoly on major exports.

[e] Another concept, of beta convergence, which is used in the literature, is conditional convergence, and this applies if the growth rate of the real per capita income is negatively related to the starting level of the per capita income after holding all or some variables, such as initial levels of human capital, measures of government policies, the propensities to save and so on.

Table 1. Mean and standard deviations of real per capita income (in US dollars) for pre- versus. post-liberalisation for liberalising countries.

Country	Regime[1]	Mean	S.D.
Asia			
Sri Lanka	0 (14)	455.172	100.600
	1 (17)	615.085	157.657
India	0 (24)	253.561	44.640
	1 (7)	412.619	36.314
Korea	0 (16)	3630.711	946.176
	1 (15)	9486.862	2242.461
Malaysia	0 (18)	2089.272	449.363
	1 (13)	3918.501	728.413
Nepal	0 (21)	157.745	14.236
	1 (10)	217.054	15.405
Philippines	0 (16)	1050.143	112.447
	1 (15)	1080.420	55.139
Thailand	0 (16)	1012.108	197.725
	1 (15)	2323.264	546.681
Turkey	0 (19)	2023.182	237.085
	1 (12)	2827.912	248.088
Africa			
Botswana	0 (10)	1092.630	305.004
	1 (21)	2893.180	706.175
Burundi	0 (20)	181.666	15.778
	1 (11)	170.590	28.840
Cameroon	0 (23)	737.693	164.921
	1 (8)	631.814	28.555
Chad	0 (20)	226.544	30.781
	1 (11)	223.931	13.390
Benin	0 (20)	359.739	17.960
	1 (11)	373.147	22.976
Gambia	0 (20)	359.605	26.983
	1 (11)	356.769	11.406
Ghana	0 (15)	406.617	56.887
	1 (16)	364.694	27.131
Kenya	0 (23)	320.342	29.934
	1 (8)	337.167	5.499
Mali	0 (18)	276.715	24.058
	1 (13)	261.342	13.495
Mauritania	0 (22)	476.582	25.326
	1 (9)	472.890	17.563
Morocco	0 (14)	1002.796	105.842
	1 (17)	1294.059	80.943

(*Continued*)

Table 1. (*Continued*)

Country	Regime[1]	Mean	S.D.
Guinea-Bissau	0 (17)	208.096	11.533
	1 (14)	225.191	21.265
Tunisia	0 (19)	1503.757	233.357
	1 (12)	2066.391	229.057
Uganda	0 (6)	232.421	8.786
	1 (13)	288.670	39.928
Latin America			
Argentina	0 (21)	6948.110	487.883
	1 (10)	7654.575	598.305
Bolivia	0 (5)	935.178	67.042
	1 (26)	912.586	84.107
Brazil	0 (21)	3723.707	564.847
	1 (10)	4531.346	224.347
Chile	0 (6)	2332.340	173.957
	1 (25)	3407.165	1103.221
Colombia	0 (16)	1698.472	170.111
	1 (15)	2217.813	159.957
Cost Rica	0 (16)	2790.541	235.588
	1 (15)	3256.176	386.527
El Salvador	0 (19)	1581.090	230.729
	1 (12)	1586.262	153.155
Guatemala	0 (18)	1401.183	121.431
	1 (13)	1441.880	77.957
Guyana	0 (18)	765.679	79.305
	1 (13)	787.998	138.594
Honduras	0 (21)	675.086	45.854
	1 (10)	708.285	14.476
Mexico	0 (17)	2883.331	385.485
	1 (14)	3318.087	229.311
Nicaragua	0 (21)	742.644	194.945
	1 (10)	430.854	19.174
Paraguay	0 (19)	1540.729	294.476
	1 (12)	1807.281	45.299
Peru	0 (21)	2438.033	198.557
	1 (10)	2187.844	211.387
Uruguay	0 (20)	4476.467	427.245
	1 (11)	5752.776	521.702

Note: Numbers of years are given in parentheses.
[1] 0 and 1 denote pre- and post-liberalisation period, respectively.

capita incomes or products. We consider two periods, liberalised and pre-liberalised. For the pre-liberalised period, we consider the average annual growth in the real per capita income and relate it with the base period real per capita income. For each of the 36 countries we have observations for the liberalised and pre-liberalised periods. We thus have two cross-sections for the liberalised and pre-liberalised periods. We can classify the data by regions and relate income growth with the initial real per capita income for each of the two periods. We obtain the slope coefficient, which is called the beta coefficient. Formally.

$$\mathrm{GY}_{it}^{\mathrm{PL}} = \alpha_0^{\mathrm{PL}} + \alpha_1^{\mathrm{PL}} \log(Y_{i0})^{\mathrm{PL}} + \varepsilon_{it}^{\mathrm{PL}} \tag{1}$$

and

$$\mathrm{GY}_{it}^{\mathrm{L}} = \beta_0^{\mathrm{L}} + \beta_1^{\mathrm{L}} \log(Y_{i0})^{\mathrm{L}} + \varepsilon_{it}^{\mathrm{L}}, \tag{2}$$

GY_{it} is the annual average growth in the real per capita income, and Y_{i0} is the real per capita income in the base period. ε_{it} is the error term, while PL and L superscripts refer to the pre-liberalised and liberalised periods, respectively.

The estimated beta coefficient should be strictly negative when indicating convergence. In Table 2, we present these results for each of the two periods. We used the year of liberalisation based on the Sachs–Warner study. Sometimes, gradual liberalisation starts before the announced year of liberalisation, and this is considered by varying the year of liberalisation. There are some very unrealistic assumptions at times in Sachs–Warner, and therefore, we have used the classification of the liberal and non-liberal period for some countries on the basis of the known time period when the trade restrictions have not been tightened. For Asian economies, there is no evidence of accelerating or decelerating convergence after liberalisation. In none of the countries has liberalisation made any significant impact on convergence. During the liberalised period, there is no significant beta coefficient, and the sign is positive for Asia and Latin America. For African economies, there is a significant divergence as shown by the beta[f] coefficient in Table 2.

[f] We varied the liberalisation period as if it started two years prior to actual liberalisation. We then conducted the regression analysis using the data for the liberalised and non-liberalised regimes and found that there was no evidence of convergence or divergence for Latin American economies. Overall, the results do not differ from those in Table 2.

Table 2. Differences in income convergence rates for pre- versus post-liberalisation for liberalising countries (see estimated Eqs. (1)[1] and (2)[2]).

Region	Number of observations		Estimated coefficient (t-statistics)		
	Pre-liberal	Post-liberal	α_1	β_1	$\beta_1 - \alpha_1^3$
Asia	9	9	0.0103	0.0055	−0.0048
			(2.1954)*	(1.1378)	(−2.1461)**
Africa	14	15	0.0206	0.0154	−0.0052
			(1.3220)	(2.6176)**	(−1.2065)
Latin America	15	16	0.0039	0.0055	0.0015
			(0.4359)	(1.5487)	(0.6336)

Note: The convergence rates are estimated using the OLS regression with t-statistics in parentheses.

[1] $t = 0$ is the base year set at 1970 for all the liberalising countries except for Bolivia. Bolivia regulated its economy in 1980. Sri Lanka liberalised its economy in 1977 until 1983, and re-liberalised in 1991; the base years for Sri Lanka are 1970 and 1984.

[2] The base year for post-liberalisation period varies when each economy was liberalised.

[3] t-statistics is reported for testing the null hypothesis of $\alpha_1 = \beta_1$.

*Significance at the 10 percent level.

**Significance at the 5 percent levels.

Sigma Convergence by Regions and Control Group

The second concept concerns cross-sectional dispersion. In this context, convergence occurs if the dispersion measured by the standard deviation of the natural logarithm of the real per capita income across a group of countries or regions declines over time. Convergence of the first kind, namely poor countries tending to grow faster than the rich ones, tends to generate convergence of the second kind, but this process could be offset by new disturbances that lead to an increase in dispersion. We measure the per capita income dispersion among the liberalised and non-liberalised groups in two different ways. The first is the standard deviation of the natural log of the per capita income among a group of countries. For this dispersion measure, our equation to be estimated is the following:

$$\sigma_{rt} = \alpha_1 + \alpha_2(d_r) + \beta_1(t) + \beta_2(t)(d_r) + e_{rt}, \tag{3}$$

where d_r is a dichotomous variable equal to 1 if the time period is a liberalised period while it equals zero for the non-liberalised period. t indexes the time in years. e_{rt} is an error term, where variance varies by r. σ_{rt} is the standard deviation of the natural log of the per capita income among the liberalising countries for regime r at time t. The rate of change in income dispersion for pre-liberalisation is given by β_1, and for the post-liberalisation period it is given by $\beta_1 + \beta_2$. In both regimes, income convergence (divergence) is represented by negative (positive) slope coefficients. The single-difference β_2 indicates whether post-liberalisation convergence differs from that of pre-liberalisation.

We classify the data into three regions, Asia, Africa and Latin America, and for each region we obtain the standard deviation of log of the per capita income for the liberalised and non-liberalised period. We have 30 standard deviations for the liberalised period for each region and 30 for the non-liberalised period. Thus, we have 60 observations for each region. The coefficient β_1 is positive for Africa and Latin America. This suggests that for each of these regions, the standard deviation of log of the real per capita income is increasing in the pre-liberalisation period. For African economies, there is a divergence in the pre-liberalisation period, and this does not change in the post-liberalisation period. The above methodology is referred to as the single-difference approach. We find evidence of significant convergence[g] for Asian and Latin American economies in the post-liberalisation period (Table 3).

The other approach is the difference-in-differences approach, where we have some control group. For Asia, we may have Latin America, or Africa as the control group. Let subscript j denote the country group, with $j = 1$ for the treatment group and $j = 0$ for some control group. Then the equation to be estimated is the following:

$$\sigma_{rt}^{j} = \alpha_1 + \alpha_2(d_r) + \alpha_3(d^j) + \alpha_4(d_r^j) + \beta_1(t) + \beta_2(t)(d_r) + \beta_3(t)(d^j) + \beta_4(t)(d_r^j) + e_{rt}^{j}. \quad (4)$$

In the above equation, the dichotomous variable d^j indicates the control group where $j = 1$ for the treatment group and $j = 0$ for the control group;

[g] The above results used the standardised standard deviation for the number of countries in each group in each year. If this is not used, the results are vastly different. We believe that as the number of countries increase in the liberalisation regime the dispersion may increase but it may not be directly proportionate to the number of countries. This procedure does not assume smoothness in σ_{rt}.

Table 3. Differences in income convergence rates for pre-versus post-liberalisation (see estimated equation (3)[1]). Estimated equation[1]: $\sigma_{rt} = \alpha_1 + \alpha_2(d_r) + \beta_1(t) + \beta_2(t)(d_r) + e_{rt}$.

Case name	Pre-liberalisation convergence rate, β_1	Post-liberalisation convergence rate, $\beta_1 + \beta_2$	Difference in convergence rates, β_2	Number of observations
Asia	−0.0006	−0.0176	−0.0170	55
	(−1.1524)	(−7.0272)**	(−6.6347)**	
Africa	0.0011	0.0072	0.0061	50
	(8.1107)**	(1.5146)	(1.2773)	
Latin America	0.0182	−0.0267	−0.0449	60
	(10.8473)**	(−10.8210)**	(−15.0509)**	

Note: The dependent variable is standardized by dividing by the square root of the number of countries in each group in each year. The convergence rates are estimated using the OLS regression. t-statistics are reported in parentheses for robust standard errors. Standard deviations for post-liberalization for Africa are not available until 1980.

**Significance at the 95 percent levels.

[1] Number of countries used to calculate σ in each equation is different for the pre- and post-liberalization period. For Asia: 12 (1970–1976), 11 (1977–1983), 12 (1984 and 1985), 9 (1986 and 1987), 8 (1988), 7 (1989 and 1990), 5 (1991–1993) and 4 (1994–1999) for the pre-liberalisation period. For Africa: 25 (1970–1979), 24 (1980 and 1981), 25 (1982 and 1983), 24 (1984), 23 (1985 and 1986), 22 (1987), 21 (1988), 19 (1989), 15 (1990 and 1991), 14 (1992) and 12 (1993–1999) for the pre-liberalisation period. For Latin America: 18 (1970–1975), 17 (1976–1979), 18 (1980–1984), 17 (1985), 15 (1986), 14 (1987), 12 (1988), 9 (1989), 8 (1990), 3 (1991–1999) for the pre-liberalisation period.

the dichotomous variable d_r^j equals one if both $j = 1$ and $r = 1$ and zero otherwise and e_{rt}^j is an error term whose variance varies with both j and r. Equation (4) estimates a separate intercept term and convergence rate for income dispersion. The effect of trade liberalisation on income convergence can be calculated as the difference-in-differences of the estimated coefficients. The difference in convergence rates within the liberalising group for the pre- and post-liberalisation period is given by β_2. The similar difference within the control group is given by $\beta_2 + \beta_4$. Thus, the difference-in-differences is given by β_4. If trade liberalisation tends to converge (diverge) incomes among the liberalising economies, then β_4 is positive (negative). Any cross-regime time effect is captured by β_2, while any time-invariant differences in convergence between two groups are captured by β_3. We report the results of different control groups for each region and find that (Table 4) there is a significant evidence of convergence of Asian economies against Latin America as a control group.[h] For Asia against Africa and Latin America against Africa, as the control group, there is significant divergence in the post-liberalisation regime. These results are very mixed, and there is no consistent pattern.

Sigma convergence using panel data

The second measure of dispersion in income captures how quickly each country's income level is converging to the average level of that country's group. Consider a country like Malaysia, which belongs to the Asian region. We measure the deviations of Malaysia's real per capita income from the mean of Asia in each time period.

Let

$$Y_{it} - \bar{Y}_t = \mu(Y_{it-1} - \bar{Y}_{t-1}), \tag{5}$$

where Y_{it} is country i's log real income per capita in year t, $\bar{Y}_t$ is the average of Y_{it} for each period and μ is a parameter relating the average income gap from one year to the next. Define $W_{it} = Y_{it} - \bar{Y}_t$ and $\Delta W_{it} = (W_{it} - W_{it-1})$, and Eq. (5) can then be manipulated to obtain Eq. (6) as follows:

$$\Delta W_{it} = \delta_1(W_{it-1}) + \delta_2(d_r) + \gamma_i + v_{it}, \tag{6}$$

where $\delta_1 < 0$ represents the rate of convergence of Y_{it} to $\bar{Y}_t$ (with $\mu - \delta_1 = 1$). The larger is δ_1 in absolute value, the faster is the rate of convergence. γ_i is the country effect. For the single-difference analysis, we can write Eq. (6) as

$$\Delta W_{it} = \delta_1(W_{it-1}) + \delta_2(d_r) + \delta_3(W_{it-1})(d_r) + \gamma_i + V_{rit}, \tag{7}$$

where r is the regime (liberalisation versus pre-liberalisation) index and d_r is defined as before. V_{rit} is the error term whose variance changes according to r. The parameter δ_3 indicates whether post-liberalisation convergence differs from that of pre-liberalisation. In Eqs. (6) and (7), liberalisation dummies have been used in Table 5. This is because the period of liberalisation in each country was different. Moreover, the estimated model is on panel

[h] When the role of target and control groups was reversed, the results did not change excepting that the sign of β_4 changed, retaining the same magnitude as expected.

Table 4. Differences in income convergence rates for pre- versus post-liberalisation (see estimated Eq. (4)[1]).

Region	Control group	Difference in-differences,[2] parameter: β_4	Number of observations	Number of control countries
Asia	Africa and Latin America	0.0060 (1.0241)	165	49
Africa	Asia and Latin America	0.0386 (7.0617)**	165	34
Latin America	Asia and Africa	−0.0398 (−6.5124)**	165	43
Asia	Africa	−0.0231 (−4.2462)**	105	29
Asia	Latin America	0.0279 (7.1097)**	115	20
Latin America	Africa	−0.0510 (−9.0284)**	110	29

Note: The dependent variable is standardised by dividing by the square root of the number of countries in each group in each year. Standard deviations for post-liberalisation for Africa are not available until 1980.

[1] Number of countries used to calculate σ in each equation is different for the pre- and post-liberalisation period. For Asia: 12 (1970–1976), 11 (1977–1983), 12 (1984 and 1985), 9 (1986 and 1987), 8 (1988), 7 (1989 and 1990), 5 (1991–1993) and 4 (1994–1999) for the pre-liberalisation period. For Africa: 25 (1970–1979), 24 (1980 and 1981), 25 (1982 and 1983), 24 (1984), 23 (1985 and 1986), 22 (1987), 21 (1988), 19 (1989), 15 (1990 and 1991), 14 (1992) and 12 (1993–1999) for the pre-liberalisation period. For Latin America: 18 (1970–1975), 17 (1976–1979), 18 (1980–1984), 17 (1985), 15 (1986), 14 (1987), 12 (1988), 9 (1989), 8 (1990), 3 (1991–1999) for the pre-liberalisation period.

[2] The convergence rates, β_4, are estimated using the OLS regression. t-statistics are reported in parentheses for robust standard errors.

**Significance at the 5 percent level.

data where fixed effects and random effects are allowed for. Pure cross-section analyses could give inconsistent results because they suffer from the omitted variable and endogeneity biases. One issue that arises from the use of panel data is whether the individual effect is considered to be fixed or random. On the one hand, although the random effect estimation addresses the endogeneity issue by instrumenting potentially exogenous variables, it also assumes that individual country effects are uncorrelated

Table 5. Differences in income convergence rates for pre- versus post-liberalisation (see estimated equations (6) and (7)).

Region	Number of countries (obs.)	Eq.	Estimated coefficient (t-statistics)			Convergence /divergence
			δ_1	δ_2	δ_3	
Asia	12	(6)	−0.0417	0.0075		Convergence
	(348)		(−3.4974)**	(1.6279)		pre-liberalisation
		(7)	−0.0398	0.0078	−0.0013	Convergence
			(−2.9227)**	(1.6502)*	(−0.3003)	pre-liberalisation
Africa	26	(6)	−0.0784	0.0071		Convergence
	(754)		(−6.6702)**	(1.1843)		pre-liberalisation
		(7)	−0.0948	0.0064	0.0182	Divergence
			(−6.8679)**	(1.0573)	(2.2508)**	post-liberalisation
Latin	20	(6)	−0.0466	0.0082		Convergence
America	(580)		(−3.8365)**	(2.0166)**		pre-liberalisation
		(7)	−0.0539	0.0080	0.0070	Convergence
			(−3.9627)**	(1.9773)**	(1.1870)	pre-liberalisation

Note: The coefficients are estimated using panel data estimation with fixed effects. t-statistics are reported in parentheses.

*Significance at the 10 percent level.

**Significance at the 5 percent level.

with the exogenous variables, an assumption that is sometimes violated.[i] On the other hand, the fixed effect method deals successfully with the correlated effect problem, yet it fails to account for potential endogeneity of regressors. Nickell (1981) shows that due to the correlation between the time-varying component of the error term and the lagged dependent variable, in a finite dynamic model with fixed T, the parameter estimates under fixed effects will be biased and inconsistent. This problem is corrected in the GMM estimation presented in Table 6 with a dynamic model (Arellano and Bond, 1991).

The results of Eqs. (6) and (7) suggest that (Table 5), there is no evidence of acceleration or deceleration in convergence for Asia in the post-liberalisation period while for Africa there is evidence of a slow down in divergence. In all three regions, there exists evidence of convergence in real per capita incomes during the pre-liberalisation period, and an autonomous

[i] The Hausman test suggests that in Table 5 random effects model is rejected.

Table 6. Dynamic models estimated by panel fixed effects and the GMM estimation: $\Delta W^j_{rit} = \gamma_i + \delta_1(W^j_{rit-1}) + \delta_2(W^j_{rit-1})(d_r) + \delta_3(W^j_{rit-1})(d^j) + \delta_4(W^j_{rit-1})(d^j_r) + v^j_{rit}$.

Models	Country (number of countries) number of observations	Control group (number of countries)	Lagged variable	Income lag	Income lag *liberal dummy δ_2	Income lag *control group dummy δ_3	Income Lag *control *liberal dummy δ_4	Constant	R^2 (SEE)	DW (LM)	AC(1) Wald χ^2	AC(2) Sargan χ^2
Panel model fixed effects	Asia (12) 928	Latin America (20)	—	−0.55** (−4.3612)	0.0074 (1.3360)	0.0161 (0.7988)	−0.0070 (−0.9396)	—	0.133 (0.038)	1.440 (35.735)	—	—
GMM estimation	Asia (12) 928	Latin America (20)	0.2535 (4.36)	−0.2416** (−4.59)	0.0051 (1.61)	−0.0226 (0.32)	0.0063 (0.83)	−0.0001 (−0.21)			−2.97 (11.90)	−1.90 (20.7)
Panel model fixed effects	Asia (12) 1102	Africa (26)	—	−0.0934** (−7.5832)	0.0187** (2.5825)	0.0540** (2.3062)	−0.0182* (−1.9006)		0.133 (0.049)	1.888 (0.179)		
GMM estimation	Asia (12) 1102	Africa (26)	−0.00674 (−1.22)	−0.1921** (−3.19)	0.0052 (0.52)	−0.1578 (−1.54)	0.0193 (0.67)	−0.0002 (−0.27)			−4.40 (33.41)	−1.23 (36.9)
Panel model fixed effects	Latin America (20) 1334	Africa (26)		−0.0934** (−7.5455)	0.0187** (2.5696)	0.0379 (1.8542)*	−0.0112 (−1.1057)		0.144 (0.049)	1.796 (1.766)		
GMM estimation	Latin America (20) 1334	Africa (26)	−0.0089 (−0.12)	−0.265** (−3.09)	−0.011 (−0.81)	−0.091 (−0.71)	0.020 (1.51)	0.0005 (0.07)			−3.66 (37.98)	−1.23 (41.3)

Note: LM is the test for heteroscedasticity. AC(1) and AC(2) refer to first-and second-order serial correlation tests in dynamic models. Wald χ^2 with five degrees of freedom was always significant indicating the valid model. Sargan χ^2 with 377 degrees of freedom satisfied the overidentifying restrictions. All dynamic models were estimated with one lag and two lags using Arellano and Bond (1991) generalized method of moments (GMM) estimation. Panel models were estimated using the fixed effect version as country dummies were always significant.

*Siginificance at the 10 percent level.

** Significance at the 5 percent level.

improvement in the growth rate is significant in Latin America. For the difference-in-differences equation, let superscript j indicate the country group. This gives

$$\Delta W^j_{rit} = \gamma_i + \delta_1(W^j_{rit-1}) + \delta_2(W^j_{rit-1})(d_r) + \delta_3(W^j_{rit-1})(d^j) + \delta_4(W^j_{rit-1})(d^j_r) + v^j_{rit}, \tag{8}$$

where all variables are defined as before and v^j_{rit} is an error term (whose variance varies by both j and r). There will also be country effects, which are denoted as γ_i. The effect of trade liberalisation can be obtained by using the difference-in-differences of the estimated rates, and this equals δ_4 here. If liberalisation tends to converge (diverge) incomes among the liberalising countries, then δ_4 is positive. Any cross-regime effect common to both groups of countries is captured by δ_2, while any time-invariant differences in convergence between groups is captured by δ_3.

Using the lagged dependent variables the model in Eq. (8) is modified. Instead of estimating the fixed effects model in the GMM estimation, a first differenced model is estimated. We employ a panel data estimator that addresses the issues of endogeneity and omitted variable biases. The estimator is the differenced GMM estimator proposed by Hansen (1982). The estimator is obtained in two steps. First, we take first differences from the dynamic model in Eq. (8), which eliminates the individual country effect γ_i. Then, we instrument all the right-hand variables using their lagged values. The first step deals with the omitted variable bias eliminating the need to make any probabilistic assumptions of the country effect. The second step eliminates inconsistency arising from potential endogeneity of the regressors.

The only difference between pre- and post-liberalisation across the two groups is trade liberalisation. In the absence of trade liberalisation, the parameter δ_4 would be zero. Control countries should be very similar to the treatment group in any difference-in-differences approach. Different control groups have different number of countries, and the choice of the country is constrained by the data availability. It is not possible to state that control groups and treatment groups are similar excepting that the structural difference is taken into consideration by country dummies, which are removed in the first-differenced GMM methodology.

In Table 6, we find some evidence of divergence in real per capita incomes after liberalisation for Asian economies against Africa as the control group.

Summary and Conclusions

This study is one of the few that has examined the impact of trade liberalisation on convergence of real per capita incomes in developing economies. We have used the concept of beta convergence for a group of economies and treated them in a regional framework. We did not find any evidence of significant beta convergence in the liberalised period as compared to the pre-liberalised period for Asian and Latin American economies. For African economies, there is significant beta divergence in the liberalisation period.

We used two measures of sigma convergence, one where year-by-year standard deviations of log of real per capita incomes were computed, and the other where the real per capita income of the country was taken as deviation from the regional mean income. This measures how quickly the country's real per capita income catches up with the regional mean income. Both these measures were used without referring to the control group, and this approach of single difference suggested that there was significant divergence during the pre-liberalisation period for Africa. This implies that trade liberalisation seems to have diverged per capita incomes from the regional mean incomes and the measure of dispersion shows a slight increase in the post-liberalisation period for Africa. There was some slight evidence of acceleration in convergence during the post-liberalisation period for Latin America and Asia. When we considered the control group against which the impact of liberalisation was measured using the above two measures of sigma convergence, we found no consistent pattern of convergence or divergence. Much of the evidence based on the single-difference approach as presented in Table 3 suggests that trade liberalisation converges incomes among liberalisers in Asia and Latin America. The use of panel data methodology is made with respect to the second measure of sigma convergence, and the GMM estimation using the Arellano–Bond estimation is carried out on the dynamic model. We summarise various results in Table 7.

We tend to go for the single-difference approach, and using Table 7, we conclude that there is a significant acceleration in convergence in real per

Table 7. Summary results of hypothesis tests.

Model		Significant acceleration in convergence	Significant deceleration in convergence	No change in divergence	Significant acceleration in divergence	Significant deceleration in divergence	No change in convergence
Beta convergence	Africa	—	—	—	Yes	—	
Sigma convegence[1]	Africa	–1	—	—	Yes[b]	—	
	Asia	Yes[a]	—	—	—	—	
	Latin America	Yes[a]	—	—	—	—	
Sigma convergence[2]	Asia–Africa			Yes[d]	Yes[c]		
	Asia–Latin America	Yes[c]					Yes[d]
	Latin America–Africa				Yes[c]		Yes[d]

[1] Single-difference approach is used: (a), Table 3 results and (b) Table 5 results.
[2] Is the difference-in-differences approach: (c) Table 4 results and (d) Table 6 results.

capita incomes in post-liberalisation period in the Asian and Latin American regions while there is a significant divergence in real per capita incomes for the African economies during the post-liberalisation period.

A major limitation of double differencing is the lack of similarity between the treatment group and the control group. It is not obvious how to select the control group, and as a result, we have tried a variety of control groups. The other is the intensity of liberalisation, and this is less likely to remain the same two to three years after liberalisation. The study only considers the onset of liberalisation, and as we have no information on tariff cuts during different periods by each country we are unable to consider this effect.

References

Arellano, M and S Bond (1991). Some tests of specification for panel data: Monte Carlo evidence and application to employment equations. *Review of Economic Studies*, 58, 277–297.

Baldwin, RE (1992). Measuring dynamic gains from trade. *Journal of Political Economy*, 100(2), 223–251.

Barro, RJ and X Sala-i-Martin (1992). Convergence. *Journal of Political Economy*, 100(2) 223–251.

Barro, RJ and X Sala-i-Martin (1995). *Economic Growth*. New York. McGraw Hill Inc.

Bernard, AB and CI Jones (1996). Comparing apples to oranges: productivity convergence and measurement across industries and countries. *American Economic Review*, 1216–1238.

Ben David, D (1993). Equalizing exchange: Trade liberalisation and income convergence. *Quarterly Journal of Economics*, 108, 653–679.

Ben David, D (1996). Trade and convergence among countries. *Journal of International Economics*, 40, 279–298.

Deardorff, AV (1986). Firless firwoes: How preferences can interfere with theorems of international trade. *Journal of International Economics*, 20, 131–142.

Hansen, L (1982). Large sample properties of generalized method of moments estimators. *Econometrica*, 50, 1029–1054.

Matsuyama, K (1996). Why are there rich and poor countries? Symmetry breaking in the world economy. *Journal of Japanese and International Economics*, 10(4), 419–439.

Meyer, BD (1994). Natural and quasi-experiments in economics. NBER Technical Working Paper, p. 170.

Nickell, S (1981). Biases in dynamic models with fixed effects. *Econometrica*, 49, 1417–1426.

Rassekh, F and H Thompson (1998). Micro convergence and macro convergence: Factor price equalization and per capita income. *Pacific Economic Review*, 3, 3–11.

Sachs, J and A Warner (1995). Economic reform and the process of global integration. *Brookings Papers of Economic Activity*, 1, 1–18.

Samuelson, P (1971). Ohlin was right. *Swedish Journal of Economics*, 365–384.

Slaughter, M (2001). Trade liberalisation and per capita income convergence: A difference-in differences analysis. *Journal of International Economics*, 55, 203–228.

Stiglitz, JE (1970). Factor price equalization in a dynamic economy. *Journal of Political Economy*, 78, 456–488.

Tsangarides, CG (2002). On cross country growth and convergence: Evidence from Africa and OECD countries. *Journal of African Economies*, 10(4), 355–389.

Chapter 7

Dynamics of the Relationship Between the Terms of Trade and the Trade Balance in Developing Countries of Asia, Africa and Latin America

Ashok Parikh* and Miyuki Shibata

University of East Anglia, Norwich, UK

Introduction

Backus *et al.* (1994) analysed the relationship between the terms of trade (price of importable in terms of exportable) and the trade balance for 11 developed economies. They found an empirical regularity, namely an S-shaped lead and lag correlation between the trade balance and the terms of trade. They then supported their finding with a stochastic general equilibrium model in which simulation of the model produces results confirming the S-curve. This study extends the analysis to 59 less developed economies. Terms of trade data were not available for all the 59 countries, so real exchange rates data were used. Moreover, the study uses annual data from 1970 to 1999 rather than quarterly or monthly data over a shorter period. Developing countries are very different in structure, and hence a similar regularity in the relationship between the terms of trade and the trade balance may not exist. Many developing countries were not open economies

* The author is grateful to Leverhulme Trust for the award of Emeritus Fellowship which has facilitated this study. The authors would like to express their gratitude to Mr. David Bailey for editing the chapter.

throughout the above period, and so we intend to examine the relationship separately for the period when liberalisation took place.

The terms of trade and the trade balance are important macro-indicators of development. The trade balance determines in part net foreign exchange receipts, while the terms of trade determine the purchasing power of a country's exports. The lead and lag correlation between the terms of trade and the trade balance indicates co-movement of these variables as the economy responds to exogenous shocks. Similarly, the lead and lag correlation between the real exchange rate and the trade balance is expected to show co-movement as a country adjusts its nominal exchange rate from time to time under a fixed exchange rate system. The S-curve is closely related to the J-curve, which was established to show the relationship between the trade balance and a real devaluation. Indeed, in a two-good model, the terms of trade equal real exchange rate.[a] Senhadji (1998) used quarterly data for less developed economies and found the existence of the S-shaped relationship between the terms of trade and the trade balance. The S-curve was derived from a general equilibrium model based on a real business cycle model, and the simulation in the study mimicked the empirical S-curve using plausible values of parameters in the model. This study is, however, an empirical rather than a theoretical one. Given *a priori* information, it is difficult to justify the assumptions of the stochastic general equilibrium model for a large group of developing economies. Our aim is to discover whether the relationships found for developed economies exist for LDCs, where the underlying economic structure is very much constrained.

The study is organised as follows: the second section provides information on the data, preliminary analysis and a historical review of the literature. The third section analyses the dynamic relationship between the terms of trade and the trade balance and examines some of the business cycle properties of the data. The fourth section examines the relationship between real exchange rates and the trade balance, while Section 5 considers the data period in two regimes and studies the relationship for the liberalised period

[a] We also look at the relationship between the income terms of trade and the trade balance of a few countries as the data on barter terms of trade were not compiled in UNCTAD statistics. These results can be obtained from the authors.

and the non-liberalised period. The last section summarises the conclusions of the study.

Data, Adjustments and Review

The relation between the terms of trade and the trade balance and/or the current account has received a lot of attention in the past (Laursen and Metzler, 1950; Harberger, 1950). Obstfeld and Rogoff (1995) provided a survey of various issues pertaining to the relationship between the terms of trade and the current account. The conclusions remained uninformative as they depended upon the values of key parameters of the model. The relationship remains an empirical issue, and this can be adequately captured by performing an empirical study.

The list of variables includes private consumption (c), gross domestic investment (i), exports (x), imports (m), net exports divided by GDP (nx), the terms of trade defined as the implicit import price deflator divided by the export price deflator (pm) and GDP. The data sources are UNCTAD (*Handbook of Trade Statistics*) and IMF (*International Financial Statistics*). The series are all annual and span the period from 1970 to 1999 or 1996 except for a few exceptions. The data have been detrended using the Hodrick–Prescott filter. Appendix Table 1 lists the information for country codes, the names of Asian, African and Latin American countries in the sample and information on data availability.

Hodrick–Prescott decomposition

The method of decomposing a series into a trend and stationary component has been developed by Hodrick and Prescott (1997). We observe the values of y_1 to y_T and want to filter the trend (T_t) and stationary component $y_t - T_t$. Consider the sum of squares

$$\frac{1}{T}\sum_{t=1}^{T}(y_t - T_t)^2 + \frac{\lambda}{T}\sum_{t=2}^{T-1}[(T_{t+1} - T_t) - (T_t - T_{t-1})]^2. \qquad (1)$$

The problem is to select a T_t sequence to minimise the sum of squares. In the minimisation problem, λ is an arbitrary constant reflecting the cost or penalty of incorporating fluctuations into the trend. In many applications,

λ is set equal to 100. Increasing the value of λ tends to smooth out the trend. If $\lambda = 0$, the sum of squares is minimised when $y_t = T_t$, i.e., the trend is equal to y_t itself. As $\lambda \to \infty$, the trend approaches a linear time trend. Intuitively, for large values of λ, the Hodrick–Prescott decomposition forces the change in the trend (i.e., $\Delta T_{t+1} - \Delta T_t$) to be as small as possible.

The advantage of the Hodrick–Prescott decomposition is that it can extract the same trend for a set of variables. This is useful since many real business cycle models indicate that all variables have the same stochastic trend.

pm is the barter terms of trade and is defined as the import unit value divided by the export unit value. *nx* is the ratio of the trade balance to GDP, both measured in current prices, and is taken from two sources, namely the World Economic Outlook of the International Monetary Fund and the UNCTAD of the United Nations. Ytot is the income terms of trade and is obtained from UNCTAD, *Handbook of Trade and Development Statistics*. RER is the real exchange rate obtained from the IMF. An increase in the value of RER implies real exchange rate depreciation. In combining series from all sources we obtain data for 59 countries.

Tables 1A–1C report some business cycle properties for the main national account variables. The business cycle properties of a variable are summarised by three statistics: its relative volatility, its cyclical behaviour with GDP, and its autocorrelation. The table also reports the contemporaneous correlation between *pm* and *nx*. A negative value implies the existence of the Harbeger–Laursen–Metzler (H–L–M) effect. This negative relationship results directly from the Keynesian consumption function: a deterioration in the terms of trade (i.e., increase in *pm*) induces a decrease in income and a less than proportional decline in consumption ($mpc < 1$). Therefore, saving and consequently net exports decline.

Obstfeld (1982) and Svensson and Razin (1983) showed that the correlation between the terms of trade and the trade balance depended on the persistence of terms of trade shocks. They find that the H–L–M effect results only with transitory shocks, as consumers borrow abroad to smooth out the effect of these shocks. Permanent terms of trade shocks leave net exports unchanged. This view embeds the permanent income hypothesis in the model.

Table 1A. Relative volatility, co-movement and autocorrleation of macro-variables, Asia: 14 countries.

	Relative volatility								Co-movement								Autocorrelation					Correlation	
	c	i	x	m	nx	pm	Ytot	rer	c	i	x	m	nx	pm	Ytot	rer	GDP	nx	pm	Ytot	rer	$pm-nx$	$\text{rer}-nx$
B'desh[1]	1.21	5.15	5.19	4.28	0.45	N/A	3.71	3.64	0.72	0.65	0.07	−0.34	0.42	N/A	0.52	0.42	0.36	0.28	N/A	0.37	0.53	N/A	0.28
Cyprus	N/A	N/A	1.63	1.06	0.37	N/A	1.64	1.04	N/A	N/A	−0.21	0.15	−0.45	N/A	0.62	−0.20	0.53	0.20	N/A	0.32	0.53	N/A	−0.10
Egypt[1]	1.32	4.05	9.94	8.89	1.34	N/A	4.79	7.23	0.02	0.20	−0.21	−0.21	0.12	N/A	0.11	−0.02	0.70	0.16	N/A	0.39	0.67	N/A	−0.21
India	1.19	2.41	4.17	4.47	0.29	4.53	3.80	2.55	0.78	0.50	0.00	−0.07	0.08	0.27	0.25	−0.07	0.23	0.31	0.37	0.48	0.43	−0.30	0.24
Jordan[1]	1.20	2.25	2.40	1.71	0.87	1.09	1.34	0.84	0.65	0.40	−0.66	−0.33	0.01	0.45	0.09	−0.43	0.70	0.48	0.06	−0.23	0.55	−0.08	−0.21
Korea	0.58	2.96	3.42	2.37	0.72	1.90	3.32	2.00	0.73	0.86	−0.04	−0.21	0.14	−0.41	0.62	−0.52	0.56	0.44	0.50	0.44	0.70	−0.52	0.20
Malaysia	1.93	4.61	2.25	3.49	1.50	N/A	3.55	1.63	0.85	0.93	0.12	0.46	−0.45	N/A	0.54	−0.23	0.64	0.46	N/A	0.23	0.55	N/A	−0.13
Nepal[1]	1.30	6.56	8.51	4.40	1.09	N/A	N/A	2.75	0.69	0.11	0.26	−0.49	0.44	N/A	N/A	0.30	−0.11	0.40	N/A	N/A	0.32	N/A	0.49
Pakistan[1]	2.94	2.85	12.2	8.81	1.01	6.16	5.58	6.74	0.60	0.53	−0.24	−0.07	−0.11	0.18	0.46	−0.36	0.42	0.26	0.34	0.03	0.43	−0.39	0.46
Papua NG[1]	1.26	3.84	3.08	2.84	1.83	N/A	N/A	1.33	0.55	−0.37	0.53	−0.55	0.59	N/A	N/A	−0.33	0.56	0.39	N/A	N/A	0.45	N/A	−0.33
Philippines	0.80	3.66	1.88	2.24	0.49	N/A	1.76	1.30	0.86	0.93	0.08	0.68	−0.63	N/A	0.34	−0.26	0.73	0.36	N/A	0.13	0.39	N/A	0.22
Sri Lanka[1]	2.00	6.17	6.08	8.58	1.86	6.06	4.36	5.01	0.81	0.39	0.05	0.13	−0.11	−0.03	0.24	0.19	0.48	0.54	0.45	0.39	0.55	−0.57	−0.32
Thailand	1.29	3.47	3.14	3.45	0.76	2.73	4.33	1.15	0.68	0.87	0.34	0.66	−0.52	0.01	0.57	−0.40	0.74	0.29	0.34	0.61	0.36	−0.17	0.19
Turkey[1]	1.12	3.02	6.65	5.12	0.40	2.50	N/A	3.65	0.82	0.73	−0.42	−0.17	−0.14	−0.65	N/A	−0.49	0.51	0.01	0.64	N/A	0.63	−0.22	0.00

All variables are in real terms.

c is the private consumption (constant 1995 US$), and i is the gross domestic investment (constant 1995 US$), both from World Development Indicators (World Bank). x and m are exports and imports at current US$ deflated by current GDP in US$, all from the United Nations. nx is net exports divided by GDP.

pm is the import unit value over the export unit value, from *International Financial Statistics* (IMF). Ytot is income terms of trade and is compiled by the United Nations, while rer is real exchange rate from *International Financial Statistics*.

All variables, except nx, are in natural logs, and all variables are HP filtered.

The series are annual and for 1970–1996 unless otherwise noticed with.[1] As for the rer series, the data is for 1970–1995.

[1] Names and years for the missing data are indicated in parenthesis after country names below.

Bangladesh (rer 1970); Egypt (c 1970–1973); Jordan (c 1970–1975, i 1970–1975); Nepal (c 1970–1974, i 1970–1972); Pakistan (c 1982, i 1982); Papua New Guinea (rer 1970); Sri Lanka (c 1983), and Turkey (c 1970–1986, i 1970–1986, pm 1985–1988).

Corr(Ytot, nx) can be obtained from the authors.

Table 1B. Relative volatility, co-movement and autocorrelation of macro-variables, Africa: 25 countries.

	Relative volatility								Co-movement								Autocorrelation					Correlation	
	c	*i*	*x*	*m*	*nx*	*pm*	Ytot	rer	*c*	*i*	*x*	*m*	*nx*	*pm*	Ytot	rer	GDP	*nx*	*pm*	Ytot	rer	*pm* − *nx*	rer − *nx*
Botswana[1]	2.88	3.01	3.26	1.59	2.21	N/A	N/A	1.76	0.51	0.68	−0.02	0.09	−0.12	N/A	N/A	−0.09	0.47	0.35	N/A	N/A	0.45	N/A	0.51
B'na Faso[1]	1.92	7.71	15.6	5.26	2.55	3.22	10.1	6.28	0.56	0.26	0.05	−0.04	0.15	−0.14	0.00	−0.53	−0.08	0.28	−0.13	0.08	0.36	−0.21	−0.33
Burundi	1.13	5.57	5.45	2.75	0.63	N/A	N/A	1.57	0.59	0.52	0.03	0.11	−0.04	N/A	N/A	0.38	0.35	0.24	N/A	N/A	0.29	N/A	0.17
Cameroon	1.36	2.49	3.32	1.98	0.42	N/A	3.35	N/A	0.79	0.70	−0.47	0.25	−0.49	N/A	0.19	N/A	0.49	0.30	N/A	0.44	N/A	N/A	N/A
CAF	1.62	7.27	8.13	6.36	0.86	N/A	6.80	5.45	0.72	0.13	0.08	0.05	0.06	N/A	0.01	0.11	0.36	0.01	N/A	−0.48	0.56	N/A	0.12
Chad[1]	N/A	N/A	2.57	2.76	0.61	N/A	2.70	1.49	N/A	N/A	0.12	0.63	−0.43	N/A	0.57	−0.29	0.58	0.11	N/A	0.31	0.38	N/A	−0.32
C. d'Ivoire	1.24	4.81	2.33	1.18	0.78	N/A	2.46	3.07	0.53	0.55	−0.09	0.14	−0.15	N/A	0.38	−0.28	0.16	0.40	N/A	0.45	0.57	N/A	0.71
Gambia[1]	2.60	5.30	6.52	3.87	2.10	N/A	6.88	1.73	−0.05	−0.20	0.43	0.05	0.20	N/A	0.54	0.03	0.00	0.38	N/A	0.25	0.44	N/A	0.54
Ghana	1.45	3.90	6.24	6.68	1.46	N/A	3.77	9.17	0.92	0.36	0.28	0.26	0.05	N/A	0.46	0.34	0.42	−0.14	N/A	0.47	0.70	N/A	0.10
Kenya	2.78	5.00	4.51	3.16	1.05	3.57	4.30	2.74	0.61	0.62	−0.51	0.06	−0.40	0.08	0.06	−0.50	0.69	0.12	0.33	0.21	0.29	−0.46	0.29
Madagascar	1.07	6.25	4.90	4.01	0.69	N/A	3.21	2.87	0.72	0.86	0.14	0.48	−0.34	N/A	0.10	0.12	0.34	0.07	N/A	0.20	0.27	N/A	0.31
Malawi[1]	1.92	5.20	2.72	3.06	1.09	N/A	2.94	2.99	0.65	0.33	−0.19	−0.04	−0.04	N/A	0.34	−0.48	0.59	0.54	0.45	−0.13	0.20	N/A	0.56
Mauritania[1]	4.48	11.5	6.27	5.59	3.18	N/A	15.5	N/A	0.18	0.24	0.12	−0.24	0.17	N/A	0.20	N/A	−0.12	0.52	N/A	0.14	N/A	N/A	N/A
Mauritius	1.73	3.78	2.76	2.00	0.88	2.73	3.81	1.37	0.66	0.84	0.20	0.48	−0.28	−0.39	0.59	−0.39	0.64	0.37	0.55	0.57	0.58	−0.34	0.29
Morocco	1.12	4.72	4.52	3.87	0.90	3.19	4.11	3.26	0.81	0.41	−0.28	−0.18	−0.02	−0.10	−0.10	−0.19	−0.15	0.35	0.18	0.51	0.66	−0.10	−0.26
Niger	1.71	4.62	2.10	1.90	0.24	N/A	2.72	1.56	0.77	0.36	0.37	0.43	−0.04	N/A	0.57	−0.21	0.53	−0.05	N/A	0.52	0.46	N/A	−0.38
Rwanda[1]	0.72	1.49	1.64	1.35	0.24	N/A	2.34	0.71	0.73	0.35	0.21	0.34	−0.23	N/A	0.36	0.14	0.20	−0.27	N/A	0.17	0.55	N/A	−0.22
Senegal	0.84	3.11	5.41	3.79	0.89	N/A	4.43	4.16	0.62	0.49	0.20	−0.20	0.53	N/A	0.51	−0.18	0.14	0.40	N/A	0.06	0.50	N/A	−0.35
SierraL'ne[1]	1.75	N/A	7.55	5.39	0.83	N/A	6.07	2.89	0.53	N/A	−0.21	−0.17	−0.04	N/A	−0.07	−0.33	0.56	0.42	N/A	0.12	0.30	N/A	0.01
Sudan[1]	N/A	N/A	4.67	4.57	0.67	N/A	1.80	4.97	N/A	N/A	0.28	0.27	−0.26	N/A	0.05	0.25	0.58	0.53	N/A	0.42	0.29	N/A	−0.25
Tanzania[1]	1.81	3.30	7.25	8.06	2.25	N/A	4.99	5.69	−0.34	0.73	0.49	0.43	−0.26	N/A	0.22	0.42	0.58	0.45	N/A	0.08	0.71	N/A	−0.20
Togo	2.44	5.97	3.74	3.67	1.17	N/A	3.25	2.35	0.05	0.70	0.43	0.66	−0.26	N/A	0.39	−0.28	0.35	0.18	N/A	0.03	0.45	N/A	0.35
Tunisia[1]	1.15	4.54	5.11	3.68	0.90	4.90	7.93	1.97	0.53	0.56	0.05	−0.08	0.11	−0.09	0.13	−0.10	0.09	0.25	0.45	0.51	−0.13	−0.19	−0.16
Uganda[1]	1.03	2.96	5.71	7.41	0.91	N/A	6.81	6.56	0.66	0.53	−0.25	−0.38	0.09	N/A	−0.07	−0.09	0.60	0.12	N/A	0.45	0.53	N/A	0.42
Zimbabwe	1.80	3.75	1.66	2.30	0.70	N/A	N/A	1.23	−0.05	0.63	−0.35	0.10	−0.21	N/A	N/A	0.03	0.55	0.43	N/A	N/A	0.26	N/A	−0.27

All variables are in real terms.

c is the private consumption (constant 1995 US$) and *i* is the gross domestic investment (constant 1995 US$), both from World Development Indicators (World Bank). *x* and *m* are exports and imports at current US$ deflated by current GDP in US$, all from the United Nations. *nx* is net exports divided by GDP.

pm is the import unit value over the export unit value, from *International Financial Statistics* (IMF). Ytot is income terms of trade and is compiled by the United Nations, while rer is real exchange rate from *International Financial Statistics*. All variables, except *nx*, are in natural logs, and all variables are HP filtered.

The series are annual and for 1970–1996 unless otherwise noticed with.[1] As for the rer series, the data is for 1970–1995.

[1]Names and years for the missing data are indicated in parenthesis after country names below. Botswana (*c* 1970–1981, *i* 1970–1981, rer 1970–1973); Burkina Faso (rer 1970–1982); Chad (rer 1970–1982); Gambia (*x* 1996, *m* 1996, *nx* 1996); Malawi (rer 1970–1979); Mauritania (*c* 1991 and 1994, *i* 1994), Rwanda (rer 1994), Sierra Leone (*c* 1970–1979); Sudan (*x* 1996, *m* 1996, *nx* 1996); Tanzania (*c* 1970–1987, *i* 1970–1987); Tunisia (*pm* 1988–1996, rer 1970–1982) and Uganda (*c* 1970–1981, *i* 1970–1981, rer 1970–1980). Corr(Ytot, *nx*) can be obtained from the authors.

Table 1C. Relative volatility, co-movement and autocorrelation of macro-variables, Latin America: 20 countries.

	Relative volatility								Co-movement								Autocorrelation					Correlation	
	c	i	x	m	nx	pm	Ytot	rer	c	i	x	m	nx	pm	Ytot	rer	GDP	nx	pm	Ytot	Rer	$pm-nx$	rer $-nx$
Argentina[1]	1.92	2.96	4.59	5.63	0.47	N/A	2.88	6.97	0.31	0.88	−0.40	0.52	−0.67	N/A	−0.09	−0.45	0.45	0.38	N/A	0.22	0.35	0.43	0.45
Barbados[1]	N/A	N/A	4.64	1.99	0.85	N/A	4.96	0.73	N/A	N/A	−0.51	0.02	−0.62	N/A	−0.42	0.57	0.59	0.34	N/A	0.63	0.53	N/A	−0.74
Bolivia[1]	1.06	4.15	3.97	5.15	0.93	N/A	4.22	2.44	0.77	0.62	0.18	0.31	−0.16	N/A	0.40	−0.18	0.87	0.09	N/A	0.07	0.33	N/A	−0.01
Brazil[1]	1.27	2.64	3.16	3.29	0.34	3.64	4.38	3.58	0.26	0.94	−0.32	0.12	−0.48	0.13	0.12	−0.17	0.64	0.35	0.38	0.10	0.65	−0.73	0.75
Chile	1.71	3.46	3.20	2.04	0.47	N/A	2.30	2.79	0.93	0.66	−0.55	0.08	−0.70	N/A	0.32	−0.67	0.57	0.31	N/A	−0.01	0.48	N/A	0.45
Colombia	1.05	5.00	8.36	5.46	1.39	6.96	5.61	5.42	0.91	0.30	0.27	0.38	−0.03	−0.03	0.26	−0.19	0.64	0.58	0.37	0.31	0.78	−0.35	0.66
Cost Rica	1.41	4.35	2.78	2.57	0.74	N/A	2.16	3.10	0.91	0.82	−0.36	0.17	−0.57	N/A	0.57	−0.57	0.67	0.17	N/A	0.43	0.31	N/A	0.27
DomRepub	1.92	4.27	6.70	4.45	0.80	N/A	5.29	4.98	0.55	0.60	0.35	0.39	−0.23	N/A	0.47	−0.06	0.27	−0.09	N/A	0.31	0.27	N/A	−0.54
El Salvador	1.56	3.51	2.62	2.18	0.49	N/A	2.54	1.49	0.88	0.80	0.56	0.52	0.15	N/A	0.59	0.19	0.83	−0.12	N/A	0.39	0.15	N/A	−0.09
Fiji[1]	2.50	3.46	3.43	2.81	0.98	N/A	N/A	1.32	0.51	0.64	0.13	0.46	−0.43	N/A	N/A	−0.49	0.29	0.06	N/A	N/A	0.48	N/A	0.37
Guatemala	0.87	4.43	3.06	4.13	0.62	N/A	3.06	2.66	0.98	0.67	0.42	0.54	−0.28	N/A	0.44	−0.02	0.85	0.14	N/A	0.23	0.50	N/A	−0.33
Guyana[1]	2.15	3.89	2.39	3.08	1.77	N/A	2.35	5.00	0.41	0.61	0.40	0.20	0.10	N/A	0.61	0.09	0.74	0.04	N/A	0.25	0.57	N/A	−0.51
Haiti	N/A	3.87	3.58	4.51	0.89	N/A	N/A	2.15	N/A	0.60	−0.18	−0.30	0.19	N/A	N/A	−0.23	0.43	0.14	N/A	N/A	0.38	N/A	−0.11
Honduras	1.06	5.17	2.79	3.75	0.76	N/A	3.15	2.99	0.62	0.63	0.48	0.22	0.15	N/A	0.55	0.05	0.58	0.14	N/A	0.57	0.40	N/A	−0.33
Jamaica	2.32	3.98	3.63	2.97	1.13	N/A	2.50	2.87	0.43	0.48	−0.11	−0.17	0.17	N/A	0.34	−0.19	0.61	0.33	N/A	0.41	0.37	N/A	0.02
Mexico	1.29	4.01	5.24	4.52	0.73	N/A	5.04	3.60	0.95	0.85	−0.33	0.04	−0.47	N/A	0.61	−0.68	0.63	0.57	N/A	0.75	0.32	N/A	0.80
Nicaragua[1]	1.46	3.08	3.82	2.40	0.85	N/A	2.00	8.71	0.29	0.48	−0.07	0.07	−0.07	N/A	0.52	−0.23	0.53	0.02	N/A	0.38	0.20	N/A	−0.20
Paraguay	1.76	3.42	6.34	2.99	0.80	N/A	5.68	3.13	0.53	0.83	−0.26	−0.11	−0.12	N/A	−0.05	−0.24	0.76	0.39	N/A	0.51	0.30	N/A	0.61
Peru	1.04	3.27	3.59	2.53	0.56	N/A	2.17	2.47	0.87	0.71	−0.46	−0.01	−0.31	N/A	−0.10	0.15	0.60	0.44	N/A	0.43	0.55	N/A	0.49
Uruguay	1.42	4.41	3.19	2.01	0.49	N/A	2.17	3.31	0.88	0.89	−0.71	0.09	−0.73	N/A	0.46	−0.75	0.66	0.48	N/A	0.14	0.57	N/A	0.72

All variables are in real terms.

c is the private consumption (constant 1995 US$) and i is the gross domestic investment (constant 1995 US$), both from World Development Indicators (World Bank). x and m are exports and imports at current US$ deflated by current GDP in US$, all from the United Nations. nx is net exports divided by GDP.

pm is the import unit value over the export unit value, from *International Financial Statistics* (IMF).

Ytot is income terms of trade and is compiled by the United Nations, while rer is real exchange rate from *International Financial Statistics*.

All variables, except nx, are in natural logs, and all variables are HP filtered.

The series are annual and for 1970–1996 unless otherwise noticed with.[1] As for the rer series, the data is for 1970–1995.

[1]Names and years for the missing data are indicated in parenthesis after country names below:

Argentina (c 1980–1992, pm 1970–1989); Barbados (x 1996, m 1996, nx 1996); Bolivia (x 1996, m 1996, nx 1996); Brazil (rer 1970–1979); Fiji (c 1986–1988 and 1990–1993, i 1986–1988 and 1990–1993); Guyana (c 1989–1991, rer 1993–1995) and Nicaragua (i 1979, rer 1970–1971).

Corr(Ytot, nx) can be obtained from the authors.

The business cycle properties of the main national account variables are summarised by three relevant statistics. Relative volatility is defined as the ratio of the standard deviation of a variable to the standard deviation of GDP. The cyclical behaviour of a variable is defined by the variable's correlation with GDP, and the persistence property is defined by the autocorrelation of a variable. We also provide the contemporaneous correlation between the real exchange rate and the normalised trade balance (trade balance to GDP ratio). Tables 1A–1C show the behaviour of various macro-variables for the 1970–1996 or 1970–1999 period. We have used the constant price GDP for estimating the relative volatility, and for most indicators this is lower with the constant price GDP than the current price GDP deflated by the import unit value.

The results in Table 1A, 1B and 1C can be summarised as follows:

(a) Overall consumption is smoother than income for Korea, the Philippines, Rwanda, Senegal and Guatemala.
(b) Most of the countries have more volatile consumption than income. This probably reflects more noise in the consumption data as less developed countries have underdeveloped financial markets, and this in turn offers less opportunity for consumption smoothing.
(c) Relative volatility in Asian, African and Latin American countries' investment is considerably more and most often three to four times larger than the constant price GDP.
(d) Exports and imports are more volatile than the current price GDP. The trade balance to GDP ratio has as expected less volatility compared to the individual components of the trade balance. Income terms of trade and real exchange rates have standard deviations exceeding one on time series of filtered data.
(e) Most of the co-movements described by the correlation between components and GDP are positive as expected. The real exchange rate and the trade balance to GDP ratio are negatively correlated with GDP. Most of the major components (c, i, x and m) of GDP show a pro-cyclical behaviour. Ytot has a pro-cyclical behaviour (positive contemporaneous correlation with GDP), while nx has mostly negative correlation (countercyclical) with GDP. rer and GDP have a negative contemporaneous correlation. Depreciation implies that rer goes up, so depreciation and GDP are negatively correlated.

(f) GDP is most often positively autocorrelated and similarly nx and rer are positively autocorrelated. rer and nx are negatively correlated, and similarly pm and nx are negatively contemporaneously correlated. Higher import prices lead to a lower trade balance as a proportion of GDP.

Dynamic Relationship Between Terms of Trade and Trade Balance

In this section, we study the lead and lag correlations between the terms of trade and the trade balance. All the data are in US dollars. We have two sources of data on the trade balance and nx. These are from the United Nations and World Economic Outlook database of IMF. The United Nations data are based on the physical inflow and outflow of goods and services, while trade statistics from the IMF are based on the observed payments and receipts for imports and exports of a given country. There is a considerable time lag between physical flows and financial transactions, and hence the two sets of figures are drastically different for a majority of countries on a year-to-year basis. The graphs for the lead and lag relationships, between the terms of trade and net exports, and between the real exchange rate and net exports, are shown in Figs. 1 and 2, respectively. The graphs indicate the correlation coefficients on the vertical axis (corr(pm_t, nx_{t+k})) and the number of lags (k) on the horizontal axis. The left of 0 expresses the relationship between nx and the future pm, and the right of 0 expresses the relationship between nx and the past pm and 0 expresses the contemporaneous relationship between nx and pm, which may be interpreted as an instantaneous response. The same is true for corr(rer_t, nx_{t+k}).

To examine whether there are any patterns in graphs, we categorise the graphs according to the signs of correlation coefficients of nx with pm or rer of the future ($k = -3, -2, -1$), current ($k = 0$) and the past ($k = 1, 2, 3$). The diagram will have $k = 0$ in the middle. A pattern of (+), (−), (+) will indicate that the diagram is V-shaped with a positive correlation between nx and future pm (or rer), a negative correlation between current nx and current pm (or rer) and a positive correlation between nx and past pm (or rer).

Lead and Lag Correlations Between pm and nx

pm is the barter terms of trade defined as the import unit price deflated by the export unit price. An increase in pm would discourage imports and should lead to decrease in imports in the long run, and hence the long-run

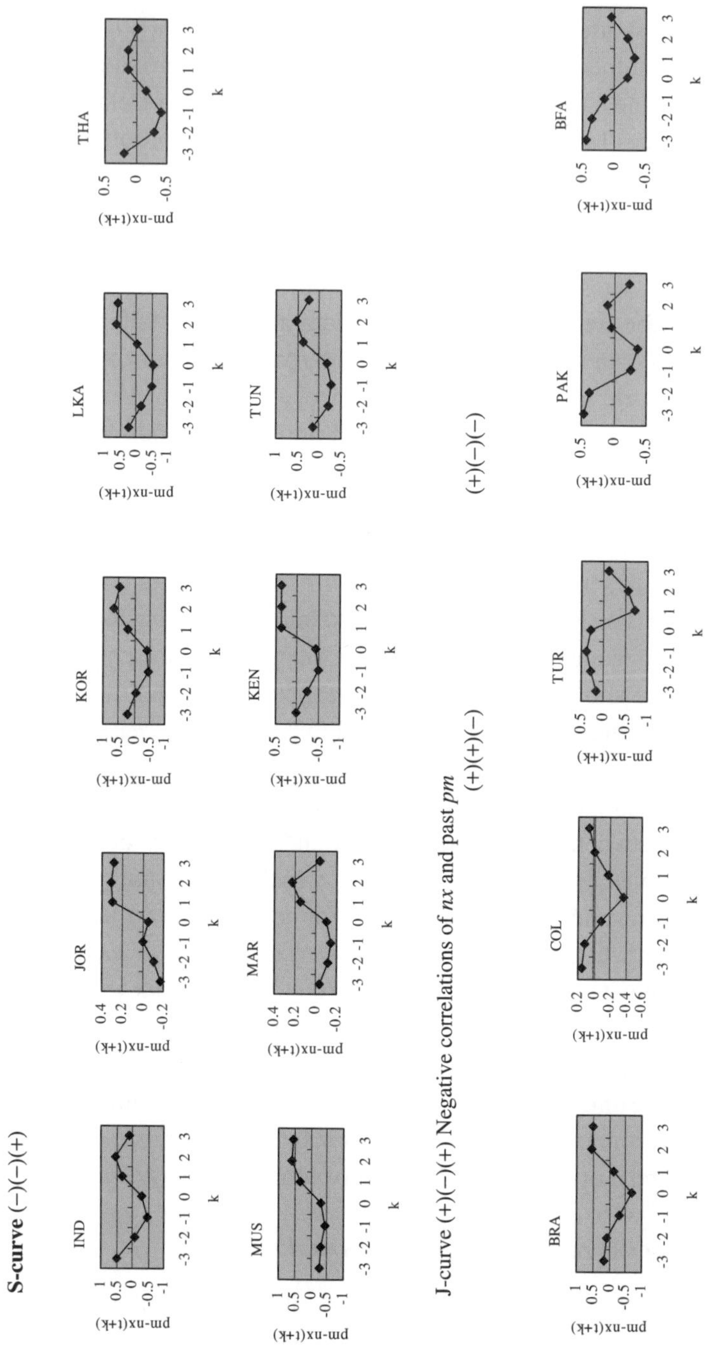

Figure 1. Lead and lag correlation between terms of trade (pm) and net export (nx).

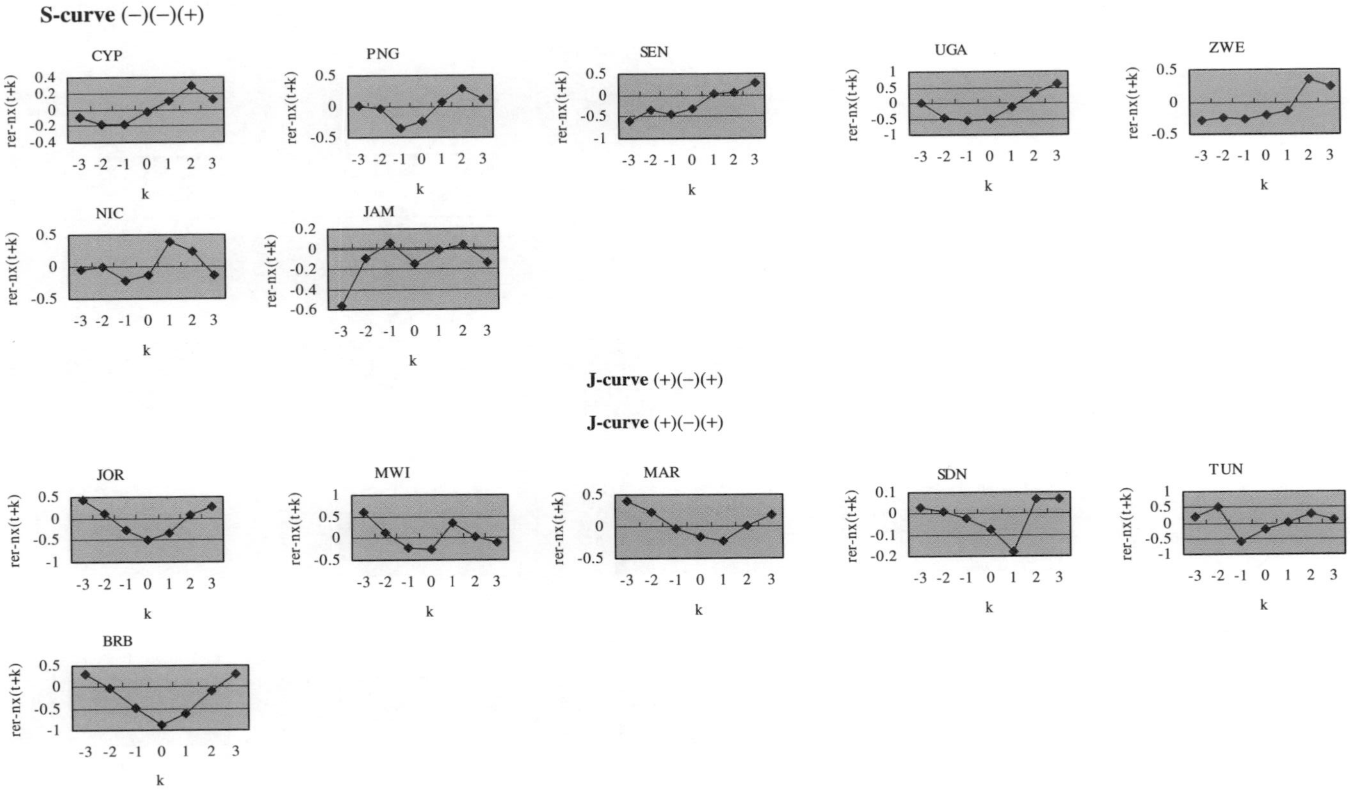

Figure 2. Lead and lag correlation between real exchange rate (rer) and nx.

Positive correlations of *nx* and past rer. (−)(+)(+)

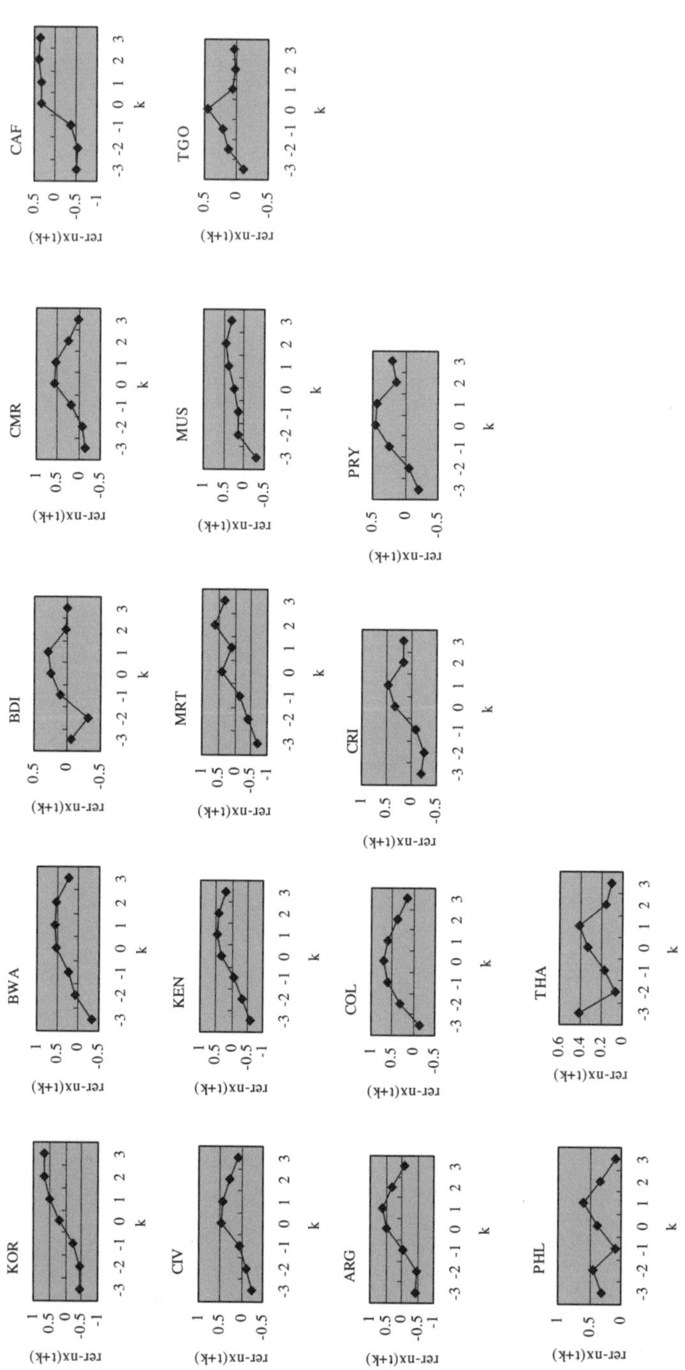

Figure 2. *(Continued)*.

Negative correlations of *nx* and past rer

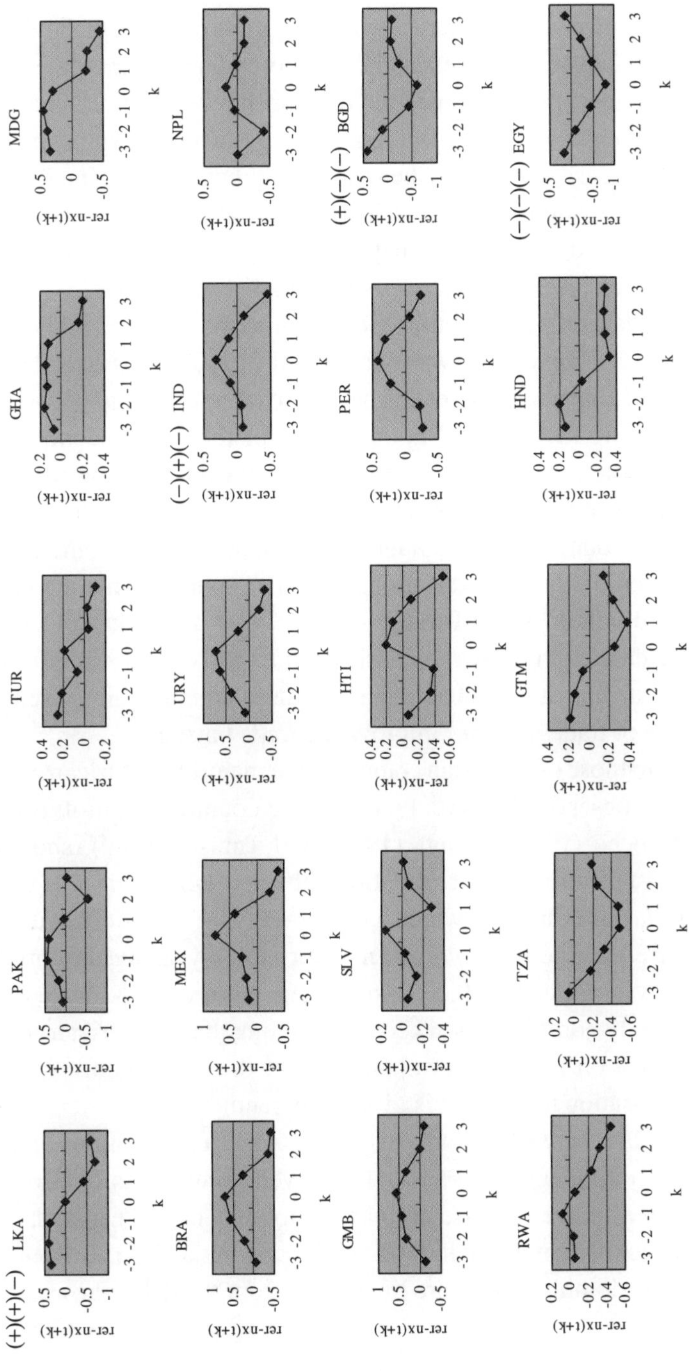

Figure 2. *(Continued).*

relationship between nx and past pm is likely to be positive. In the short run, when import demands are inelastic, the import value will increase with the increase in import prices. Hence the relationship between nx and current pm could be negative in the short run. If there is a trade surplus, px would eventually increase, and hence the relationship between nx and future pm is negative. We would expect the relationship to show the (−), (−), (+) shape if we plot the correlations between (pm_t, nx_{t+k}). This curve will be S-shaped if the correlation decreases with higher values of k.

We used data on pm from the IMF (barter terms of trade), while data on the trade balance come from two sources, IMF (1970–1999) and UN (1970–1996). Figure 1 presents the results based on the relationship between pm_t and nx_{t+k} using the United Nations data. For the Asian economies, the correlation pattern between pm_t and nx_{t+k} revealed that the majority of the Asian countries had the observed S-curve regardless of the source of data. India, Jordan, Korea, Thailand and Sri Lanka followed the observed S-curve pattern in the United Nations data. The countries that did not have the expected pattern were Turkey (+), (+), (−) and Pakistan (+), (−), (−). In the case of these two countries, net exports did not improve with an increase in pm. It is probable that for these countries improvement in barter terms of trade does not improve the trade balance.

Similar to those of the Asian countries, the majority of African countries followed the observed S-curve. Four of these countries, Mauritius (before 1970), Morocco (1984), Kenya (1993) and Tunisia (1989), showed the (−), (−), (+) pattern on the correlation between pm_t and nx_{t+k}. The only exception was Burkina Faso which had the (+), (−), (−) pattern. Although it has (+) correlation between pm and nx after a three-year lag, the correlation coefficient was very small (0.039), so the curve is a weak J-shape. Burkina Faso is the only non-liberalised economy among the five African countries for which data on pm were available. As for the four countries, the year when liberalisation took place is given in parentheses.

We had data on pm for only two Latin American economies, namely Brazil and Colombia. Brazil has the observed S-curve. As for Colombia, nx improves after the increase in pm but only with three-year lags, and the correlation coefficient is small (0.054). The shape is a V-curve. Both Brazil (1991) and Colombia (1986) are liberalised from the dates shown.

Relationship Between the Real Exchange Rates and the Trade Balance

In a two-good economy, the terms of trade obviously will equal the real exchange rate. In a multi-good export and import structure, the relationship will differ, and hence there is a need to examine the nature of the relationship in long and short run. In the long run, an increase in rer (depreciation) would be associated with higher nx (the positive relationship between nx and past rer), while in the short run, when imports are inelastic, nx would deteriorate with the higher price level for imports, and hence the negative relationship between nx and current rer will emerge. This is the J-curve effect. Kulkarni and Bhatia (2000) discovered that there was a J-curve relationship between the exchange rate and the balance of payments in the Philippines, Kenya, Japan, Indonesia, Mexico and Spain. A trade surplus will be offset by an eventual real exchange rate appreciation (the negative relationship between nx and future rer). Similar to the relationship between pm and nx, we expect (−), (−), (+) as the correlation pattern between rer_t and nx_{t+k}. This curve will be S-shaped if the correlation decreases with higher values of k.

Figure 2 shows the lead and lag relationship between rer_t and nx_{t+k} based on the IMF data. Only three countries, namely Cyprus, Papua New Guinea and Jordan, out of 14 countries, followed the observed S-curve (or J-curve) pattern. Amongst these three, the two economies, Cyprus and Jordan, are the early liberalisers as they liberalised before 1970. Among the remaining nine countries, Korea (1986) (−), (+), (+), Thailand (1986) and Philippines (1986) (+), (+), (+) had their net exports improved after rer depreciation but did not have the initial negative impact on nx. The remaining eight countries revealed that their nx deteriorated following the rer depreciation; Sri Lanka (1991), Pakistan, Turkey (1989), Malaysia (1988)[b] (+), (+), (−) and India (1994), Nepal (1991) (−), (+), (−) for the long run, while Bangladesh (+), (−), (−) and Egypt (−), (−), (−) for both short run and long run. This may be due to inflexibility in production in these economies or to their being close to the outside world. In fact, Bangladesh and Egypt are the two economies that have not liberalised their economies until now.

[b] The graph for Malaysia is not included in Fig. 2, due to space limitation.

For African economies, the correlation between rer_t and nx_{t+k} does not decrease with higher k, so the curve does not have an S-shape even when it has the expected (−), (−), (+) or (+), (−), (+) relations. We find some evidence of a J-curve for Senegal, Uganda (1988) and Zimbabwe on the (−), (−), (+) pattern. Malawi, Morocco (1984), Sudan and Tunisia (1989) have the expected J-curve on the basis of the (+), (−), (+) pattern of correlation.

Nine out of 25 countries of Africa have the (−), (+), (+) shape, implying that net exports improved after rer depreciation but did not suffer the initial negative impact on trade balance. Botswana (1980), Burundi (1990), Cameroon (1993), Central African Republic, Côte d'Ivoire, Kenya (1993), Mauritania (1992), Mauritius (before 1970) and Togo all fall into this category of the (−), (+), (+) pattern of correlation between rer_t and nx_{t+k}.

The remaining nine countries had observed deterioration in their net exports following rer depreciation.[c] Ghana (1985), Madagascar, Niger, Burkina Faso (+), (+), (−) and Gambia (1990) (−), (+), (−) showed deterioration in net exports as a result of rer depreciation in the long run, while Rwanda, Tanzania, Chad and Sierra Leone (1990) (+), (−), (−) exhibited such a pattern in both the short and long run.

We find that there is no clear pattern between liberalisation and the S-shape or J-shape pattern between rer_t and nx_{t+k} for the African countries. For the Asian countries, we find that liberalised economies tend to follow S-curve or J-curve, while less liberalised economies tend to have a feature that the trade balance deteriorates with rer depreciation.

In the case of Latin American economies (Fig. 2), Nicaragua (1991) and Jamaica (1989) both have the observed S-curve relationship between rer_t and nx_{t+k}. Barbados has the observed J-effect (+), (−), (+), but the correlation does not decrease with k, and it turns up with V-curve.

Four out of 20 Latin American economies have the (−), (+), (+) shape; the economy had its net exports improved after rer depreciation but did not have the initial negative impact on nx. Argentina (1991), Costa Rica (1986), Colombia (1986) and Paraguay (1989) belong to this group. The remaining 13 countries had observed deterioration in their nx following

[c] The graphs for Niger, Burkina Faso, Chad and Sierra Leone are not presented, due to space limitation.

rer depreciation.[d] Brazil (1991), Mexico (1987), Uruguay (1990), Chile (1976) and Dominican Republic had the (+), (+), (−) pattern and El Salvador (1989), Haiti, Peru (1976), Fiji and Guyana (1988) had the (−), (+), (−) pattern, indicating nx deterioration in the long-run. Guatemala (1988), the Honduras (1991) and Bolivia (1985) had the (+), (−), (−) pattern, indicating nx deterioration in both the short and the long run.

On the whole, rer does not have the S-shape relationship with nx for most of the Latin American economies, due to strong ties with the US economy and US dollar. The past rer and nx are negatively correlated for 13 countries in a sample of 20 economies. The contemporaneous relationship between rer and nx is positive for 14 economies, and hence there is no plausible J-shape relationship for the majority of the countries of Latin America.

Is Relationship Between Terms of Trade and Trade Balance Different in Liberalised Economies?

It is conceivable that countries that are liberalised might not have constraints similar to the less liberalised economies. The countries where there are strict import controls might have different behaviour with respect to exports and imports, and when import prices are low, they might import the maximum permissible with the foreign exchange available to buy imports. On the other hand, liberalised economies might not have any foreign exchange constraint, and as a result, when import prices are low and the demand for imports is more elastic, they could contribute to deficits on the trade account. Terms of trade improvement in a liberalised environment may contribute to deficits in trade balances, while in a non-liberalised structure, we should expect the terms of trade improvement to lead to an improvement in trade balances. The other possibility is that when import prices are high and the demand for imports is elastic, the country might postpone buying imports, and this in turn could improve the balance of trade. Deterioration in the terms of trade can lead to an improvement in the trade balance in a liberalised environment if the demand for imports is elastic.

---

[d] The graphs for Chile, Dominican Republic, Fiji, Guyana and Bolivia are not presented in Fig. 2, due to space limitation. All the eliminated graphs are available from the authors.

We, therefore, have no way to find out the consequences of liberalisation other than empirically. We first conducted Augmented Dickey–Fuller (ADF) tests on the HP-filtered data of $\log(pm/px)$ and nx. These data are from the United Nations. The HP-filtered variables have already eliminated the stochastic trend and contain only cyclical and random components. Both the HP-filtered series will be stationary, and the ADF tests support this conclusion. We then looked at the derivation of the long-run relationship between the terms of trade and the trade balance. The most suitable model is the Autoregressive Distributed[e] lag (ADL) model for each country, and we estimated the ADL model using four lags of Cpm (cyclical component of $\log(pm/px)$) and Cnx (cyclical component of nx). We used the Akaikie and Schwarz–Bayes criterion to find the most parsimonious form of the ADL model for each country, and for most countries we found that ADL(1,1) was the best fitting model. These results are presented in Table 2. We then derived the long-run relationship from ADL(1,1). For Brazil, Colombia, Sri Lanka, Thailand and Burkina Faso, the sign of the long-run Cpm was negative and not often significant. Detailed results of all the estimated parameters are shown in Table 2. Burkina Faso was never liberalised, and it still has a negative and significant coefficient. Brazil was liberalised during the period, and it also has a negative and significant coefficient. For almost all other economies, the long-run coefficient was not significant and often with incorrect sign, indicating that the improvement in terms of trade (decline in Cpm) in the long-run deteriorates the trade balance. For Korea, a deterioration in the current terms of trade (that is, increase in Cpm) leads to a decline in the trade balance, while deterioration in the last period's terms of trade leads to an improvement in the trade balance. As the last period's effect dominates over the current period, we find the long-run relationship with positive sign giving a perverse relationship between terms of trade improvement and the trade balance. If import prices fall in relation to export prices, there can be a greater rise in imports

[e] Bahmani-Oskooee and Alse (1995) used the co-integration approach and did not find any co-integration between the unit root non-stationary trade balance and terms of trade variables for 24 countries. The authors used quarterly data of the floating exchange rate period and concluded that import tariffs or export subsidies will have no long-run impact on the trade balance.

Table 2. Short- and long-run relationships between terms of trade and trade balance on HP-filtered data regression coefficients, t-ratios and test statistics of residuals.

Name of the country/model	Constant	$Cnx(-1)$	Cpm	$Cpm(-1)$	R^2(SEE)	Long-run Cpm	AR[1] test/ARCH	Normal/reset	Het[2]/het * x^3
Brazil/	−0.0006	0.3678	−0.07***	0.0362**	0.6164	−0.051	0.86 (0.44)	2.15 (0.34)	0.82 (0.57)
ADL (1,1)	(−0.31)	(1.91)	(−5.24)	(2.03)	(0.0098)	(−2.16)	2.25 (0.15)	2.25 (0.15)	0.74 (0.66)
Colombia/	0.0003	0.6194***	−0.077**	0.0399	0.4632	−0.096	1.78 (0.19)	1.087 (0.58)	0.712 (0.65)
ADL (1,1)	(0.068)	(3.70)	(−2.29)	(1.12)	(0.0205)	(−0.96)	0.056 (0.815)	0.587 (0.45)	0.512 (0.84)
Burkina Faso/	−0.0007	0.2616	−0.2257	−0.2362	0.2239	−0.6255*	0.697 (0.51)	8.015 (0.018)	14.375 (0.000)
ADL (1,1)	(−0.0067)	(1.32)	(−1.47)	(1.54)	(0.0574)	(−1.83)	0.334 (0.57)	0.20 (0.65)	11.49 (0.0001)
India/	0.00008	0.2966	−0.0223*	0.0343**	0.3605	0.0171	0.008 (0.99)	4.013 (0.13)	0.858 (0.51)
ADL (1,1)	(0.075)	(1.51)	(−1.71)	(2.85)	(0.0061)	(0.712)	0.811 (0.38)	0.411 (0.52)	0.861 (0.58)
Jordan/	−0.0017	0.5070**	−0.0669	0.2565*	0.3392	0.3846	0.305 (0.85)	2.237 (0.32)	2.15 (0.90)
ADL (1,1)	(−0.135)	(2.92)	(−0.477)	(1.84)	(0.0646)	(0.917)	0.298 (0.59)	0.42 (0.52)	3.86 (0.92)
Korea/	0.0011	0.4599**	−0.24***	0.275***	0.6362	0.0676	0.368 (0.70)	0.063 (0.97)	3.39 (0.02)
ADL (1,1)	(0.341)	(2.82)	(−3.91)	(4.44)	(0.0165)	(0.458)	4.07 (0.057)	0.82 (0.37)	2.01 (0.13)
Kenya/	0.0009	0.0753	−0.18***	0.183***	0.524	0.0004	1.251 (0.31)	0.763 (0.68)	2.34 (0.08)
ADL (1,1)	(0.022)	(0.41)	(−3.52)	(3.74)	(0.023)	(0.006)	0.078 (0.78)	0.085 (0.77)	1.76 (0.17)
Morocco/	0.0008	0.3563*	−0.0298	0.0585	0.1675	0.044	0.56 (0.58)	3.21 (0.20)	2.28 (0.09)
ADL (1,1)	(0.15)	(1.81)	(−0.538)	(1.05)	(0.0273)	(0.391)	0.025 (0.88)	0.88 (0.36)	1.72 (0.19)
Mauritius/	−0.0008	0.3505*	−0.20***	0.251***	0.598	0.0752	1.335 (0.28)	11.13 (0.004)	1.22 (0.35)
ADL (1,1)	(−0.15)	(2.28)	(−3.60)	(4.78)	(0.0295)	(0.785)	3.397 (0.08)	5.41 (0.03)	1.16 (0.40)
Sri Lanka/	0.0151	0.561***	−0.16***	0.159***	0.5986	−0.0100	0.0286 (0.97)	10.11 (0.006)	0.397 (0.87)
ADL (1,1)	(0.278)	(3.23)	(−3.32)	(3.11)	(0.0277)	(−0.072)	0.0003 (0.98)	0.138 (0.71)	0.38 (0.92)
Thailand/	0.00	—	−0.0467	—	0.0285	−0.0467	1.319 (0.287)	3.102 (0.212)	0.560 (0.579)
Static			(−0.857)		(0.0213)	(−0.857)	0.192 (0.665)	0.477 (0.496)	0.560 (0.579)

Notes: *Significant at 10 percent level; **Significant at 5 percent level; ***Significant at 1 percent level.

[1]The LM test for autocorrelation up to order 2.

[2]This is the test for heteroscedasticity using an auxiliary regression of residual squares on explanatory variables and their squares.

[3]This uses explanatory variables, their squares and cross-products.

Data source used is from the United Nations.

than exports, leading to a deterioration of the trade balance in developing economies.

We decided to introduce the interaction between Cpm and a liberal variable in the ADL(1,1) regression model. Pakistan and Burkina Faso were never liberalised in the sample period, while Jordan and Mauritius were liberalised all the time in the sample. For other countries, we introduced interactions in the model, and excepting for two countries, the results did not change. The interaction between Cpm and the liberalisation variable was not significant excepting for Morocco and Thailand. Liberalisation significantly improved the trade balance, i.e., the increase in terms of trade (increase in import prices in relation to export prices) reduced the balance of trade when the liberalisation regime was in operation. For Morocco, the coefficient was −0.234 (t-statistic, −2.30), while for Thailand the coefficient was −0.97 (t-statistic, −3.71), and this indicates that liberalisation contributed to the improvement in the trade balance in these two countries. In other countries, either the period of liberalisation was not long enough such as India (1991 or 1994) or liberalisation did not progress smoothly and restrictions on imports were maintained during the liberalisation regime.

Summary and Conclusions

Studies in the past on the relationship between the terms of trade and the trade balance concentrated on the estimation of import demand elasticities. Few studies have looked at the relationship between the terms of trade and the trade balance to establish a direct link. Our study has considered the data from developing economies of Asia, Africa and Latin America over three decades and has analysed the dynamic behaviour of the terms of trade and net exports.

Backus *et al.* (1994) found that the lead and lag correlation between the trade balance and terms of trade is S-shaped. To some extent we find support of this hypothesis for a few countries. We also examined whether there was any long-run relationship between the terms of trade and the trade balance using autoregressive distributed lag models on the stationary time series. Stationarity was achieved by using the Hodrick–Prescott filter. We found that for two countries improvement in the terms of trade improve the trade balance. We also find that the relationship of the trade balance with the last period's terms of trade was perverse, indicating that the improvement in terms of trade in the last period deteriorated the trade balance. The hypothesis that liberalisation could bring a developing economy to a more flexible economic structure and as a result one may find that terms of trade improvements could lead to improvement in the trade balance was tested. For Morocco and Thailand, the relationship supported this hypothesis. Constraints on the availability of data over the entire period on the barter terms of trade remained one of the limitations of the study.

References

Backus, DK, PJ Kehoe and FE Kydland (1994). Dynamics of the trade balance and the terms of trade: The J-curve? *American Economic Review*, 84(1), 84–103.

Bahmani-Oskooee, M and J Alse (1995). Is there any long-run relation between the terms of trade and trade balance. *Journal of Policy Modelling*, 17(2), 199–205.

Harberger, AC (1950). Currency depreciation, income and balance of trade. *Journal of Political Economy*, 58, 47–60.

Hodrick, RJ and EC Prescott (1997). Post-war US business cycles: An empirical investigation. *Journal of Money, Credit and Banking*, 29, 1–16.

Kulkarni, KG and A Bhatia (2000). Empirical evidence of the J-curve hypotheses. *Indian Economic Journal*, 49(3), 43–50.

Laursen, S and LA Metzler (1950). Flexible exchange rates and the theory of employment. *Review of Economics and Statistics*, 32, 281–299.

Obstfeld, M (1982). Aggregate spending and terms of trade: Is there a Laursen-Metzler effect? *Quarterly Journal of Economics*, 97, 251–270.

Obstfeld, M and K Rogoff (1995). The intertemporal approach to the current account. In *Handbook of International Economics*, 3. Chapter 34, Amsterdam: North Holland.

Sachs, J and A Warner (1995). Economic reform and the process of global integration. *Brookings Papers on Economic Activity*, 1, 1–118.

Senhadji, AS (1998). Dynamics of the trade balance and the terms of trade in LDCS: The S-curve. *Journal of International Economics*, 46, 105-131.

Svensson, LEO and A. Razin (1983). The terms of trade, spending and the current account: The Harberger–Laursen–Matzlet effect. *Journal of Political Economy*, 91, 97–125.

Appendix

Table 1. Names of countries included with available data on terms of trade and real exchange rate.

		Liberal	*pm*	rer
Asia				
Bangladesh	BGD	Non		1
Sri Lanka	LKA	1991	1	1
Cyprus	CYP	1970		1
India	IND	1994	1	1
Jordan	JOR	1970	1	1
Republic of Korea	KOR	1986	1	1
Malaysia	MYS	1988		1
Nepal	NPL	1991		1
Pakistan	PAK	Non	1	1
Papua New Guinea	PNG	Non		1
Philippines	PHL	1986		1
Thailand	THA	1986	1	1
Turkey	TUR	1989	1	1
Egypt	EGY	Non		1
	Sum		7	14
Africa				
Botswana	BWA	1980		1
Burundi	BDI	1990		1
Cameroon	CMR	1993		1
Central African Rep.	CAF	Non		1
Chad	TCD	1990		1
Gambia	GMB	1990		1
Ghana	GHA	1985		1
Côte d'Ivoire	CIV	Non	1	1
Kenya	KEN	1993	1	1
Madagascar	MDG	Non		1
Malawi	MWI	Non		1
Mauritania	MRT	1992		
Mauritius	MUS	1970	1	1
Morocco	MAR	1984	1	1
Niger	NER	Non		1
Rwanda	RWA	Non		1
Senegal	SEN	Non		1
Sierra Leone	SLE	Non		1
Zimbabwe	ZWE	Non		1

(*Continued*)

Table 1. (*Continued*)

Asia		Liberal	*pm*	rer
Sudan	SDN	Non		1
Togo	TGO	Non		1
Tunisia	TUN	1989	1	1
Uganda	UGA	1988		1
Tanzania	TZA	Non		1
Burkina Faso	BFA	Non	1	1
	Sum		5	25
Latin America				
Argentina	ARG	1991		1
Barbados	BRB	1970		1
Bolivia	BOL	1985		1
Brazil	BRA	1991	1	1
Chile	CHL	1976		1
Colombia	COL	1986	1	1
Costa Rica	CRI	1986		1
Dominican Rep.	DOM	Non		1
El Salvador	SLV	1989		1
Fiji	FJI	Non		1
Guatemala	GTM	1988		1
Guyana	GUY	1988		1
Haiti	HTI	Non		1
Honduras	HND	1991		1
Jamaica	JAM	1989		1
Mexico	MEX	1987		1
Nicaragua	NIC	1991		1
Paraguay	PRY	1989		1
Peru	PER	1991		1
Uruguay	URY	1990		1
	Sum		2	20

Notes: The year of liberalisation is given in the second column. The period of liberalisation when it started was obtained from Sachs and Warner (1995). A country is classified as closed if it fails any one of the following five criteria: non-tariff barrier coverage; tariff rates; black market premia on exchange rates; overall economic system — socialist or capitalist and the extent of government intervention in the export sector.

pm = import unit value (index US$, 1995 = 1, IFS75) divided by export unit value (index, US$, 1995 = 1, IFS,74), collected from IFS CD-Rom.

rer = real exchange rate (index, 1985 = 1, IMF), 1970–1995.

Number 1 next to the country code indicates the data availability.

Chapter 8

Relationship Between Trade Liberalisation, Economic Growth and Balance of Payments in Developing Countries*

Ashok Parikh[1] and Corneliu Stirbu[2]

[1] *University of East Anglia, Norwich, UK*
[2] *HWWA, Hamburg, Germany*

Introduction

The objectives of this study are to analyse the relationship between trade liberalisation and economic growth using country- and region-level information for developing countries of the world. Trade liberalisation could generate more imports than exports, leading to deterioration in trade balance. Does deteriorating trade balance affect economic growth at a country level? There are many other factors which could affect both economic growth and trade balance, and this is considered using a simple balance of payments constrained model of Thirlwall (1979). This study is different from previous studies in at least three respects: (a) it uses the balance of payments constrained growth model in a behavioural form with liberalisation and oil prices as exogenous variables; (b) it uses the latest available data on real GDP in PPP terms and growth rates from Summers *et al.* (2001) and (c) liberalisation index is used for three decades from two different studies namely Sachs–Warner (1995) and Wacziarg (2001).

* The authors would like to thank Dr. Katja Michaelowa for her helpful comments, which have improved the chapter considerably. The first author would like to express gratitude to Leverhulme Trust for the Emeritus award that has facilitated this study.

Previous research in this field tends to give conflicting results. Some studies show that the countries that went for liberalisation programmes have improved their export performance (Thomas, 1991; Weiss, 1992; Joshi and Little, 1996; Helleiner, 1994; Bleaney, 1999; Ahmed, 2000). On the other hand, other studies have found little evidence of a relationship between trade liberalisation and economic growth (UNCTAD, 1989; Agosin, 1991; Clarke and Kirkpatrick, 1992; Greenaway and Sapsford, 1994; Shafaedin, 1994; Jenkins, 1996). On the import side, there is a strong positive impact of trade liberalisation on the growth of imports and this impact is through the sensitivity of price and income changes (Melo and Vogt, 1984; Bertola and Faini, 1991).

Many analysts believed that trade policy openness and higher ratios of trade volumes were positively correlated with economic growth until Rodriguez and Rodrik (2000) raised some concerns about the robustness of these results. Conclusions of various studies remained sensitive to difficulties in measuring openness, statistically sensitive specifications and collinearity of protectionist policies with other poorly executed policies in developing economies. Ocampo and Taylor (1998) provided views from the theoretical side whether trade liberalisation in developing economies would lead to economic growth, and their conclusion was that there are problems on productivity growth and income distribution on account of liberalisation program and hence it might not necessarily lead to higher economic growth. Wacziarg (2001) attempted the measurement of liberalisation variables as Sachs and Warner classification posed problems on their categorisation of open and closed economies. Like Wacziarg, this study uses the updated data on income levels (Summers *et al.*, 2001), which provide the basic information to examine the relationship between trade openness and economic growth before and after liberalisation and study the relationship between investment, liberalisation and time period elapsed from liberalisation. Both the aggregate region-level and country-level study for selected countries are attempted. The data period of our interest ranges from 1970 to 2000, and during this period the relationship between trade balance and economic growth may have undergone changes from one decade to the next in many regions of the world. We intend to analyse whether region-level growth and trade balance are affected by liberalisation. Timing of liberalisation within a country could also affect the relationship.

Dollar and Kray (2004) have shown that the growth pattern of countries that have liberalised have shown acceleration in their real income, and in the 1990s, globalising developing countries grew at 5 percent per capita, rich countries at 2.2 percent and non-globalising developing countries at only 1.4 percent. Their view is that the countries that have gone on the globalisation path are catching up with rich countries while non-globalisers are lagging behind. Irwin and Trevio (2002) following Frankel and Romer (1999) conclude that the countries that trade more as a proportion of their GDP have higher incomes even after controlling for the endogeniety of trade. Overall, it appears that trade contributes to improvement in real income and per capita growth; however, if trade is not combined with adequate policies to balance imports against exports, it could generate the balance of trade and balance of payments deficits, leading to deterioration in the growth of real incomes.

Conceptually, balance of payments deficits is equivalent to current account deficits. A current account deficit can be defined as the country's excess of investment over savings. However, the saving and investment flows reported in many national income accounts do not conform closely to the theoretically correct concepts of saving and investment when international capital mobility is extensive. Historically, current account balances were small in the post-1945 period initially because of official restrictions on international capital movements, with most industrialised countries' currencies inconvertible until 1959. After the early 1970s, net international capital flows have expanded as a result of petrodollar recycling and the removal of many industrial country restrictions on international payments following the adoption of floating exchange rates and technological evolution in the financial industry. As capital flows have increased from developing to developed countries after 1970s, trade deficits do not result into current account deficits as capital flows dampen the impact of trade deficits on the domestic economy in the short run. However, in the long run, the loan and service payments could increase the burden on the domestic economy, leading to debt crises and unfavourable effects on economic growth.

There is a plausible link between economic growth and the external balance, and this was noted in the literature on two-gap models (Chenery and Bruno, 1962) and the balance of payments constrained economic growth (Thirlwall, 1979). These models are static, and in the dynamic context, the role of exports is not only to earn extra foreign exchange but also to create the domestic market because the latter would allow the industry to operate at full capacity while the former would generate surplus foreign exchange. A country's trade performance is influenced by a large number of domestic factors, including its structural characteristics, resource endowments and policies. External economic environment is no less important in determining the country's trade balance. These vary considerably from country to country, and a full account of such influences requires a detailed country specific analysis. As the detailed country analysis is not the purpose of this study, the scope of this research is confined to examine the impact of a number of common factors namely the global demand, terms of trade, trade and financial liberalisation and exchange rate regimes on the trade balance to GDP percentages. These factors would have presumably influenced the trade and growth performance of a large number of low- and medium-income developing countries. Slow growth of the developed countries' markets and continued restrictions of access in areas of export interest to developing countries tend to add to trade deficits in developing countries by slowing the pace of their export earnings and leading to terms of trade losses. Trade liberalisation widens the deficits as in the short run this produces an upsurge in imports, where protection was excessive and the import-substitution strategies were not successful. The lack of coordination between exchange rate management and trade liberalisation can lead to trade deficits. Financial liberalisation leading to capital account liberalisation tends to aggravate payment difficulties by discouraging investment in traded-goods industries.

This empirical study intends to provide a long-run relationship between economic growth and liberalisation at a country level and also attempts to study the relationship between trade balance and GDP growth incorporating several exogenous global factors that can have influence on domestic economic growth and the balance of payments. The other objective is to examine and assess quantitatively the impact of trade liberalisation for

14 selected economies that have liberalised at different points of time during the 1970–1991 period. As our quantitative analysis covers a large number of African, Asian and Latin American developing economies, the panel data are used to study the behavioural relationship between trade balance and GDP growth under liberalisation, changes in terms of trade and growth in the world market demand. As the growth of GDP and trade balance are endogenous variables we propose to estimate the model equation by using the instrumental variable estimation for panel data. It is also proposed to look at policies to alleviate the effects of trade and financial liberalisation on trade deficits of developing economies. A simple indicator of liberalisation and openness does not distinguish between slow and fast growing countries. Dichotomous policy indicators such as liberalisation dummy have serious disadvantages as they do not consider the intensity of liberalisation and time period elapsed from the date of liberalisation. A subsample of developing countries is examined with detailed information on the broader economic and political context of trade reforms.

This study is organised as follows: In the second section, we present a review and describe our data set, dates of liberalisation, openness indicator and various other variables. In the third section, the relationships between trade balance and liberalisation and openness and liberalisation along with liberalisation time period when the country was liberalised are presented for three different periods and three different regions. In the fourth section, the relationship based on determinants of trade balance and current account is presented. Trade liberalisation, growth, advanced countries' growth and terms of trade are used in a panel framework, where individual countries form a sample. In the fifth section, some tentative conclusion on the evidence that the balance of trade and economic growth are negatively related for a large number of developing countries is presented. This evidence supports the hypothesis that faster growth with liberalisation could create balance of trade problems. There does not exist a great deal of evidence on current account balances being affected by economic growth. In the sixth section, 14 countries are selected in a panel study, and determinants of trade balance and current accounts are used. In the last section, some conclusions are drawn.

External Deficits and Growth in Developing Countries: A Review of Long-term Trends[a]

All developing countries and territories

The ratio of the current account deficit to gross domestic product (GDP) has been relatively stable for developing countries[b] taken as a group over the past decade and a half, although it has fluctuated between 1 and 3 percent (Fig. 1). This contrasts sharply with the 1970s, where developing countries faced strong fluctuations in their current account but experienced a surplus in most of the years. Developing countries' trade account has

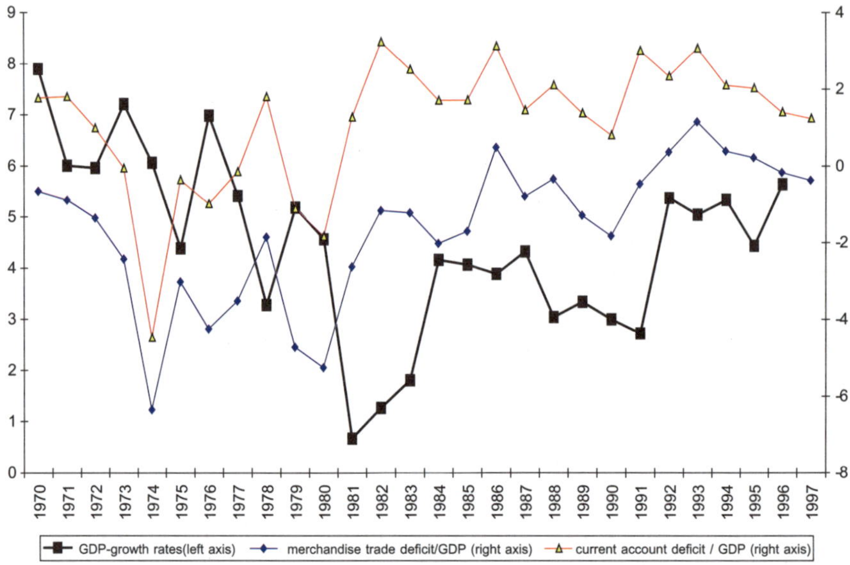

Figure 1. GDP, growth rates, merchandise trade deficit/GDP ratio and current account/GDP ratio of developing countries and territories, 1970–1997%.
Source: UNCTAD database.

---

[a] A large part of the second section is presented in UNCTAD (1999) *Trade and Development Report.*

[b] Given that data on the current account for the 1970s with a comprehensive coverage of developing countries is available only from the IMF's World Development Outlook database, this section makes use of the IMF's country group convention, i.e., Hong Kong, China SAE, the Republic of Korea, Singapore and Taiwan, Province of China, are not included in the group of developing countries.

moved by and large in parallel with their current account. It is inferred from Table 1, however, that the early 1990s was the first period during which developing countries had a trade deficit for several consecutive years. This has caused the average (group) trade account position to be worse during the 1990s than in previous periods, with an only slight difference compared with the 1980s but a very large one compared with the 1970s. The rate of growth in developing countries has fluctuated substantially over the past three decades: an average growth rate of about 6 percent — but with significant fluctuations around a downward trend — during the 1970s was followed by a sharp drop in GDP growth at the beginning of the 1980s. GDP growth was relatively stable at around 3 to 4 percent during the second half of the 1980s and subsequently rose to an average of about 5 percent during the first half of the 1990s. By taking the evidence on external deficits and GDP growth together, it seems that for developing countries the external deficits and financial requirements associated with any given growth rate have been larger over the past few years compared to earlier periods.[c]

Non-fuel-exporting developing countries excluding China

The evolution of the current account position in the non-fuel-exporting developing countries excluding China has been largely determined by the

[c] The evolution of the world market price for crude oil has strongly influenced the external position and rate of growth of developing countries, with significantly different implications for fuel- and non-fuel-exporting countries. The difference in the experience between these two country groups has of course been marked most in the years immediately following the two oil-price hikes in 1973 and 1979 but has been very distinct also over the past few years when the price of oil declined drastically. Given the strong dependence of the major fuel-exporting developing countries on just one export item with a strongly fluctuating price on the world market, they face very specific problems. Therefore, the remainder of this analysis will focus on non-fuel exporting developing countries. The People's Republic of China will also be excluded from the following analysis for two reasons. First, China may be characterised best as an economy in transition which over the past few years has undergone a change in nature of the way in which the economy functions comparable to that of the transition economies in Central and Eastern Europe which are also excluded from the analysis. Second, given that China alone accounts for about 15 percent of GDP of all developing countries, its external accounts have often moved opposite to those of the group of developing countries as a whole and China's growth rate has been very substantially higher than that of most other developing countries over the past few years, its inclusion would introduce a bias to the analysis.

Table 1. Trade account to GDP ratio and GDP growth: 1989–1996 compared with 1970–1979 (excluding 1974–1975).

		Improving trade account				Deteriorating trade account			
		More than 10%	5–10%	2–5%	0–2%	0–2%	2–5%	5–10%	More than 10%
Rising growth	More than 5% growth				Chile **China**				Uganda
	3–5%	PNG					Cyprus	Guyana	Ghana *Kuwait*
	1–3%	Benin	Chad			**Argentina** Bangladesh **India** Mauritania Niger Uruguay	**Thailand**		Jamaica Nepal
	0–1%	Guinea-Bissau Jordan Singapore			Pakistan			**Malaysia** **Peru** Sri Lanka	El Salvador
Falling growth	0–1%				Senegal	Guinea Madagascar	Bolivia *Indonesia* *Iran*	Liberia Zimbabwe	Nicaragua Sudan Tanzania
	1–3%	Barbados Burkina Faso *Nigeria* *Syria*		Fiji *Venezuela*	Costa Rica	CAR **Colombia** Tunisia	Honduras Mali Mauritius **Turkey**	Guatemala	Dominican Rep. *Libya* Zambia

(*Continued*)

Table 1. (*Continued*).

	Improving trade account				Deteriorating trade account			
	More than 10%	5–10%	2–5%	0–2%	0–2%	2–5%	5–10%	More than 10%
3–5%	Trinidad and Tobago	**Korea**	Hong Kong	**Mexico** Sierra Leone **Taiwan** Togo	Kenya Malawi Morocco		**Philippines**	Paraguay
More than 5%	Botswana Congo	*Algeria* Cameroon *Gabon*	**Brazil** Cote d'Ivorie *Ecuador*			Zaire	**Egypt** Haiti Rwanda	Burundi Gambia *Iraq* *Saudi Arabia*

Notes: 14 big countries in bold (defined as the largest GDP in 1990–1995 and GDP greater than US$60 billion in 1997 excluding the major oil-exporting countries, as well as Hong Kong, Singapore). 12 major oil-exporting countries in italics. Nine main manufactures underlined.
All data from ETS except data on current GDP are from World Development Indicators for Ghana, India, Jamaica, Malaysia, Mauritania, Nigeria, Papua New Guinea, Rwanda, Sierra Leone, Sri Lanka, Thailand, Trinidad and Tobago and Zimbabwe. As no data on current GDP are available for 1996 for Barbados, Bolivia, Gambia, Iran, Iraq, Liberia, Libya, Saudi Arabia and Sudan; the second period comprises only 1989–1995 for these countries.

evolution of their trade and income accounts, while their balances on services and current transfers have not been subject to important changes over the past three decades.[d] During the 1970s and the 1990s, high trade deficits were the main factor behind the rising current account deficit. By contrast, the rising burden of interest payments associated with developing countries' increased external indebtedness caused a strong deterioration in their incomes' account during the early 1980s. The consequent deterioration of their current account was offset by an improvement in their trade account (as can be seen in Fig. 1 by the increased difference between the current and the trade account during the 1980s).[e] Figure 2 uses mean values of trade balance and current account deficits to GDP percentages. It can be seen that there is an increased difference between current account and trade deficits after 1990. Figures 3a–3c refer to regional mean values of trade balance to GDP, the regional current account balance to GDP and regional growth rates for three regions, Africa, Asia and Latin America. For each region, the number of countries differs.

A comparison of the average external positions and growth rates for these three periods reveals a similar general pattern for developing countries as a whole, as well as for several subgroups.[f] Between the 1970s and the 1980s, developing countries reduced their external trade deficits by about 2–3 percentage points but experienced a drop in the rate of growth by about 2 percentage points; by contrast, between the 1980s and the 1990s, their trade deficits increased strongly with the rate of growth remaining by and

[d] The GDP ratio of the services account has fluctuated between 0 and −0.5 percent, while that of the current transfers has fluctuated between 1.5 and 2.0 percent. With the fuel-exporting developing countries included, the average services/GDP ratio varies from −0.8 to −3.0 percent and that of the current transfer/GDP ratio 0 to 0.8 percent. For detailed empirical evidence, see Table A31 in International Monetary Fund, *World Economic Outlook*, various issues.

[e] Fuel-exporting developing countries experienced a sharp deterioration in the services account following the first oil-price shock, which explains why in Fig. 1 the discrepancy between the GDP ratios of the trade deficit and the current account deficit widened already during the second half of the 1970s.

[f] Given the fact that for many countries country-specific data on the current account are available only from the mid-1980s onwards, the view presented in this paragraph refers only to the trade account. However, since the available data at the aggregate level show that trade and curent account positions have moved by and large in parallel, it seems reasonable to assume that this conclusion indirectly applies to the current account.

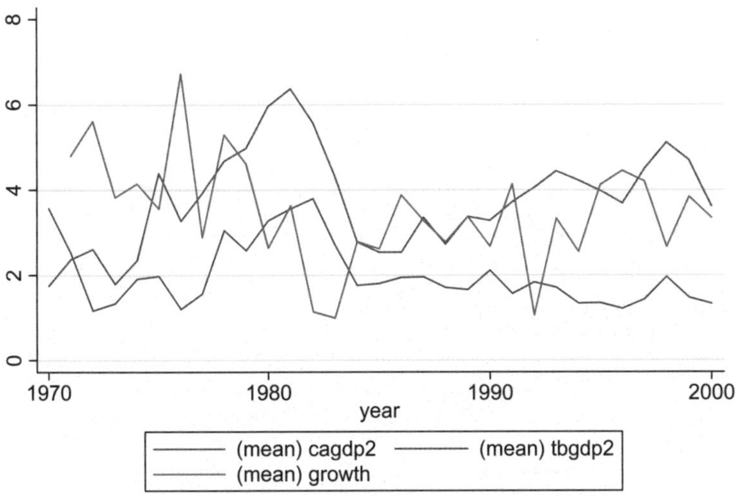

Figure 2. Relationship between growth rates, trade balance and current account to GDP percentages, (means of 75 countries: 1970–2000).
Note: Deficits positive and surplus negative.

large unchanged. There are a few notable exceptions from this basic pattern of a similar deficit/GDP ratio and a lower growth rate in the 1990s compared with the 1970s:

- the average external trade position of developing countries including the major fuel-exporting countries has worsened throughout the period;
- the group of non-fuel-exporting countries in sub-Saharan Africa has experienced a worsening of both its external position and its growth rate;
- the group of non-fuel developing Asia excluding China raised its growth rate while improving its external position during the 1980s; it is the only region for which the relationship in the first half of the 1990s is not substantially different from that in the 1970s.

Similar movements in the trade account/GDP ratios can be caused by different trends in exports and imports. Export and import value indices give

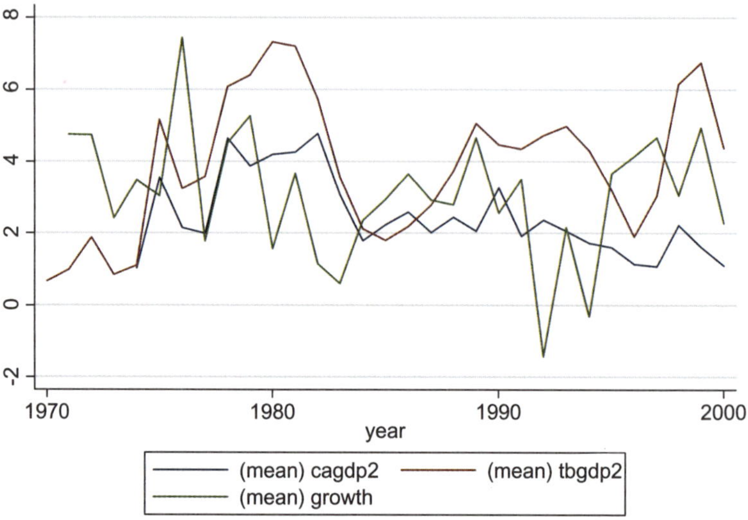

Figure 3a. Relationship between growth rate and trade balance and current account to GDP percentages — Africa (36 countries).
Note: Deficits positive and surplus negative.

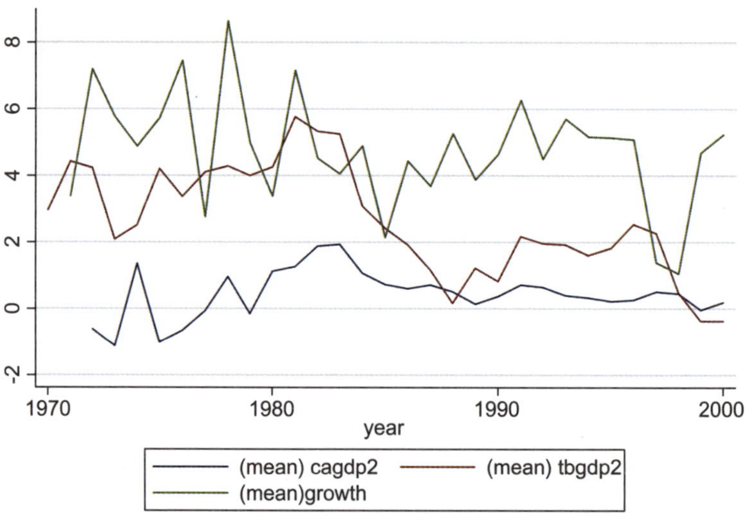

Figure 3b. Relationship between growth rate and trade balance and current account to GDP percentages — Asia (16 countries).
Note: Deficits positive and surplus negative.

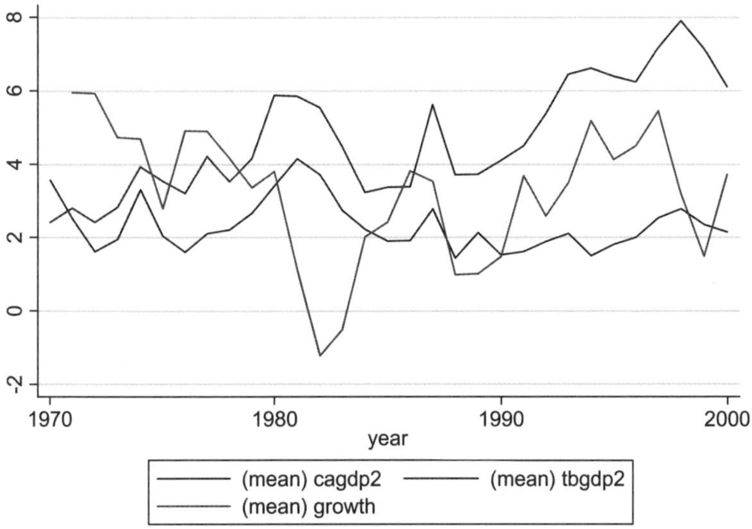

Figure 3c. Relationship between growth rate and deficit — Latin America (23 countries).
Note: Deficits positive and surplus negative.

some indication as to whether an improvement in a trade balance of the country was achieved by an increase in exports, a decrease in imports, or both. Statistical evidence shows that after a continuous increase of both exports and imports in developing countries during the 1970s, their exports stagnated and their imports dropped during the first half of the 1980s (Tables 2A and 2B). By contrast, both imports and exports have risen strongly since 1986. Looking at regional subgroups suggests that the drastic improvement in the trade balance of non-fuel developing America during the 1980s was due to a slight increase in exports but mainly due to a very substantial compression of imports. This contrasts sharply with the experience of non-fuel developing Asia excluding China whose trade balance improved in the 1980s due mainly to a very strong increase in exports. Hence, while import compression is likely to have choked economic growth in developing America, rising imports were associated with rising growth and rising exports in developing Asia. Sub-Saharan Africa is the other developing region that experienced strong import compression during the 1980s and,

Table 2A. Average annual growth rates of import and export values, selected developing country groups, 1970–1996, percentages.

	1970–1979 less 1974–1975		1982–1988		1989–1996	
	Exports	Imports	Exports	Imports	Exports	Imports
Developing countries and territories	22.0	18.6	2.0	2.6	11.7	12.4
Non-fuel developing countries	21.6	17.9	9.0	5.5	12.1	13.4
Non-fuel developing countries excl. China	21.4	17.5	8.8	4.8	11.7	13.5
Non-fuel sub-Saharan Africa	14.0	13.4	3.2	1.0	6.2	6.1
Non-fuel developing America	18.8	15.0	2.9	−1.9	9.7	13.9
Non-fuel developing Asia and Oceania	26.5	21.8	12.9	9.6	13.2	13.9
China	25.7	28.2	12.3	16.4	15.9	12.8

Source: UNCTAD database.

contrary to the situation in developing America, this experience has not improved much over the past few years.[g]

We consider the 1980–1989 decade and compare it with the 1990–1999 decade as far as trade balance and current account deficits are concerned for

[g] The pattern of adjustment regarding the combination between the external trade position and growth has not been uniform across developing countries. As already mentioned, it can be expected that rising (falling) growth is associated with a deteriorating (improving) trade account/GDP ratio. An improving trade account/GDP ratio accompanied by rising growth may be called an unusual and virtuous combination, while falling growth accompanied by a deteriorating trade account/GDP ratio is clearly unsustainable. Given that a good part of the 1980s can be considered as a period of crisis and adjustment and hence as exceptional for developing countries, it appears most appropriate to compare the past few years with the 1970s. Looking at trends in external trade and growth at the level of individual developing countries shows that 34 out of the 84 countries that are included in the analysis have had on average a worse position in both external trade and growth over the past few years compared to the 1970s; 23 countries have had the "normal" but adverse experience of an improving trade position and falling growth; 18 countries had the "normal" and positive experience of rising growth combined with a deteriorating trade position, while only nine developing countries have succeeded in improving both the external trade position and GDP growth (UNCTAD, 1999).

Table 2B. Average annual growth rates of import and export volumes selected developing country groups, 1970–1996, percentages.

	1970–1979 less 1974–1975		1982–1988		1989–1996	
	Exports	Imports	Exports	Imports	Exports	Imports
Developing countries and territories	6.9	5.9	4.7	1.2	8.2	9.3
Sub-Saharan Africa	6.4	7.0	0.8	−6.8	3.6	2.4
Developing America	6.3	3.0	2.8	−4.5	6.7	9.1
South and South-East Asia	15.2	8.5	11.7	9.0	11.4	11.6
Non-fuel developing countries	10.6	4.9	8.6	3.9	11.6	10.0

Source: *UNCTAD Handbook of International Trade and Development Statistics*, various years.

developing countries. There was a strong improvement in external balance of developing countries. While the improvement in the external accounts during the crisis and the adjustment period of the early 1980s were associated mainly with import compression and falling growth, the relationship between external accounts and growth became virtuous and very unusual for the short period between 1983 and 1985 when external accounts improved with rising growth. Then, there was a strong deterioration in the external position between the years 1987–1988 and the mid-1990s with a swing back to a deficit level similar to that of the previous decade. Two features of the post-1987 period stand out. (i) The 1987–1990 period was characterised by increasing external deficits and slowing growth, i.e., a constellation, which is clearly unsustainable in the long run. During this period many developing countries also underwent a regime change in their trade policy in the sense that they dismantled quantitative restrictions and reduced tariffs, and that they maintained this stance in spite of a worsening trade account. In other words, they stopped using trade policy measures for balance of payments purposes. (ii) Even though economic growth in developing countries picked up moderately after 1990, the rates achieved are associated with higher external deficits (to GDP ratios) than in previous periods. This means that over the past decade there was an increase in the external financing requirement associated with any given growth rate. As a matter of fact, the relationship between growth and the external position of the past few years mimics that of the period prior to the economic crisis of the early 1980s.

By contrast, both imports and exports have risen strongly since 1986. Looking at regional subgroups suggests that the drastic improvement in the trade balance of non-fuel developing America during the 1980s as due to a slight increase in exports but mainly due to a very substantial compression of imports. This contrasts sharply with the experience of non-fuel developing Asia excluding China whose trade balance improved in the 1980s due mainly to a very strong increase in exports — contrary to developing America, imports also increased. Hence, while import compression is likely to have choked economic growth in developing America, rising imports were associated with rising growth and rising exports in developing Asia. Sub-Saharan Africa is the other developing region that experienced strong import compression during the 1980s and, contrary to the situation in developing America, this experience has not improved very much over the past few years.

Individual country experience

The external trade position deteriorated in the majority of countries, while the majority of countries experienced rising growth rates between the 1980s and the 1990s. However, 15 out of the 29 countries with a deteriorating external trade position and rising growth between the 1980s and the 1990s are in developing America (Table 3). It is also noteworthy that, between the 1980s and the 1990s, all the developing countries that have been affected most by the recent financial crisis (i.e., Brazil, Indonesia, Korea, Malaysia and Thailand) experienced a worsening in their external trade position and thus an increase in their external financing requirements.

Perhaps, a somewhat surprising feature is that Singapore is the only main exporter of manufactures whose external trade position improved between the 1980s and the 1990s, while that of Hong Kong, Korea, Malaysia, Mexico, Taiwan, Thailand and Turkey worsened. It should not be forgotten, however, that exports with a comparatively high-income elasticity of

Table 3. Trade account to GDP ratio and GDP growth: 1989–1996 compared with 1982–1988.

		Improving trade account				Deteriorating trade account			
		More than 10%	5–10%	2–5%	0–2%	0–2%	2–5%	5–10%	More than 10%
Rising growth	More than 5% growth		*Syria*	*Libya*	*Iran*			Guinea Guyana	Sudan
	3–5%	PNG Singapore	Jordan *Trinidad and Tobago*	*Gabon*		**Argentina**	Bolivia	Guatemala Liberia **Malaysia** Nicaragua **Philippines** Uganda	El Salvador
	1–3%	Benin *Nigeria*	*Saudi Arabia*	Mali	Niger	*Ecuador*	**Chile** Fiji *Indonesia* **Peru** **Thailand**	*Kuwait* **Mexico**	Mauritania Tanzania
	0–1%			*Venezuela*	Bangladesh **Colombia** Sri Lanka Tunisia	Cote d'Ivorie	Dominican Rep. Honduras Jamaica Nepal	Paraguay	
Falling growth	0–1%	Guinea Bissau	*Congo*	CAR **China** Senegal	**India**		Costa Rica Zambia	Malawi	Ghana
	1–3%	Burkina Faso		**Pakistan**	*Algeria* Cyprus Morocco	**Brazil** Kenya **Turkey**	Hong Kong **Korea** Madagascar	Mauritius Zimbabwe	Gambia

(Continued)

Table 3. (*Continued*).

	Improving trade account				Deteriorating trade account			
	More than 10%	5–10%	2–5%	0–2%	0–2%	2–5%	5–10%	More than 10%
3–5%		Chad	Togo		Barbados **Egypt** Haiti	Sierra Leone	**Taiwan**	
More than 5%	Cameroon	*Iraq*			Botswana Democratic Rep. of Congo Rwanda	Burundi		

Notes: 18 big countries in bold (defined as the largest GDP in 1990–1995 and GDP greater than US$ 60 billion in 1997 excluding the major oil-exporting countries, as well as Hong Kong, Singapore). Nine major oil-exporting countries in italics. Nine main exporters of manufactures underlined.
All data from ETS except data on current GDP are from World Development Indicators for Ghana, India, Jamaica, Malaysia, Mauritania, Nigeria, Papua New Guinea, Rwanda, Sierra Leone, Sri Lanka, Thailand, Trinidad and Tobago and Zimbabwe. As no data on current GDP are available for 1996 for Barbados, Bolivia, Gambia, Iran, Iraq, Liberai, Libya, Saudi Arabia and Sudan; the second period comprises only 1989–1995 for these countries.

demand encompasses a much broader spectrum than manufactures. Some countries in the sample have been able to increase exports of agro-industrial goods, such as Chile, where export earnings from fruit and fishery and forestry products have, together, come to rival those from copper, and this has helped them to achieve both increased growth and an improved external position between the 1970s and the 1990s.

World growth and terms of trade

World growth, and in particular growth in developed countries, experienced a marked and secular decline in the early 1970s. But, while developed countries were still growing at an annual average rate of about 3 percent during the 1970s and 1980s, their rate of growth slowed down to an average rate of below 2 percent during the 1990s. One consequence of this has been a decline in the demand for exports from developing countries as many of the export items serve as inputs for production to the manufacturing industries in developed countries. This decline in the demand for their exports has been particularly harmful for developing countries over the past few years when many have adopted an export-led growth strategy. The combination of slow growth in the demand and the attempt by many developing countries to capture the same export markets is likely to lead to a situation of falling terms of trade for developing countries. Falling terms of trade for many developing countries have indeed resulted in a decline in the purchasing power of their exports.

Economies with a relatively specialised export structure are more vulnerable to adverse terms of trade shocks so that the sustainable level of their current account deficit tends to be lower than that of economies with a more diversified export structure. As is well known, many developing countries continue to be heavily dependent on a narrow range of primary commodities for their export earnings. Despite temporary primary commodity price hikes — most recently in the mid-1990s — most developing countries have been subject to a downward trend in their terms of trade over the medium and long term. There is strong statistical evidence suggesting that the decline in commodity prices since the early 1980s has been mostly of a secular and persistent nature and that only a small part is attributable to reversible cyclical forces. Moreover, there is evidence that suggests that the volatility in commodity prices has risen steadily and considerably since the early 1970s (Reinhart and Wickham, 1994). There can be little doubt that both these movements have had detrimental impacts on economic growth and investment in developing countries.

The adverse impact of the recent financial crises in the Asian economies on the demand for primary commodities has added further to the decline in the terms of trade of commodity-exporting countries, and the expectation is that commodity prices will remain depressed well into the 21st century (World Bank, 1998).

An obvious policy conclusion from the above is that developing countries need to strive for diversification with a view to raising the proportion of manufactures in their exports. However, even those developing countries for which manufactures have been the main source of export earnings have not succeeded in obtaining a lasting improvement in their terms of trade; the terms of trade of these countries have fallen on average by somewhat over 1 percent per annum since the beginning of the 1980s.[h] Output expansions of low-technology manufactured goods with no barriers to entry in the world market have resulted in falls of export prices for developing countries.[i]

Trade liberalisation and growth in exports and imports

It is convenient to distinguish the immediate impact of trade liberalisation on the growth rate of imports and exports from its more medium-term impact, because exports usually pick up only after a time lag. Data for 14 countries were obtained to look at the growth in exports and imports immediately

---

[h] UNCTAD (1995, Table 2.5). The group of developing countries classified as major exporters of manufactures includes Brazil, Hong Kong (China), Malaysia, Mexico, the Republic of Korea, Singapore, Taiwan (Province of China), Thailand, Turkey and the former Yugoslavia.

[i] This notion of a "commoditisation" of some manufactured goods refers to the fact that there are few or no barriers to enter the markets of such low-technology manufactures and output expansions induce price falls. A possible explanation of this phenomenon regards the entry of China into global markets as a major exporter of manufactured products after 1985. It has been argued, for example, that this has resulted in an approximately 20 percent decline in the terms of trade of developing countries' manufactured exports between the mid-1980s and the mid-1990s (Wood, 1997).

after liberalisation and few years after liberalisation. Regarding the period immediately following trade liberalisation, imports grew faster than exports in all 10 countries from Latin America as well as in Kenya; the other four African countries show a more balanced development (Table 4). In a medium-term period after trade liberalisation, by contrast, exports and

Table 4. Growth of imports and exports and movements of real exchange rates after trade liberalisation in selected developing countries.

Name of country/region	Year of regime change in trade policy	First two years after regime change in trade policy			Subsequent 10 years[1]		
		Growth[2] of		Real exch. rate[3]	Growth[2] of		Real exch. rate[3]
		Exports	Imports		Exports	Imports	
Latin America							
Argentina	1991	2	65	87	22	13	76
Brazil	1990	2	5	110	8	33	104
Chile	1976	17	31	98	9	4	119
Colombia	1991	2	24	93[4]	14	12	75
Mexico	1986	6	18	93	15	16	64
Asia							
Malaysia	1988	18	32	103[4]	18	18	104[4]
Philippines	1986	15	18	107[4]	15	19	98[4]
Thailand	1986	31	32	98	17	19	86
Turkey	1989	5	15	85	11	18	82
Africa							
Ghana	1985	22	18	141[4]	12	21	247[4]
Kenya	1993	12	21	82	n.a.	n.a.	n.a
Morocco	1984	7	2	157[4]	7	9	119[4]
Tunisia	1989	16	13	103[4]	9	9	100[4]
Uganda	1988	−21	−25	136[4]	35	39	242

Notes:
[1] Subsequent (under10) years until 1996, where the regime change was after 1986.
[2] Annual average growth of value in percent.
[3] Index of average real exchange rate with the dollar unless otherwise indicated (year of regime change =100), and increase in the index indicates depreciation.
[4] Real effective exchange rate.
Source: UNCTAD database, except real effective exchange rates which are from *International Financial Statistics*.

imports grew at about the same speed, except in Brazil, where imports grew very significantly stronger than exports, and Argentina, where exports grew much faster than imports. However, Argentina's imports had grown at a rate of over 60 percent during the period immediately following liberalisation, compared to a 2 percent growth of exports, so that it is not surprising that the rate of import growth slowed down. Looking at the two periods combined, the exports of most of the liberalising countries have not grown fast enough after trade liberalisation to compensate for the rapid growth of imports during the years immediately following trade liberalisation. This evidence suggests that trade liberalisation in developing countries has tended to lead to a deterioration in the trade account.

Trade policies and its impact on economic growth

With regard to the evolution of the level of the real exchange rate, there is a significant difference between the three regions. The currencies of the Latin American countries appreciated after trade liberalisation as they had adopted a policy of exchange rate based stabilisation — as mentioned above, except Chile for which the data mirrors the substantial devaluation in 1982. (Brazil experienced a strong appreciation of its currency in the late 1980s so that the depreciation shown in the data can be considered a slight correction of that development.) The Asian countries maintained a by and large unchanged level of their real exchange rate, except Turkey whose currency appreciated. By contrast, the African countries (except Kenya, which faced strong appreciation, and Tunisia, which maintained the pre-reform level of its real exchange rate) experienced depreciation after trade liberalisation. This phenomenon is marked most in Ghana and Uganda, but these two countries suffered from very strong overvaluation in the pre-reform period. This means that many liberalising countries have not succeeded in engineering a depreciation of the exchange rate in order to soften the need for contractionary demand policies to contain the balance of payments problems after trade liberalisation. This appears to be true in particular for those countries where the discrepancy between the growth rate of imports and that of exports is greatest during the period immediately following trade liberalisation (Argentina, Colombia, Mexico and Turkey), all of which experienced a significant appreciation of their real exchange rate. By contrast, countries, which maintained a relatively stable (and realistic) level of the real exchange, i.e., Malaysia, Philippines, Thailand and Tunisia, experienced a relatively balanced growth of their imports and exports in both periods. In addition to the level of imports, their structure has an important bearing on growth and the potential for future exports. A surge in imports of intermediate production inputs and capital goods, particularly machinery and equipment, is likely to hold very different prospects in the medium term than one dominated by consumer goods. Empirical evidence (UNCTAD, 1999) suggests that the share of capital goods in total imports increased after trade liberalisation in all four Asian developing countries, as well as in Argentina and Brazil, strongly dropped in Kenya and Mexico and remained unchanged in the other four countries. It is also interesting to note that the share of luxury goods in total imports increased in almost all of the 15 countries, and very significantly so in Argentina, Brazil, Colombia, Tunisia and Turkey. This suggests that the structure of trade liberalisation in these countries was less than optimal with regard to stimulating economic growth and exports.

Theoretical Basis of Relationship Between Trade Balance and Economic Growth

There exists extensive literature on the relationship between economic growth and external balance. The literature on two-gap models, three-gap models and World Bank and IMF models all adopt the constraints on balance of payments, savings investment and budget balances. In the two-gap models (Chenery and Bruno, 1962), the first gap relates to the resources needed for investment as external capital flows permit developing countries to invest more than their domestic savings. This alone is sometimes not sufficient to accelerate capital accumulation and economic growth, because the foreign exchange gap becomes dominant. Both investment and growth in developing countries are dependent on imported intermediate and capital goods. It is probable that even if domestic savings are sufficient to finance all the investment, a developing country may not be able to carry out investment projects if the foreign exchange available to run the projects is not adequate. Investment in this instance would be lower than that could be financed by savings generated at full employment. Hence, the production capacity would be underutilised, and incomes and savings would be reduced. Capital inflows can reduce the foreign exchange gap, allowing imports, investment and savings to be raised above the levels constrained by export earnings.[j] Bacha (1990) introduced the third gap, namely fiscal gap, and analysed the consequences of foreign resource transfers on the GDP growth rate of developing countries. The utilisation of excess capacity was not considered in the original two-gap models until Taylor (1991) brought the capacity utilisation explicitly into the analysis of foreign capital requirements for developing countries. In the three-gap models, the constrained growth rate corresponding to each gap can be derived; with respect to foreign exchange gap, one can show how a decline in foreign transfers affects the economies' growth rate in the short and medium run. Basically, the model is static and does not go far enough to analyse the complex process of dynamics of capital accumulation, trade balance and economic growth.

Ranaweera (2003) provides a summary of the three-gap model of the World Bank and a critique of the single constraint model of Thirlwall (1979) and Thirlwall and Hussain (1982). Thirlwall (1979) proposed a balance of payments constrained growth model where the dynamic foreign trade multiplier of Harrod became the law for providing the sustainable growth.[k]

---

[j] Two-gap models treat one gap as being more binding than the other, and this provides a lower limit on growth, given the available capital flow. The Chenery–Strout (1966) model provided an absorptive capacity constraint stating the peak capital inflow a developing country could absorb. Bacha (1984) was the first to mention that the two gaps were identical to the internal and external balances of open economy macroeconomics in a developing country framework. A three-gap model provides a general framework under which the role and significance of domestic private and public sector saving as well as foreign saving can be assessed. Rapid growth in exports, improvement in the trade position and declining external debt levels would make the foreign exchange constraint redundant in some economies, and the model that permits interaction between capacity expansion and capacity utilisation will become more realistic, given the structural constraints and bottlenecks the growth process would generate.

[k] It postulates that the most binding constraint on growth in an open economy is likely to be the balance of payments. It argues that the balance of payments position of a country is the main constraint on economic growth, because it imposes a limit on the demand to which supply can adapt.

According to this law, the growth rate for a developing economy is the rate of growth in real exports divided by the income elasticity of the demand for imports. Earlier versions (1979) did not introduce capital flows until Thirlwall and Hussain (1982) augmented the model with the capital flows. The model was still incomplete as debt service was not included in the derivation of growth or capital requirements. Elliott and Rhodd (1999) incorporated the debt servicing in Thirlwall–Hussain's model. Despite some of these modifications, various criticisms can be levied against the model as it is still not a complete model; it leaves out the savings–investment gap, the fiscal gap and the monetary implication of the balance of payments. The Thirlwall–Hussain model does not show foreign exchange requirements relating to the maintenance of a desired or target level of reserves. However, in the absence of any other model that can be easily implemented to study liberalisation, we cast the basic Thirlwall–Hussain model in behavioural equations and estimate the reduced form to study the impact of liberalisation, terms of trade and oil prices on GDP growth. The basic model of Thirlwall is presented here.

$$m = \varepsilon(p_{\mathrm{f}} - e - p_{\mathrm{d}}) + \pi y, \tag{1}$$

$$x = \beta(p_{\mathrm{d}} + e - p_{\mathrm{f}}) + \sigma w, \tag{2}$$

$$p_{\mathrm{f}} + m = p_{\mathrm{d}} + e + x. \tag{3}$$

In the above equations, m is the rate of growth of real imports, x is the rate of growth of real exports, y is the rate of growth of the real income, w is the rate of growth of the world income, p_{f} is the rate of change in the foreign price of imports, p_{d} is the rate of change in domestic prices and e is the rate of change of exchange rate of foreign currency per unit of domestic currency. The model's parameters are: ε is the price elasticity of demand for imports ($\varepsilon < 0$), β is the price elasticity of demand for exports ($\beta < 0$), π is the income elasticity of demand for exports ($\pi > 0$) and σ is the income elasticity of demand for imports ($\sigma > 0$). The model yields the rate of growth as the sum of two effects: (i) terms of the trade effect and (ii) the effect of growth of the world income.

$$y = \frac{(1 + \beta + \varepsilon)(p_{\mathrm{d}} + e - p_{\mathrm{f}}) + \sigma w}{\pi}. \tag{4}$$

If terms of trade remain unchanged and the current account is balanced,[1] then the balance of payments constrained real income growth is given by

$$y = \frac{\sigma w}{\pi}. \tag{5}$$

As mentioned before, other authors incorporated debt servicing and capital inflows in the above model. Equation (4) or (5) yields the long-run growth constrained by the balance of payments. Krugman (1989) provides a simple rule (45 degree rule) that the relative rates of growth in a domestic economy against a foreign economy are equivalent to the relative income elasticity of exports and imports. The fundamental logic in this rule is that if countries are basically alike, then the prices of their typical traded outputs should be identical, and apparent income elasticities will be such as to make continued price equality possible.

As this study is with a view to examine the impact of trade liberalisation we intend to incorporate liberalisation (LIBER), oil prices (GROIL), long-term debt (GDEBT), debt servicing (DEBTSIMP) and world interest rate (CINTEREST) in their influence on growth. Similarly, we examine the impact of liberalisation, terms of trade and oil prices on economic growth, separately. In the basic equation (4) we introduce liberalisation and the oil-price rise as exogenous variables to study the trade balance over time. Terms of trade do not remain constant over time in reality, so our behavioural equation (6) also has PPI, the terms of trade effect.

$$\begin{aligned} \text{GROWTH}_{it} = {} & \alpha_{0i} + \alpha_{1i}\text{PPI}_{it} + \alpha_{2i}\text{ADVGR}_{it} \\ & + \alpha_{3i}\text{LIBER}_{it} + \alpha_{4i}\text{GROIL}_{it} + \varepsilon_{it}, \\ & i = 1, 2 \ldots, 42(\text{countries}); \\ & t = 1, 2 \ldots, 31(\text{time periods}). \end{aligned} \tag{6}$$

[1] In the short run countries can run balance of payments deficits financed by capital inflows, but they cannot finance ever increasing deficits. Deficits above a certain percentage of GDP trigger signals in the international markets that force the countries to adjust. Likewise, the terms of trade or real exchange rate fluctuate in the short run, but in the long run it appears to remain stable.

The other alternative model which we estimated was the following:

$$\begin{aligned}\text{GROWTH}_{it} = {} & \beta_{0i} + \beta_{1i}\text{PPI}_{it} + \beta_{2i}\text{ADVGR}_{it} + \beta_{3i}\text{LIBER}_{it} \\ & + \beta_{4i}\text{GROIL}_{it} + \beta_{5i}\text{GDEBT}_{it} + \beta_{6i}\text{DEBTSIMP}_{it} \\ & + \beta_{7i}\text{CINTEREST} + \upsilon_{it}, \\ & \quad i = 1, 2 \ldots, 42(\text{countries}); \\ & \quad t = 1, 2 \ldots, 31(\text{time periods}). \end{aligned} \tag{7}$$

In Eq. (7), we consider the determinants of balance of payments, which includes both current and capital account transactions. Long-term debt and service payments on accumulated debt as a proportion to total payments are introduced as separate explanatory variables. Equation (6) uses the explanatory variables that determine trade balance, while Eq. (7) uses the explanatory variables that are approximate determinants of balance of payments. The results of these estimated behavioural equations are discussed in the next section.

Liberalisation and Growth Relationship

Data for this study are from various sources, the main ones being the *International Financial Statistics*, the *Penn World Tables* and Wacziarg's study on liberalisation and growth and the Sachs–Warner measure of liberalisation. Trade balance and current account figures are obtained from the IMF issues, while an openness indicator and a liberalisation dummy for the 1990–1999 period were taken from Wacziarg (2001). Means and standard deviations of GROWTH, TBGDP1 (trade balance to GDP in %), TBGDP2 (defined as deficits in positive %), CAGDP1 (current account to GDP in %) and CAGDP2 (defined as deficits in positive %) for each country are presented in Annex 1. Growth, investment and openness can be stimulated under liberalisation if the appropriate conditions prevail in the economies under consideration.[m] The year of liberalisation and the time

[m] Edwards (1993) considers the openness–growth relationship using existing indicators. Overall, nine indicators were used: (i) The Sachs–Warner index; (ii) the World Bank Integration index; (iii) the Edward Leamer Openness index; (iv) the average black market premium; (v) the average tariff rate as developed by Barro and Lee; (1994); (vi) the average coverage of non-tariff barriers (Barro and Lee); (vii) the Heritage Foundation index of distortions; (viii) the ratio of total revenues on trade taxes to total trade and (ix) the regression index of

period elapsed from liberalisation are used as two separate variables affecting investment, growth and openness. The openness indicator is the ratio of imports plus exports to GDP, while investment rate is in percentage and growth rate in total real GDP at PPP rates in dollar terms for the countries under consideration. The openness indicator does not have impact of tariff reductions excepting that some of these are reflected in exports and imports.

Panel Study: Liberalisation, Growth and Trade Balance Relationships

Both fixed and random effect models were estimated using a binary liberalisation indicator, defined by the dates of liberalisation and the time period elapsed from liberalisation. Timing effect[n] (Table 5) of liberalisation (LIBERTM) is significant as in the 1970–1979 period, trade balance to GDP deteriorated in the first period, improved in the second period and the impact was not significant in the last period.

Table 6 presents regionwise relationships for the entire period 1970–2000. In most cases, our choice based on the Hausman test rejects the random effect model. Liberalisation promotes growth, openness and investment in Asian countries. Trade balance tends to deteriorate with economic growth in Asian economies, while there is no such evidence for either Latin American or African economies. For Latin American economies, the direct impact of liberalisation is to increase the trade deficits, while for African economies liberalisation has improved trade balance in a bivariate relationship. There is a mixed bag of results at a regional level as the data and

---

Holger Wolf on import distortions. His conclusion on various measures was that "inspite of significant efforts and ingenuity, there has not been too much progress in this area". There existed a positive relationship between trade intensity and growth performance on the basis of the cross-country plot of average annual growth rate against the average annual growth rate in trade.

[n] Timing effect was introduced by looking at the number of years before and after liberalisation. If the country was liberalised in 1976, it gets the value of 1 for that year, and it rises to 24 in year 2000, while for 1975, the year before liberalisation is given the value of −1. Different countries were liberalised at different times, so the variable time elapsed from liberalisation and time period prior to liberalisation (negative number of years) capture the timing effect. We could define dummy variables for different decades for liberalisation, but this was not considered important.

number of observations differ. For the earlier period, there were not many observations on trade balance for a large number of African economies, and this could have led to the conclusion that there is no significant relationship between liberalisation and growth. The between country regression indicates that the liberalisation contributes positively to growth in African

Table 5. Multivariate relationship between trade balance, GDP growth, timing of liberalisation and liberalisation year using panel data.

	Region	Time period	Model	Constant	LIBER	LIBERTM
GROWTH	Developing countries	1970–1979	FE	2.34 (1.60)	8.68*** (2.23)	−0.08 (−0.83)
	Developing countries	1980–1989	FE	2.54*** (4.30)	0.96 (0.82)	0.02 (0.27)
	Developing countries	1990–1999	FE	1.71** (2.46)	2.69*** (3.00)	−0.06 (−0.77)
OPENK	Developing countries	1970–1979	FE	51.13*** (12.45)	11.38 (0.98)	−0.89*** (−3.42)
	Developing countries	1980–1989	FE	57.19*** (48.20)	−0.68 (−0.29)	−0.74*** (−3.80)
	Developing countries	1990–1999	FE	58.97*** (35.06)	−3.76* (−1.74)	1.50 (7.59)
KI	Developing countries	1970–1979	FE	14.77*** (15.69)	−2.55*** (−0.96)	0.33 (0.55)
	Developing countries	1980–1989	FE	10.63*** (35.54)	2.74*** (4.60)	−0.40*** (−8.28)
	Developing countries	1990–1999	FE	11.22*** (26.10)	2.47*** (4.47)	−0.06 (−1.17)
TBGDP1	Developing countries	1970–1979	FE	−5.82*** (−7.30)	1.01 (0.49)	0.19*** (3.74)
	Developing countries	1980–1989	FE	−1.33*** (−3.80)	−1.99*** (−2.77)	−0.43*** (−7.39)
	Developing countries	1990–1999	FE	−2.71*** (−6.53)	−0.61 (−1.24)	0.05 (1.15)
CAGDP1	Developing countries	1970–1979	FE	−3.44*** (−3.55)	0.71 (0.31)	0.12 (1.45)
	Developing countries	1980–1989	FE	−0.74* (−3.33)	−1.65*** (−3.61)	−0.35*** (−9.49)
	Developing countries	1990–1999	FE	−2.40*** (−7.24)	1.23*** (2.95)	0.01 (0.25)

(Continued)

Table 5. (*Continued*).

	Region	Time period	Model	Constant variable	Growth	LIBER	LIBERTM
CAGDP1	Developing countries	1970–1979	FE	−3.99*** (−3.88)	−0.05* (−1.70)	2.05 (0.86)	−0.16** (−1.95)
	Developing countries	1980–1989	FE	−0.81*** (−3.57)	0.03 (1.57)	−1.69*** (−3.69)	0.35*** (9.51)
	Developing countries	1990–1999	FE	−2.46*** (−7.35)	0.028 (1.29)	1.16*** (2.76)	−0.01 (−0.18)
TBGDP1	Developing countries	1970–1979	FE	−5.63*** (−6.45)	−0.04 (−1.28)	1.78 (0.84)	−0.18*** (−3.00)
	Developing countries	1980–1989	FE	−1.25*** (−3.50)	−0.30 (−1.12)	−1.96*** (−2.72)	0.43*** (7.38)
	Developing countries	1990–1999	FE	−2.56*** (−6.18)	−0.07*** (−2.90)	−0.32 (−0.64)	−0.06 (−1.57)

Note: ***Significant at 1 percent; **significant at 5 percent; *significant at 10 percent.

economies. On the other hand, investment responds negatively to liberalisation.[o]

Now, the relationship between growth and liberalisation at a country level is examined first. For the 1970–2000 period, growth with the liberalisation variable, trade balance to GDP (TBGDP1) and current account to GDP (CAGDP1) with the liberalisation variable is related to examine the extent to which liberalisation alone explains each of these macro-variables at a country level. Both TBGDP1 and CAGDP1 are no longer deficits but *recorded* trade balance and current account balances to GDP. Only significant results on the liberalisation coefficient are presented in Table 7. For five countries, liberalisation has a positive and significant effect on growth. For 12 countries, trade balance worsens with liberalisation. Impact varies from the 0.23 point decline for Brazil in the trade balance to GDP to the 7.18 point decline for Nicaragua. For three countries, the impact of liberalisation on current account to GDP percentages is negative and significant. The investment to GDP ratio rises with liberalisation in about 10 countries, and the impact varies from the 1.74 point increase to the 6.05 point increase in the investment to GDP percentage. Openness and liberalisation are highly interrelated, and hence it is found that the impact of

[o] This kind of contradiction is bound to be observed when the role of other variables is not allowed in a simple bivariate relationship. The omitted variable tends to exaggerate the impact of the included variable if the omitted variable is positively correlated with the liberalisation variable.

Table 6. Regionwise relationships between growth and liberalisation and other variables using panel data.

Region	Dependant	Time period	Number of observations	Model	Constant	Liberalisation dummy	Growth	Hausmann test χ^2
Africa	GROWTH	1970–2000	774	FE	3.22***	0.27		14.42
					(10.47)	(0.48)		
			26	BE	1.33**	5.84***		
					(2.36)	(4.13)		
	TBGDP1	1970–2000	487	FE	−3.78***	1.09**		0.76
					(−19.38)	(2.54)		
			26	BE	−3.22**	−2.00		
					(−2.36)	(−0.57)		
	CAGDP1	1970–2000	580	RE	−3.24***	1.71***		0.42
					(−6.71)	(5.28)		
			26	BE	−2.81***	0.57		
					(−3.53)	(0.34)		
	OPENK	1970–2000	801	FE	71.12***	−9.52***		n/a
					(69.15)	(−4.93)		
			26	BE	48.02	61.10		
					(5.09)***	(2.52)		
	KI	1970–2000	801	FE	10.61***	−1.99***		14.95
					(46.97)	(−4.70)		
			26	BE	6.87***	9.36*		
					(3.33)	(1.77)		
	TBGDP1	1970–2000	603	FE	−3.91***		0.01	1.65
					(−23.96)		(0.69)	
			36	BE	−2.34		−0.43	
					(−1.39)		(−1.09)	

(*Continued*)

Table 6. (*Continued*).

Region	Dependant	Time period	Number of observations	Model	Constant	Liberalisation dummy	Growth	Hausmann test χ^2
	CAGDP1	1970–2000	771	RE	−2.68***		0.03	0.05
					(−6.85)		(1.73)	
			35	BE	−2.82***		0.07	
					(−3.96)		(0.36)	
Asia	GROWTH	1970–2000	390	RE	4.41***	0.85		3.39
					(9.52)	(1.55)		
			13	BE	3.67***	2.06**		
					(5.94)	(2.41)		
	TBGDP1	1970–2000	391	RE	−2.30**	−0.44		0.25
					(−2.10)	(−0.65)		
			13	BE	−0.50	−3.35		
					(−0.13)	(−0.60)		
	CAGDP1	1970–2000	328	RE	−0.38	−0.06		0.00
					(−1.60)	(−0.23)		
			13	BE	−0.37	−0.07		
					(−1.00)	(−0.13)		
	OPENK	1970–2000	328	RE	40.08***	23.25***		0.01
					(4.97)	(8.00)		
			13	BE	41.43***	21.05		
					(2.72)	(0.99)		

(*Continued*)

Table 6. (*Continued*).

Region	Dependant	Time period	Number of observations	Model	Constant	Liberalisation dummy	Growth	Hausmann test χ^2
	KI	1970–2000	403	FE	15.13***	2.17***		4.24
					(33.79)	(3.33)		
			13	BE	10.07***	10.44**		
					(3.02)	(2.24)		
	TBGDP1	1970–2000	459	RE	−2.17		−0.13***	0.15
					(−1.28)		(−3.16)	
			16	BE	1.04		−0.79	
					(0.18)		(−0.68)	
	CAGDP1	1970–2000	396	FE	−0.56***		0.01	1.10
					(−4.38)		(0.03)	
			16	BE	−1.10**		0.12	
					(−2.12)		(1.11)	
L.A	GROWTH	1970–2000	599	RE	2.87***	0.43		0.25
					(8.33)	(1.04)		
			20	BE	2.52***	1.21		
					(3.32)	(0.76)		
	TBGDP1	1970–2000	538	RE	−2.51**	−2.09***		0.01
					(−2.46)	(−8.46)		
			20	BE	−2.80	−1.36		
					(−1.30)	(−0.29)		

(*Continued*)

Table 6. (*Continued*).

Region	Dependant	Time period	Number of observations	Model	Constant	Liberalisation dummy	Growth	Hausmann test χ^2
	CAGDP1	1970–2000	500	RE	−2.40***	0.45**		0.20
					(−4.73)	(2.34)		
			20	BE	−3.09**	1.80		
					(−2.25)	(0.71)		
	OPENK	1970–2000	618	FE	58.23***	12.47***		0.62
					(47.73)	(6.43)		
			20	BE	35.31	66.31		
					(1.26)	(1.11)		
	KI	1970–2000	619	FE	14.43***	0.14		0.65
					(58.26)	(0.36)		
			20	BE	16.18***	−3.91		
					(7.17)	(−0.81)		
	TBGDP1	1970–2000	568	RE	−4.97***		−0.06**	0.14
					(−3.18)		(−2.44)	
			23	BE	−2.70		−0.75	
					(−0.70)		(−0.70)	
	CAGDP1	1970–2000	571	FE	−2.26***		−0.02	16.98
					(−17.99)		(−0.76)	
			23	BE	−4.03***		0.55*	
					(−4.22)		(1.86)	

Note: ***Significant at 1 percent; **significant at 5 percent; *significant at 10 percent.

Table 7. Bivariate relationship between growth, TBGDP1, CAGDP1, investment and openness with liberalisation at a country level, 1970–1999.

Country	Time period	Dependant	Number of observations	Constant	LIBER	Adj R-squared
Argentina	1970–2000	GROWTH	30	0.28 (0.22)	5.23 (2.33)	0.1325
Chile	1970–2000	GROWTH	30	−1.08 (−0.42)	6.09 (2.17)	0.1130
Dominican Republic	1970-2000	GROWTH	30	4.45 (7.29)	2.90 (2.60)	0.1659
India	1970–2000	GROWTH	30	4.34 (7.44)	2.19 (1.81)	0.0729
Madagascar	1970–2000	GROWTH	30	0.88 (1.95)	2.61 (2.35)	0.1353
Argentina	1970–2000	TBGDP1	31	−0.99 (−3.83)	−1.44 (−3.17)	0.2323
Bolivia	1970–2000	TBGDP1	19	0.85 (1.37)	−2.48 (−3.17)	0.3342
Brazil	1970–2000	TBGDP1	17	0.22 (8.32)	−0.23 (−6.76)	0.7364
Dominican Republic	1970-2000	TBGDP1	30	−3.99 (−9.06)	−5.62 (−6.59)	0.5942
Gambia	1970–2000	TBGDP1	29	−7.77 (−6.28)	−5.50 (−3.09)	0.2337
Guatemala	1970–2000	TBGDP1	29	−0.88 (−2.53)	−1.99 (−3.99)	0.3475
Honduras	1970–2000	TBGDP1	20	−2.05 (−3.68)	−5.57 (−5.00)	0.5580
Jamaica	1970–2000	TBGDP1	30	−9.19 (−9.10)	−5.63 (−3.38)	0.2641
Nicaragua	1970–2000	TBGDP1	23	−2.57 (−2.99)	−7.18 (−4.92)	0.5137
Peru	1970–2000	TBGDP1	31	0.37 (1.12)	−2.72 (−4.72)	0.4149
El Salvador	1970–2000	TBGDP1	27	−0.81 (−2.58)	−6.09 (−11.71)	0.8397
Uruguay	1970–2000	TBGDP1	31	−0.47 (−1.18)	−1.71 (−2.54)	0.1535
Columbia	1970–2000	CAGDP1	31	0.58 (1.53)	−1.20 (2.23)	0.1167
Nicaragua	1970–2000	CAGDP1	24	−6.03 (−7.14)	−2.15 (−1.64)	0.0686

(*Continued*)

Table 7. (*Continued*).

Country	Time period	Dependant	Number of observations	Constant	LIBER	Adj R-squared
Uganda	1970–2000	CAGDP1	20	−0.67	−1.39	0.3670
				(−2.15)	(−3.47)	
Chile	1970–2000	KI	31	11.51	4.50	0.0854
				(5.56)	(1.95)	
Costa Rica	1970–2000	KI	31	13.99	2.30	0.2183
				(26.78)	(3.06)	
Gambia	1970–2000	KI	31	4.99	2.81	0.2404
				(8.03)	(3.24)	
Honduras	1970–2000	KI	31	10.76	6.05	0.5301
				(18.49)	(5.90)	
India	1970–2000	KI	31	11.39	1.60	0.4662
				(77.98)	(5.21)	
Peru	1970–2000	KI	31	15.94	3.37	0.1622
				(21.74)	(2.61)	
El Salvador	1970–2000	KI	31	6.46	1.99	0.2945
				(19.15)	(3.68)	
Uganda	1970–2000	KI	31	1.54	1.74	0.6766
				(10.90)	(7.99)	
Argentina	1970–2000	OPENK	31	10.17	10.64	0.7934
				(18.14)	(10.78)	
Bolivia	1970–2000	OPENK	30	34.45	8.16	0.2502
				(18.88)	(3.27)	
Chile	1970–2000	OPENK	31	26.74	18.04	0.3638
				(7.03)	(4.26)	
Central African Rep.	1970–2000	OPENK	31	72.08	9.77	0.1902
				(44.05)	(2.84)	
Cameroon	1970–2000	OPENK	31	41.92	5.46	0.0897
				(30.04)	(1.99)	
Costa Rica	1970–2000	OPENK	31	47.56	33.24	0.5518
				(12.67)	(6.16)	
India	1970–2000	OPENK	31	16.77	7.53	0.7642
				(46.43)	(9.91)	
Jamaica	1970–2000	OPENK	31	86.40	26.39	0.6649
				(40.94)	(7.78)	
Sri Lanka	1970–2000	OPENK	31	63.99	20.36	0.5643
				(34.92)	(6.31)	
Mexico	1970–2000	OPENK	31	23.19	27.08	0.4647
				(6.40)	(5.20)	

(*Continued*)

Table 7. (*Continued*).

Country	Time period	Dependant	Number of observations	Constant	LIBER	Adj R-squared
Nicaragua	1970–2000	OPENK	31	58.01	50.38	0.5202
				(11.74)	(5.79)	
Peru	1970–2000	OPENK	31	22.51	4.59	0.4119
				(40.55)	(4.69)	
Philippines	1970–2000	OPENK	31	39.46	32.50	0.7349
				(17.20)	(9.18)	
Paraguay	1970–2000	OPENK	31	38.45	43.36	0.7610
				(14.00)	(9.82)	
El Salvador	1970–2000	OPENK	31	37.37	15.38	0.3904
				(17.56)	(4.50)	
Tunisia	1970–2000	OPENK	31	81.48	9.34	0.2735
				(49.16)	(3.51)	
Uganda	1970–2000	OPENK	31	14.65	17.29	0.4159
				(6.19)	(4.73)	
Uruguay	1970–2000	OPENK	31	23.23	16.31	0.7817
				(24.89)	(10.41)	

Note: All regression coefficients with respect to the liberalisation variable are significant.

liberalisation in opening trade is large and highly significant for 18 countries.

Next, the hypothesis whether growth was determined by changes in terms of trade, real exchange rate changes, percentage change in oil prices and liberalisation was tested. Using Eq. (6), the hypothesis was tested whether the above determinants of growth are significant at a country level. In most of the cases, individual coefficients of changes in terms of trade, advanced countries' growth rate and percentage change in oil prices were insignificant. The liberalisation variable was significant and positive in a few cases. Similarly, the hypothesis was tested whether growth was determined by the determinants of current account, and no strong evidence was found in favour of long-term debt and/or debt service ratio or interest rate influencing the growth rate for majority of countries.[p]

Some of these results at individual country levels do not support the hypothesis suggested by gap models or the balance of payments constrained

[p] These results can be obtained from the authors.

growth model. It is found that trade liberalisation is sometimes associated with worsening of trade balance, which is consistent with the foreign exchange gap model. However, for some countries and overall, trade liberalisation promotes growth, and growth is not constrained by balance of payments. This can be explained by the recent developments in international capital markets, which facilitate the financing of the savings investment gap much more easily than 30 or 40 years ago. Foreign direct investment movement has become much larger to countries that have appropriate infrastructure and necessary political institutions. Since FDI flows to new emerging market economies have increased drastically, foreign exchange gaps are less constraining than in the earlier era of 1960s.

Effect of Trade Liberalisation and Growth on Trade Balance and Current Account

The effect of trade liberalisation on the trade balance and current account of the balance of payments is ambiguous irrespective of the framework used for the analysis of the balance of payments. The impact of liberalisation on trade performance is measured using monetary units because it is the nominal gap which measures a country's shortage of foreign exchange and by how much a country requires to borrow to sustain growth in case liberalisation worsens the payments on current account. Relative prices are introduced by making use of terms of trade variables. We do not have data on nominal (barter) terms of trade, and hence we have to use the income terms of trade meaning thereby the index of purchasing power of exports. An income variable is introduced as growth in real income in Purchasing Power Parity terms. Liberalisation improves growth performance as our results demonstrate in the previous section. We also use the interaction dummy between liberalisation and growth, which takes the value of 1 for post-liberalisation growth and 0 otherwise. If the sign of this variable is negative, then it has raised the growth rate, which in turn has raised import growth and worsened the trade balance/balance of payments. The coefficient on the shift dummy variable (LIBER) should be regarded as pure liberalisation effect on trade balance, independent of liberalisation working through its impact on growth performance. Liberalisation could interact with PPI (LIBPPI) meaning thereby that liberalisation increases imports in the short run and could affect import prices more than export prices, leading to adverse terms of trade. A negative coefficient with LIBPPI would mean that liberalisation leads to probably worsened terms of trade, contributing to a fall in trade balance if the sign of LIBPPI is negative. We also have to consider different sizes of nations, and this is done by using the trade balance to GDP (TBGDP) ratios in percentage terms. The following equations are estimated using panel data.

$$\begin{aligned}\left(\frac{\text{TB}}{\text{GDP}}\right)_{it} &= \delta_1 + \delta_2(\text{ADVGR})_{it} + \delta_3(\text{GROWTH})_{it} + \delta_4(\text{PPI})_{it} \\ &\quad + \delta_5(\text{LIBER})_{it} + \delta_6(\text{LIBGROWTH})_{it} + \delta_7(\text{LIBPPI})_{it} \\ &\quad + \delta_8(\text{LIBADVGR})_{it} + \varepsilon_{it}, \\ &\qquad i = 1, 2 \ldots, 42 \quad \text{and} \quad t = 1, 2, \ldots, 31 \end{aligned} \tag{8}$$

and

$$\begin{aligned}\left(\frac{\text{CA}}{\text{GDP}}\right)_{it} &= \varphi_1 + \varphi_2(\text{ADVGR})_{it} + \varphi_3(\text{GROWTH})_{it} + \varphi_4(\text{PPI})_{\text{it}} \\ &\quad + \varphi_5(\text{LIBER})_{it} + \varphi_6(\text{LIBGROWTH})_{it} \\ &\quad + \varphi_7(\text{LIBPPI})_{it} + \varphi_8(\text{LIBADVGR})_{it} + \varphi_9(\text{DEBT})_{it} \\ &\quad + \varphi_{10}\left(\frac{\text{DEBT}}{\text{GDP}}\right)_{it} + \varphi_{11}(\text{CINTEREST})_{it} + \zeta_{it}, \\ &\qquad i = 1, 2 \ldots, 42 \quad \text{and} \quad t = 1, 2, \ldots, 31. \end{aligned} \tag{9}$$

The above two equations are similar to Eqs. (6) and (7) as (6) uses the determinants of trade balance while (7) uses the determinants of current account balance as mentioned before. In Table 8A, we provide the results based on multiple linear regression whether there exists any relationship of trade balance with liberalisation and growth. Only significant relationships are presented in Table 8A. Trade balance deteriorates with liberalisation in a few countries if the country has experienced liberalisation during the 1970–2000 period, while for other countries, such as Chile, Costa Rica, India, Kenya, Mauritius, El Salvador and Uganda, the relationship is positive. For many other countries, the relationship is significantly negative. When we examine slope coefficient with respect to domestic growth, the relationship is negative for many countries, although on a country-by-country basis the

Table 8A. Relationship of TBGDP1 with liberalisation and domestic growth country-level study: 1970–1999.

Country	Constant	LIBER	Growth	Adj R-squared
Argentina	1.05	−1.12	−0.07	0.3103
	(4.12)	(−2.31)	(−1.92)	
Bangladesh	−.033	—	0.05	0.1678
	(−2.89)	—	(2.50)	
Bolivia	0.79	−1.86	−0.27	0.4389
	(1.38)	(−2.38)	(−2.04)	
Brazil	0.17	−0.23	0.01	0.8382
	(7.14)	(−8.44)	(3.23)	
Barbados	−13.67	—	0.19	0.0999
	(−23.06)	—	(2.05)	
Chile	−2.76	2.56	−0.09	0.0655
	(−2.50)	(1.97)	(−1.11)	
Cote D'Ivore	4.01	—	−0.28	0.1315
	(4.20)	—	(−1.77)	
Cameroon	−1.70	—	−0.003	0.0621
	(−4.38)	—	(−0.08)	
Columbia	−1.62	0.86	0.21	0.1281
	(−2.97)	(1.92)	(1.98)	
Costa Rica	−3.77	1.41	−0.10	0.0627
	(−5.64)	(1.81)	(−0.94)	
Dominican	−5.53	−6.45	0.32	0.6604
Republic	(−7.93)	(−7.48)	(2.54)	
Egypt	−5.31	1.58	−0.12	−0.0142
	(−5.19)	(0.99)	(−0.76)	
Gambia	−8.17	−5.04	−0.02	0.1747
	(−4.59)	(−2.64)	(−0.09)	
Guatemala	−0.84	−1.93	−0.03	0.3013
	(−1.54)	(−3.69)	(−0.27)	
Honduras	−3.16	−5.04	0.23	0.6291
	(−4.00)	(−4.60)	(2.04)	
India	−0.31	0.33	−0.04	0.1413
	(−2.65)	(2.23)	(−1.99)	
Jamaica	−9.03	−5.79	−0.004	0.2462
	(−8.29)	(−3.34)	(−0.02)	
Jordan	−21.09	—	−0.74	0.1160
	(−6.33)	—	(−2.13)	
Kenya	−4.06	1.51	−0.06	0.1564
	(−7.80)	(2.06)	(−0.94)	

(*Continued*)

Table 8A. (*Continued*).

Country	Constant	LIBER	Growth	Adj R-squared
Mauritius	−4.56	1.51	0.005	0.1288
	(−8.59)	(2.50)	(0.09)	
Madagascar	−1.72	−0.77	0.06	−0.0693
	(−6.41)	(−0.78)	(0.54)	
Mexico	1.21	−1.21	−0.32	0.3794
	(2.41)	(−2.36)	(−4.33)	
Malaysia	4.60	—	−0.22	0.0046
	(3.10)	—	(−1.06)	
Nicaragua	−2.41	−7.04	−0.19	0.5628
	(−2.81)	(−5.01)	(−1.96)	
Pakistan	−1.23	—	−0.14	0.0402
	(−2.16)	—	(−1.47)	
Peru	0.32	−2.51	−0.04	0.4000
	(0.94)	(−4.23)	(−0.82)	
Philippines	−1.61	−0.88	−0.06	−0.0006
	(−2.80)	(−1.27)	(−0.59)	
Paraguay	−2.75	−1.01	0.15	0.0940
	(−4.18)	(−1.23)	(1.56)	
Sierra Leone	−0.87	−5.97	−0.01	0.8310
	(−2.59)	(10.58)	(−0.23)	
El Salvador	0.87	5.97	0.014	0.8310
	(2.59)	(10.58)	(0.23)	
Thailand	−0.62	—	−0.22	0.2887
	(−1.32)		(−3.57)	
Tunesia	−6.10	0.89	0.13	0.0352
	(−8.75)	(1.40)	(1.26)	
Uganda	−5.93	4.91	−0.33	0.6137
	(−8.35)	(5.19)	(−2.31)	
Uruguay	−0.36	−1.51	−0.09	0.1786
	(−0.87)	(−2.20)	(−1.46)	

Note: Choice of results is based on at least one of the coefficients being significant at the 5% level.

relationship is not strong as many negative slope coefficients with respect to growth are not statistically significantly different from zero.

In Table 8B, we examine the relationship between current account to GDP percentages and liberalisation and domestic economic growth. There were only 10 countries for which one of the variables namely liberalisation or growth had a significant coefficient. For Colombia, the relationship

Table 8B. Relationship of CAGDP1 with liberalisation and domestic growth country-level study: 1970–1999.

Country	Constant	LIBER	Growth	Adj. R-squared
Cote D'Ivore	−5.63	4.38	0.25	0.3790
	(−8.08)	(3.49)	(2.13)	
Columbia	2.12	−1.67	−0.32	0.2975
	(3.31)	(−3.29)	(−2.62)	
Costa Rica	−5.28	2.91	−0.05	0.3728
	(−8.70)	(3.86)	(−0.50)	
Dominican	−1.90	1.72	−0.10	0.1386
Republic	(−3.39)	(2.57)	(−0.96)	
Gambia	−8.42	8.34	0.37	0.3384
	(−3.26)	(3.33)	(1.03)	
Honduras	−4.38	1.43	0.05	0.1889
	(−11.76)	(2.82)	(0.84)	
Jamaica	−4.36	1.94	0.15	0.0652
	(−5.46)	(1.71)	(0.83)	
Paraguay	−3.48	2.95	0.10	0.6314
	(−8.60)	(6.69)	(2.04)	
Tunisia	−2.36	1.56	−0.03	0.2657
	(−4.00)	(3.22)	(−0.26)	
Uganda	−0.75	−1.39	0.012	0.3394
	(−2.10)	(−3.39)	(0.50)	

Note: Choice of results is based on at least one of the coefficients being significant at the 5% level.

was positive. Liberalisation improved the CAGDP for 8 of 10 countries, and it was only Uganda and Colombia that the CAGDP worsened due to liberalisation.

Tables 9A and 9B record the results of growth equations using country-level data. We find that growth is significantly related to annual change in terms of trade and liberalisation as the goodness-of-fit statistic is very high. However, due to multicollinearity, individual coefficients are not significant. For Bolivia, liberalisation is significant. Liberalisation indeed plays a positive role in improving the country's growth rate for Argentina, Bolivia and Chile.

In Table 9B, we regress growth on terms of trade changes, liberalisation, debt service to exports and annual change in interest rate as these

Table 9A. Growth related to GRPPI, LIBER, LIBGRPPI.

Country	Constant	GRPPI	LIBER	LIBGRPPI	Adj. R-squared
Argentina	−0.69	−0.01	2.16	−0.01	0.7953
	(−0.88)	(−0.29)	(1.25)	(−0.10)	
Bolivia	−1.16	0.16	2.76	−0.08	0.4498
	(−1.20)	(0.86)	(2.07)	(−0.44)	
Chile	−14.32	−0.16	19.55	0.17	0.5446
	(−2.31)	(−1.26)	(3.17)	(1.33)	

Note: Choice of results is based on R-squared being significant at the 5% level.

Table 9B. Growth related to GRPPI, LIBER, DEBTSR, CINTEREST.

Country	Constant	GRPPI	LIBER	DEBTSR	CINTEREST	Adj. R-squared
Argentina	0.09	0.01	2.35	−3.62	−0.01	0.7657
	(0.03)	(0.12)	(1.24)	(−0.42)	(−0.59)	
Chile	9.38	0.01	—	−3.77	−0.006	0.5770
	(2.87)	(0.65)		(−0.24)	(−0.32)	
Columbia	0.27	0.08	1.42	12.16	−0.01	−0.4273
	(0.09)	(0.94)	(0.53)	(1.05)	(−0.64)	
Costa Rica	10.26	0.34	−0.82	−20.45	−0.006	0.4749
	(2.35)	(2.29)	(−0.40)	(−1.61)	(−0.31)	
India	5.45	0.03	3.69	−7.47	0.002	0.5437
	(2.53)	(0.87)	(3.21)	(−0.68)	(0.26)	
Mexico	6.94	0.16	−2.88	−20.16	−0.02	0.5514
	(2.12)	(2.50)	(−1.32)	(−1.53)	(−1.33)	
Thailand	10.01	0.06	—	−38.87	0.01	0.4657
	(2.89)	(3.72)		(−2.12)	(0.60)	
Uganda	5.20	−0.27	−11.17	39.46	0.02	0.6051
	(1.03)	(−1.82)	(−3.38)	(1.08)	(0.63)	

Note: Choice of results is based on R-squared being significant at the 5% level.

are determinants of current account balance. Liberalisation plays a positive role in the Indian economy, while for Uganda, liberalisation reduces growth. Higher debt service payments reduce economic growth and higher world interest rates reduce growth.

Table 10 shows the results of regional analysis, where the developing countries of Africa, Asia and Latin America are separately considered. Both fixed and random effect models are estimated. Our choice is for fixed effect

Table 10. Determinants of trade balance and current account balance on panel data (all countries).

Dependent variable/ model	Constant	Growth	GRPPI	LIBER	ADVGROWTH	LIBGROWTH	LIBGR PPI	DEBTSR	GLTDOL	CINTEREST	R-square/No. of observations
TBGDP1/	−2.7393***	−0.0748**	0.0308***	−1.1699***	0.0293	−0.0352	−0.0223***				0.0626/
FIXED	(−14.80)	(−2.75)	(4.47)	(−3.72)	(1.37)	(0.76)	(−2.82)				985
TBGDP1/	−2.7443***	−0.0677**	0.0140***	−1.2001***	0.0299	−0.0463					0.0546/
FIXED	(−14.84)	(−2.49)	(4.03)	(−3.80)	(1.39)	(−1.00)					985
TBGDP1/	−2.6988***	−0.0871***	0.0311***	−1.2918***	0.0294		−0.0228***				0.0620/
FIXED	(−15.00)	(−3.96)	(4.53)	(−4.77)	(1.37)		(−2.90)				985
CAGDP1/	−2.4038***	−0.0050	0.0017**	0.5334***	0.0246**			2.3891***	−0.0088**	0.00013	0.0524/
FIXED	(−10.41)	(−0.39)	(2.14)	(3.20)	(2.04)			(2.63)	(−2.42)	(0.09)	916
Africa											
TBGDP1/	−4.0064***	−0.2558	0.0469***		0.0561*	0.1184*	−0.0352***				0.1528/
FIXED	(−18.54)	(−0.91)	(6.03)		(1.85)	(1.74)	(−3.26)				295
CAGDP1/	−3.5147***	0.0293	0.0203***	1.2950***				5.6057***		0.0021	0.1428/
FIXED	(−10.29)	(1.24)	(3.76)	(3.99)				(2.90)		(0.65)	295
CAGDP1/	−3.9137***	0.0281	0.0042	1.2042***				6.3799***	−0.0105*	0.0023	0.1173/
FIXED	(−7.47)	(1.17)	(1.28)	(3.53)				(3.22)	(−1.93)	(0.70)	295
Asia											
TBGDP1/	−1.6984*	−0.3302***	0.0088	−0.4468							0.0759/
FIXED	(−1.95)	(−4.37)	(1.17)	(−0.40)							255
Latin America											
TBGDP1/	−1.9509***	−0.1025***	0.0252***	−2.6912***		0.1829***	−0.0163*				0.1861/
FIXED	(−10.94)	(−3.30)	(2.98)	(−8.72)		(3.38)	(−1.68)				435
TBGDP1/	−1.9623***	−0.0921***	0.0129***	−2.6933***		0.1668***					0.1805/
FIXED	(−10.99)	(−3.02)	(3.04)	(−8.71)		(3.12)					435

Note: ***Significant at 1 percent; **significant at 5 percent; *significant at 10 percent.

models, and these results for all countries for which data are available indicate that liberalisation has a strong negative effect on trade balance to GDP, while liberalisation improves the current account to GDP ratio. Surprisingly, an increasing debt-service ratio (to total payments) improves current account, while the growth in long-term debt reduces the current account balance. The most important result in this table is the negative relationship between TBGDP1 and GROWTH. Higher economic growth in a developing economy by 1 percent tends to deteriorate trade balance by 0.06–0.08 point of the TBGDP percentage. For Africa, growth is not a significant determinant of TBGDP1. The annual change in terms of trade and liberalisation interacted with the terms of trade change are the most significant variables. Liberalisation possibly leads to higher imports and deteriorates terms of trade. For Asia, growth deteriorates TBGDP1, and similarly, for Latin America, the same result holds. Liberalisation interacted with growth improves TBGDP1. There were no significant relationships between CAGDP1 and growth and other variables for Latin America or Asia. The above regional differences are likely to arise due to perhaps omitted variables, misspecification of the true dynamic structure through a static model and differences in behaviour of economic agents in each geographical region or country. Our aim was to consider a general framework under which the relationship between trade balances, economic growth, terms of trade and advanced countries' growth rates can be considered.

Study on the Basis of 14 Selected Countries

An attempt can be made to date the change in policy from when on trade policy has not been tightened. This has been done for 15 countries.[q] — five countries from Latin America, Argentina (1991), Brazil (1991), Chile (1976), Colombia (1991) and Mexico (1986); five countries from Asia, Korea (1986), Malaysia (1988), Philippines (1986), Thailand (1986) and Turkey (1989); and five countries from Africa, Ghana (1985), Kenya (1993), Morocco (1984), Tunisia (1989) and Uganda (1988). However, isolation of the impact of this regime change on the liberalising country's trade account is made difficult by the fact that trade liberalisation has in some cases

[q] The classification is based on data from three studies: Little *et al.* (1993) and Sachs and Warner (1995). See also Dean *et al.* (1994).

been preceded or accompanied by exchange rate devaluation or a move towards a more flexible exchange rate regime. Therefore, an evaluation of the changes in imports and exports following trade liberalisation also needs to take exchange rate changes into account. Turkey was excluded because no data on income terms of trade were available.

We now present the results of panel data estimation designed to obtain the relation between economic growth and trade balance in developing countries and the effect of liberalisation on this relation. These results can also be used in constructing scenarios to estimate payment deficits that could be associated with faster growth in developing countries than has so far been achieved, and hence of their external financing requirements. The model is specified by taking the ratio of trade balance to income (TBGDPIMF and TBGDP from UNCTAD) as the dependent variable, and the growth rate (GROWTH) and the purchasing power of exports (i.e., income terms of trade) (PPI) of developing countries and the growth rate of developed countries (DEVWD) as explanatory variables. Income rather than barter terms of trade is used to capture the effects of both relative prices and export volumes and to assess the impact of liberalisation on import propensity.[r] Liberalisation (LIB) is used as a dummy variable and is expected to capture the joint effects of exchange rate appreciation and instability resulting from capital account liberalisation as well as the impact of import liberalisation. The regression equations are estimated on the basis of panel data estimation techniques using the information for 14 countries over 30 years, i.e., from 1970 to 1999. The equations are estimated alternatively as random effect and fixed effect models. The Hausman test supports the random effect model implying that the intercepts are uncorrelated with the explanatory variables.[s] In general, cross-section and time-series data on their own yield very different estimates of a model. If pooled cross-section

[r] Since the TB/GDP percentage incorporates the barter terms of trade and the export volume, in this formulation the impact of income terms of trade on the trade balance works through import volumes. The model has also been estimated using the net barter terms of trade. The latter had a positive and significant impact on the trade balance, and the effect of other explanatory variables were broadly similar to those obtained with the income terms of trade. However, unlike the specification reported here, liberalisation had no effect on the relation between barter terms of trade and trade balances.

[s] These models using panel data analysis differ according to whether they treat intercept parameters as random or fixed across the sample. The estimators in the random effect model

and time-series data are available, we have more information, and this in turn avoids a number of problems encountered with either cross-section or time-series alone. One method of reducing the omitted-variable bias is to use a panel instead of the standard cross-country data. Panel estimation controls for differences in time-invariant, unobservable country characteristics, thereby removing any bias resulting from the correlation of these characteristics with the explanatory variables. As a first hypothesis, LIBERAL is used as an intercept shift, i.e., it adds to trade deficits by a constant amount independent of the values of the explanatory variables.

We show the results of various estimation procedures in Tables 11A–11C. In Table 11A, we show the result of fixed effect versus random effect models. Two dependent variables are used alternately. In each case, the Hausman test favours the random effect model. Analysing the results of the random effect model, we find that the increase in growth by 1 percent will contribute to 0.19 percentage point to the trade deficit, while a similar improvement in growth will contribute to current account deficit by 0.15 percentage point *ceteris paribus*. The faster growth in developed economies tends to reduce the deficit, and 1 extra percentage point growth in the developed world will improve the trade balance to GDP by 0.79 percentage point and current account by 0.51 percentage point. An increase in oil prices tends to have a negative effect on both current account and trade balance as oil-producing economies are not in our sample. Liberalisation significantly improves current account, but on its own liberalisation does not have a significant effect on trade balance. The improvement in terms of trade on its own improves both trade balance and current account, but when liberalisation impact is considered along with the improvement in terms of trade, the impact of improvement in terms of trade on trade balance is considerably reduced.

In Table 11B, we deal with the problem of endogenity of growth variable. Growth might depend upon the investment to GDP ratio and initial level GDP at constant prices in each country. We therefore adopt the instrumental variable (IV) approach to the estimation of random effect models. Our

---

are the generalised least squares estimators, and they combine the within- and between-country estimators using the corresponding residual variances as weights. For elementary panel data techniques see Johnston (1996). For special treatment of panel data models, see Wooldridge (2002).

Table 11A. 14 countries study: fixed effect model (levels).

Name of the variable	Dependent variable					
	TBGDPIMF		CAGDP		TBGDP	
	Fixed effect (regression coefficient and t-statistic)	Random effect (regression coefficient and t-statistic)	Fixed effect (regression coefficient and t-statistic)	Random effect (regression coefficient and t-statistic)	Fixed effect (regression coefficient and t-statistic)	Random effect (regression coefficient and t-statistic)
GROWTH	−0.1909	−0.1899	−0.1546	−0.1476	−0.2359	−0.2367
	(−4.04)	(−4.04)	(−3.31)	(−3.33)	(−4.31)	(−4.35)
DEVWD	0.7962	0.7963	0.5232	0.5147	0.8398	0.8397
	(5.14)	(5.16)	(3.42)	(3.37)	(5.03)	(5.05)
OILPR	−0.0158	−0.0161	−0.0966	−0.0979	−0.0544	−0.0548
	(−0.63)	(−0.64)	(−3.87)	(−3.95)	(−2.00)	(−2.02)
PPI	0.0521	0.0524	0.0432	0.0453	0.0484	0.0487
	(5.80)	(5.86)	(4.87)	(5.20)	(5.04)	(5.10)
LIBERAL	1.3848	1.4066	2.9799	2.8914	0.8518	0.9029
	(1.35)	(1.37)	(2.93)	(2.96)	(0.69)	(0.73)
LIBPPI	−0.0384	−0.0387	−0.0334	−0.0346	−0.0352	−0.0355
	(−4.12)	(−4.17)	(−3.62)	(−3.84)	(−3.32)	(−3.38)
CONSTANT	−7.8661	−7.9037	−6.4088	−6.5366	−7.4548	−7.4717
	(−8.11)	(−4.78)	(−6.68)	(−6.78)	(−7.14)	(−3.97)
σ_u	4.6672	5.0264	0.9528	0.6680	5.1617	5.8883
σ_e	3.9283	3.9283	3.8840	3.8840	4.1691	4.1691
ρ	0.5853	0.6208	0.0567	0.0287	0.6052	0.6661
R^2	0.2447	0.1611	0.1999	0.2011	0.2314	0.1236
$F(6,400)$	21.60		15.27		$F(6.344) = 17.24$	
No. observations	420	420	420	420	364	364
Wald $\chi^2(6)$		131.20		99.52		104.84
Hausman test $\chi^2(6)$		0.51		0.8090		0.14

Table 11B. 14 countries study: random effect model estimated by error component two-stage least squares (levels).

Name of the variable	Dependent variable		
	TBGDPIMF	CAGDP	TBGDP
	Random effect (regression coefficient and t-statistic)	Random effect (regression coefficient and t-statistic)	Random effect (regression coefficient and t-statistic)
GROWTH	−0.4544	−0.1864	−0.8657
	(−1.81)	(−1.73)	(−2.19)
DEVWD	0.9511	0.5365	1.1738
	(4.46)	(3.41)	(3.95)
OILPR	−0.0393	−0.1175	−0.0849
	(−1.29)	(−4.51)	(−2.15)
PPI	0.0482	0.0462	0.0388
	(4.42)	(5.16)	(2.71)
LIBERAL	2.9100	3.9767	1.4357
	(2.34)	(3.70)	(0.91)
LIBPPI	−0.0400	−0.0413	−0.279
	(−3.45)	(−4.18)	(−1.87)
CONSTANT	−6.3564	−5.9801	−4.3984
	(−3.71)	(−5.45)	(−1.75)
σ_u	4.1154	0.0	5.6418
σ_e	8.3764	7.7642	8.1394
ρ	0.1945	0.0	0.3245
R^2	0.0804	0.1743	0.0767
No. observations	336	336	336
Wald $\chi^2(6)$	70.16	69.84	57.49

Instrumented: Growth instruments used: DEVWD, OILPR, LIBERAL, LIBPPI, growth(−2) INV and GDPCONSTANT.

test does not reject the hypothesis of zero correlation between country effects and the error term. For each of the three dependent variables we estimate random effect models with the IV procedure (Baltagi, 1995). Our results marginally worsen with respect to the growth variable when it is treated endogenous and the two-stage estimator is derived. Most of the other coefficients have the same signs as in Table 11A, and income terms of trade have a positive impact in improving trade balance to GDP or current

Table 11C. 14 countries study: dynamic model estimated by Arellano–Bond panel data estimation and first-differenced regression by instrumental variable estimation.

Name of the variable	TBGDPIMF		CAGDP		TBGDP	
	Fixed effect (regression coefficient and t-statistic)	Random Effect (regression coefficient and t-statistic)	Fixed effect (regression coefficient and t-statistic)	Random effect (regression coefficient and t-statistic)	Fixed effect (regression coefficient and t-statistic)	Random effect (regression coefficient and t-statistic)
Lagged dependent (1)	0.5680	0.0759	0.5487	0.1987	0.4061	−0.0157
	(10.64)	(0.16)	(9.20)	(0.37)	(5.29)	(−0.06)
Lagged dependent (2)	−0.0097		−0.0132		0.0467	
	(−0.15)		(−0.20)		(0.59)	
GROWTH	−0.2201	−0.2214	−0.1987	−0.2084	−0.1831	−0.1621
	(−3.77)	(−3.10)	(−3.37)	(−2.56)	(−4.80)	(−3.04)
GROWTH(−1)	−0.1720	−0.2123	−0.1846	−0.2142	−0.1964	−0.1791
	(−3.48)	(−5.22)	(−3.30)	(−5.48)	(−5.99)	(−3.66)
DEVWD	0.5799	0.4218	0.4837	0.3922	0.6899	0.4392
	(4.60)	(3.90)	(3.76)	(3.39)	(3.72)	(3.29)
DEVWD (−1)	−0.1264	0.1097	0.0217	0.1314	0.1030	0.2118
	(−0.83)	(0.45)	(0.13)	(0.55)	(0.71)	(1.11)
OILPR	−0.0336	−0.0838	−0.0882	−0.0838	−0.0190	−0.0542
	(−1.41)	(−2.40)	(−3.47)	(−2.28)	(−0.66)	(−1.18)
PPI	0.0274	0.0452	0.0174	0.0444	0.0317	0.0622
	(2.75)	(3.63)	(2.40)	(3.37)	(3.18)	(3.95)
LIBERAL	1.4257	4.7564	0.5540	5.0263	2.0059	3.0977
	(1.20)	(2.63)	(0.64)	(2.74)	(1.48)	(1.31)

(Continued)

Table 11C. *(Continued)*.

Name of the variable	TBGDPIMF		CAGDP		TBGDP	
	Fixed effect (regression coefficient and t-statistic)	Random Effect (regression coefficient and t-statistic)	Fixed effect (regression coefficient and t-statistic)	Random effect (regression coefficient and t-statistic)	Fixed effect (regression coefficient and t-statistic)	Random effect (regression coefficient and t-statistic)
LIBPPI	−0.0190	−0.0371	−0.0138	−0.0378	−0.0249	−0.0256
	(−2.06)	(−2.85)	(−2.01)	(−2.67)	(−2.54)	(−1.43)
CONSTANT	−0.0723	−0.0757	0.0649	−0.0476	−0.0852	−0.4353
	(−1.53)	(−0.40)	(1.49)	(−0.24)	(−1.05)	(−1.76)
AC order 1	−3.04		−3.01		−2.15	
	(0.0023)		(0.0026)		(0.0317)	
AC order 2	0.55		0.44		−1.16	
	(0.5793)		(0.6597)		(0.2452)	
No. of observations	378	364	378	364	322	308
Wald $\chi^2(10)$	1434.36		994.32		3009.36	
Sargan test $\chi^2(403)$	1.22		0.12		1.55	
R-square		0.2340		0.3758		0.0358
σ_u		4.5319		1.1238		5.5742
σ_e		3.2846		3.4883		3.9661
ρ		0.6556		0.0940		0.6639

Instrumented: Lagged dependent variable, all variables in first differences.

Instruments used: growth, lagged growth, DEVWD, lagged DEVWD, OILPR, PPI, LIBERAL, LIBPPI, and lag3 of the dependent variable.

Note: In the dynamic model, results of robust standard errors are used.

account to GDP percentages. The model is static and does not have lagged variables. This is now corrected in Table 11C.

We estimate two further models, one, a dynamic model with two period lags, and the other, the first-differenced model by using the instrumental variable technique. We write the equation for a dynamic model in the following form:

$$y_{it} = \delta_1 y_{it-1} + \delta_2 y_{it-2} + \mathbf{X}_{it}\mathbf{B} + \alpha_i + \eta_t + \varepsilon_{it}, \quad i = 1, 2 \ldots, 14, \ t = 1, 2, \ldots, 30 \tag{10}$$

y_{it} is the trade balance or current account to GDP in percentages, $\mathbf{X}_{it}$ is a set of explanatory variables namely liberaliasation, growth in real GDP, purchasing power of exports (terms of trade) and intereactions of purchasing power of exports with liberalisation and growth rate in real GDP in developed economies. η_t is the effects of time or year dummies and may be represented as cyclical impacts on trade balance to GDP percentages. We expect the sign of the coefficients to be positive with respect to purchasing power of exports and growth in developed economies, while we expect negative sign with respect to growth in real GDP and oil prices.

Even if y_{it-1} and ε_{it} are not correlated, if t does not approach infinity (t=30 in our case) then estimation by fixed effects or random effects is not consistent even if n (number of countries) goes to infinity. Arellano and Bond (1991) suggest an alternative procedure that corrects not only for the bias introduced by the lagged endogenous variable, but also permits a degree of endogeneity in the other regressors such as the growth variable on the right-hand side variable as a subset of **X** matrix. The Generalised Method of Moments Estimator first differences each variable and then use lagged values of each of the variables as instruments. Specifically,

$$\Delta y_{it} = \delta_1 \Delta y_{it-1} + \delta_2 \Delta y_{it-2} + \Delta\mathbf{X}_{it}\mathbf{B} + \Delta\varepsilon_{it}. \tag{11}$$

The first three observations are lost due to lags and differencing. Assuming that ε_{it} are not autocorrelated for each i at $t = 4$, y_{i1} and y_{i2} are valid instruments for lagged variables. Similarly, at $t = 5$, y_{i1}, y_{i2} and y_{i3} are valid instruments. We thus estimate the dynamic model using the above procedure.[t] For the first-differenced model, we explicitly use the instruments for the growth variable namely the investment to GDP ratio, GDP at constant prices of the last period and the growth variable lagged by three periods. We discuss these results using the 14-country sample with 30 observations for each country.

In the first-differenced model, the second lag is not used. All the variables are in the first-differenced form. The second lagged variable is not significant. Of the two results for each dependent variable we prefer the first-differenced version as it captures endogeneity of some so-called exogenous regressors. For the dynamic model, the signs of the estimated coefficients are in agreement with our *a priori* views. Growth has a negative and significant coefficient, and its impact is slightly less on current account to GDP percentages than on the trade balance to GDP percentage. The growth in the developed world in the current period acts as a cushion for averting the current account deficit while liberalisation helps to improve current account, but liberlisation with income terms of trade tends to worsen the current account and trade balance to GDP percentages. When we control for relevant factors, we find that the impact of the 1 percent increase in growth rate in developing countries tends to worsen the trade balance to GDP percentage by 0.22 points, while the current account deteriorates by 0.20 points. When this effect is combined with the last period growth, the impact on both trade balance and current account is much larger and it is nearly 0.40 points.

Summary and Conclusions

In recent research on trade liberalisation, not much attention has been given to the issue of imports, the balance of trade and current account of the balance of payments. It is conceivable that trade liberalisation may lead to faster growth of imports than exports if the countries were highly protected in pre-liberalised period. The faster growth in imports in relation to exports could have serious implications for the balance of trade, and this in itself could constrain economic growth in some of the developing economies.

[t] The Monte Carlo simulation has shown that for panels with t=5 or 6, the bias of the coefficients of the lagged dependent variable can be significant, although the bias for the coefficients on other right-hand side variables tends to be minor.

Trade liberalisation may promote growth on the one hand from the supply side through a more efficient allocation of resources, while it may constrain growth from the demand side unless a balance between exports and imports can be maintained through trade policies such as real exchange rate depreciation or deficits in the short run can be financed by capital inflows.

Our study encompassed three decades and about 42 developing countries dispersed over three geographical regions of Asia, Africa and Latin America. Our tentative findings are on the relationship between liberalisation and growth and liberalisation, growth and trade balance or current account, while other factors affecting these relationships are taken into consideration. Overall, liberalisation contributes significantly to economic growth, openness and investment rates over periods 1970–1979 and 1990–1999. Liberalisation worsens trade deficits while it improves current account deficits when the entire period is considered. Economic growth in a domestic economy reduces current account deficits in the 1980–1989 period, while it has no significant relationship in earlier or latter decades. Trade deficits tend to rise with economic growth in Asian economies, while there is no such evidence for either Latin American or African economies. Our country-level study did not permit us to reach unambiguous conclusions. For five countries, liberalisation has a positive and significant effect, while for 12 countries, trade balance tends to worsen with liberalisation. When Thirlwall's basic equation was used in a behavioural form at a country level, we did not find that the growth was significantly constrained by changes in terms of trade, advanced countries' growth rates or annual percentage change in oil prices. Liberalisation indeed has a positive effect on growth in many economies. We examined the relationship of trade balance to GDP and the current account to GDP percentage while including control variables namely terms of trade, liberalisation, advanced countries' growth rates and interactions of each of the variables with liberalisation. We found that trade balance obviously deteriorates with liberalisation and economic growth, and hence countries would have difficulty in reaching potential or planned growth in the subsequent periods after liberalisation. Deterioration in trade balance could impact on economic growth in subsequent periods. Current account balances, however, did not deteriorate with the impact of liberalisation and economic growth for many economies.

We found that trade balance obviously deteriorates with liberalisation and economic growth, and hence some of these countries would have difficulty in reaching potential or planned growth in the periods after liberalisation. Deterioration in trade balance could impact on economic growth in subsequent periods. Current account balances, however, did not deteriorate with the impact of liberalisation and economic growth for many economies. The direct impact of trade liberalisation on trade balance was not significant. Growth had a negative relationship with trade balance in a dynamic model applied to panel data. However, domestic economic growth was not a significant determinant of current account balances. This would imply that for a large number of countries, foreign direct investment may have increased to such an extent that despite the increase in trade deficit, economic growth continues without its harmful effects on current account balance.

Means and standard deviations of variables

Country	Variables (%)		1970–2000	1970–1979	1980–1989	1990–1999
Argentina	TBGDP2	Mean/SD	0.53(1.35)	0.56(0.87)	1.11(1.24)	0.77(1.74)
(10)	CAGDP2	Mean/SD	0.21(0.17)	0.06(0.38)	0.50(0.15)	0.30(0.08)
	GROWTH	Mean/SD	2.02(6.22)	2.86(4.38)	1.53(6.02)	5.06(6.78)
Antigua	TBGDP2	Mean/SD	28.98(8.42)	12.36(1.82)	29.97(7.33)	32.89(2.99)
(11)	CAGDP2	Mean/SD	6.34(5.99)	4.51(3.39)	9.88(7.37)	3.33(3.08)
	GROWTH	Mean/SD	4.10(5.47)	1.52(3.42)	5.58(5.56)	2.79(5.81)
Burundi	TBGDP2	Mean/SD	2.31(1.57)	0.84(1.16)	3.50(1.33)	2.61(1.05)
(12)	CAGDP2	Mean/SD	1.03(0.80)	—	1.55(1.01)	0.76(0.63)
	GROWTH	Mean/SD	0.59(8.47)	1.20(6.40)	2.74(7.96)	0.83(7.54)
Benin	TBGDP2	Mean/SD	8.96(3.87)	9.61(4.76)	—	8.61(−)
(13)	CAGDP2	Mean/SD	3.17(2.72)	4.02(1.36)	3.45(4.00)	2.38(1.51)
	GROWTH	Mean/SD	3.20(3.91)	1.53(3.49)	3.38(5.28)	4.30(2.42)
Burkina	TBGDP2	Mean/SD	2.95(0.30)	2.95(0.37)	—	—
Faso (14)	CAGDP2	Mean/SD	1.40(1.05)	2.36(1.23)	1.18(0.67)	0.66(0.60)
	GROWTH	Mean/SD	3.50(3.58)	4.01(3.38)	3.19(4.84)	3.56(2.63)
Bangladesh	TBGDP2	Mean/SD	0.10(0.39)	0.27(0.56)	0.12(0.31)	0.03(0.28)
(15)	CAGDP2	Mean/SD	0.51(0.53)	0.94(0.79)	0.78(0.56)	0.11(0.26)
	GROWTH	Mean/SD	3.66(4.40)	1.79(7.03)	4.14(3.42)	4.68(1.23)
Bolivia	TBGDP2	Mean/SD	0.71(2.02)	1.55(0.53)	−0.63(1.60)	1.96(1.87)
(17)	CAGDP2	Mean/SD	2.33(1.21)	2.90(1.93)	2.34(1.28)	2.14(0.90)
	GROWTH	Mean/SD	2.56(3.05)	4.97(1.74)	−0.58(2.96)	3.55(0.85)
Brasilia	TBGDP2	Mean/SD	−0.08(0.13)	—	−0.25(0.05)	0.012(0.004)
(18)	CAGDP2	Mean/SD	0.002 (0.008)	0.002 (0.0005)	0.004 (0.013)	0.0009 (0.001)
	GROWTH	Mean/SD	4.20(4.37)	8.01(3.33)	2.93(4.24)	1.90(3.37)

Country	Variables (%)		1970–2000	1970–1979	1980–1989	1990–1999
Barbados	TBGDP2	Mean/SD	12.92(2.76)	11.66(1.64)	11.71(2.05)	14.80(2.71)
(19)	CAGDP2	Mean/SD	1.42(2.79)	4.15(1.42)	0.53(1.94)	−0.60(2.46)
	GROWTH	Mean/SD	3.70(5.24)	5.39(4.86)	4.45(6.75)	1.28(3.41)
Botswana	TBGDP2	Mean/SD	1.99(8.75)	8.93(3.50)	1.56(11.34)	−1.82(4.13)
(20)	CAGDP2	Mean/SD	−0.30(6.58)	5.00(3.19)	0.55(8.69)	−3.81(2.27)
	GROWTH	Mean/SD	9.51(6.09)	14.30(7.82)	8.45(4.08)	6.26(2.91)
Central	TBGDP2	Mean/SD	0.32(0.26)	0.18(0.17)	0.60(−)	—
African	CAGDP2	Mean/SD	1.40(0.74)	0.95(0.19)	1.47(0.75)	1.50(0.92)
Rep. (21)	GROWTH	Mean/SD	−0.52(7.19)	0.63(3.23)	−0.57(5.73)	−1.63(11.13)
Chile	TBGDP2	Mean/SD	0.91(2.53)	2.08(2.12)	0.17(3.55)	0.61(1.36)
(22)	CAGDP2	Mean/SD	2.68(2.59)	2.57(2.01)	4.07(3.41)	1.54(1.09)
	GROWTH	Mean/SD	4.00(6.10)	2.58(8.24)	3.08(6.30)	6.09(3.44)
Cote d'Ivoire	TBGDP2	Mean/SD	−2.59(2.30)	−1.74(1.27)	−4.00(3.02)	—
(24)	CAGDP2	Mean/SD	3.89(3.59)	4.72(3.08)	5.40(4.42)	2.35(2.22)
	GROWTH	Mean/SD	2.73(4.83)	6.67(3.55)	0.34(5.56)	1.97(3.01)
Cameroon	TBGDP2	Mean/SD	1.65(1.25)	1.20(1.29)	2.17(1.04)	—
(25)	CAGDP2	Mean/SD	2.01(1.17)	1.60(0.50)	2.49(1.14)	1.41(1.24)
	GROWTH	Mean/SD	3.55(6.61)	6.90(6.96)	3.42(7.73)	0.41(3.90)
Colombia	TBGDP2	Mean/SD	0.43(1.19)	0.007(0.59)	0.92(1.45)	0.47(1.32)
(27)	CAGDP2	Mean/SD	0.006(1.60)	0.35(0.95)	−1.30(1.53)	0.99(1.47)
	GROWTH	Mean/SD	3.87(2.09)	5.60(1.73)	3.37(1.50)	3.01(2.18)
Cape Verde	TBGDP2	Mean/SD	20.82(4.03)	22.96(3.55)	17.28(1.18)	—
(29)	CAGDP2	Mean/SD	3.75(9.16)	0.41(3.79)	1.48(2.00)	7.39(13.66)
	GROWTH	Mean/SD	5.23(7.69)	0.98(7.99)	8.79(8.95)	4.74(3.89)
Costa Rica	TBGDP2	Mean/SD	3.46(2.17)	5.08(1.76)	2.15(1.95)	3.25(1.93)
(30)	CAGDP2	Mean/SD	3.66(2.16)	6.44(2.22)	4.09(2.17)	2.40(1.03)
	GROWTH	Mean/SD	3.75(3.65)	5.85(1.73)	1.52(4.33)	4.24(3.33)
Dominican	TBGDP2	Mean/SD	5.49(3.24)	2.28(1.41)	5.09(1.03)	8.60(1.63)
Rep (32)	CAGDP2	Mean/SD	1.95(1.62)	2.76(1.25)	2.24(1.79)	1.26(0.83)
	GROWTH	Mean/SD	5.32(3.07)	6.29(2.60)	3.85(1.99)	5.69(4.02)
Ecuador	TBGDP2	Mean/SD	−0.92(1.60)	0.005(1.29)	−1.67(1.39)	−0.95(1.75)
(34)	CAGDP2	Mean/SD	1.85(1.91)	2.60(1.88)	2.39(1.66)	1.39(1.84)
	GROWTH	Mean/SD	3.88(5.39)	9.42(4.67)	1.69(4.22)	1.28(3.53)
Egypt	TBGDP2	Mean/SD	5.37(3.54)	3.96(4.09)	8.07(3.22)	4.27(1.62)
(35)	CAGDP2	Mean/SD	0.86(1.31)	2.85(0.08)	1.38(0.88)	−0.19(0.86)
	GROWTH	Mean/SD	4.71(4.20)	3.27(7.07)	6.03(2.60)	4.70(1.22)
Ethiopia	TBGDP2	Mean/SD	1.70(1.14)	0.64(0.55)	2.80(0.70)	2.06(0.56)
(36)	CAGDP2	Mean/SD	0.62(0.67)	0.86(0.14)	0.96(0.70)	0.26(0.58)
	GROWTH	Mean/SD	2.80(6.24)	3.14(1.55)	1.79(8.32)	2.74(6.80)
Fiji	TBGDP2	Mean/SD	6.81(3.41)	10.36(2.90)	5.73(3.76)	5.83(0.72)
(37)	CAGDP2	Mean/SD	1.67(2.64)	3.92(−)	1.25(3.54)	1.87(1.47)
	GROWTH	Mean/SD	3.08(4.91)	5.66(3.82)	1.46(6.26)	2.37(3.57)
Gabon	TBGDP2	Mean/SD	−5.72(2.48)	−5.72(2.48)	—	
(38)	CAGDP2	Mean/SD	−0.20(6.99)	−4.02(2.86)	2.45(8.86)	−2.09(4.43)
	GROWTH	Mean/SD	3.65(9.63)	6.66(11.09)	2.73(12.96)	2.06(2.89)
Ghana	TBGDP2	Mean/SD	−0.15(1.51)	−0.35(1.91)	0.06(1.04)	—
(39)	CAGDP2	Mean/SD	1.26(1.20)	0.24(1.15)	1.10(1.24)	1.91(0.87)
	GROWTH	Mean/SD	2.86(5.77)	1.97(9.38)	2.59(4.16)	3.21(2.23)

Country	Variables (%)		1970–2000	1970–1979	1980–1989	1990–1999
Guinea	TBGDP2	Mean/SD	0.55(1.11)	0.77(1.22)	0.03(0.86)	0.20(−)
(40)	CAGDP2	Mean/SD	1.08(0.76)	—	1.26(0.67)	1.01(0.81)
	GROWTH	Mean/SD	2.86(3.54)	2.16(4.82)	2.21(3.97)	4.23(0.96)
Gambia, The	TBGDP2	Mean/SD	10.42(5.48)	6.04(5.25)	10.45(3.98)	15.26(2.42)
(41)	CAGDP2	Mean/SD	1.90(5.63)	16.45(1.90)	0.56(3.13)	−0.06(2.31)
	GROWTH	Mean/SD	3.74(3.89)	4.11(3.66)	4.01(3.55)	2.61(4.42)
Guinea-Bissau	TBGDP2	Mean/SD	10.62(4.78)	13.86(2.85)	11.79(3.88)	4.87(1.18)
(42)	CAGDP2	Mean/SD	11.97(4.96)	—	15.17(2.75)	8.78(4.67)
	GROWTH	Mean/SD	5.18(15.54)	9.85(15.01)	1.66(12.83)	4.71(19.43)
Grenada	TBGDP2	Mean/SD	17.71(3.00)	14.78(1.06)	19.91(1.47)	—
(44)	CAGDP2	Mean/SD	6.04(6.66)	−0.39(1.04)	2.82(7.23)	10.54(2.86)
	GROWTH	Mean/SD	3.86(3.86)	4.21(6.30)	4.61(4.23)	2.86(3.44)
Guatemala	TBGDP2	Mean/SD	1.84(1.66)	0.81(0.83)	0.92(1.46)	3.32(0.99)
(45)	CAGDP2	Mean/SD	1.63(0.73)	1.33(0.95)	1.64(0.86)	1.65(0.62)
	GROWTH	Mean/SD	3.48(2.36)	5.63(1.88)	1.61(2.29)	3.37(1.04)
Guyana	TBGDP2	Mean/SD	1.63(3.04)	1.40(3.33)	2.65(0.84)	—
(46)	CAGDP2	Mean/SD	8.23(2.74)	5.82(2.98)	10.17(2.15)	7.13(1.18)
	GROWTH	Mean/SD	1.59(7.91)	2.29(6.90)	−2.39(7.52)	4.94(8.08)
Honduras	TBGDP2	Mean/SD	3.44(3.24)	2.04(1.80)	2.06(1.65)	6.73(3.05)
(48)	CAGDP2	Mean/SD	3.70(1.39)	4.43(0.66)	4.27(1.70)	2.69(0.75)
	GROWTH	Mean/SD	3.34(4.14)	5.68(5.16)	3.08(2.60)	1.50(3.94)
Haiti	TBGDP2	Mean/SD	3.28(1.18)	2.56(1.06)	4.03(0.81)	3.85(1.01)
(49)	CAGDP2	Mean/SD	1.09(1.25)	0.82(0.95)	2.15(1.13)	0.18(0.74)
	GROWTH	Mean/SD	5.19(10.05)	2.91(4.24)	−0.13(3.55)	13.37(13.86)
Indonesia	TBGDP2	Mean/SD	−2.52(1.91)	−3.43(2.52)	−2.73(1.69)	−1.41(0.83)
(50)	CAGDP2	Mean/SD	0.01(0.06)	—	0.03(0.09)	0.0004(.0005)
	GROWTH	Mean/SD	5.97(3.77)	7.76(1.65)	6.03(2.30)	4.42(5.67)
India	TBGDP2	Mean/SD	0.44(0.35)	0.25(0.27)	0.82(0.32)	0.26(0.12)
(51)	CAGDP2	Mean/SD	−0.005(0.038)	−0.03(0.09)	0.0004(0.0001)	0.0002(0.0001)
	GROWTH	Mean/SD	4.85(2.90)	2.62(3.93)	6.03(1.10)	5.71(2.20)
Jamaica	TBGDP2	Mean/SD	11.25(5.13)	8.18(3.75)	10.49(3.93)	14.44(5.13)
(53)	CAGDP2	Mean/SD	3.31(2.93)	3.21(3.92)	4.63(3.34)	2.06(1.73)
	GROWTH	Mean/SD	0.99(4.34)	0.75(6.51)	1.73(3.81)	0.46(2.74)
Jordan	TBGDP2	Mean/SD	25.50(13.87)	33.93(13.61)	29.85(12.55)	13.20(2.49)
(54)	CAGDP2	Mean/SD	1.96(3.44)	0.55(4.25)	3.04(3.50)	2.02(2.49)
	GROWTH	Mean/SD	5.78(7.29)	9.50(9.87)	3.55(7.08)	5.05(3.59)
Kenya	TBGDP2	Mean/SD	3.94(1.78)	4.62(2.08)	4.35(1.72)	2.77(0.96)
(55)	CAGDP2	Mean/SD	1.87(2.15)	3.40(2.94)	2.40(2.28)	0.72(0.76)
	GROWTH	Mean/SD	4.59(5.17)	8.30(7.68)	4.07(2.91)	2.02(1.77)
Korea	TBGDP2	Mean/SD	1.37(2.75)	3.55(1.59)	0.63(2.48)	0.25(2.86)
(57)	CAGDP2	Mean/SD	0.04(0.13)	0.12(0.25)	0.04(0.13)	0.02(0.06)
	GROWTH	Mean/SD	7.16(4.22)	8.55(2.59)	7.25(4.20)	5.76(5.45)
Sri Lanka	TBGDP2	Mean/SD	2.14(1.43)	1.11(1.35)	3.08(1.60)	2.30(0.38)
(59)	CAGDP2	Mean/SD	1.32(0.90)	0.97(0.66)	1.80(1.21)	1.01(0.38)
	GROWTH	Mean/SD	3.96(2.52)	3.03(1.76)	4.59(2.43)	3.93(3.16)
Morocco	TBGDP2	Mean/SD	3.63(1.74)	4.05(2.68)	3.83(1.39)	3.05(0.61)
(62)	CAGDP2	Mean/SD	0.51(0.85)	0.56(1.25)	0.68(1.09)	0.32(0.27)
	GROWTH	Mean/SD	3.75(4.91)	5.39(2.02)	3.79(4.68)	2.61(6.82)

Country	Variables (%)		1970–2000	1970–1979	1980–1989	1990–1999
Madagascar	TBGDP2	Mean/SD	1.70(1.13)	1.32(1.31)	1.87(1.20)	2.14(0.46)
(63)	CAGDP2	Mean/SD	2.76(2.02)	2.13(2.82)	3.46(2.51)	2.49(0.31)
	GROWTH	Mean/SD	1.32(2.43)	0.85(2.85)	1.23(2.31)	1.65(2.42)
Mexico	TBGDP2	Mean/SD	0.64(1.66)	1.40(0.56)	−0.98(1.65)	1.40(1.35)
(64)	CAGDP2	Mean/SD	−0.006(0.04)	0.002(−)	−0.02(0.06)	0.002(0.001)
	GROWTH	Mean/SD	3.85(3.55)	6.22(1.91)	1.98(4.02)	3.09(2.88)
Mali	TBGDP2	Mean/SD	3.54(2.15)	3.54(2.15)	—	—
(65)	CAGDP2	Mean/SD	3.34(1.28)	2.74(2.10)	3.88(1.06)	3.04(0.64)
	GROWTH	Mean/SD	3.07(5.64)	4.90(5.20)	0.31(6.22)	4.18(5.15)
Mozambique	TBGDP2	Mean/SD	3.75(0.73)	—	—	3.75(0.73)
(66)	CAGDP2	Mean/SD	3.51(0.71)	—	3.77(0.43)	3.21(0.86)
	GROWTH	Mean/SD	0.72(8.32)	0.69(10.44)	−1.84(8.85)	2.67(5.62)
Mauritania	TBGDP2	Mean/SD	0.09(5.31)	3.84(3.32)	−2.05(5.17)	—
(67)	CAGDP2	Mean/SD	5.19(4.78)	7.04(1.37)	8.19(4.19)	0.81(3.17)
	GROWTH	Mean/SD	1.34(7.67)	2.94(8.11)	−1.07(6.46)	2.32(8.52)
Mauritius	TBGDP2	Mean/SD	2.94(2.15)	2.96(2.29)	2.92(2.13)	—
(68)	CAGDP2	Mean/SD	1.22(1.63)	3.35(1.43)	1.10(1.82)	0.58(0.72)
	GROWTH	Mean/SD	5.36(4.15)	6.31(6.17)	4.43(4.10)	5.18(1.49)
Malawi	TBGDP2	Mean/SD	3.42(2.20)	4.72(2.01)	2.23(2.22)	3.51(1.74)
(69)	CAGDP2	Mean/SD	4.63(3.29)	7.70(4.25)	3.54(2.74)	4.95(3.17)
	GROWTH	Mean/SD	4.56(7.77)	7.75(6.53)	2.01(2.55)	4.70(11.41)
Malaysia	TBGDP2	Mean/SD	−3.15(3.23)	−4.20(2.92)	−3.66(2.60)	−1.18(3.43)
(70)	CAGDP2	Mean/SD	0.03(1.27)	−0.26(2.81)	0.14(0.38)	0.09(0.28)
	GROWTH	Mean/SD	6.66(2.99)	7.53(2.90)	5.62(3.38)	6.83(2.80)
Niger	TBGDP2	Mean/SD	1.07(0.83)	1.07(0.83)	—	—
(71)	CAGDP2	Mean/SD	3.24(1.91)	3.80(2.35)	3.45(2.06)	2.34(0.82)
	GROWTH	Mean/SD	1.35(7.17)	1.10(10.30)	0.45(7.61)	1.92(2.95)
Nigeria	TBGDP2	Mean/SD	−4.63(6.11)	−6.47(8.28)	−2.83(5.77)	−4.58(2.78)
(72)	CAGDP2	Mean/SD	—	—	—	—
	GROWTH	Mean/SD	1.38(8.95)	3.85(10.07)	1.63(7.48)	1.04(7.43)
Nicaragua	TBGDP2	Mean/SD	5.07(4.78)	0.75(2.45)	6.20(1.52)	9.47(3.32)
(73)	CAGDP2	Mean/SD	6.93(3.28)	0.02(3.28)	7.90(1.48)	8.21(1.92)
	GROWTH	Mean/SD	0.20(7.27)	0.85(10.46)	−0.95(7.07)	−0.31(2.92)
Nepal	TBGDP2	Mean/SD	2.69(0.77)	1.73(0.37)	2.95(0.49)	2.96(0.80)
(74)	CAGDP2	Mean/SD	0.89(0.55)	0.06(0.33)	1.00(0.46)	1.13(0.43)
	GROWTH	Mean/SD	4.31(3.19)	4.00(2.98)	4.14(4.59)	4.63(1.84)
Pakistan	TBGDP2	Mean/SD	1.97(1.30)	2.15(1.50)	2.75(1.17)	1.06(0.35)
(75)	CAGDP2	Mean/SD	0.43(0.69)	1.39(0.96)	0.48(0.60)	0.03(0.10)
	GROWTH	Mean/SD	5.26(2.50)	4.58(2.91)	7.47(1.43)	3.73(1.42)
Panama	TBGDP2	Mean/SD	14.19(3.83)	17.04(3.18)	12.45(4.67)	13.06(1.34)
(76)	CAGDP2	Mean/SD	2.20(3.96)	5.56(1.32)	0.66(4.88)	2.47(2.92)
	GROWTH	Mean/SD	3.67(4.82)	4.51(2.25)	2.78(7.94)	3.81(2.41)
Peru	TBGDP2	Mean/SD	0.51(1.96)	−0.30(2.15)	−0.51(1.29)	2.24(1.10)
(77)	CAGDP2	Mean/SD	0.18(0.71)	0.48(2.05)	0.28(0.52)	0.002(0.0006)
	GROWTH	Mean/SD	2.15(6.34)	3.08(3.79)	−0.07(9.18)	3.41(4.92)

Country	Variables (%)		1970–2000	1970–1979	1980–1989	1990–1999
Philippines (78)	TBGDP2	Mean/SD	2.15(1.87)	1.65(1.06)	1.84(0.98)	3.36(2.37)
	CAGDP2	Mean/SD	0.04(0.32)	0.41(0.71)	−0.01(0.31)	0.0007(0.001)
	GROWTH	Mean/SD	3.52(3.46)	5.74(1.31)	1.90(4.58)	3.04(2.82)
Papua New Guinea (79)	TBGDP2	Mean/SD	−0.10(4.15)	0.94(3.92)	2.51(2.43)	−3.65(3.37)
	CAGDP2	Mean/SD	1.48(2.95)	−1.09(1.22)	3.82(2.14)	0.03(2.37)
	GROWTH	Mean/SD	2.57(6.47)	4.10(6.81)	1.25(3.68)	2.52(8.45)
Paraguay (80)	TBGDP2	Mean/SD	2.17(1.81)	1.14(1.17)	2.25(1.75)	4.06(1.58)
	CAGDP2	Mean/SD	1.66(1.75)	2.24(0.87)	2.75(1.78)	0.38(1.24)
	GROWTH	Mean/SD	4.46(4.12)	7.46(3.66)	4.10(3.98)	2.82(3.05)
Rwanda (81)	TBGDP2	Mean/SD	2.80(1.46)	1.04(0.58)	4.30(0.63)	2.98(0.44)
	CAGDP2	Mean/SD	1.01(1.23)	−0.44(1.74)	1.84(0.63)	0.85(0.89)
	GROWTH	Mean/SD	2.78(16.06)	5.30(5.43)	3.33(5.13)	−0.23(27.59)
Senegal (82)	TBGDP2	Mean/SD	4.72(1.73)	4.72(1.73)	—	—
	CAGDP2	Mean/SD	3.83(1.95)	3.53(1.84)	5.30(1.81)	2.53(1.03)
	GROWTH	Mean/SD	2.75(5.08)	2.41(6.31)	2.46(6.40)	3.09(2.38)
Sierra Leone (84)	TBGDP2	Mean/SD	2.54(2.39)	3.23(2.05)	2.64(3.09)	1.25(1.47)
	CAGDP2	Mean/SD	2.16(3.13)	5.96(2.85)	1.52(3.33)	1.33(1.29)
	GROWTH	Mean/SD	0.27(6.49)	−1.13(7.02)	3.46(5.08)	−2.48(6.50)
Salvador, El (85)	TBGDP2	Mean/SD	3.07(3.26)	0.29(1.04)	1.56(0.81)	6.73(1.55)
	CAGDP2	Mean/SD	0.95(0.89)	0.44(1.49)	1.23(0.95)	0.84(0.50)
	GROWTH	Mean/SD	2.08(4.44)	3.98(3.05)	−1.77(5.15)	4.22(1.91)
Seychelles (87)	TBGDP2	Mean/SD	27.22(4.99)	31.36(−)	27.74(5.45)	27.53(2.13)
	CAGDP2	Mean/SD	6.62(3.68)	3.21(1.94)	8.13(3.01)	6.47(4.07)
	GROWTH	Mean/SD	4.44(7.23)	9.04(6.28)	1.43(9.31)	3.53(3.71)
Syria (88)	TBGDP2	Mean/SD	4.41(4.53)	7.04(3.16)	6.52(4.13)	0.67(2.47)
	CAGDP2	Mean/SD	0.33(1.67)	−1.10(3.40)	1.27(1.35)	−0.15(0.88)
	GROWTH	Mean/SD	6.21(10.21)	8.81(15.95)	4.11(9.29)	6.15(3.34)
Chad (89)	TBGDP2	Mean/SD	2.46(0.69)	2.46(0.69)	—	—
	CAGDP2	Mean/SD	0.63(1.01)	1.14(0.87)	0.17(1.04)	1.24(0.55)
	GROWTH	Mean/SD	1.61(14.40)	6.74(17.47)	−2.52(15.60)	1.37(10.38)
Togo (90)	TBGDP2	Mean/SD	5.42(5.48)	4.90(6.92)	9.33(1.01)	4.47(1.53)
	CAGDP2	Mean/SD	3.50(3.55)	6.86(6.33)	2.01(1.35)	2.97(0.71)
	GROWTH	Mean/SD	1.11(8.75)	0.15(11.30)	4.25(7.91)	−0.83(7.30)
Thailand (91)	TBGDP2	Mean/SD	2.02(1.71)	2.16(0.51)	2.28(1.15)	1.99(2.54)
	CAGDP2	Mean/SD	0.10(0.37)	0.53(0.75)	0.007(0.10)	0.001(0.002)
	GROWTH	Mean/SD	6.18(4.35)	6.94(2.98)	6.80(2.85)	4.91(6.50)
Trinidad and Tobago (92)	TBGDP2	Mean/SD	−2.13(5.53)	−0.82(7.46)	−3.06(4.42)	−1.90(4.47)
	CAGDP2	Mean/SD	−0.0001(4.69)	−4.20(4.04)	2.09(4.83)	0.004(3.53)
	GROWTH	Mean/SD	2.74(8.17)	4.93(6.41)	1.07(6.61)	2.32(11.26)
Tunisia (93)	TBGDP2	Mean/SD	5.00(1.68)	5.33(2.56)	5.04(1.28)	4.73(0.77)
	CAGDP2	Mean/SD	1.73(1.40)	3.83(1.35)	1.77(1.27)	0.91(0.54)
	GROWTH	Mean/SD	5.31(3.18)	7.37(3.61)	3.88(3.43)	5.00(1.57)
Turkey (94)	TBGDP2	Mean/SD	2.89(1.32)	2.71(1.44)	2.25(0.98)	3.45(1.13)
	CAGDP2	Mean/SD	0.07(0.25)	0.16(0.38)	0.06(0.27)	0.02(0.10)
	GROWTH	Mean/SD	4.22(4.00)	4.74(3.49)	4.05(3.94)	3.69(4.90)

Country	Variables (%)		1970–2000	1970–1979	1980–1989	1990–1999
Tanzania	TBGDP2	Mean/SD	5.76(2.04)	5.08(2.65)	6.55(1.92)	5.75(1.22)
(96)	CAGDP2	Mean/SD	4.57(1.92)	3.41(3.12)	4.10(1.44)	5.67(1.43)
	GROWTH	Mean/SD	2.47(10.47)	4.68(4.09)	0.29(16.74)	2.48(6.92)
Uganda	TBGDP2	Mean/SD	4.81(2.63)	6.97(2.03)	—	3.00(1.63)
(97)	CAGDP2	Mean/SD	1.51(1.11)	—	1.07(1.36)	1.95(0.56)
	GROWTH	Mean/SD	4.18(8.43)	−0.59(8.32)	5.99(11.45)	6.73(1.68)
Uruguay	TBGDP2	Mean/SD	1.08(1.95)	0.99(1.22)	−0.04(2.31)	2.06(1.67)
(98)	CAGDP2	Mean/SD	0.98(1.50)	2.25(1.32)	1.23(1.86)	0.40(0.99)
	GROWTH	Mean/SD	2.08(5.17)	2.81(3.23)	0.17(7.37)	3.68(3.69)
Zambia	TBGDP2	Mean/SD	−5.69(6.03)	−9.51(6.28)	−2.26(2.31)	−0.29(1.18)
(102)	CAGDP2	Mean/SD	3.14(4.38)	−0.07(1.28)	3.35(5.25)	4.63(2.88)
	GROWTH	Mean/SD	1.58(4.00)	2.27(4.98)	1.33(3.51)	0.98(3.96)
Zimbabwe	TBGDP2	Mean/SD	1.07(1.35)	−1.43(−)	0.88(1.45)	1.68(0.70)
(103)	CAGDP2	Mean/SD	2.32(1.83)	1.35(3.19)	2.62(1.81)	1.77(0.90)
	GROWTH	Mean/SD	3.40(5.67)	3.93(6.57)	5.00(4.85)	2.07(5.51)
World	TBGDP2	Mean/SD	3.77(1.17)	3.22(6.97)	3.76(7.25)	4.10(3.76)
	CAGDP2	Mean/SD	2.101(0.75)	2.15(3.23)	2.02(3.44)	1.59(2.02)
	GROWTH	Mean/SD	3.50(1.27)	4.61(6.82)	3.49(6.61)	3.30(3.49)

Variables

ADVGR	growth rate in developed countries (%)
CA	current account
CAGDP	current account balance to GDP
CAGDP1	current account balance to GDP (%)
CAGDP2	cagdp*(−1) = current account deficits to GDP (%) (+ve)
CG	government share of CGDP
CGDP	Real gross domestic product per capita (current prices)
CI	investment share of CGDP
CINTEREST	annual percentage change in world interest rate (%)
DEBRSIMP	debt service as a percentage of total imports (%)
DEBT	long-term outstanding debt (US$ mil.)
GDEBTSIMP	percentage change in debt service in total imports of goods and services (%)
GROIL	annual percentage change in oil price (%)
GROWTH	annual percentage change in real GDP using Heston, Summer and Aten's purchasing power parity real GDP
INTEREST	world interest rate
KI	investment share of RGDPL
LIBADVGR	liberalisation dummy interacting with developed countries growth rates (%)
LIBER	liberalisation dummy taking the value 1 when the country was liberalised
LIBERTM	time period elapsed from date of liberalisation
LIBGROWTH	liberalisation dummy interacting with growth in country under consideration
LIBPPI	liberalisation dummy interacting with income terms of trade (index)
OIL	crude oil price
OPENK	openness as a percentage to constant price GDP (%)
OPENNESS	exports plus imports as a share of GDP (%)
PPI	income terms of trade = (value of exports/unit value of imports) * 100
RERI	real exchange rate
TB	trade balance

TBGDP	trade balance to GDP
TBGDP1	trade balance to GDP (%)
TBGDP2	TBGDP* (−1) = trade deficits to GDP % (+ve)

References

Agosin, M (1991). Trade policy reform and economic performance: A review of the issues and some preliminary evidence. UNCTAD Discussion Papers, No. 41, Geneva.

Ahmed, N (2000). Export responses to trade liberalisation in Bangladesh: A cointegration analysis. *Applied Economics*, 32, 1077–1084.

Arellano, M and SR Bond (1991). Some tests of specification for panel data: Monte Carlo evidence and an application to employment equations. *Review of Economic Studies*, 58, 277–297.

Bacha, EL (1984). Growth with limited supplies of foreign exchange: A reappraisal of the two-gap model. In *Economic Structure and Performance*, Essays in honour of H.B. Chenery, M Syrquin, L Taylor and L Westphal (eds.). New York: Academic Press.

Bacha, EL (1990). A three-gap model of foreign transfers and the GDP growth rate in developing countries. *Journal of Development Economics*, 32, 279–296.

Barro, RJ and JW Lee (1994). Sources of economic growth. *Carnegie-Rochester Conference Series on Public Policy*, 40, 1–46.

Bertola, G and R Faini (1991). Import demand and non-tariff barriers: The impact of trade liberalisation. *Journal of Development Economics*, 34, 269–286.

Bleaney, M. (1999). Trade reform, macroeconomic performance and export growth in ten Latin American countries 1979–1995. *Journal of International Trade and Economic Development*, 8, 89–105.

Chenery, H and M Bruno (1962). Development alternatives in an open economy: The case of israel. *The Economic Journal*, 72(285), 79–103.

Chenery, H and A Strout (1966). Foreign assistance and economic development. *American Economic Review*, 56, 149–179.

Clarke, R and C Kirkpatrick (1992). Trade policy reform and economic performance in developing countries: Assessing the empirical evidence. In *Industrial and Trade Policy Reform in Developing Countries*, R Adhikari, C Kirkpatrick and J Weiss (eds.). Manchester: Manchester University Press.

Dollar, D and A Kray (2004). Trade, growth and poverty. *Economic Journal*, 114(493), F22–F49.

Dean JM, S Desai and J Riedel (1994). Trade policy reform in developing countries since 1985: A review of the evidence. World Bank Discussion Paper No. 267, Washington, DC.

Elliott, DR and R Rhodd (1999). Explaining growth rate differences in highly indebted countries: An extension to Thirlwall and Hussain. *Applied Economics*, 31(9), 1145–1148.

Edwards, S (1993). Openness, trade liberalisation, and growth in developing countries. *The Journal of Economic Literature*, 31, 1358–1393.

Frankel, JA and D Romer (1999). Does trade cause growth? *The American Economic Review*, 89(3), 379–399.

Greenaway, D and D Sapsford (1994). What does liberalisation do for exports and growth? *Weltwirtschaftliches Archiv*, 130, 152–174.

Helleiner, G (ed.) (1994). *Trade Policy and Industrialisation in Turbulent Times.* London: Routledge, p. 31.

International Monetary Fund, *World Economic Outlook*, various issues.

Irwin, DA and M Tervio (2002). Does Trade Raise Income? Evidence from the Twentieth Century. *Journal of International Economics*, 58, 1–18.

Jenkins, R (1996). Trade performance and export performance in Bolivia. *Development and Change*, 27, 693–716.

Johnston, J (1996). *Econometric Methods.* New York: McGraw Hill.

Joshi, V and IMD Little (1996). *India's Economic Reforms 1991–2001.* Oxford: Oxford University Press.

Krugman, P (1989). Differences in income elasticities and trends in real exchange rates. *European Economic Review*, 33, 1031–1054.

Little, IMD, RN Cooper, WM Corden and S Rajapatirana (1993). *Boon, Crisis and Adjustment. The Macroeconomic Experience of Developing Countries.* New York: Oxford University Press.

Melo, O and MG Vogt (1984). Determinants of the demand for imports of Venezuela. *Journal of Development Economics*, 14, 351–358.

Ocampo, JA and L Taylor (1998). Trade liberalisation in developing economics: Modest benefits but problems with productivity growth, macro prices and income distribution. *Economic Journal*, 108, 1523–1546.

Ranaweera, T (2003). Alternative paths to structural adjustment in Uzbekistan in a three-gap framework. World Bank Policy Research, Working Paper 3145, Washington, DC.

Reinhart, C and P Wickham (1994). Commodity prices — cyclical weakness or secular decline? IMF Working Papers 94/7, International Monetary Fund.

Rodriguez, F and D Rodrik (2000). Trade policy and economic growth: A skeptic's guide to the cross-national evidence. *National Bureau of Economic Research* (NBER), No. 7081, Cambridge, MA.

Sachs, J and A Warner (1995). Economic reform and the process of global integration. *Brookings Papers on Economic Activity*, 1, 1–118.

Shafaedin, SM (1994). The impact of trade liberalisation on exports and GDP in least developed countries. UNCTAD Discussion Papers, No. 85, Geneva.

Summers, R, A Heston and B Aten (2001). *Penn World Table Version 6.0.* Center for International Comparisons at the University of Pennsylvania (CICUP).

Taylor, L (1991). *Foreign Resource Flows and Developing Country Growth.* Research for Action 8, World Institute of Development Economics Research, United Nations University, Helsinki.

Thirlwall, AP (1979). The balance of payments constrained growth as an explanation of international growth rate differences. *Banca Nazionale del Lavoro Quarterly Review*, 128, 44–53.

Thirlwall, AP and NM Hussain (1982). The balance of payments constraint, capital flows and economic growth rate differences between developing countries. *Oxford Economic Papers*, 34(3), 498–509.

Thomas, V, J Nash and S Edwards (1991). *Best Practices in Trade Policy Reform.* Oxford: Oxford University Press.

UNCTAD (1989). *Trade and Development Report 1989*, Geneva.

UNCTAD (1995). *Handbook of International Trade and Development Statistics*, Geneva.

UNCTAD (1999). *Trade and Development Report*, Geneva.

Wacziarg, R (2001). Measuring the dynamic gains from trade. *World Bank Economic Review*, 15(3), 393–429.

Weiss, J (1992). Export response to trade reforms: Recent Mexican experience. *Development Policy Review*, 10, 43–60.

Wood, A (1997). Openness and wage inequality in developing countries: The Latin American challenge to East Asian conventional wisdom. *World Bank Economic Review,* 11(1).

Wooldridge, JM (2002). *Econometric Analysis of Cross Section and Panel Data.* Massachusetts: Cambridge University Press.

World Bank (1998). *Global Economic Perspectives 1998/99.* Washington, DC: World Bank.

Chapter 9

Relationship between Trade Liberalisation, Growth and Balance of Payments in Developing Countries: An Econometric Study*

Ashok Parikh

University of East Anglia, Norwich, UK

Introduction

The objectives of this study are to examine the impact of liberalisation on economic growth and then the extent to which economic growth influences trade balances and current accounts of a group of developing countries in different regions of the world. Has liberalisation changed the relationship between economic growth and trade balance due to its differing effects on economic growth in various developing regions over different time periods? Previous research in this field tends to give conflicting results. Some studies show that the countries that went for liberalisation programmes have improved their export performance (Thomas *et al.* 1991; Joshi and Little, 1996; Helleiner, 1994; Bleaney, 1999; Ahmed, 2000). On the other hand, other studies have found little evidence of a relationship

* This study was prepared while the author was visiting the Hamburg Institute of International Economics, Hamburg, Germany. The author wishes to thank Dr. Carsten Hefeker and participants at the seminar for their useful comments, the Leverhulme Trust for the Emeritus award, Dr. T. R. Gourvish for improving the paper, the referees and editor of "*International Trade Journal*" for their helpful comments and Dr. Gurleen Popli for her statistical assistance.

between trade liberalisation and economic growth (UNCTAD, 1989; Clarke and Kirkpatrick, 1992; Greenaway and Sapsford, 1994; Shafaedin, 1994; Jenkins, 1996). On the import side, there is a strong positive impact of trade liberalisation on the growth of imports, and this impact is effected through the sensitivity of price and income changes (Melo and Vogt, 1984; Bertola and Faini, 1991). Thirlwall and Santos-Paulino (2004) found that the impact of liberalisation differs as between highly protected countries, and less protected countries, and the response to liberalisation on economic growth was very high when liberalisation was adopted in a highly protected environment. The positive effect of trade liberalisation on import growth was far greater in the more highly protected industries in the period before liberalisation and showed that the impact of a more liberalised trade regime, independent of duty reductions, raised import growth by more than exports. Thirlwall and Santos-Paulino found that import growth increased by about 6 percent per annum, while export growth rose by less than 2 percent per annum. This precipitated a worsening of the trade balance by over 2 percent of GDP; however, the impact on current account was only about 0.8 percent of GDP on average. Their overall conclusion was that free trade and flexible exchange rates do not always ensure that unemployed domestic resources are easily converted into scarce foreign exchange. Dollar and Kray (2004) have shown that the growth pattern of countries that have liberalised have shown an acceleration in their real income. In the 1990s, globalising developing countries grew by 5 percent per capita, rich countries by 2.2 percent and non-globalising developing countries by only 1.4 percent. Their view is that the countries that have followed a globalisation path are catching up with rich countries while non-globalisers are lagging behind. Irwin and Trevio (2002) following the study of Frankel and Romer (1999) conclude that the countries that trade more as a proportion of their GDP have higher incomes even after controlling for the endogeneity of trade. On the one hand, trade contributes to an improvement in real income and per capita growth, while on the other hand, if trade is not combined with adequate policies to balance imports against exports, it could generate balance of trade and balance of payments deficits. Greenaway *et al.* (2002) found that trade liberalisation did not have growth enhancing effects, and their evidence was mixed. When a dynamic panel framework was used, they found that liberalisation had an impact on economic growth with a lag.

Rodriguez and Rodrik (2000) raised some concerns about the robustness of the positive relationship between liberalisation and economic growth. Their liberalisation variable was based on the Sachs-Warner (1995) classification. Wacziarg (2001) used a different classification of liberalisation, and also made use of updated data on income levels (Summers *et al.* 2001). This study uses updated data on income levels and studies the relationship between liberalisation and economic growth. Moreover, the study is extended to examine the impact of liberalisation and economic growth on the trade balance and current accounts of a group of developing countries at a regional level. Wacziarg (2001) did not study the impact on the balance of payments, while Thirlwall and Sanots-Paulino did not provide any theoretical model to conduct an empirical study and did not use the latest panel data techniques in a dynamic model.

Measurement of liberalisation and openness indicators is imperfect in most studies. Liberalisation is measured as a dichotomous variable, which fails to distinguish between the intensity of liberalisation and the time period elapsed from the date of liberalisation. Before obtaining a liberalisation variable, a subsample of developing countries with detailed information on broader economic and political context of trade reforms was collected, and our large sample results are interpreted in the context of country case studies. Details on country case studies can be obtained from the author.

In the second section, static panel data models are used to examine the relationship between liberalisation and domestic economic growth and the impact of liberalisation and domestic growth on the trade balance. In the third section, a model linking the trade balance or current account to domestic growth is provided. The model is based on the consumption smoothing principle for the economy and follows a dynamic optimisation model under a current account constraint. In the fourth section, the dynamic model is estimated using the dynamic panel data technique. Economic growth is an endogenous variable, and our estimation procedure takes this into account. In the fifth section, a regional analysis for two regions, namely Africa and Latin America (including Asian countries), is undertaken, and some of the contrasting features of the results are shown. A separate analysis for a group of Asian countries was not possible since the number of Asian countries in our sample was too small. In the last section, some policy conclusions are drawn.

Liberalisation and Growth Relationship

Data for this study are derived from various sources, the main ones being the *International Financial Statistics*, the *Penn World Tables*, Wacziarg's study on liberalisation and growth and the Sachs–Warner measure of liberalisation. Trade balance and current account figures are obtained from the IMF issues, while an openness indicator and liberalisation dummy for the 1990–1999 period was taken from Summers, Heston and Aten (2001) and Wacziarg, respectively. Means and standard deviations of growth, TBGDP1 (trade balance to GDP in %) and CAGDP1 (current account to GDP in %) for each country are presented in Annex 1 of Chap. 8. For the cross-sectional study, the data on various variables were taken from Barro and Lee (1994), Banks (2001) and Summers, Heston and Aten (2001). At the outset 75 developing countries dispersed over different regions of the world, namely Africa, Asia and Latin America. Almost all Eastern European and developed market-oriented economies were excluded. Growth, investment and openness can be stimulated under liberalisation if the right conditions prevail in the economies under consideration.[a] The year of liberalisation and the time period elapsed from liberalisation are used as two separate variables affecting investment, growth and openness. The openness indicator is the ratio of imports plus exports to GDP, the investment rate is expressed as a percentage of GDP, and the growth rate of per capita GDP is expressed in real terms in cross-section regressions. Growth rates in the panel study refer to the growth rate in total real GDP at PPP rates in dollar terms for the countries under consideration. Variables used in the cross-sections and panel study are fully summarized in Appendices 1 and 2. Means and

[a] Edwards (1993) considers the openness–growth relationship using existing indicators. Overall, nine indicators were used: (i) the Sachs–Warner index; (ii) the World Bank Integration index; (iii) the Edward Leamer Openness index; (iv) the average black market premium; (v) the average tariff rate as developed by Barro and Lee (1994); (vi) the average coverage of non-tariff barriers (Barro and Lee); (vii) the Heritage Foundation index of distortions; (viii) the ratio of total revenues on trade taxes to total trade and (ix) the regression index of Holger Wolf on import distortions. His conclusion on various measures was that "inspite of significant efforts and ingenuity, there has not been too much progress in this area". There existed a positive relationship between trade intensity and growth performance on the basis of the cross-country plot of average annual growth rate against the average annual growth rate in trade.

standard deviations of various variables for the countries of the sample by time periods can be obtained from the author.

Panel study: liberalisation, growth and trade balance relationships

Both fixed effect and random effect models (Table 1A) were estimated on a binary liberalisation indicator, defined by the dates of liberalisation. The growth in real GDP was regressed on a liberalisation dummy for the entire period, and for three separate periods, namely 1970–1979, 1980–1989 and 1990–1999. For a period-by-period analysis a change in the pattern of relationship between trade balance to GDP ratios and current account to GDP ratios is examined. For the whole period, there exists a significant negative relationship between trade balance and economic growth. The behaviour of current account with respect to GDP growth is the reverse of the trade balance relationship. For a decade-by-decade relationship, we find that growth reduces current account deficits in the 1980–1989 period, while it has no significant relationship in earlier or later periods. Liberalisation has a deleterious effect upon the trade balance, while growth, current account and investment rate are all encouraged by liberalisation. The timing effect of liberalisation (Table 1B) is negative and significant in periods 1970–1979 and 1980–1989 on a openness indicator, while the impact of the timing effect on trade balance to GDP revealed a deterioration in the first period, an improvement in the second period and became insignificant in the last period. A similar analysis was conducted at a regional level, and some of the summary results are provided here. Detailed results can be obtained from the author. Liberalisation clearly promotes growth, openness and investment in Asian countries. The trade balance tends to deteriorate with economic growth in Asian economies, while there is no such evidence for either Latin American or African economies. For Latin American economies, the direct impact of liberalisation is to reduce the trade balance, while for African economies, liberalisation has improved the trade balance. We have a mixed bag of results at a regional level as the data and number of observations differed.[b]

[b] The relationship between trade balance and GDP growth rates differs between Latin American and East Asian regions because of the lack of establishment of new trading regions in Latin America and slow growth in these countries as compared to East Asia.

Table 1A. Bivariate relationship between trade balance, GDP growth and liberalisation year using panel data.

1970–1999: developing countries: regression coefficients and t-statistic						1970–1979: developing countries: regression coefficients and t-statistic					
Dependent	Model	Constant	LIBER	Growth	Hausmann test χ^2	Model	Constant	LIBER	Growth	Hausmann test χ^2	Dependent
GROWTH	FE	3.46***	0.28		17.65[1]	FE	3.38***	8.23**		2.18	GROWTH
		(17.73)	(0.88)				(5.60)	(2.14)			
TBGDP1	RE	−3.02***	−0.82***		0.06	FE	−3.15***	−0.17		0.63	TBGDP1
		(−4.34)	(−3.46)				(−8.93)	(−0.08)			
CAGDP1	RE	−2.40***	0.91***		0.27	RE	−2.42***	0.85		0.07	CAGDP1
		(−8.24)	(5.62)				(−5.67)	(0.85)			
OPENK	RE	61.84***	4.05***		2.00	RE	63.74***	7.31		0.05	OPENK
		(13.06)	(3.20)				(9.49)	(0.74)			
KI	FE	13.17***	−0.56**		76.58[1]	RE	13.67***	0.4426		2.69	KI
		(83.37)	(−2.10)				(12.92)	(0.23)			
TBGDP1	RE	−4.04***		−0.04**	1.52	FE	−3.34***		0.001	52.10[1]	TBGDP1
		(−5.18)		(−2.37)			(−18.21)		(0.04)		
CAGDP1	FE	−2.11**		0.02	6.38[1]	RE	−2.13**		−0.0051	0.29	CAGDP1
		(−27.67)		(1.65)			(−5.79)		(−0.24)		
1980–1989: developing countries: regression coefficients and t-statistic						1990–1999: developing countries: regression coefficients and t-statistic					
GROWTH	FE	2.52***	1.11		1.49[1]	FE	1.87***	1.93***		0.91	GROWTH
		(6.91)	(1.10)				(3.00)	(2.72)			
TBGDP1	RE	−3.25***	0.40		0.36	RE	−2.94***	−0.83**		0.24	TBGDP1
		(−3.98)	(0.64)				(−4.06)	(−2.00)			
CAGDP1	FE	−2.29**	0.40		1.21	FE	−2.32***	1.13***		0.72[1]	CAGDP1
		(−14.71)	(0.92)				(−8.12)	(3.45)			
OPENK	FE	59.77***	−5.11***		3.86	FE	61.90***	5.98***		4.02[1]	OPENK
		(79.88)	(−2.46)				(38.35)	(3.24)			

(Continued)

Table 1A. (*Continued*).

1980–1989: developing countries: regression coefficients and t-statistic						1990–1999: developing countries: regression coefficients and t-statistic					
Dependent	Model	Constant	LIBER	Growth	Hausmann test χ^2	Model	Constant	LIBER	Growth	Hausmann test χ^2	Dependent
KI	FE	12.35***	0.311		9.92[1]	FE	10.87***	2.14***		8.49[1]	KI
		(63.17)	(0.57)				(27.75)	(4.79)			
TBGDP1	FE	−3.90***		−0.03	5.41[1]	RE	−4.22***		−0.03*	0.04	TBGDP1
		(−23.50)		(−1.33)			(−5.01)		(−1.81)		
CAGDP1	FE	−2.42***		0.002	21.28[1]	RE	−1.86***		0.031**	0.22	CAGDP1
		(−21.00)		(0.13)			(−6.43)		(2.25)		

Note: ***significant at 1 percent; **significant at 5 percent; *significant at 10 percent.
[1]Random effect is rejected, t-statistic in parentheses.

Table 1B. Multivariate relationship between trade balance, GDP growth, timing of liberalisation and liberalisation year using panel data.

	Region	Time period	Model	Constant	LIBER	LIBERTM
GROWTH	Developing countries	1970–1979	FE	2.34 (1.60)	8.68*** (2.23)	−0.08 (−0.83)
	Developing countries	1980–1989	FE	2.54*** (4.30)	0.96 (0.82)	0.02 (0.27)
	Developing countries	1990–1999	FE	1.71*** (2.46)	2.69*** (3.00)	−0.06 (−0.77)
OPENK	Developing countries	1970–1979	FE	51.13*** (48.20)	11.38 (−0.29)	−0.89*** (−3.80)
	Developing countries	1990–1999	FE	58.97*** (35.06)	−3.76* (−1.74)	1.50*** (7.59)
KI	Developing countries	1970–1979	FE	14.77*** (15.69)	−2.55 (−0.96)	0.33 (0.55)
	Developing countries	1980–1989	FE	10.63*** (35.54)	2.74*** (4.60)	−0.40*** (−8.28)
	Developing countries	1990–1999	FE	11.22*** (26.10)	2.47*** (4.47)	−0.06 (−1.17)
TBGDP1	Developing countries	1970–1979	FE	−5.82*** (−7.30)	1.01 (0.49)	−0.19*** (−3.74)
	Developing countries	1980–1989	FE	−1.33*** (−3.80)	−1.99*** (−2.77)	0.43*** (7.39)
	Developing countries	1990–1999	FE	−2.71*** (−6.53)	−0.61 (−1.24)	−0.05 (−1.15)
CAGDP1	Developing countries	1970–1979	FE	−3.44*** (−3.55)	0.71 (0.31)	−0.12 (−1.45)
	Developing countries	1980–1989	FE	−0.74*** (−3.33)	1.65*** (3.61)	−0.35*** (−9.49)
	Developing countries	1990–1999	FE	−2.40*** (−7.24)	1.23*** (2.95)	−0.01 (−0.25)

Note: ***Significant at 1 percent; **significant at 5 percent; *significant at 10 percent; t-statistic in parentheses.

Table 2 reports the results of cross-country regressions. These allow the possibility of using some political[c] and other variables in the regression

[c] Socio-political and environmental variables have played a crucial role in economic development, growth and international trade. Countries that maintain permanent peace, domestic and political stability, and are endowed with abundant resources including a skilled labour force have a high potential for growth and development. Socio-political variables cannot be

Table 2. Cross-section regressions using two periods: regression coefficients, t-statistic and R^2 using various models.

Explanatory variables[1]	1970–1989						1990–1999					
	(1)	(2)	(3)	(4)	(5)	(6)	(1)	(2)	(3)	(4)	(5)	(6)
LRGDPCH70/	0.1694	0.0401	−1.2976***	−1.3161***	−1.4763***	−1.3681***	1.2078***	2.2549***	1.7564*	−0.4094	−0.3832	−0.3533
LRGDPCH89	(0.44)	(0.05)	(−2.82)	(−3.01)	(−3.24)	(−3.12)	(3.22)	(6.15)	(1.72)	(−0.60)	(−0.52)	(−0.48)
LIBERAL70–89/				1.1909***	1.1833**	1.02259**				−1.1253*	−1.2435*	−0.8937
LIBERAL90–99				(2.81)	(2.56)	(2.27)				(−1.81)	(−1.90)	(−1.23)
POL					−0.5981	−0.7461					0.3658	0.2968
					(−1.12)	(−1.44)					(0.50)	(0.41)
SEC70/SEC85			0.8014	0.4480	1.9431	−0.3708			6.1405**	6.0446**	6.3279**	5.7521**
			(0.41)	(0.23)	(1.03)	(−0.19)			(2.11)	(2.54)	(2.50)	(2.23)
PRI70/PRI85			0.8922	0.5009	0.2077	0.5949			−4.5141**	−0.6065	−0.6625	−0.5047
			(0.72)	(0.42)	(0.17)	(0.50)			(−2.14)	(−0.33)	(−0.35)	(−0.26)
GVDXE7084/			−0.1166***	−0.1142***	−0.1098***	−0.1158***			−0.0145	−0.0587	−0.0633	−0.0633
CG8998			(−3.53)	(−3.63)	(−3.34)	(−3.61)			(−0.24)	(−1.11)	(−1.17)	(−1.17)
REVCOUP7085/			−0.9109	−1.1062	−0.7022	−0.4516			−0.8107	−0.9353	−0.9953	−1.1495
REV8998			(−1.15)	(−1.47)	(−0.77)	(−0.52)			(−0.90)	(−0.97)	(−1.00)	(−1.15)
ASSASS7085/			−0.1024	−0.1993	−0.1910	−0.1313			0.0339	0.6849**	0.7338**	0.7185**
ASSASS8998			(−0.34)	(−0.69)	(−0.63)	(−0.45)			(0.13)	(2.00)	(2.09)	(2.04)
PPI70DEV/			0.3020	0.2081	0.0188	0.1606			0.8334	−0.8953	−0.8759	−0.7300
PPI89DEV			(0.71)	(0.51)	(0.04)	(0.39)			(0.80)	(−1.20)	(−1.12)	(−0.92)
INV7089/			0.1443***	0.1307***	0.1133***	0.1298***			0.0313	0.0330	0.0310	0.0316
INV8998/			(3.49)	(3.31)	(2.73)	(3.24)			(0.52)	(0.57)	(0.52)	(0.53)
DENSI60/			0.0061***	0.0055**		0.0060***						0.0031
DENSI80			(2.74)	(2.54)		(2.76)						(1.08)
Intercept7089/	−0.3575	1.4941	9.6684***	9.9575***	11.7713***	10.66***	−8.2728***	−16.91***	−11.2308	3.8959		2.704
Intercept9099	(−0.12)	(0.26)	(2.88)	(3.11)	(3.51)	(3.30)	(−2.80)	(−5.77)	(−1.51)	(0.82)		(0.49)
Adj R-sq.	−0.0113	−0.0383	0.4344	0.5804	0.5450	0.5989	0.1306	0.6120	0.6076	0.2394	0.2280	0.2304
Number of observations 1970–1989/ 1990–1999	73	28	63	62	63	61	71	26	24	64	62	62

Note: ***Significant at 1 percent; ** significant at 5 percent; *significant at 10 percent; t-statistics in parentheses.
[1]Explanatory variables for 1990–1999 are shown in the same column with the same symbol with 1989 or 1990 base year.

models. The liberalisation dummy enters highly significantly with a magnitude of about 1.18–1.20 percentage point of annual growth during 1970–1989. This is much smaller than that in Wacziarg's paper and it could be due to the non-inclusion of developed countries in the sample. The Sachs–Warner study suggests that open economies tend to converge unconditionally while closed economies do not. Openness, base-year real GDP, investment rate, density of population and government consumption to GDP are all highly significant in the remaining results provided in Table 2. The openness variable is not significant for the 1990–1999 period, and liberalising economies do not show any convergence. Our conclusion is that the openness measure could be quite weak for the period under study.[d]

Effect of trade liberalisation and growth on trade balance and current account

The impact of trade liberalisation on the trade balance and current account of the balance of payments is ambiguous irrespective of the framework used for the analysis of balance of payments. In the elasticity approach to balance of payments, the effect of liberalisation will depend upon the price elasticities of exports and imports. If the impact is measured in foreign currency, export earnings will increase if the price elasticity is greater than 1, and import payments will increase if the price elasticity is less than 1 in absolute terms. In the absorption approach to balance of payments, the effect of liberalisation will be realised through real income changes. Even if real income increases,

---

easily quantified. Political scientists have constructed indices measuring key socio-political conditions in each economy. Many such variables were employed in the literature to capture the presence or absence of political stability, economic freedom, corruption, democracy, economic efficiency and other conditions affecting economic performance of countries.

[d] The date based indicator of liberalisation was used in a three-period analysis using a panel of three cross-sections. A panel was constructed with three periods, 1970–1979, 1980–1989 and 1990–1998, in order to estimate the effects of the openness indicator on growth over a longer span of time. The estimated coefficient on the liberalisation variable lies between insignificant and 1.19. For the period 1989–1998 the liberalisation coefficient is not significantly different from zero. In Table 3, when estimates are constrained, it was found that liberalisation has an effect on growth, and the impact for 1 unit change is 1.62 percent point change on growth. The conditional convergence hypothesis holds. An extreme political repression tends to reduce economic growth, while an increase in density of population increases economic growth.

Table 3. Regression coefficients, z-statistic: Arellano–Bond dynamic panel estimation 1980–1999 (42 countries unbalanced panel).

Name of the variable	TBGDP1[1]		CAGDP1[1]		TBGDP1[2]		CAGDP1[2]	
	Coefficient	z-statistic[3]	Coefficient	z-statistic[3]	Coefficient	z-statistic[3]	Coefficient	z-statistic[3]
TBGDP1[4](−1)	0.7335***	29.44			0.7028***	6.16		
CAGDP1[4](−1)			0.5198***	8.00			0.4436***	7.92
GROWTH[4]	−0.0346*	−1.93	0.0020	0.12	−0.0360	−1.32	−0.0123	−0.64
GROWTH[4](−1)					−0.0335**	−2.23	0.0039	0.45
PPI	0.0142***	3.35	0.0021	1.69	0.0141**	2.79	0.0072**	2.38
LIBER	0.3167	0.54	−0.3442*	−1.90	0.7189	1.10	0.4942	1.08
LIBPPI[4]	−0.0104**	−2.35			−0.0053*	−1.79		
ADVGR	0.0018	0.14	0.0234***	3.02	0.0569**	2.17	0.0266	1.31
ADVGR(−1)					−0.1083	−3.61	−0.0733***	−3.08
LIBGROWTH[4]	0.0129	0.43						
DEBTSR			1.3365	0.78			1.2015	0.79
GLTDOL			−0.0058**	−2.12			0.0062	0.95
CINTEREST			0.0025	1.91			0.0025	0.84
CONSTANT	0.0489**	2.76	0.0373**	2.78	0.0351	0.53	0.1315**	2.22
First-order AC	−12.94(0.000)		−3.04(0.0024)		−3.10(0.0019)		−3.82(0.0001)	
Second-order AC	1.88(0.0604)		1.22(0.2208)		1.07(0.2845)		0.71(0.48)	

(*Continued*)

Table 3. (*Continued*).

Name of the variable	TBGDP1[1]		CAGDP1[1]		TBGDP1[2]		CAGDP1[2]	
	Coefficient	z-statistic[3]	Coefficient	z-statistic[3]	Coefficient	z-statistic[3]	Coefficient	z-statistic[3]
Wald[5] χ^2			247.98(8DF)		359.03(23DF)		3025.52(25DF)	
Number of obs.	888		849		537		692	
Sargan[6] test χ^2	655.35(0.00)		35.82(1.00)		15.10(1.00)		15.72(1.00)	

***Significant at 1 percent level; **significant at 5 percent level; *significant at 10 percent level.

[1]Time dummies are not used.

[2]Time dummies used.

[3]z-statistic follows a normal distribution and 5 percent critical value is -1.96 or $+1.96$.

[4]For the growth and lagged TBGDP1 or CAGDP1 variable two period lags are used as instruments. This includes the interactions of liberalisation with the right-hand side variables.

[5]The Wald test is the test of the null hypothesis that all coefficients excepting the constant and time dummies are zero.

[6]The Sargan test of overidentifying restrictions is from the two-step estimation.

the balance of payments may not improve if the absorption propensity is greater than unity. If trade liberalisation reduces prices, this will increase real absorption through a real balance effect and money illusion, but it could increase absorption if there is a redistribution of income to the traded goods sector where the propensity to save is higher than that in the non-traded sector. In the monetary approach to balance of payments, the liberalisation could affect both the demand and the supply of real money balances. Rose and Ostry (1989) conducted an analysis of the impact of tariff changes on real trade balance and have found no statistically significant effect.

The impact of liberalisation on trade performance is measured using monetary units, because it is the nominal gap which measures a country's shortage of foreign exchange and by how much a country requires to borrow to sustain growth in case liberalisation worsens the payments on current account. Relative prices are introduced by making use of the terms of the trade variable. Data on nominal (barter) terms of trade are not available for a large number of sample countries, and hence we have to use the available information on the income terms of trade meaning thereby the index of purchasing power of exports. An income variable is introduced as the growth in real income and is expressed in purchasing power parity terms. Liberalisation improves growth performance as our results have demonstrated in the previous section. It is probable that liberalisation in a country could interact with economic growth, and hence an interaction between domestic economic growth and the dummy variable for liberalisation is constructed. If the sign of this variable is negative in the trade balance relationship then it has raised the growth rate, which in turn has raised import growth and worsened the trade balance/balance of payments. The coefficient on the shift dummy variable (LIBER) should be regarded as the pure liberalisation effect on trade balance, independent of liberalisation working through its impact on growth performance. The nations differ in size, and this is resolved by using trade balance to GDP ratios in percentage terms (TBGDP1).

Theoretical Base of Current Account and GDP Growth Relationship

In this section, a dynamic model is proposed to study the relationship between GDP growth and trade balance to GDP ratios. Thirlwall and

Santos-Paulino (2004) examined the relationship between trade balance and GDP growth but did not provide any theory for the relationship. This theoretical model is largely designed for developed countries but it provides a framework for studying the relationship between trade balance and GDP growth rates when the debt–GDP ratio is constant. Moreover, a theory consistent empirical relationship between trade balance and GDP growth rates is formulated and estimated in the latter section.

We consider a small open economy inhabited by a representative agent with an infinite time horizon. The economy starts in period t and continues forever. We normalise population size to unity. The utility function for infinite period is

$$U(t) = \sum_{s=t}^{\infty} \beta^{s-t} U(C_s), \tag{1}$$

where C_s is consumption in period s and β is the discount rate. Deriving the t period-budget constraint, the current account with constant interest rate is

$$CA_t = B_{t+1} - B_t = Y_t + rB_t - C_t - G_t - I_t, \tag{2}$$

where CA is the current account, B is the net foreign assets accumulated on prior dates, I is the investment and is equivalent to changes in the capital stock, C is the consumption, G is the government expenditure and t refers to the time period.

There is an accounting equivalence between the net export surplus in the current account and the negative value of the capital account. The current account balance as defined in Eq. (2) is the change in the net foreign assets position between two periods.

If output is determined by $Y = AF(K)$, i.e., output is a function of capital K (accumulated over previous periods) with A as the given technology, the utility function after substitution for consumption in period s will be

$$U_t = \sum_{s=t}^{\infty} \beta^{s-t} U[(1+r)B_s - B_{s+1} + A_s F(K_s) - (K_{s+1} - K_s) - G_s]. \tag{3}$$

One finds two necessary conditions for maximizing U_t with respect to B_{s+1} and K_{s+1} for every period $s \geq t$:

$$U'(C_s) = (1 + r)\beta U'(C_{s+1}), \tag{4}$$

$$A_{s+1}F'(K_{s+1}) = r. \tag{5}$$

These are called the consumption (Euler) equation (4), and the equality between the marginal product of capital and the world interest rate (5). $U'(C_s)$ and $F'(K_{s+1})$ are the marginal utility of consumption and the marginal product of capital (associated with technology of the period), respectively. The relevant infinite-horizon budget constraint[e] is

$$\sum_{s=t}^{\infty}\left(\frac{1}{1+r}\right)^{s-t}(C_s + I_s) = (1 + r)B_t + \sum\left(\frac{1}{1+r}\right)^{s-t}(Y_s - G_s). \tag{6}$$

Generally, there are inherent uncertainties that will affect consumption and investment decisions. In a stochastic environment, we make the assumption of rational expectations and can replace the utility maximization over time under certainty with the expected utility maximization over an infinite time period corresponding to Eq. (1). Rearranging the budget constraint and writing $TB_s = Y_s - C_s - I_s - G_s$ as the economy's trade balance in Eq. (6) we obtain

$$-(1 + r)B_t = \sum_{s=t}^{\infty}\left(\frac{1}{1+r}\right)^{s-t} TB_s. \tag{7}$$

The trade balance is the net output transferred to foreigners in each period. Suppose $Y_{s+1} = (1 + g)Y_s$, where $g > 0$ is the growth rate in output, and that the economy maintains a steady debt-output ratio (B_s/Y_s) so that $B_{s+1} = (1 + g)B_s$. The current account identity would imply a steady imbalance of $B_{s+1} - B_s = gB_s = rB_s + TB_s$, which yields

$$\frac{TB_s}{Y_s} = \frac{-(r - g)B_s}{Y_s} = \frac{-B_s}{Y_s/r - g}. \tag{8}$$

[e] This is based on the assumption that lenders will not permit an individual to die with unpaid debts and it would not be optimal for the individual to disappear leaving unused resources. Given the infinite time horizon, the countries are assumed to have the same behaviour as individuals.

To maintain a constant debt–GDP ratio the country needs to pay out the excess of interest over its growth rate. Alternatively, the necessary trade surplus as a proportion of GDP is equivalent to the ratio of the debt to the world market value of a claim on the economy's entire future. The relationship between the trade balance as a proportion to GDP and the country's growth rate is positive.[f] There are, however, possibilities of a negative relationship between economic growth and trade balances. This can happen if the behaviour of output is non-stationary.

If output follows a stochastic process

$$Y_{t+1} - Y_t = \varphi(Y_t - Y_{t-1}) \tag{9}$$

with $0 < \varphi < 1$, then output will be a non-stationary random variable, where

$$Y_t = Y_{t-1} + \sum_{s=-\infty}^{t} \varphi^{t-s} \varepsilon_s . \tag{10}$$

In the above equation, permanent output fluctuates more than the current output level. Consumption smoothing implies that an *unexpected* increase in output causes an even greater *increase* in consumption. Hence, a positive output innovation in this case implies a current account deficit.

The other possibility is the one where there is a trend productivity growth, and a small developing economy is growing faster than the world economy. In this case, the debt–GDP ratio increases forever, which is unstable. This is because a country is promoting higher growth now at the cost of future economic growth. In this case, higher economic growth could lead to trade balance deficits and/or current account deficits. Under our dynamic framework, the debt–GDP ratio could increase if there is a positive output shock or the domestic growth rate[g] is higher than that of the world

[f] The slow growing economies are likely to suffer a debt burden in the short run. In 1991, the slow growing Argentina and Nigeria had external debt as 3.9 and 4.8 percent of GDP, respectively, while for fast growing Thailand the proportion was only 0.2 percent (Obstfeld and Rogoff, 1997).

[g] It is now a well-known proposition that with integrated global capital markets there can be no intercountry differences in returns to capital (risk-adjusted), and as capital flows to the country where the rate of return is higher, the cross-country differences in marginal products of capital would disappear leading to a convergence in output per worker. This proposition

economy. Productivity shocks[h] can occur through terms of trade shocks and also through the liberalisation policy in a developing economy. A temporary deterioration in terms of trade can cause a current account deficit, whereas a permanent deterioration would cause an immediate shift to the new lower consumption level consistent with the external balance.[i]

The model does not use explicitly real exchange rate changes that could come through liberalisation and the adopted policies of the countries experiencing liberalisation. Consumption and investment plans will be sensitive to changes in real exchange rates, and trade liberalisation may contribute to improvements in the expected future growth path. If the expected future growth path is raised by adequate reforms along with liberalisation, it is rational for forward-looking agents to increase present and future consumption and invest more. This will indeed worsen the savings–investment balance and would worsen the trade and current account balances. Countries in this case would have higher real exchange rates and build-up of debt, but this will be consistent with the presented model with rational forward-looking agents in which inter-temporal budget constraints are satisfied. Some of the regression results of the static model in the second section are consistent with this conclusion, where higher economic growth leads to deterioration in the trade and current account balances.

If we assume that the world real rate of interest[j] is not constant but is equal to the growth rate in developed economies, then we have a model

---

has been empirically tested, and a plausible conclusion to draw from the debate is that there is convergence in output per worker, but it has been very slow (see Table 2, coefficient of LRGDPCH70 and LRGDPCH89).

[h] In the representative agent model, higher productivity growth will tend to weaken the current account as people borrow today against higher future incomes. In the overlapping generation model, productivity growth could raise the labour income of young workers but does not affect the wage incomes of older workers. As young savers will count more heavily in aggregate saving than old dissavers, saving will tend to rise and the current account to improve (Obstfeld, 1995).

[i] We do not distinguish between permanent and temporary deterioration in terms of trade in the empirical study because many developing countries over a long period export primary commodities and terms of trade either have moved against primary products or have not changed drastically during the last 30 years.

[j] The world rate of interest on loans provided by the World Bank and other multilateral bodies charge the interest rate prevailing in developed countries. In the long run, growth rates and real interest rates are not likely to diverge from each other.

equation for the trade balance to GDP ratio, where $CA = B_{s+1} - B_s = rB_s + TB_s$, and the ratio of current account to GDP is equivalent to $TB/\mathrm{GDP} + rB/\mathrm{GDP} = F$ (GDP growth, productivity shocks). As productivity shocks are caused by terms of trade changes, growth in the developed world and liberalisation regimes, these are considered to be determinants of productivity shocks in the trade balance to GDP ratios.

$$TB/\mathrm{GDP} = F(\text{GDP growth, terms of trade, growth in industrial countries, liberalisation}). \tag{11}$$

The above equation provided a reduced form relationship, which can be estimated from the available sample information. Moreover, under a stochastic framework when output follows a non-stationary path, the relationship between trade balance and output growth becomes negative.[k]

For current account to GDP percentages, the world interest rate that is determined by the growth rate in developed countries is used. So, the following is our estimating equation for *CA*/GDP:

$$CA/\mathrm{GDP} = F(\text{World interest rate, GDP growth, terms of trade, liberalisation}), \tag{12}$$

where the world interest rate is determined by the growth rate in developed economies.

In the above relationships, interactions between liberalisation and GDP growth and liberalisation and terms of trade are expected. The marginal effect of GDP growth on *TB*/GDP will be negative (or positive according to stationary output behaviour) as developing countries are likely to grow faster than developed countries, and their import propensity will be higher than export propensity in the short run. Moreover, the marginal impact of the terms of trade will be positive as a favourable change in the terms of trade of developing economies will lead to an improvement in the *TB*/GDP ratio.

---

[k] Liberalisation could introduce non-stationarity in output behaviour which we unfortunately could not investigate with merely 30 observations for each country and in some cases it is even less. Moreover, liberalisation could bring structural change, and even when the unit root hypothesis was not rejected it could be due to liberalisation leading to economy wide changes and repercussions. Hence we have not used unit root tests to discover non-stationarity in output behaviour.

The higher growth in developed economies will improve the trade balance to GDP ratio as the developing countries are likely to export more to the developed world (since growth in the industrialised world creates demand for commodities and raw materials including intermediate products).

Trade Balance and Growth Relationships, Structural Change and Dynamic Panel Models

The estimation of the following two static models was conducted first. Both fixed effect and random effect models[1] were estimated without any lags.

$$\begin{aligned}\left(\frac{TB}{\text{GDP}}\right)_{it} &= \delta_1 + \delta_2(\text{ADVGR})_{it} + \delta_3(\text{GROWTH})_{it} + \delta_4(\text{PPI})_{it}\\ &\quad + \delta_5(\text{LIBER})_{it} + \delta_6(\text{LIBGROWTH})_{it}\\ &\quad + \delta_7(\text{LIBPPI})_{it} + \delta_8(\text{LIBADVGR})_{it} + \varepsilon_{it},\\ &\quad i = 1, 2\ldots, 42 \text{ and } t = 1, 2, \ldots, 31 \end{aligned} \tag{13}$$

and

$$\begin{aligned}\left(\frac{CA}{\text{GDP}}\right)_{it} &= \varphi_1 + \varphi_2(\text{ADVGR})_{it} + \varphi_3(\text{GROWTH})_{it} + \varphi_4(\text{PPI})_{it}\\ &\quad + \varphi_5(\text{LIBER})_{it} + \varphi_6(\text{LIBGROWTH})_{it}\\ &\quad + \varphi_7(\text{LIBPPI})_{it} + \varphi_8(\text{LIBADVGR})_{it} + \varphi_9(\text{DEBT})_{it}\\ &\quad + \varphi_{10}\left(\frac{\text{DEBT}}{\text{GDP}}\right)_{it} + \varphi_{11}(\text{CINTEREST})_{it} + \zeta_{it},\\ &\quad i = 1, 2\ldots, 42 \text{ and } t = 1, 2, \ldots, 31 \end{aligned} \tag{14}$$

The equation for a dynamic model is in the following general form:

$$\begin{aligned} y_{it} &= \delta_1 y_{it-1} + \delta_2 y_{it-2} + \mathbf{X}_{it}\mathbf{B} + \alpha_i + \eta_t + \varepsilon_{it},\\ &\quad i = 1, 2\ldots, 42, t = 1, 2, \ldots, 31 \end{aligned} \tag{15}$$

[1] These models using the panel data analysis differ according to whether they treat intercept parameters as random or fixed across the sample. The estimators in the random effect model are the generalized least squares estimators, and they combine the within- and between-country estimators using the corresponding residual variances as weights. For elementary panel data techniques see Johnston (1996). For special treatment of panel data models, see Baltagi (1995) and Wooldridge (2002).

y_{it} is the trade balance or current account to GDP in percentages, $\mathbf{X}_{it}$ is a set of explanatory variables, namely liberalisation, growth in real GDP, purchasing power of exports (terms of trade), and interactions of liberalisation with purchasing power of exports and of liberalisation with the growth rate in real GDP in developing and developed economies. η_t is the effect of time or year dummies and may be represented as the cyclical impact on trade balance to GDP percentages. When the dependent variable is current account to GDP percentages, the debt related variables are used, namely debt service to payments ratios, the annual growth in accumulated long-term debt and the percentage change in world interest rates.[m]

The sign of the coefficients is expected to be positive with respect to the purchasing power of exports and growth in developed economies, while it is expected to be negative with respect to growth in real GDP and oil prices. Two-year lags are used on the assumption that lags are not likely to be longer.

Even if y_{it-1} and ε_{it} are not correlated, and t does not approach infinity ($t = 31$ in our case), then estimation by fixed or random effects is not consistent even if n (number of countries) approaches infinity. Arellano and Bond (1991) suggest an alternative procedure that corrects not only for the bias introduced by the lagged endogenous variable, but also permits a degree of endogeneity in the other regressors (such as the growth variable on the right-hand side variable as a subset of the **X** matrix). The Generalized Method of Moments Estimator first differences each variable and then uses the lagged values of each of the variables as instruments. Specifically,

$$\Delta y_{it} = \delta_1 \Delta y_{it-1} + \delta_2 \Delta y_{it-2} + \Delta \mathbf{X}_{it}\mathbf{B} + \Delta \varepsilon_{it}. \quad (16)$$

The first three observations are lost due to lags and differencing. Assuming that ε_{it} are not autocorrelated for each i at $t = 4$, y_{i1} and y_{i2} are valid instruments for lagged variables. Similarly, at $t = 5$, y_{i1}, $y_{i2}$and y_{i3} are

[m] We expect the current account to deteriorate with an increase in debt, increase in service payments and an increase in world interest rates. Expected signs are negative with respect to each one of them.

valid instruments. We thus estimate the dynamic model using the above procedure.[n]

Results of Arellano–Bond estimation on the whole sample for the entire period and subperiods

In Table 3, the results of dynamic models are presented for the 1980–1999 period using sample data for 42 countries. The panel is unbalanced as we do not have data for all the years for all countries. Data for the earlier periods were not consistently available, and hence we have excluded period 1970–1979. Our study is over the 1980–1999 period. First differences remove the fixed effects, and given the dynamics, lagged effects on changes in TBGDP1 and CAGDP1 are introduced in the respective trade balance and current account equations. It is found that both growth and lagged growth effects are negative on trade balance. This also confirms the hypothesis that faster domestic growth affects the trade balance adversely. Liberalisation increases current account deficits as in Table 3. Overall liberalisation impacts adversely upon trade balances, but its effects come through the terms of trade interaction with liberalisation. In Table 3, liberalisation is used as a dummy, and also a slope dummy, where it is interacting with income terms of trade. This means that liberalisation affects terms of trade, and the terms of trade with liberalisation has a negative impact on trade balance. In Table 3, TBGDP1 and CAGDP1 equations are also estimated with time dummies in the last four columns, while the first four columns do not use time dummies. Time dummies indicate that there are autonomous effects, and such effects could be correlated with country-invariant advanced countries' growth rates. The terms of trade have significant positive effects on trade balance, but the interaction with the liberalisation variable has a negative effect (Table 3).

---

[n] The Monte Carlo simulation has shown that for panels with $t = 5$ or 6, the bias of the coefficients of the lagged dependent variable can be significant, although the bias for the coefficients on other right-hand side variables tends to be minor.

Regional Analysis and Subperiod Models

It might be worthwhile to look at the results by regions and by subperiods. Is there any evidence of a change in the relationship between trade balance and economic growth over different subperiods? Our UNCTAD (1999) study demonstrated that the relationship between trade balance and GDP growth could have changed from one decade to the next. In order to study this aspect, the estimates of periods 1980–1989 and 1990–1999 are examined using the data of as many countries as possible. The estimation is based on panel data using the Blundell–Bond (1998) dynamic panel estimator. We now do not estimate the current balance to GDP equation. All results refer to TBGDP1, and they are obtained using the system GMM and the equation GMM[o] as they are explained in Bond (2000). These results are presented in Table 4. Terms of trade have significant effects on trade balance during the 1980–1989 period with the two-step system GMM. The growth variable does not have a significant relationship with TBGDP1, and this means that although the relationship is negative, it does not have harmful effects on trade balance. Liberalisation on its own does not have a significant impact on TBGDP1 during the 1980–1989 period. There seems to be significant evidence that the relationship between trade balance and GDP growth is negative in the 1990–2000 decade, while although the relationship is negative, it is not significant for the previous decade. Liberalisation tends to have a negative impact on TBGDP1 over period 1990–2000. Pursuit of trade liberalisation by South East Asian countries contributed to high growth during the last two decades. This is the case for South Korea, Taiwan, and Hong Kong, Singapore. The two most populous countries in the World, China[p] and India, also achieved phenomenal increases in their rates of growth by pursuing for the first time, trade liberalisation policies, particularly with

[o] The first-differenced GMM estimator (equation GMM) and the extended GMM estimator (system GMM) were studied through Monte Carlo experiments by Blundell and Bond, and they showed that the extended estimator has a much smaller finite sample bias and much greater precision when estimating autoregressive parameters using persistent series. Both level and first-differenced instruments are used in the system GMM, while the equation GMM uses only the instruments in level form.

[p] China is excluded from our sample of countries because it has not adopted the market system and it is hard to state that it was a liberalised economy in any of the time periods.

Table 4. Blundell–Bond dynamic panel estimators with the system GMM and difference GMM for TBGDP1 of 42 countries.

Name of the variable	1980–1989				1990–1999			
	System GMM		DIFF-GMM		System GMM		DIFF-GMM	
	Coefficient	*t*-statistic	Coefficient	*t*-statistic	Coefficient	*t*-statistic	Coefficient	*t*-statistic
TBGDP1(−1)	0.9127***	20.49	0.7017***	3.41	0.9439***	13.98	0.5016***	5.38
GROWTH	−0.0400	−1.52	−0.0263	−1.24	−0.0862*	−1.72	−0.1214***	−2.66
GROWTH(−1)					−0.0423	−0.82	−0.1011***	−3.70
PPI	0.0109***	2.12	0.0093	1.37	0.0053***	3.17	0.0068**	2.36
ADVGR	0.0777	1.61	0.1101	3.28	0.0054	0.17	−0.0287	−1.28
LIBER	−1.2012	−1.20	−0.8278	−0.89	−1.2442	−1.13	−1.1325	−1.55
Year 1981/1991	−0.3207	−0.41	0.1045	1.12	−0.3207	−0.41	−0.1405	1.39
Year 1982/1992	1.3381	1.66	1.6162***	3.20	1.3381	1.66	−0.2950	−0.74
Year 1984/1993	0.1346	0.36	0.3341	0.84	0.1346	0.36	−0.3708	−1.28
Year 1985/1994	0.4103	0.92	0.8166**	2.03	0.4103	0.92	0.5598*	1.75
Year 1986/1995	0.5796	0.90	1.2355***	3.33	0.5796	0.90		
Year 1987/1996							0.3268	0.95
Year 1988/1997	−0.6310	−1.75*	−0.4255	−1.28	−0.6310	−1.75*		
Year 1989/1998	0.2055	0.49	0.1876	0.47	0.2055	0.49	0.0695	0.22
Year 1999					−0.1174	−0.20	0.0965	0.21
Constant	−1.0411	−1.58	—		−1.0411	−1.58	—	

(Continued)

Table 4. (*Continued*).

Name of the variable	1980–1989				1990–1999			
	System GMM		DIFF-GMM		System GMM		DIFF-GMM	
	Coefficient	*t*-statistic	Coefficient	*t*-statistic	Coefficient	*t*-statistic	Coefficient	*t*-statistic
AR(1)	−2.76(0.006)***		−2.31(0.021)***		−2.76(0.006)***		2.59(0.01)***	
AR(2)	1.05(0.294)		1.09(0.274)		1.05(0.294)		−1.05(0.293)	
Hansen test	$\chi^2(101) = 26.87(1.00)$		$\chi^2(96) = 23.68(1.00)$		$\chi^2(101) = 26.87(1.00)$		$\chi^2(112) = 19.54(1.00)$	
No. of obs.	301		259		301		226	

*** Significant at 1 percent level; **significant at 5 percent level, *significant at 10 percent level.

Notes:

1. Year dummies are included.
2. Asymptotic standard errors, asymptotically robust to heteroscedasticity, are used to report *t*-statistic.
3. The first-order AC and the second-order AC are tests of the first-order and the second-order serial correlation in the first-differenced residuals, asymptotically distributed as $N(0,1)$ under the null of no serial correlation.
4. Hansen is a test of overidentifying restrictions, asymptotically distributed as χ^2 under the null of instrument validity, with degrees of freedom reported in parentheses.
5. The instruments used in each equation are GMM (DIFF)-$\text{TBGDP}_{it-2\ldots}\text{TBGDP}_{i1}$, $\text{GROWTH}_{it-1}\ldots\text{GROWTH}_{i1}$, $\text{PPI}_{it-1}\ldots\text{PPI}_{i1}$ and $\text{ADVGR}_{it-1}\ldots\text{ADVGR}_{i1}$.

the Association of South East Asian economies (IMF, World Economic Outlook and World Bank, 1998).

Table 5 reports results for African countries for two subperiods 1980–1989 and 1990–1999 and also a comparative study of 1980–1999 for Africa and Latin American including Asian regions. For the first period, all time dummies were insignificant. In an unbalanced panel when observations are differenced out, very few observations are left for each of the periods, namely 1980–1989 and 1990–1999. The lagged dependent variable has a small coefficient although significant. The sign of the growth variable for the 1990–1999 decade is negative and significant but not for the 1980–1989 period. Liberalisation has a negative and significant coefficient for the 1990–2000 time period, and an increase in liberalisation may lead to a 1.95 percentage point decline in trade balance, *ceteris paribus*. For the first period, advanced countries' growth has a significant role to play in improving trade balance. Overall, it is found that the relationship is different between the two periods, and our hypothesis about liberalisation[q] and domestic growth both having deteriorating impacts on trade balance in the 1990–1999 decade is confirmed. Africa is the continent that has suffered from droughts, civil war, AIDS, limited international trade and has been the recipient of insignificant Foreign Direct Investment. Economic growth was lowest in the African continent.

The results of the entire sample for African and Latin American economies including Asian countries are also presented in the same table. For the African economies, growth in OECD or advanced countries plays a positive and significant role in improving trade balance. This may imply that the behaviour overall is very different between two periods for African economies. For Latin American (including Asian) economies, growth has a negative impact on the trade balance; an increase in income terms of trade

[q] We used other variations of the equations for current account and trade balance variables. Growth was never significantly related to trade balance or current account in the first period. Liberalisation has reduced both trade account and current account balances in Africa in the 1990–2000 period. The dominant negative effect on trade balance comes from its interactions with terms of trade. Liberalisation may deteriorate terms of trade as imports expand at a faster rate and import prices might rise faster than export prices, leading to deterioration in terms of trade, and this in turn could lead to trade balance deterioration. For African economies, liberalisation interacting with growth has a positive impact on trade balance.

Table 5. Regression coefficients, t-statistic of Bond–Blundell dynamic panel estimation, for Africa 1980–1989, 1990–1999, and, 1980-1999 and Latin America, 1980–1999: with or without time dummies.

Name of the variable	Africa				Africa		Latin America and Asia	
	TBGDP1: 1980–1989		TBGDP1: 1990–1999		TBGDP1: 1980–1999			
	One step DIF-GMM		One step DIF-GMM		DIF-GMM		DIF-GMM	
	Coefficient	t-statistic	Coefficient	t-statistic	Coefficient	t-statistic	Coefficient	t-statistic
TBGDP1(−1)	0.3494***	3.92	0.2903*	1.73	0.6066***	9.34	0.6769***	6.00
GROWTH	−0.0073	−0.26	−0.0718	−1.52	0.0105	0.42	−0.0700***	−4.11
GROWTH (−1)	−0.0115	−0.42	−0.1128**	−2.31	−0.0033	−0.14		
PPI	0.0176**	2.57	−0.0004	−0.12	0.0038	0.99	0.0062***	3.31
LIBER	−0.3272	−0.60	−1.9490**	−2.42	−0.4239	−0.77	−0.0717	−0.27
ADVGR	0.0716**	2.06	0.0253	0.56	0.1185**	2.38	0.0285*	1.71
Year 1992/1983			−1.3665**	−2.20			1.9878***	3.79
Year 1993/1984			−1.6351**	−2.77			1.2090**	2.93
Year 1994/1985			−0.3903	−0.66			1.9316**	2.81
Year 1996/1986			−0.1397	−0.17			1.6710***	3.42
Year 1997/1987			−0.1139	−0.17			1.7521***	3.90
Year 1998/1988			−1.0755*	−1.70			1.1654**	2.25
Year 1999/1989			0.2431	0.36			1.6514***	4.29
Year—/1990							0.8303**	2.68
Year—/1993[1]					−1.4840**	−1.97		
Constant	—	—	—	—			0.0088	0.15

(Continued)

Table 5. *(Continued)*.

Name of the variable	Africa				Africa		Latin America and Asia	
	TBGDP1: 1980–1989		TBGDP1: 1990–1999		TBGDP1: 1980–1999			
	One step DIF-GMM		One step DIF-GMM		DIF-GMM		DIF-GMM	
	Coefficient	*t*-statistic	Coefficient	*t*-statistic	Coefficient	*t*-statistic	Coefficient	*t*-statistic
First-order AC	−2.92(0.004)		−1.40(0.162)		−4.36(0.000)		−2.79(0.005)	
Second-order AC	−1.12(0.26)		−0.16(0.871)		1.14(0.255)		0.85(0.394)	
Number of obs.	77		35		139		398	
Hansen test χ^2	76.68(0.115)		46.89(0.210)		131.23(0.064)		2.91(1.00)	

[1]Only significant year effects are reported. ***Significant at 1 percent; **significant at 5 percent level; *significant at 10 percent level.

Notes:

1. Year dummies are included in the second period, and as they were insignificant in the first period, they were excluded.
2. Asymptotic standard errors, asymptotically robust to heteroscedasticity, are used to report *t*-statistic.
3. The First-order AC and the second-order AC are tests of the first-order and the second-order serial correlation in the first-differenced residuals, asymptotically distributed as $N(0,1)$ under the null of no serial correlation.
4. Hansen is a test of overidentifying restrictions, asymptotically distributed as χ^2 under the null of instrument validity, with probability values reported in parentheses.
5. The instruments used in each equation are GMM (DIF)-$\text{TBGDP}_{it-2\ldots}\text{TBGDP}_{i1}$, $\text{GROWTH}_{it-2}\ldots\text{GROWTH}_{i1}$, $\text{PPI}_{it-1}\ldots\text{PPI}_{i1}$ and $\text{ADVGR}_{it-1}\ldots\text{ADVGR}_{i1}$.

improves trade balance, liberalisation is not significant and the dynamic model is plausible. Many time dummies for Latin America and Asian countries are significant, so there is a great deal of autonomous effect on trade balance, and, as anticipated, the effect is positive up to 1988, and as we mentioned before this was the period when both trade balance and economic growth improved.

In Table 6, the results of Latin American countries combined with Asian countries are presented for trade balance equations for the two different periods. It is found that the growth coefficients are not significant for the

Table 6. Regression coefficients, t-statistic Bond–Blundell dynamic panel estimation 1980–1999: Latin America and Asia.

Name of the variable	TBGDP1: 1980–1989: DIF GMM		TBGDP1: 1990–2000: DIF GMM	
	Coefficient	t-statistic	Coefficient	t-statistic
TBGDP1(−1)	0.7473***	4.90	0.5066***	8.49
GROWTH	−0.0547	−1.41	−0.1679***	−3.65
GROWTH(−1)	−0.0377	−1.28	−0.0905**	−2.62
PPI	0.0103**	2.04	0.00985***	4.87
LIBER	−0.7098	−1.10	0.8669	1.22
ADVGR	0.1278***	3.44	−0.0408	1.65
Constant	0.1078	1.34	−0.2158**	−2.21
First-order AC	−2.22(0.027)		−2.46(0.014)	
Second-order AC	1.46(0.145)		−0.43(0.668)	
Number of obs.	182		177	
Sargan Test χ^2	10.63(1.00)		10.35(1.00)	

***Significant at 1 percent level; **significant at 5 percent level; *significant at 10 percent level.

Notes:

1. Year dummies are included.
2. Asymptotic standard errors, asymptotically robust to heteroscedasticity, are used to report t-statistic.
3. The first-order AC and the second-order AC are tests of the first-order and the second-order serial correlation in the first-differenced residuals, asymptotically distributed as $N(0,1)$ under the null of no serial correlation.
4. Sargan is a test of overidentifying restrictions, asymptotically distributed as χ^2 under the null of instrument validity, with degrees of freedom reported in parentheses.
5. The instruments used in each equation are GMM (DIF)-$TBGDP_{it-2}$...$TBGDP_{i1}$, $GROWTH_{it-2}$...$GROWTH_{i1}$, PPI_{it-1}...PPI_{i1} and $ADVGR_{it-1}$...$ADVGR_{i1}$.

first period, while for the second period they are highly significant and negative suggesting that growth deteriorates trade balance. The decade of 1990–1999 for Latin America[r] shows a worsening of trade balance, and this is captured to some extent in time dummies. Latin America has not shown very high growth like ASEAN economies during the last decade because no new trade block has emerged to pursue trade liberalisation. MERCOSUR was established in 1991 and consisted of only four countries. The growth in advanced countries improves trade balance in Latin American and Asian economies. Terms of trade have a positive impact on trade balance in both periods, while liberalisation on its own is not significant in either period. Again, when two periods are studied separately and with the first-differencing procedure, the number of observations is small. The method of the system GMM did not provide significant results on a large number of variables.

Summary and Conclusion

Our study has many limitations as data inadequacies dominate the model estimation. The measures of trade liberalisation such as Sachs–Warner (1995) or Wacziarg (2001) do not take into account different intensities of liberalisation in different time periods. Our study has not considered liberalisation attempted by any developed economy. Tariff and non-tariff barriers on a significant scale exist in developed countries for agricultural products largely exported by developing economies.

Nevertheless, we argue that liberalisation would lead to higher economic growth if trade reforms are carried out and political stability prevails. A diverse set of countries have experienced different effects of liberalisation, and this is reflected in our regional study. One of the major issues emerging from this study is the adverse impact of liberalisation and economic growth on trade balances of developing countries, which implies that

[r] We only considered trade balance to GDP, and two models, one with time dummies and the other without time dummies are estimated. Growth is significantly negatively related to trade balance in both models. What we can infer here is that faster economic growth in Asian and Latin American countries would lead to a decline in trade balance as import growth far exceeds export growth. Surprisingly, growth in advanced countries does not remove pressure on trade balance or current account balance.

the capital financing requirements would increase in the presence of trade deficits in the short and medium run for developing economies. Globalization has made both developing and developed countries highly interdependent. If developing countries were to catch up with developed countries in their per capita income, enormous flows of multilateral and private capital may be needed from developed countries by way of capital financing. Our study seems to indicate that there are differing patterns on trade deficits across various geographical regions and also during the decade of 1990–1999. Trade liberalisation has increased the imports of many developing countries, and although after the initial phase of import growth exports picked up in some developing countries, on the whole, it remained insufficient to narrow the trade deficits. Rapid liberalisation was sometimes followed by large inflows of capital, currency appreciation and mounting trade deficits, but it often ended up with a crisis involving reversal of capital inflows, collapse and overshooting of exchange rates, sharp cuts in imports and a deep economic contraction.

We find that trade liberalisation does have a significant relationship with economic growth and/or trade deficits in the short to medium run. Our significant relationship between liberalisation and trade deficits and economic growth and trade deficits is for Latin American and Asian economies for the latter decade. This seems to indicate that their capital financing requirements are much higher than what the world community has been able to provide and rapid liberalisation has often caused financial crisis and debt problems in Latin American and some Asian economies.

References

Ahmed, N (2000). Export responses to trade liberalisation in Bangladesh: A cointegration analysis. *Applied Economics*, 32, 1077–1084.

Arellano, M and SR Bond (1991). Some tests of specification for panel data: Monte Carlo evidence and an application to employment equations. *Review of Economic Studies*, 58, 277–297.

Baltagi, B (1995). *Econometric Analysis of Panel Data.* New York: John Wiley & Sons.

Banks, A (2001). Cross-national time-series data archive (CNTS). Centre for Social Analysis, State University of New York, Binghamton.

Barro, RJ and JW Lee (1994). Sources of economic growth. *Carnegie-Rochester Conference Series on Public Policy*, 40, 1–46.

Bertola, G and R Faini (1991). Import demand and non-tariff barriers: The impact of trade liberalisation. *Journal of Development Economics*, 34, 269–86.

Bleaney, M (1999). Trade reform, macroeconomic performance and export growth in ten Latin American countries 1979–1995. *Journal of International Trade and Economic Development*, 8, 89–105.

Blundell, R and S Bond (1998). Initial conditions and moment restrictions in dynamic panel data models. *Journal of Econometrics*, 87, 115–143.

Bond, S (2002). Dynamic panel data models: A guide to micro data methods and practice. Institute of Fiscal Studies, London, Paper 09/02.

Clarke, R and C Kirkpatrick (1992). Trade policy reform and economic performance in developing countries: Assessing the empirical evidence, In *Industrial and Trade Policy Reform in Developing Countries*, R Adhikari, C Kirkpatrick and J Weiss (eds.), Manchester: Manchester University Press.

Dollar, D and Kray A (2004). Trade, growth and poverty. *Economic Journal,* 114(493), F22–F49.

Edwards, S (1993). Openness, trade liberalisation, and growth in developing countries. *Journal of Economic Literature*, 31, 1358–1393.

Frankel, JA and D Romer (1999). Does trade cause growth? *American Economic Review*, 89(3), 379–399.

Greenaway, D and D Sapsford (1994). What does liberalisation do for exports and growth? *Weltwirtschaftliches Archiv*, 130, 152–174.

Greenaway, D, W Morgan and P Wright (2002). Trade liberalisation and growth in developing countries. *Journal of Development Economics*, 67, 229–244.

Helleiner, G (ed.) (1994). *Trade Policy and Industrialisation in Turbulent Times.* London: Routledge.

International Monetary Fund, *World Economic Outlook*, various issues.

Irwin, DA and M Tervio (2002). Does trade raise income? Evidence from the twentieth century. *Journal of International Economics*, 58, 1–18.

Jenkins, R (1996). Trade performance and export performance in Bolivia. *Development and Change*, 27, 693–716.

Johnston, J (1996). *Econometric Methods*. New York: McGraw Hill.

Joshi, V and IMD Little (1996). *Indias Economic Reforms 1991–2001.*Oxford: Oxford University Press.

Melo, O and MG Vogt (1984). Determinants of the demand for imports of venezuela. *Journal of Development Economics*, 14, 351–358.

Obstfeld, M (1995). The intertemporal approach to the current account. In *Handbook of International Economics, 3*, G Grossman and K Rogoff (eds.), Chapter 34. Amsterdam, Netherlands: North Holland.

Obstfeld, M and K Rogoff (1997). *Foundations of International Macroeconomics.* Cambridge, MA: Academic Press.

Rodriguez, F and D Rodrik (2000). *Trade Policy and Economic Growth: A Skeptic's Guide to the Cross-National Evidence*. National Bureau of Economic Research, (NBER) No. 7081. Cambridge, MA: MIT Press.

Rose, A and J Ostry (1989). Tariffs and the macroeconomy: Evidence from the USA. International Finance Discussion Papers 365, Board of Governors of the Federal Reserve System, US.

Sachs, J and A Warner (1995). Economic reform and the process of global integration. *Brookings Papers on Economic Activity*, 1, 1–118.

Shafaedin, SM (1994). The impact of trade liberalisation on exports and GDP in least developed countries. UNCTAD Discussion Papers No. 85, Geneva.

Summers, R, A Heston and B Aten (2001). *Penn World Table Version 6.0*. Center for International Comparisons at the University of Pennsylvania (CICUP).

Thirlwall, T and A Santos-Paulino (2004). The impact of trade liberalisation on exports, imports and the balance of payments of developing countries. *Economic Journal*, 114(493), F50–F73.

Thomas, V, J Nash and S Edwards (1991). *Best Practices in Trade Policy Reform*. Oxford: Oxford University Press.

UNCTAD (1989). *Trade and Development Report 1989*. Geneva, Switzerland: United Nations.

UNCTAD (1999). *Trade and Development Report 1999*. Geneva, Switzerland: United Nations.

Wacziarg, R (2001). Measuring the dynamic gains from trade. *World Bank Economic Review*, 15(3), 393–429.

Wacziarg, R and KH Welch (2003). *Trade Liberalisation and Growth: New Evidence*. National Bureau of Economic Research, (NBER) No. 10152. Cambridge, MA: MIT Press.

Wooldridge, JM (2002). *Econometric Analysis of Cross Section and Panel Data*. Cambridge, MA: The MIT Press.

World Bank (1998). *Global Economic Perspectives 1998/99*. Washington, DC: World Bank.

Appendix A. Variables

ADVGR	growth rate in developed countries (%)
CA	current account
CAGDP	current account balance to GDP
CAGDP1	current account balance to GDP (%)
CG	government share of CGDP
CGDP	real gross domestic product per capita (current prices)
CI	investment share of CGDP
CINTEREST	annual percentage change in world interest rate (%)
DEBRSIMP	debt service as a percentage of total imports (%)
DEBT	long-term outstanding debt (US$ mil.)

GDEBTSIMP	percentage change in debt service in total imports of goods and services (%)
GROIL	annual percentage change in oil price (%)
GROWTH	annual percentage change in real GDP using Summers, Heston and Aten's purchasing power parity real GDP
INTEREST	world interest rate
KI	constant price investment as a share of real GDP (based on Laspeyer's index)
LIBADVGR	liberalisation dummy interacting with developed countries growth rates (%)
LIBER	liberalisation dummy taking the value 1 when the country was liberalised
LIBERTM	time period elapsed from date of liberalisation
LIBGROWTH	liberalisation dummy interacting with growth in country under consideration
LIBPPI	liberalisation dummy interacting with income terms of trade (index)
OIL	crude oil price
OPENK	exports plus imports at constant prices as a percentage to constant price GDP (%)
OPENNESS	exports plus imports as a share of GDP (%)
PPI	income terms of trade = (value of exports/unit value of imports)* 100
RERI	real exchange rate
TB	trade balance
TBGDP	trade balance to GDP
TBGDP1	trade balance to GDP (%)

Names and sources of variables: sources and descriptions of the variables used in the regression

GROWTH	Real per capita growth rate of GDP per year for example G7089=(log(GDP89)–log(GDP70))/19; periods 1970–1989, 1980–1989, 1989–1998. Summers, Heston and Aten (2001)
LRGDPCH	Real GDP per capita in (1996 international prices). *Source*: Summers, Heston and Aten (2001)
LIBER_SW_1970–1989	Openness indicator for 1970–1989
LIBER_SW_*xx*	Cross-sectional openness indicator constructed from Sachs and Warner's liberalisation dates for $xx = 1970, 1980, 1989$
LIBER_WW_1990–1999	Openness indicator for 1990–1999, constructed by Wacziarg and Welch (2003)
POL	Composite dummy variables indicating extreme political repression and unrest: Sachs and Warner (1995)
SEC	Secondary school enrolment rate, 1970, 1980, 1985. *Source*: Barro and Lee (1994)
PRI	Primary school enrolment rate, 1970, 1980, 1985. *Source*: Barro and Lee (1994)

GVXDXE	Ratio of government consumption spending net of spending on the military and education to real GDP, averaged 1970–1984, *Source*: Barro and Lee (1994)
CG	Ratio of real government consumption expenditure to real GDP for periods 1970–1980, 1980–1989 and 1989–1998. *Source*: Summers, Heston and Aten (2001)
REVCOUP	Number of revolutions and coups per year, averaged over period 1970–1985. *Source*: Barro and Lee (1994)
REVOL	Number of revolutions per year, averaged over periods 1970–1980, 1980–1989 and 1990–1998. *Source*: Banks (2001)
ASSASS	Number of assassinations per million population per year, averaged over the relevant period, 1970–1985, 1970–1980, 1980–1989 and 1989–1998. *Source*: Banks (2001)
PPIDEV	The deviation of the log of the price level of investment (PPP investment divided by exchange rate relative to the United States) from the cross-country sample mean in 1970. *Source*: Summers, Heston and Aten (2001)
INV	Ratio of real gross domestic investment (public and private) to real GDP, averaged over period 1970–1989. *Source*: Barro and Lee (1994)
DENSI	Population (in thousands) divided by land area (in square meters), 1960, 1970, 1980. *Source*: Summers, Heston and Aten (2001) (population data) and CIA World Factbook (land area)
Fixed and random effects models	
GROWTH	Real per capita growth rate of GDP per year (annual data). *Source*: Summers, Heston and Aten (2001)
INVESTMENT	Investment rate. *Source*: Heston, Summers and Aten (2001)
OPENNESS	Ratio of imports plus exports to GDP. *Source*: Summers, Heston and Aten (2001)

Chapter 10

Instability and Volatility of Capital Flows to Developing Countries*

Alberto Gabriele[1], Korkut Boratav[2] and Ashok Parikh[3]

[1]*UNCTAD, Geneva*

[2]*University of Ankara, Turkey*

[3]*University of East Anglia, Norwich, UK*

Introduction

Despite the recent recovery in capital flows towards developing countries, some of their characteristics have generated serious problems. As these flows are increasingly concentrated in a small group of emerging markets, most developing countries have been facing a severe scarcity of external resources, while for the minority endowed with some measure of access to international financial markets, volatility and sustainability remain the key issues. Financial liberalisation has helped to create new channels for resource transfers from the developed world, but it has also generated conditions wherein such transfers can easily be reversed with serious consequences in terms of instability.

The present study depicts, discusses and analyses some of the issues related to capital movements between developed and developing countries.

* The authors would like to thank Dr. Yilmaz Akyuz for discussions on a number of issues raised in this chapter, the referees for their constructive comments and Ms. Jan Anderson for editing the chapter. Ms. Erna Borneck and Petra Hoffman provided competent statistical assistance.

The second section is an overview of the recent controversies on external financial liberalisation. The third section surveys the post-1970 developments in capital inflows to developing countries, their main components and their contribution to development finance. The fourth section examines the instability and volatility of total inflows and their components using two different statistical measures. The fifth section concentrates on a particular type of capital movement, i.e., short-term, arbitrage-seeking capital flows to emerging market economies. This analysis requires specific conceptualization, definition and data generation from balance of payments statistics. In the sixth section, a similar analysis of volatility and instability of short-term inflows and outflows to emerging market economies is undertaken. The penultimate section discusses the policy implications of the foregoing analysis and is followed by a summary and conclusions.

The Controversy on External Financial Liberalisation

Since the early 1980s, the majority of academic economists, international financial institutions and most policy makers in the developing countries have tended to agree on the favourable impact of domestic and external financial liberalisation in developing countries. However, the sobering experience of the Asian crisis has reopened the controversy on the merits and drawbacks of financial liberalisation.

The main arguments put forward in order to advocate financial liberalisation as the natural and inevitable complement to trade liberalisation stem from the traditional faith in the intrinsic efficiency, fairness, and self-regulating capacity of markets. With very few exceptions these are believed to produce economic outcomes far superior to those which might arise from even the best intentioned and technically sophisticated state-mandated controls and interventions. The liberalisation and opening up of capital accounts are expected to lead to an optimal worldwide allocation of capital. Financial flows towards developing countries will soar, attracted by higher returns on investment in economies characterised by low capital/labour ratios and thereby high marginal productivity of capital. From the point of view of the recipient developing country, financial flows from abroad allow for smoothing the consumption/investment pattern according to an optimal inter-temporal path, leading to higher investment and growth rates. Capital flows towards developing countries arise from structural conditions that are unlikely to change dramatically for a long period of time, as differences in per capita capital endowments remain substantial in spite of a long-run trend towards convergence. Therefore, sizeable trade and current account deficits are expected to be a permanent feature of the economic scenario in developing countries. Moreover, the sustainability of large deficits is made easier by reductions in transaction costs and by the enhanced international mobility of goods, services and financial flows.

The advocates of liberalisation concede that the increased capacity to borrow bestowed on domestic agents by the dismantling of previous restrictions can by itself magnify default risks. However, they recommend a certain graduality in the liberalisation process which should be accompanied or, better, preceded by an overall strengthening of the banking and financial institutions and by an improvement in the surveillance and regulatory capacities of the authorities. A position similar to that sketched above is, for instance, put forward by Fischer (1998). Eichengreen and Mussa (1998) also conclude their discussion on this issue with an endorsement for "prudent" capital account liberalisation. They argue that, as a matter of principle, "the first-best response is to eliminate the domestic distortion at its source, and not to restrict capital flows" (p. 29). However, they concede that information asymmetries intrinsic to the operation of capital markets are often severe and intractable. Hence, the most recommendable policy course towards financial liberalisation might require market-friendly tax and tax-like instruments aimed at influencing certain types of transactions by altering relative prices, while avoiding, whenever possible, a return to administrative controls.

On the other side of the debate, an increasing number of economists deny the advisability of capital account liberalisation as a natural and coherent complement to current account liberalisation. Their core argument rests on the fundamental asymmetry between markets of goods and services on the one hand, which can be assumed by and large to work in a relatively efficient and predictable manner, and financial markets on the other hand, which are plagued by an array of nontrivial imperfections. The reasons are well known and Rodrik (1998), for instance, mentions a few of them:

- Asymmetric information and implicit guarantees lead to moral hazard and excessive lending for risky projects;

- A mismatch can arise in financial institutions between short-term and long-term instruments, which can provoke bank runs and financial panic;
- Asymmetric herding behaviour on the part of money managers routinely leads to excess volatility and contagion effects, also reverberating on asset prices. Crises can arise not only due to policy-induced macroeconomic distortions, but also due to the intrinsic malfunctioning of markets. Indeed, the recent Asian experience suggests that a crisis can occur even where fundamental macroeconomic equilibria appear to be under control.

Theoretical and empirical contributions to this line of thought are numerous. Agenor and Aizerman (1998) interpret the contagion effect as an increase in the volatility of shocks. Calvo (1999) analyzes the interaction between informed and uninformed investors in capital markets. Asymmetric information can lead uninformed investors to misinterpret informed investors' actions (such as selling emerging market securities to meet margin calls caused by routine operations in developed countries' markets), generating financial panic[a] and ultimately resulting in declining output in developing countries. Cooper (1998) argues that free international capital movements are incompatible with both fixed and floating exchange rates, and hence at least some controls should be kept in place unless countries are ready to fix their exchange rate permanently to a major currency, as did Argentina. Kregel (1999) explores the causal linkages between financial globalisation, large capital flows to developing countries, and banking and balance of payments crises.

A study by Lensink *et al.* (1998) focuses not on emerging markets but on a group of very poor and financially very underdeveloped countries, traditionally characterised by strong financial repression. The authors estimate, by means of a simulation analysis carried out on a group of African countries, the likely impact of different financial liberalisation policies on capital flight, as well as some other direct and indirect effects of these policies. According to the authors' results, all three financial liberalisation

[a] These phenomena may occur through the emergence of multiple equilibria and give rise to multiplier effects. However, multiple equilibria are not a necessary condition, as the same basic causal chain can also ensue under equilibrium uniqueness.

measures considered (interest rate deregulation, decrease in reserve requirements and a change in exchange rate policies) do have an impact on capital flight, but this impact is "very tiny" in size. Moreover, interest rate deregulation in particular, the most widely applied financial deregulation measure, also has an inflationary effect (via Neo-Structuralist cost-push story) and may stimulate capital flight in the short, if not the long run. These results are particularly relevant as they apply to countries traditionally considered among the most financially repressed in the world, and hence those which should benefit most from the removal of such extreme distortions through liberalisation. The authors conclude that "Financial liberalisation policies *per se* may not be the panacea for reducing capital flight" (pp. 1363–1364).

Calvo *et al.* (1996) emphasise the importance of a conservative fiscal stance, the need of multiple policy tools, the limited effectiveness of sterilisation and the overall complex nature of the problem of how to deal with capital flows.

Finally, it is worth referring to some recent, mainly empirical contributions emerging from the IMF, the main advocate of the present value of financial liberalisation. Their results confirm the seriousness of the problems linked with financial liberalisation and the possibility that capital controls might be of some use under special circumstances, although the conclusions uphold the institutional belief in the superiority of non-interventionist and market-friendly policy options. Bikhchandani and Sharma (2000) review recent research findings on herd behavior in financial markets. They argue that in emerging markets, where the phenomenon is more relevant, more empirical work is warranted to achieve definitive conclusions, due largely to the intrinsic difficulties inherent in measuring the phenomenon. Caramazza *et al.* (2000) investigates empirical evidence on financial contagion in 61 emerging markets and finds that indicators of vulnerability to international financial spillovers and financial fragility are highly significant thus explaining the regional concentration of the Mexican, Asian, and Russian crises. Nagasayu (2000) analyzes data on exchange rates and stock indices in the Philippines and Thailand, finding ample evidence of cross-country correlation and the impact of contagion on these countries' financial crises. Cerra and Saxena (2000) use a Markov-switching model to show that contagion from exchange rate pressures and stock market instabilities in Thailand and Korea contributed to the Indonesian financial crisis.

On capital controls, Ariyoshi *et al.* (2000) state that on the one hand no single measure is universally effective, and although there is a trade off between selective controls, the effectiveness of these tends to be partial and short-lived. On the other hand, the more comprehensive controls, while having a stronger impact, are more costly, administratively complex and burdensome. They conclude that capital controls cannot substitute for sound macroeconomic policies (p. 34) and that strong prudential policies can allow for successful capital account liberalisation and can thus be an alternative to capital controls themselves.[b] Another study by Lopez-Mejia (1999) concludes that controls, especially those on short-term inflows, can be of some use, as was shown by the experience of Chile,[c] Colombia and Malaysia.[d] Zee (2000), as an alternative to traditional quantity-based capital controls, proposes a price-based withholding tax on all capital inflows, which he argues would be difficult to evade and cheaper to implement than quantitative capital controls.

It stems clearly from this brief review of the debate that even the most ardent opponents of the liberalisation of capital flows are not in favour of financial autarky, nor do they deny the potential benefits to developing countries of some degree of access to foreign savings. The controversy rather focuses on the evaluation of the trade-off between such benefits and the macroeconomic risks that can arise from the instability, unpredictability and pro-cyclical impact of capital flows, contributing to the emergence of financial crises and to systematic inappropriate selection in investment projects.

---

[b] In their review of case studies, the authors acknowledge that the two countries in their sample which applied long-standing and extensive capital controls (India and China) appear to have achieved at least the narrow policy goal of reigning in external capital flows, although the impact of controls on their overall economic performance is unclear.

[c] The Chilean experience, with market-friendly tax-based controls on capital inflows, is actually the most thoroughly studied in the developing world, with widely diverging conclusions being reached by different observers. Edwards (1998), for instance, referring to quantitative evidence stemming from previous research, argues that capital controls should not be considered a key ingredient of Chile's success.

[d] Other important references amongst the mushrooming literature on international capital flows and the respective merits and drawbacks of liberalisation and controls are, for instance, Dooley, 1995; Reisen, 1996; Kaminsky and Reinhart, 1996; Johnson, 1998; Bird, 1998; Knight and Scacciavillani, 1998; Lopez-Mejia, 1999, Nolan and Xiaogang, 1998.

Trends in Capital Flows to Developing Countries

The recent increase in global capital flows[e] to developing countries constitutes essentially a recovery (in terms of inflows/GDP ratios) in comparison to a decline in the 1980s and is concentrated in a few emerging markets. From a qualitative point of view, its potential positive development impact is severely undermined by at least three factors, all of which are relatively new and typical of the 1990s. First, there has been a surge in offsetting financial transactions such as reserve accumulation and capital outflows by residents. Second, the share of FDI which corresponds to "real" new green-field investment in productive capacities has declined, while that linked to one-off mergers and acquisitions, and especially privatisation, has gone up. Third, as will be analysed in detail in the fourth section, instability in capital flows has increased.[f] During most of the 1980s, capital inflows to developing countries were negative, but since the beginning of the 1990s they have achieved a growth of about 12 percent per annum in real terms. However, capital inflows are now more concentrated in a few emerging markets than before the debt crisis, particularly in China. The share of total net capital inflows going to the 20 countries that belong to this group rose from around 50 percent in the 1970s and 1980s to over 90 percent in the 1990s. Conversely, the share going to Africa dropped dramatically.

The composition of capital flows also shifted in favor of private flows: These were about two-thirds of total flows in the 1970s, fell to 54 percent in the 1980s, but rose thereafter until reaching about 80 percent in the 1990s (see Table 1). Conversely, ODA to developing countries reached a

---

[e] In this chapter, the following definitions are adopted for various types of international capital flows, in accordance with the IMF balance of payments terminology:

Capital inflows: acquisition of domestic assets by non-residents (sales are treated as negative inflows).

Net capital inflows: acquisitions minus sales of domestic assets by non-residents.

Capital outflows: acquisition of foreign assets by residents (sales are negative outflows).

Net capital outflows: acquisition minus sales of foreign assets by residents.

Net capital flows: sum total of net capital inflows plus net capital outflows.

Net transfers: net capital inflows less net factor payments abroad, including interest payments on external debt and profit remittances.

[f] Most financial data quoted in this section are taken from the World Bank, 1999, and UNCTAD secretariat estimates and databases utilised in the preparation of the 1999 Trade and Development Report (UNCTAD, 1999). The data on short-term financial flows are from the IMF. (See below, note i).

Table 1. Percentage distribution of major components of total capital inflows to developing countries by totals of subperiods.

	1970–1979	1980–1989	1990–1996	1997–1998
Total net inflows	100.0	100.0	100.0	100.0
Official	33.7	45.8	19.7	17.7
(ODA)	(12.7)	(30.7)	(11.6)	(7.2)
(Other official)	(21.0)	(15.1)	(8.1)	(10.5)
Private	66.3	54.2	80.3	82.3
(FDI)	(9.1)	(14.3)	(30.3)	(47.9)
(Portfolio equity)	(0.0)	(0.5)	(10.2)	(6.5)
(Bonds)	(2.1)	(1.7)	(11.2)	(9.8)
(Bank loans)	(48.1)	(29.8)	(25.1)	(16.6)
(Other private)	(7.0)	(7.9)	(3.5)	(1.5)

Source: World Bank, World Development Finance CD Rom.

peak in relative terms in 1986 (i.e., 25 percent) and the peak in absolute figures was attained in 1991 (i.e., $28.7 billion). Thereafter, ODA declined almost continually in absolute terms falling below the 10 percent threshold of total inflows from 1993 onwards. Other official flows have been markedly unstable, surging in particular in 1995 and 1998 due to official intervention in the Mexican and Asian crises. The composition of private flows also changed significantly. Bank loans, which previously constituted about three-quarters of the total, fell drastically after the outbreak of the debt crisis and picked up only with the major Mexican bailout in 1995. The share of total net capital inflows of both FDI and portfolio increased dramatically from 9 percent and virtually nil, respectively, in the 1970s to over 30 and 10 percent, respectively, during the 1990–1996 period.[g]

Turning to the diminishing potential of capital inflows to enhance investment and growth, the net outflows/net-inflows ratio (i.e., the share of net inflows offset by net outflows) more than doubled during the 1990s amongst developing countries as a whole. In 15 emerging markets (for which more detailed data are available)[h] this ratio grew from 14 percent in the 1980s to

[g] In the crisis years 1997–1998, FDI proved relatively resilient and increased its share of total flows to almost half of the total. On the contrary, the share of volatile portfolio flows fell dramatically (see Table 1).

[h] Argentina, Brazil, Chile, Colombia, Egypt, India, Indonesia, Malaysia, Mexico, Pakistan, Peru, the Philippines, Republic of Korea, South Africa, and Turkey. China, an atypical country in terms of capital inflows, is deliberately excluded from this sample.

23.6 percent in the 1990s, while the reserve changes/inflows ratio increased from 3 percent to 21.4 percent over the same period.[i] The increase in net outflows is mainly the product of the generalised liberalisation and globalisation trend. The surge in reserve accumulation responds to attempts by governments to combat the potentially destabilising impact of capital inflows through sterilisation, as well as setting up a monetary defense line against the eventuality of a sudden withdrawal of capital and a concomitant attack on their currencies. Conversely, the share of net inflows earmarked to the financing of current account deficits fell from 50 percent to under 30 percent between the first and second part of the 1990s in developing countries as a whole, and from 72 percent in the 1980s to 50 percent in 1990–1998 in the emerging market economies' subgroup.

Focusing in particular on short-term flows, the most volatile component of total capital flows to developing countries, the trends referred to above are further strengthened. Short-term inflows to developing countries, like total capital flows, were stagnant in the 1980s, surged in the early 1990s, but declined after 1995. Short-term outflows, which comprised about two-third of total net outflows in 1990–1998, have drained a large proportion of net inflows (in the 1980s, due to the impact of huge capital flight from Mexico, Brazil, and Argentina, these actually exceeded net inflows, generating negative net short-term flows). Not surprisingly, the leakage (i.e., the share of inflows which is not allocated to the financing of current deficits) from short-term inflows is much higher than from other components of capital flows[j] and tends to be more volatile and prone to contagion and herding effects.[k]

---

[i] The size of errors and omissions diminished in the emerging markets due to the liberalisation of some previously illegal capital exports on the part of residents, but not in developing countries as a whole.

[j] For the purpose of analysing short-term flows, for which data availability is scanty, we used the IMF data (*Balance of Payments Statistics*, various years) to set up a subgroup of 13 emerging markets for which consistent statistical information is available. This group comprises 13 of the 16 countries included in the group of emerging markets excluding Colombia, Egypt and Indonesia. Data from these two not perfectly comparable samples of emerging markets show that in the 1990s the outflow/inflow ratio for total capital flows in the 16-strong group was 24 percent, while the same ratio for short-term flows in the 13-country group was 55 percent.

[k] See the third and fourth section for a formal analysis of these characteristics of short-term flows.

As noted earlier, FDI has played an increasing role in total capital flows to developing countries: the share of total global FDI going to these countries rose during the 1990s to almost 30 percent reversing the prevailing trend of the 1980s. However, FDI is extremely concentrated (80 percent of the total) on 20 emerging markets, with three of them (China, Brazil, and Mexico) receiving almost half of the total. Cumulative FDI in China in the 1990s was about one-third of that of all developing countries. A large and increasing share of FDI is constituted by mergers and acquisitions (M&A), which by themselves represent a mere change of ownership and do not directly add to the productive capacity of the host country. Available information from UNCTAD 1997 and from the World Bank 1999 allow us to estimate tentatively that the share of M&A in the cumulative total FDI has risen from 22 percent in 1988–1991 to 72 percent in 1992–1997. This excludes China, where virtually no privatisation has occurred so far and most of the FDI has been of a greenfield nature.[1]

Instability and Volatility of Total Capital Flows and Their Components

In this section, we first introduce a terminological distinction between instability and volatility, which basically refer to the same economic phenomenon, but in some cases are conventionally associated to the different statistical indicators more appropriate for different types of time series. When applied to a stationary series, the two terms carry the same meaning and are thus identical. However, when applied to unit root non-stationary time series, the coefficient of variation of the original series is considered as an instability index, while the standard deviation of annual percentage change is considered as an indicator of volatility. The term volatility is appropriately used in the context of changes induced by a stochastic shock large enough to cause a permanent change in the economy. The stochastic shock can lead to changes in the time path of the economy, resulting in an increasing (decreasing) mean and increasing (decreasing) variance for the

---

[1] There has been a generalised shift of FDI towards the services and other non-tradable sectors. This shift might imply a relatively low potential for export expansion, with possible negative consequences on the balance of payments, as appears to have been the case in a number of countries in the 1990s. (see BIS 1998).

time series in question which are thus non-stationary, although they can be stationary in the first-, second- or third- difference form. Real shock caused by the oil price rise in 1973–1974 was regarded to be a permanent shock as it affected the trend path of many market economies in that period. When the data series has experienced such shocks, it may be better to analyze the annual percentage change of the time series under consideration, because the series in the original form can be non-stationary with non-constant mean and variance.

In the light of the above background, the coefficient of variation on the data in levels form and the standard deviation of annual percentage change in the total capital and private inflows are expected to quantitatively measure instability and volatility, respectively. The first measure would be the most appropriate when it is assumed that the original total capital and private inflows in level form are stationary. The second measure would be more suitable when it is the first differences in proportional terms in the series that are in fact stationary. Tables 2 and 3 present the findings. As the data period is very short it is not possible to conduct unit root tests since these tests are asymptotic and valid only for large samples.

Twenty-five countries were chosen for the instability and volatility analysis. The main financial flows examined are

- total private inflows-, including short-term bank loans (TPIN), defined as short-term bank loans + private net revenue flows;
- total capital inflows-, including short-term bank loans (TCIN), defined as total private inflow + official flows + IMF purchases − IMF repurchases;
- Foreign Direct Investment (FDI).[m]

In addition to the above, *total portfolio flows* (TPORT) and *total bank loans* (CBNG) were considered. These data were patchy up to 1984, and hence the analysis on the last two variables is not in this summary. Data for short-term loans (FST)[n] were available only from 1985. Data were divided into three periods: 1975–1982, 1983–1989 and 1990–1998. For total private flows and total capital flows the volatility index was compiled using the

[m] FDI flows have varied markedly amongst different countries.

[n] Short term bank loans are expected to exhibit very high instability as they tend to act counter-cyclically to minimize fluctuations in the overall inflows.

Table 2. Time-series comparisons of volatility of total capital flows and their components.

Name of the country	Standard deviation of annual percent change						Coefficient of variation of		
	TCINX 1975–1982	TPINX 1975–1982	TCINX 1983–1989	TPINX 1983–1989	TCINX 1990–1998	TPINX 1990–1998	Annual %	Change in %	
							FDI 1975–1982	FDI 1983–1989	FDI 1990–1998
Argentina	238.22	414.81	306.73	419.29	795.52	519.92	104.2	77.0	147.82
Brazil	34.6	37.32	473.38	461.39	175.61	186.85	25.7	53.5	117.38
Chile	341.71	151.86	45.62	124.31	57.29	39.86	83.5	145.9	213.09
China	111.91	156.29	52.41	96.23	57.06	64.38	282.8	48.8	145.16
Colombia	140.45	374.29	103.79	26, 666.09	159.82	120.57	82.1	46.1	214.39
Democratic Rep. of Congo	92.13	1202.00	76.13	156.47	45.22	90.87	85.1	78.9	−7317.00
Ivory Coast	52.06	94.79	460.22	180.35	826.60	721.02	47.1	57.5	−352.83
Dominican Republic	34.02	65.19	30.54	143.05	158.85	106.84	56.9	40.7	130.56
Ecuador	126.29	269.21	292.62	278.28	393.99	762.75	68.8	19.5	143.33
Egypt	80.87	101.45	15.50	24.21	71.56	406.11	99.6	29.2	414.01
Ghana	348.54	163.09	97.51	232.59	44.19	438.84	161.5	78.5	255.82
India	61.65	487.86	28.96	41.69	52.68	55.70	83.0	79.4	178.56
Kenya	98.96	371.01	37.59	205.46	818.69	246.85	65.9	76.1	356.39
Korea	31.52	45.32	387.92	445.21	133.71	195.10	49.0	72.0	151.98
Malaysia	34.79	34.35	173.28	156.27	93.02	146.36	57.5	51.6	176.60
Mexico	37.76	38.21	127.52	427.51	193.95	392.14	62.9	75.8	243.50
Nigeria	152.94	244.14	372.43	222.97	184.12	123.00	167.6	102.6	489.09
Peru	185.59	296.61	37.46	94.32	184.98	1796.92	94.7	378.6	−452.82

(Continued)

Table 2. (*Continued*).

Name of the country	Standard deviation of annual percent change						Coefficient of variation of		
	TCINX 1975–1982	TPINX 1975–1982	TCINX 1983–1989	TPINX 1983–1989	TCINX 1990–1998	TPINX 1990–1998	Annual %	Change in %	
							FDI 1975–1982	FDI 1983–1989	FDI 1990–1998
Phillipines	37.99	47.93	60.21	167.08	133.11	189.17	129.0	116.8	318.58
Thailand	58.38	61.14	208.60	229.60	55.72	68.53	74.0	93.9	177.80
Turkey	85.36	210.09	150.52	461.52	109.16	140.33	70.9	101.6	362.02
Uruguay	757.87	81.64	118.56	243.52	676.19	207.62	116.8	126.4	243.13
Venezuela	76, 669.34	1994.18	173.67	118.34	179.54	687.53	1772.0	95.3	156.76
Zambia	88.02	393.25	22.16	96.64	61.99	75.64	105.6	79.5	1208.46
Zimbabwe	1259.56	2766.21	215.74	79.76	61.53	496.42	562.5	−13.14	257.10

Notes:

1. Negative mean so only standard deviation is given.

2. For FDI, a coefficient of variation of annual percent change is provided because the size of FDI has changed drastically over three periods. The coefficients of variation of annual percent change adjust for different means.

3. The volatility indicators relative to total capital flows and total private flows were calculated from the series which did not include short-term bank loans as data for the latter have only been published by the World Bank since 1985. As total capital flows and total private flows are referred to as TCIN and TPIN, respectively, in the text (the third section), we used the acronyms TCINX and TPINX to indicate the series excluding short-term bank loans in this table.

Source: World Bank, World Development Finance CD Rom.

Table 3. Coefficients of variation as a measure of instability for different components of capital flows.

	COEV TCIN			COEV TPIN			COEV TPINX		
	1975–1982	1983–1989	1990–1998	1975–1982	1983–1989	1990–1998	1975–1982	1983–1989	1990–1998
Argentina	0.83262	1.28747	0.6373	0.96257	1.45421	0.6530	0.96257	0.7813	0.6460
Brazil	0.26324	1.02782	0.7775	0.26667	0.96231	0.6690	0.26667	1.43717	0.8160
Chile	0.89218	0.41791	0.7064	0.85806	0.72387	0.6700	0.85806	0.57583	0.6560
China	0.96547	0.55502	0.5026	1.35108	0.63569	0.5160	1.35108	0.58171	0.5290
Colombia	0.81545	0.64556	0.8224	0.89504	0.80611	0.7970	0.89504	0.63259	1.9381
Congo, Rep. (Zaire)	0.77875	1.02866	0.9172	1.15047	1.91473	−5.4960	1.15047	1.08002	−2.3775
Côte d'Ivoire	0.39378	0.68451	0.9426	0.3908	1.13664	3.03760	0.3908	2.84446	2.8170
Dominican Republic	0.29315	0.47762	0.7599	0.58748	0.95824	0.8162	0.58748	0.54538	0.7570
Ecuador	0.75613	0.3496	0.8464	0.6343	1.41842	1.0182	0.6343	0.65828	0.6740
Egypt, Arab F.	0.18005	0.18674	0.3921	0.71632	0.17546	1.7976	0.71632	0.15163	1.0608
Ghana	0.43929	0.2606	0.3183	2.34475	3.95145	0.9075	2.34475	2.61568	1.0678
India	0.64688	0.29328	0.2885	1.20087	0.48689	0.6570	1.20087	0.4875	0.4845
Kenya	0.47221	0.46431	1.1044	1.13684	1.54669	−166.588	1.13684	1.29663	−5.9701
Korea, Rep.	0.40428	9.81756	0.7154	0.4656	4.66296	0.9360	0.4656	837.72729	0.5786
Malaysia	0.82226	2.54623	0.6207	0.86877	2.29867	0.6585	0.86877	1.9593	0.4703
Mexico	0.50117	0.65224	0.4677	0.50778	1.15275	0.3249	0.50778	1.38611	0.3568
Nigeria	0.79584	0.74254	0.6034	0.8224	0.86337	0.6488	0.8224	1.75003	0.8258
Peru	0.67448	0.77982	0.7543	1.19905	1.24629	0.8784	1.19905	1.16921	0.8594
Philippines	0.23184	0.48768	0.8608	0.25233	1.06607	1.1649	0.25233	1.03771	0.7829
Thailand	0.67936	1.01129	0.6666	0.7214	1.33121	0.8669	0.7214	1.1355	0.4990

(*Continued*)

Table 3. (*Continued*).

	COEV TCIN			COEV TPIN			COEV TPINX		
	1975–1982	1983–1989	1990–1998	1975–1982	1983–1989	1990–1998	1975–1982	1983–1989	1990–1998
Turkey	0.71043	0.47289	0.8732	1.44535	0.63063	0.9302	1.44535	0.93316	0.8625
Uruguay	0.77034	1.31151	0.8622	0.69375	1.57988	1.0130	0.69375	1.39623	1.0866
Venezuela	0.77846	−6.05909	0.8988	0.79866	−3.82894	1.1588	0.79866	−2.63323	0.9929
Zambia	0.44234	0.46951	0.3576	1.67527	1.23225	3.6375	1.67527	0.59784	1.0747
Zimbabwe	1.20375	1.08094	0.7054	1.16726	−5.54455	5.4384	1.16726	−3.35364	16.3972
	COEV TPORT			COEV FDI			COEV CBNG		
Argentina	1.85266	1.3412	0.7900	1.05573	1.06221	0.4624	1.75826	2.59297	1.8385
Brazil	1.23486	−0.96846	0.6800	0.25784	0.53509	1.1874	0.36243	5.57888	3.5946
Chile	2.83623	3.45152	0.7380	0.8352	1.45931	0.7274	0.81888	0.49227	0.6934
China	2.8656	0.76497	0.9010	2.82843	0.4882	0.6140	3.29641	1.01847	2.2412
Colombia	−0.89298	1.85229	0.8740	0.82193	0.46128	0.9335	0.98252	2.11927	1.5351
Congo, Rep. (Zaire)	—	—	−1.9840	0.85195	0.79002	−11.2435	1.3812	4.41769	−2.0114
Côte d'Ivoire	−0.58152	−1.02785	2.9990	0.47158	0.57493	1.4298	0.53421	8.64004	−3.1586
Dominican Republic	—	—	3.0950	0.56957	0.40713	0.6029	1.70658	−0.62725	−2.5577
Ecuador	7.75988	−1.53547	−2.7070	0.68801	0.19481	0.5465	0.68061	1.5937	1.8935
Egypt, Arab F.	2.96629	−1.32086	1.7120	0.99663	0.29253	0.4456	1.34323	1.06336	−1.1617
Ghana	—	—	1.4900	1.61502	0.78379	0.7520	−28.21126	−16.74427	2.6847
India	2.82843	0.79351	0.7100	0.83052	0.79432	0.9060	1.20388	0.33959	1.1483
Kenya	−2.00917	—	2.1700	0.65929	0.7613	0.8924	2.01911	1.11862	−2.5748

(*Continued*)

Table 3. (*Continued*).

	COEV TPORT			COEV FDI			COEV CBNG		
	1975–1982	1983–1989	1990–1998	1975–1982	1983–1989	1990–1998	1975–1982	1983–1989	1990–1998
Korea, Rep.	0.91956	1.94525	0.6000	0.49086	0.72025	0.8239	0.8028	−5.07802	3.6139
Malaysia	2.22255	1.74132	1.1770	0.57526	0.51577	0.2061	1.16075	−3.6033	0.6264
Mexico	0.92927	−0.48884	0.9070	0.633	0.75868	0.4735	0.46194	5.79452	2.4152
Nigeria	−2.82843	—	1.4570	1.67641	1.02678	0.3685	0.88016	−1.3153	−2.0920
Peru	−2.21166	−1.98431	1.3280	0.94708	3.78557	0.8886	2.60473	2.30165	2.0367
Philippines	1.11374	−1.68554	0.8120	1.29557	1.16871	0.4858	0.39503	17.30875	−3.2808
Thailand	0.83162	1.63072	0.8530	0.74028	0.93915	0.6009	0.87306	1.24327	1.4614
Turkey	9.76933	1.69273	0.7080	0.70937	1.01673	0.1482	1.5684	1.03728	1.6893
Uruguay	2.09043	1.04974	0.7580	1.1678	1.26406	0.7731	1.04667	4.3798	−5.6052
Venezuela	1.47628	−2.1943	0.9210	17.72289	0.95282	0.9148	0.79445	−1.7177	5.2546
Zambia	−1.62781	—	—	1.05682	0.79532	0.6884	4.80891	−1.71018	1.0287
Zimbabwe	2.41753	−0.91174	−0.9180	5.6363	−1.73545	0.8605	1.83705	−2.36689	11.1248

Notes:

1. The role of portfolio flows (TPORT) and total bank loans (CBNG) increased during the last period. As the standard deviation is affected by means, we provide the coefficient of variation that adjusts for varying means across different periods.
2. A negative coefficient of variation is due to overall means being negative.
3. The coefficient of variation of Portfolio flows and total bank loans showed greater instability for the last period, as it has experienced greater fluctuations.

Source: World Bank, World Development Finance CD Rom.

standard deviation of annual percentage change. Due to the unavailability of FST data up to the mid-1980s the volatility indexes were calculated in Table 2 for the *private and total flows series which excluded short-term bank loans*, termed TPINX and TCINX, respectively.

Table 3 presents the results of the instability analysis, carried out for the same 25 countries over three periods (1975–1982, 1983–1989, 1990–1998). The stability measure is the coefficient of variation (in level form), calculated for seven categories of financial flows: TCIN, TPIN, TCINX, TPINX, TPORT, FDI and CBNG.[o]

The results presented in Table 2 show that in many countries the volatility of capital flows[p] has increased in the 1990s, while it has decreased in only a few. Argentina, Columbia, Zaire, Peru, India, Kenya, the Philippines, Venezuela, Uruguay, Zambia and Zimbabwe show an increase in volatility in both private and total capital inflows from the previous two periods. Korea, Malaysia, Thailand, Turkey and Nigeria show a decrease in volatility. For other countries there is no clear pattern.[q]

Among the Asian countries, volatility is relatively higher for Korea, Turkey, Malaysia and the Philippines with respect to Thailand. Most African countries (especially Zaire and Nigeria) show a greater degree of volatility in private capital inflows than other Asian or Latin American countries. Various factors could be responsible, for example, political instability in Zaire and Nigeria could have resulted in significant outflows on private accounts. For Thailand, the impact of the 1997 shock is captured as the latter analysis indicates. Herd behavior and contagion cannot be ruled out for Malaysia, Thailand, the Philippines and Korea. Chile has acquired more stability, and there does not seem to be any significant difference between private and

---

[o] As data on short-term bank loans are not available before the mid-1980s, the series of TPIN and TPINX, as well as those of TCIN and TCINX, are the same for period 1975–1982. This is the reason why the coefficients of variation presented in Table 3 are identical for TPIN and TPINX and TCIN and TCINX, respectively.

[p] As explained, the capital flows series analysed in Table 2 (TCINX and TPINX) do not include short-term loans, due to the non-availability of sufficient and consistent data on the latter.

[q] Comparing Table 2 and Table 3, we can observe that, for total capital inflows and private inflows, the standard deviation of annual percentage change (volatility index in Table 2) is higher for most Latin American countries than the corresponding coefficients of variation (measure of instability in Table 3).

total capital inflows. Uruguay and Peru have a very high standard deviation on the annual percentage change of FDI, and this reflects a much greater degree of volatility in comparison to the other Latin American countries.

The coefficients of variations for FDI presented in Table 3 can also be compared for three periods. For Argentina, Ghana, the Philippines, Turkey, Thailand, Uruguay and Zambia, there is a decrease in the coefficient of variation over time. There is an increase for Brazil, the Ivory Coast and Kenya.

For FDI, both mean flows and standard deviations have gone up for most countries of the sample. The standard deviation for the 1990–1998 period was greater than the corresponding mean for Brazil, Venezuela and the Ivory Coast. Instability in FDI flows is noticeably greater for the latter period in absolute terms. For the Ivory Coast, the mean is very small, and this is because of large fluctuations in FDI on a smaller base figure.[r] For the African countries, Zambia, Zimbabwe, Ghana, Kenya, Zaire and the Ivory Coast, the role of FDI is small, and mean inflows for the 1990–1998 period are not high when compared to Latin American countries. Our results demonstrate that the three regions of the developing world are, in fact, vastly different in receiving foreign capital and the behaviour of outflows is strikingly different between countries within a region. Chile seems to have experienced less volatility in total capital flows, while Mexico and Argentina showed much greater instability within the Latin American region. Our results also suggest that there is some evidence that instability overall has increased with FDI and that the sudden withdrawals of FDIs from East Asian economies during the 1997–1998 period precipitates the large change. In addition, the coefficient of variation of FDI shows, comparatively, a very large change for Thailand.

Short-Term Arbitrage-Seeking Capital Movements

It is common knowledge that there has been a significant, albeit erratic upsurge in short-term capital inflows to developing countries since 1990. This observation has sometimes been presented as a predominantly new process without making clear-cut distinctions between inflows and outflows

---

[r] In 1992, the FDI outflow from the Ivory Coast was 290 million dollars.

or between different types and categories of short term capital movements. Clarifications and elaborations in three directions will be helpful. First of all, it must be pointed out that the recent upsurge in short term inflows to developing countries is not an altogether new phenomenon. A similar expansion of such inflows in relative terms was observed during the 1970s, and since then the typical pattern has been cyclical rather than an uninterrupted upward trend. Second, it must be pointed out that the composition of short term capital movements has changed. Usually no distinction is made between different categories of short-term inflows, however commercial (trade) credits and arbitrage-seeking flows ought to be distinguished. Both are short-term, but the former is a stable component linked to the financing requirements of external trade, whereas the latter is the erratic component sensitive to inter-country differentials on returns to financial assets, exchange rate expectations and country risk-assessments for the short run. Finally, the analysis should include short-term net *outflows* by residents in addition to the usual *inflow* categories. Such outflows by residents of developing countries have expanded significantly during recent years and, as discussed later, are not confined to short-term capital movements. However, in terms of relative magnitudes and volatility, short-term outflows by residents have been much more significant than other categories. The relative gap between net short-term inflows and net short-term outflows to developing countries (i.e., net short-term flows) turns out to be much larger than other categories of capital movements.

If export credits are separated from short-term flows, what remains behind can, broadly speaking, be characterised as capital flows sensitive to international arbitrage — sometimes referred to as "hot money". Both non-residents and residents are involved in such capital flows. Non-residents' short-term transactions on the capital and financial accounts of the balance of payments constitute inflows. Two categories of non-resident agents are behind arbitrage-based capital inflows: rentiers (e.g., institutional investors) who invest in domestic assets to maximise their returns in dollar terms and banks who lend short term in foreign currency to resident banks or to domestic firms. Resident banks engage in arbitrage seeking by using the borrowed foreign exchange to lend in national currencies to domestic firms and/or to the government. Resident firms which borrow short term in foreign currencies, but spend the proceeds to cover their costs in domestic currencies, seek to minimize their credit costs — another pattern of arbitrage seeking. Interest rate differentials, exchange rate expectations and perceptions on country-risk are the relevant variables.

On the other hand, residents may engage in parallel (but reverse) capital movements abroad. For developing countries, investing in external assets is sometimes referred to as "capital flight", implying rentiers are active agents. However, recent years have also witnessed increased activities by banking entities of developing countries engaging in short-term lending activities abroad. As elsewhere in this section, cross-border transactions by non-residents registered as *liabilities* to the recipient country in balance of payments accounts will be referred to as *inflows*. Cross-border transactions by residents of the same country registered as *assets* in balance of payments accounts will be referred to as *outflows*. Unless asset liquidation and reverse transfers take place, inflows and outflows are recorded with plus and minus signs, respectively.

The individual constituents of short-term inflows undertaken by non-residents (generating liabilities to the recipient country) are portfolio investment in equity (essentially in stock markets) and short-term debt (money market) instruments (e.g., Treasury bills); short-term loans to banks and "other sectors"; changes in currency and deposits in the national currency held by external agents and other short-term external liabilities of banks. The same cross-border transactions undertaken by residents are considered outflows. Errors and omissions (EO) as recorded in balance of payments accounts are considered short-term unrecorded capital flows — a minus sign representing an outflow and *vice versa*. However, there may be magnitudes within the EO figures which may indicate unrecorded movements of residents between domestic and foreign currency (unrecorded currency switching) or unrecorded current account transactions (e.g., illegal trade).

Table 4 shows data on short-term non-commercial capital ("hot money") movements in terms of inflows, outflows and net flows-to and from thirteen emerging market economies. A number of observations can be made. In terms of *short-term inflows* (STIs), findings for emerging market economies (Table 4) are consistent with the totals (inclusive of commercial loans) depicted for all developing countries in Table 1. For both these groups, i.e., the emerging market and the larger group of developing countries, the

Table 4. Short-term net inflows (STI), net outflows (STO), and net flows (NSF) (totals of thirteen emerging market economies[1], (billion $)).

	1980–1984	1985–1989	1990–1994	1995–1998	1980–1998
STI, current $	6.1	0.21	220.2	60.4	286.9
STO, current $	−57.5	−18.1	−63.8	−140.2	−279.6
NSF, current $	−51.4	−17.9	156.4	−79.8	7.3
STI,1990 prices	6.8	−0.1	173.0	49.0	228.7
STO,1990 prices	−67.2	−19.9	−47.8	−127.1	−261.9
NSF, 1990 prices	−60.4	−20.0	125.2	−78.1	−33.3

Notes:
For concepts see the text. Individual balance of payments items (under the code numbers as set and defined by IMF, *Balance of Payments Manual 1993*) covered under STI are 4660, 4680, 4774, 4777, 4783, 4784, 4795 and 4798. Those under STO are 4610, 4630, 4724, 4727, 4733, 4734, 4745, 4748 and 4998. NSF = STI + STO. The price deflator used in rows 4–6 is UNCTAD's unit import value index for all developing countries.
[1]Argentina, Brazil, Chile, India, Korea, Malaysia, Mexico, Pakistan, Peru, the Philippines, South Africa, Thailand and Turkey. 1998 figures exclude Malaysia and therefore — being a crisis year for that country — probably underestimate outflows and overestimate inflows for the last period.
Source: IMF, *Balance of Payments Statistics*.

pattern is similar: stagnation in the 1980s, a dramatic upsurge during the early 1990s followed by a huge decline of short term inflows after 1995.

Table 4 presents two new elements, i.e., on *short-term outflows* (STOs) and *net short-term flows* (NSFs). The importance of the outflow leakage is clear when it is observed that even during the boom phase of inflows, i.e., 1990–1994, outflow/inflow ratio is 29 percent. The same ratio exceeds or approaches unity during the 1980s and the late 1990s, respectively, resulting in negative NSFs during the 1980s and 1995–1998. In terms of macro-economic conditions, the early 1980s and the post-1995 years reflect financial instability, and the 1985–1989 period covers a stagnant phase of capital inflows overall. The negative NSFs during the 1980s is a totally Latin American phenomenon: the size of the "deficit" on NSF of Argentina, Brazil and Mexico exceeds that of the whole group during the 1980–1984, period and with the addition of Peru the same is true (by an excess of 14 percent) for 1985–1989 years as well. The "explosion" in STOs from 1995 onwards, on the other hand, is much more evenly dispersed and closely related to the financial instabilities in Latin America during 1995–1996 and Asia in

Table 5. Short-term inflows and outflows under financial crises (billion $).

	Argentina and Mexico, 1995–1996	East Asia, 1997–1998
Inflows	−6.7	−48.2
Outflows	−35.4	−30.3
Net flows	−42.1	−78.5

Notes: See Table 4. East Asia includes Malaysia, Korea, the Philippines and Thailand for 1997, but only the last three countries in 1998.

1997–1998 (See Table 5). In terms of policies, the divide is between the 1980s and 1990s as reflecting the pre- and post-liberalisation of the capital account. What is striking is the fact that capital account liberalisation has affected inflows much more substantially than outflows during 1990–1994. In other words, it can be stated that, at first sight, STOs were taking place at substantial levels regardless of capital controls during the 1980s, and the significant impact of liberalisation was an upsurge in STIs in the early 1990s. However, when the financial instability phases of 1995 onwards and, more specifically, the crisis years for Mexico and Argentina (1995–1996) and East Asia (1997–1998, see Table 5) are considered, this impression will have to be corrected: outflows reach astronomical levels (i.e., above 30 billion dollars in two years) both in the Mexican/Argentinian and East Asian crises and in the former case far exceed the reversal of inflows, i.e., negative STI (see Table 5). Hence, the justification for capital controls is much more valid under conditions of financial instability than during booms in short-term inflows.

If we define the cycle of short-tem capital movements on the basis of inflows, the "normal" pattern to be expected for STOs would be a pro-cyclical one: the same variables, namely interest differentials and exchange rate movements, would presumably affect residents and non-residents similarly. Inward capital movements (regardless of residential position) would prevail during the boom phase of the cycle, and capital "flight" by residents would accompany negative inflows by non-residents under financial instability. The following section will test this hypothesis by a Granger causality analysis. However, looking into shorter intervals during the post-liberalisation phase, it is observed that STIs and STOs move in parallel fashion during crises and its immediate aftermath (Table 5), but in opposite directions (i.e., rising outflows accompanying rising inflows) during the boom. Two interpretations are possible: residents' and non-residents' evaluations on *expected* values for the variables affecting portfolio allocation decisions (e.g., on exchange rates and country-risk assessments) may diverge from each other systematically during the upsurge phase, or alternatively, after the lifting of capital controls, an initial outflow by residents takes place which creates a non-symmetrical and divergent pattern. But after a "normal" level of assets abroad by residents is attained, the expected pro-cyclical movements would be expected to prevail. In the latter case, residents' behaviour would aggravate the magnitude of upheavals and downturns. The extreme instability of short-term flows and their unsustainable character is clear-cut.

As with other categories of capital flows, leakage in the form of outflows by residents took out a significant portion of short-term inflows to developing countries. It should be emphasised, however, that leakage from short-term inflows is significantly higher than other capital movements. As discussed earlier, they exceed inflows during the 1980s. Taking the 1990s as a whole, the "leakage" (i.e., outflow/inflow) ratio for short-term capital movements equals 72.7 percent for the emerging market economies covered in Table 4. On the other hand, the outflow/inflow ratio during 1990–1998 of all capital movements for sixteen countries that belong to the same group was found to be 23.6 percent. In terms of constant (1980) prices, the totality of net short-term flows during a period of eighteen years was a negative magnitude, i.e., \$–33.3 billions (Table 4), — an average drain of \$115 million in real terms (i.e., 1980 prices) for each country. It is very clear that the post-1995 years are dominated by financial instability that has resulted in negative short-term flows. Adverse growth implications are self-evident.

Instability, Volatility Indicators and Granger Causality Analysis on Short-Term Inflows and Outflows

The aggregate investigation of short-term capital movements in the fourth section is, in this section, followed by econometric analyses of instability and volatility as well as causality between inflows and outflows both within a single country and between countries. Table 6, based on the data of Table 4, presents the findings.

Table 6. Volatility and instability indicators of short-term inflows and outflows.

		Volatility indicator					
		1980–1989	1990–1998			1980–1989	1990–1998
		Standard deviation of annual % change					
	SNF	365	124		SNF	280	313
ARG	STI	2609	4094	MEX	STI	197	471
	STO	741	2942		STO	443	2086
	SNF	173	2284		SNF	171	284
BRA	STI	1291	6675	PAK	STI	194	269
	STO	1241	2824		STO	1251	1011
	SNF	676	157		SNF	178	2810
CHI	STI	258	197	PERU	STI	551	335
	STO	124	1563		STO	297	688
	SNF	193	274		SNF	432	494
INDIA	STI	1098	161	PHI	STI	728	388
	STO	152	352		STO	258	503
	SNF	491	142		SNF	519	373
KOREA	STI	993	84	SAF	STI	1916	377
	STO	175	432		STO	190	824
	SNF	144	358		SNF	221	8190
MAL	STI	352	149	THA	STI	1492	9194
	STO	674	157		STO	266	3188
					SNF	4519	178
				TUR	STI	171	521
					STO	260	174

		Instability indicator					
		1980–1989	1990–1998			1980–1989	1990–1998
		Coefficients of variation					
	SNF	−1.40	−10.8		SNF	2.00	2.85
ARG	STI	−1.38	2.48	CHI	STI	2.95	0.86
	STO	−1.79	−1.53		STO	3.07	−2.74
	SNF	−2.24	13.14		SNF	−6.49	1.08
BRA	STI	3.74	1.65	INDIA	STI	−7.91	0.99
	STO	−1.19	−0.81		STO	−9.26	−4.58
					SNF	−5.63	−11.14
				KOREA	STI	4.47	3.3
					STO	−1.56	−1.00

(Continued)

Table 6. (*Continued*).

		Instability indicator					
		1980–1989	1990–1998			1980–1989	1990–1998
	SNF	−1.46	3.55		SNF	−2.11	0.69
MAL	STI	2.14	2.87	PERU	STI	47.15	1.22
	STO	−1.09	27.44		STO	−1.86	0.93
	SNF	−1.41	4.19		SNF	−10.00	7.7
MEX	STI	7770	1.93	PHI	STI	−36.92	1.58
	STO	−1.22	−3.01		STO	−7.86	−1.55
	SNF	2.37	1.64	SAF	SNF	−1.7	31.72
PAK	STI	0.73	1.06		STI	24.36	1.33
	STO	−1.38	−0.9		STO	−0.75	−0.96
	SNF	20.16	10.88		SNF	2.07	−7.25
THA	STI	1.33	1.68	TUR	STI	2.40	2.31
	STO	1.75	−1.63		STO	34.28	−1.90

The IMF data are used from 1980 to 1998, and two measures of the instability index for two different periods, namely 1980–1989 and 1990–1998, are compiled. There are three different flows in the statistics used i.e., net flows (positive or negative), net inflows and net outflows, all in million dollars. The first measure of instability was the coefficient of variation on the original data of each of the three variables. The second measure was the standard deviation of the annual percentage change in annual flows. Instability in the *net* short-term flow increases in the 1990s with respect to the previous decade in eight countries out of thirteen. In Malaysia, all short-term flows are unstable in the 1990s, while for many other countries they are relatively stable for STI or STO. The measure of instability does not show much difference between the pre and post liberalisation period. However, the volatility index measured by the standard deviation of annual percentage change indicates significant changes for Mexico, Brazil, Thailand, Chile, Argentina, Peru and South Africa for inflows, outflows and net flows. The 1997 crisis in Thailand is clearly reflected in these measures. We also analysed the correlation between inflows of various countries, yen/dollar exchange rates and interest rates in Japan and USA (line 60 and 61 in the IMF statistics). Most inflows were significantly negatively correlated with yen/dollar exchange rates, suggesting that when the yen depreciated the inflows tended to fall, while similarly positively correlated outflows with the yen/dollar exchange rate imply that the yen depreciation promoted outflows during the post 1990 period. There are also high positive correlations between outflows and Japanese interest rates. The outflows of Korea and Malaysia and Korea and the Philippines were highly correlated, indicating contagion in the East Asian crisis. Quite a large number of Asian economies had their inflows highly correlated in the sense they received either FDI or total capital flows during the same period from international investors.

Bivariate granger causality tests performed on short-term inflows and outflows using IMF data

The concept of the Granger causality is that the variable x causes y when past values of x have an explanatory power in a regression of a variable y on lagged values of y and x. We use this concept in our analysis of inflows, where inflows of one country are explained by inflows of another country and outflows of the country under consideration are explained by outflows of other countries. We also looked at the relationship between inflows and outflows of the same country and whether the country receiving a higher level of inflows shows a higher level of outflows or whether the Granger causality runs from inflows to outflows for the same country. There was no evidence for the latter hypothesis.

Inflows

The following linkages were significant at the 10 percent level (one means inflows to the first country, or group of countries, Granger-causes inflows to the second country, but not vice-versa).

Using both one and two period lags:

Chile, Mexico on Thailand implying that Chile's inflows Granger causes Thailand inflows and Mexican inflows Granger causes Thailand inflows. There was a two-way causality between Thailand and Philippines. Many other results were obtained using one period and two period lags separately. However, there was no discernible and significant pattern in these results. Out of the two particularly strong linkage cases mentioned above, the impact of Thailand on the Philippines, might appear very plausible (both countries are Asian, Thailand is the larger and most advanced of the two economies) but that of the two Latin American countries on Thailand is puzzling. Chile trades a lot with Asia, but the financial linkages are not very strong. Moreover, Thailand was not very much affected by Mexican crises in the 1980s and 1990s.

Outflows

We used two-year and one year lags, and the results are summarised for 2-year lags. Argentina causes Mexican outflows, and similarly Thailand and Chile also cause Mexican outflows. Korea and Thailand cause Philippine outflows, and the Philippines causes South African and Indian outflows. Korean outflows also cause Indian and South African outflows, while Indian outflows cause Thailand outflows.

Causality linkages relative to outflows are stronger and more consistent than to inflows which is consistent with expectations from theory and past experience. Outflows from Thailand and Korea, in particular, appear to exert a strong impact on outflows from other countries in Asia, but also in Latin America (Mexico) and Africa (South Africa), with both 1 and 2 year lags. Outflows from the Philippines are also remarkable for their strong short-term impact on Korea, India and South Africa.

A note of caution is necessary in the interpretation of these results. The concept of the Granger Causality is a statistical concept, and a spurious causality in a bivariate sense can result when a third factor can be the cause of the apparent causality. Moreover, *a priori* information needs to be used while interpreting the results. It is unlikely that Chile's inflows could cause Thailand's inflows with two-year lags. Such a dubious result is due to the absence of high frequency data and the nature of the statistical concept of the Granger causality.

Policy Options to Deal with Capital Flows Volatility

The results presented in the second, third and sixth sections show that capital flows to developing countries are characterised by high, rising and unpredictable volatility. Therefore, they provide robust, albeit qualified, support to those who stress the dangers of financial liberalisation in developing countries (see the first section). Hasty and indiscriminate financial liberalisation increases the liquidity of domestic borrowers (feeding domestic instability) and the potential for international contagion. Moreover, it tends to focus policy priorities towards pleasing international investors instead of concentrating on development tasks. As a result, the economic fortunes of developing countries end up as hostages to very volatile capital flows controlled by powerful domestic and international private agents, whose erratic behavior constitutes a wild card even in the presence of very orthodox policy stances and textbook macroeconomic fundamentals.

This critical view is also consistent with some stylised facts of the recent and less recent past as pointed out, for instance, by Rodrik (1998) who refers to the most recent case of the Asian crisis. In 1997, five "emerging" economies (Indonesia, Malaysia, the Philippines, South Korea and Thailand) experienced a net outflow of US$12 billion, corresponding to a one-year turnaround of more than 100 billion, or more than 10 percent of their combined GNP. This is an example of how volatile capital flows can be and of how dramatic the impact is on developing countries. Moreover, the crises in Asia, Mexico and elsewhere which have taken place with increasing virulence in the last two decades, far from being isolated and aleatory accidents, constitute a structural feature of international capitalism as has been documented by several economic historians. Kindleberger (1993), for instance, in his major work on the financial history of Western Europe, observed that financial crises appear regularly in the last four centuries, at roughly every 10 years.

However, acknowledging the existence of a problem is usually easier than finding the appropriate remedy, and capital flow regimes in developing countries are no exception. Although the calls for the outright dismissal of the relevance of economic policy making in individual countries are too far-fetched, the powerful worldwide push towards globalisation does tend, to some extent, to diminish the scope and effectiveness of interventions carried out at national level, especially in developing countries.

Among the possible interventions at national level, a distinction can be made between the maintenance, upgrading and reintroduction of capital controls and the efforts aimed at domestic institutional development in the financial and banking sectors, particularly the creation and perfecting of supervisory and regulatory agencies. The former represents a policy course diametrically opposed to that of liberalisation, while the latter is in principle compatible to some extent with financial liberalisation and could ideally reap its benefits while counteracting its risks.[s] As far as capital controls are concerned, like any policy measure their potential benefits (and drawbacks) vary from one case to another, and as a general rule their engineering should be finely tuned to the level of opening, market orientation and the relative balance of private and public economic power typical of each developing country. On the one hand, positive experiences with capital controls appear to be associated with market-friendly, marginal tax-like interventions, chiefly on capital inflows and in relatively more liberalised developing countries: Chile is typical. On the other hand, post-reform China has achieved an outstanding economic performance in a very different context of largely public control on the means of production and more generally on economic decisions, while avoiding, so far, contagion from the Asian crisis. This shows that an array of even relatively rough quantitative, administrative and directly political interventions on capital flows[t] can in fact be compatible with fast international integration and accelerated economic development, while being undoubtedly effective as a shield *vis à vis* international financial vagaries, especially during hard times.

The option of institutional development constitutes less of an alternative to capital controls than it is commonly assumed to be. As far as this development takes place at the level of those public bodies whose mandate is to govern, supervise, monitor and regulate the actions of private agents in the financial arena, it would obviously be welcome, but it would constitute yet another form, albeit more decentralised and sophisticated, of policy interference in the autonomous functioning of the market. If, alternatively, institutional development is supposed to come by the behavioural function

---

[s] It is also clear that, although this kind of institutional development can in fact be beneficial and might allow for a deeper degree of financial liberalisation in several fields, it is particularly difficult to implement in countries which by definition are relatively poorly developed in the broadest sense of the word (see footnote a).

[t] Roubini, using a methodology proposed originally by Calvo, observed that a basic measure of reserve adequacy, the M1/FX (reserves) ratio, was the highest in a group of eight Asian countries at the end of 1996. However, as was later confirmed by subsequent events, China's financial vulnerability should not be overstated, as "the ability of Chinese residents to convert domestic liquid assets into foreign currency is severely limited by widespread capital controls that are absent in most other countries of the region" (pp. 8–9).

of agents themselves (for instance, in the form of a more prudent lending policy on the part of the banks) in a *ceteris paribus* situation, it would represent on the part of agents an evolution towards a non market-based,[u] more socially responsible conduct. This change would often require them to act counter to the incentive signals coming from imperfect markets, the failures of which (adverse selection, moral hazard, herd behaviour, contagion effects and the like) have long been recognised by theory. Like all non market-based economic changes, this type of economic development cannot be expected to materialise as a product of moral exortation: barring exceptional circumstances, it can only be the product of a slow and progressive maturation of the economic and social culture. These two logically distinct forms of institutional development, which are mutually strengthening, constitute, therefore, a necessary component of overall economic development which should be pursued as a long-term policy goal by any country whether engaged in a process of financial liberalisation or not. However, in the former case it is plain that to push liberalisation to a point that is not compatible with the attainable level of institutional development would be a recipe for disaster — a type of risk that would not be present in the latter case.[v]

Finally, it might be worth commenting on the conceivable interventions at the multilateral level which could help developing countries to overcome some of the problems related to their dependency on volatile international capital flows. The long decline of the role of the ODA might be stopped and reversed, allowing developing countries to count, at least in part, on a more secure and predictable source of development finance. Moreover,

---

[u] We use the expression "non market-based" to refer to behaviour which is not totally consistent with a profit maximisation exercise exclusively based on the information on prices and quantities coming from market signals, but incorporates as well other less rigorously quantified information and other objectives. A classical example is that of large Japanese companies which are (or, at least, used to be) very reluctant to fire their employees during bad times. Such behaviour was in part due to the respect of social harmony and stability values which had a weight of their own, but tended also to improve the firms' economic performance in the long run due to hard-to-quantify factors such as the fidelity and cooperative attitude of the staff and the maintenance and building-up of firm-specific skills which would have been jeopardised by a high turnover.

[v] Of course, the choice not to liberalise at all, especially in very financially repressed, closed, and distorted economies, carries its own, different types of risks.

institutions such as the IMF and the World Bank might act in a financially expansive, countercyclical fashion, thus counteracting, for instance, herd behaviour, panic and contagion effects stemming from the private sector in moments of acute crisis, instead of magnifying these very evils as they often do. But these would be major institutional developments at international level, and as such they are easier advocated than translated in practice, as coordination and decision making in the international arena are painstakingly slow. Moreover, the interests of those very private agents who are naturally opposed to any limitation of their degrees of financial freedom weigh far more than those of the developing countries in the so-called international community. Therefore, reform of the international financial system in favour of developing countries presently constitutes little more than wishful thinking.

Summary and Conclusions

In this chapter, we examined the evolution of various components of capital flows to developing countries, focusing, in particular, on the estimate of their instability and volatility. The statistical analysis was based on the IMF and the World Bank data sources relative to different groups of developing countries. The coefficient of variation was chosen as the instability index, while the standard deviation of annual percentage change was used as a volatility index. Both instability and volatility of total capital flows and of their components have increased in the last period, 1990–1998, as compared to previous periods. Similar results were obtained with respect to short-term flows. This finding suggests that the East Asian crisis was probably due largely to herd behavior and contagion. The depreciation of the yen promoted outflows from Asia in the post-1990 period. This is reflected in covariance analysis of inflows, outflows, exchange rates (yen/dollar) and Japan and US interest rates.

Our policy conclusions are not optimistic. It is apparent that the decline in ODA has reduced the scope for developmental efforts in the South, and especially in Africa. In the majority of developing countries private capital inflows are dramatically insufficient with respect to development needs. In the relatively few, mostly middle income, developing countries where capital flows reach a sizeable amount, only a small fraction is translated into productive investment. Moreover, capital flows tend to be very volatile and thus contribute to increased macroeconomic instability and to the frequency of crises. Financial liberalisation, in the absence of an adequate institutional and regulatory framework, can be the main cause of financial crises.

The volatility in capital inflows could in principle be reduced if institutions such as the IMF and the World Bank acted in a financially expansive, counter-cyclical fashion, counteracting herd behavior, panic and contagion effects emanating from the private sector in moments of crises. At a national level, however, some policy interventions are warranted, and the role of capital controls, in particular, cannot be ignored. Policy efforts should also tend towards promoting institutional development in the financial and banking sectors, with particular attention to the creation and perfectioning of supervisory and regulatory agencies.

References

Agenor, PR and J Aizenman (1998). Contagion and volatility with imperfect credit markets. *IMF Staff Papers*, 45(2), 207–235.

Ariyoshi, AK, B Habermeier, I Laurens, J Other-Kobe, JI Canales-Kriljenko and A Kirilenko (2000). Country experiences with the use and liberalization of capital controls (advance copy). *IMF Occasional Paper No.90*, 1–186.

Bikhchandani, S and S Sharma (2000). Herd behavior in financial markets: A review. *IMF Working Paper No 48*, 1–33.

Bird, G (1998). Convertibility and volatility: The pros and cons of liberalizing the capital account. *Economic Notes*, 2, 1–33.

Calvo, G (1999). Contagion in emerging markets: When wall street is a carrier. New York University, Mimeo.

Calvo, G, L Leiderman and C Reinhart (1996). Inflows of capital to developing countries in the 1990s. *Journal of Economic Perspectives*, 10(2), 123–139.

Caramazza, F, L Ricci and R Salgado (2000). Trade and financial contagion in currency crises. *IMF Working Paper No.55* (March), 1–47.

Cerra, V and SC Saxena (2000). Contagion, monsoons, and domestic turmoil in Indonesia: A case study in the asian currency crisis. *IMF Working paper No.60*, 1–60.

Cooper, G (1998). Should capital-account convertibility be a world objective? *Should the IMF Pursue Capital Account Convertibility?* In Fisher *et al.* (eds.), Essays in International Finance, No. 207, pp. 11–19, Princeton University.

Dooley, M (1995). A survey of academic literature on controls over international capital transactions. *IMF Working Paper No. 127*, 1–38.

Edwards, S (1998). The Americas: Capital controls are not the reason for Chile's success. *Wall Street Journal*, 6 April.

Eichengreen, B and M Mussa (eds.) (1998). Capital account liberalisation — theoretical and practical aspects. *IMF Occasional Paper No. 172*, 1–33.

Fisher, S (1998). Capital-account liberalization and the role of the IMF, In *Should the IMF pursue capital account convertibility?* S Fisher *et al.* (eds.), Essays in International Finance, No. 207, pp. 1–10, Princeton University.

Johnson, RB (1998). Controls on capital movements — prudential regulations, short-term capital flows and effectiveness of controls. Paper presented to the *Seminar on Capital Account Convertibility*, Singapore Training Institute, 6 May.

Kaminsky, G and C Reinhart (1996). The twin crises: The causes of banking and balance of-payments problems. *American Economic Review*, 2, 473–500.

Kindleberger, CP (1993). *A Financial History of Western Europe*, 2nd ed., pp. 1–524, Oxford University Press, New York.

Knight, M and F Scacciavillani (1998). Capital account: What is their relevance for economic policymaking?. *IMF Working Paper No. 71*, 1–41.

Kregel, JA (1999). Globalization of private financial institutions, capital flows and global financial instability. Paper presented to the meeting of the *Association of Economists from Latin America and the Caribbean: Globalization and the Problems of Development*, Havana, January, (Mimeo).

Lensink, R, N Hermes and V Murinde (1998). The effect of financial liberalisation on capital flight in African economies. *World Development*, 26(7), 1349–1368.

Lopez-Mejia, A (1999). Large capital flows: A survey of the causes, consequences, and policy responses. *IMF Working Paper No. 17*, 1–54.

Nagasayu, J (2000). Currency crise and contagion: Evidence from exchange rates and sectoral stock indices of the Philippines and Thailand. *IMF Working Paper No. 39*, 1–39.

Nolan, P and W Xiaogang (1998). Beyond privatisation: Institutional innovation and growth in China's large state-owned enterprises. *World Development*, 27(1), 169–200.

Reisen H (1996). Managing volatile capital flows: The experience of the 1990s. *Asian Development Review*, 14(1), 72–96.

Rodrik, D (1998). Who needs capital account convertibility? In *Should the IMF pursue capital account convertibility?* S Fisher *et al.* (eds.), pp. 55–65, Essays in International Finance, No. 207.

Roubini, N (1999). The case against currency boards: Debunking 10 myths about the benefits of currency boards. New York University, Mimeo.

World Bank (1999). Global Development Finance, Vol. 1, Analysis and Summary Tables and Vol. 2. (Country Tables), CD-ROM, Washington, DC.

Zee, HH (2000). Retarding short-term capital flows through withholding tax. *IMF Working Paper No. 40*, 1–14.

SUBJECT INDEX

AUTHOR INDEX